The Shattered Self

A Psychoanalytic Study of Trauma

The Shattered Self

A Psychoanalytic Study of Trauma

Richard B. Ulman
Doris Brothers

 THE ANALYTIC PRESS

1988   Hillsdale, NJ   Hove and London

An earlier version of chapter 2 appeared in the 1987 summer issue of *The American Journal of Psychoanalysis*. Reprinted with permission of the AJP.

An earlier version of chapter 7 appeared in the April 1987 issue (15(3): 175–203) of *The Journal of the American Academy of Psychoanalysis*. Reprinted with permission of the JAAP.

The Analytic Press.
Distributed solely by

Lawrence Erlbaum Associates, Inc., Publishers
365 Broadway
Hillsdale, New Jersey 07642

Set in Century type by
Coghill Composition Co., Richmond, VA
Printed in the United States of America
by Braun-Brumfield, Ann Arbor, MI

Library of Congress Cataloging-in-Publication Data
Ulman, Richard B.
   The shattered self.

   Includes bibliographies and index.
   1. Post-traumatic stress disorder—Treatment.
2. Psychic trauma—Treatment.   3. Psychoanalysis.
I. Brothers, Doris.   II. Title.   [DNLM: 1. Psychoanalytic
Therapy.   2. Self-Assessment (Psychology)   3. Stress
Disorders, Post-Traumatic—psychology.   WM 170 U43s]
RC552.P67U46   1987   616.85′21   87-19266
ISBN 0-88163-047-0

10 9 8 7 6 5 4 3 2 1

Dedicated to the memory of Heinz Kohut

Contents

Acknowledgments

First and foremost, we want to express our deep gratitude and respect for the courageous trauma survivors who participated in our collaborative research on incest, rape, and combat trauma. Hoping that trauma survivors might receive better treatment in the future, they shared with us the horror and pain of the traumatic experiences that had shattered their worlds and forced them to attempt to restore a semblance of their former selves. Without their active cooperation, our research project and this book reporting on its findings would not have been possible.

We greatly appreciate the support of Alfred M. Freedman, M.D., Chairman of the Department of Psychiatry of New York Medical College, and a number of administrators at the Franklin Delano Roosevelt Veterans Administration Hospital, all of whom made it possible for one of us (RBU) to conduct the research with Vietnam combat veterans suffering from PTSD. In the course of conducting this phase of the research, the same author had the good fortune to work under and with Herbert Hendin, M.D., who taught him the value of conducting methodologically sound clinical research and thus conveyed the true meaning of being a scientific researcher.

We acknowledge the invaluable assistance of our two reviewers, Paul E. Stepansky, Ph.D., and Daniel H. Buie, M.D., whose constructive criticisms and suggestions helped us to achieve a degree of clarity in our thinking and writing that we hope does justice to the material. We are indebted to Eleanor Starke Kobrin, managing editor of The Analytic Press, for her care and patience in the preparation of the manuscript and the production of the book. We also wish to thank Jack

Sherin and Donald R. Ledwin, of Sherin and Matejka, Inc., for their superb design of the book jacket.

Additionally, we are very thankful for the help of Ilene Miner, coordinator for Adolescent Services at the Bellevue Pediatric Resource Center, and Anne-Marie Eriksson, Board Chair, Incest Survivors Resource Network, International, in finding young women willing to participate in the research on incest and rape trauma.

We gratefully acknowledge several well-known and senior members of the self psychology community, including Robert D. Stolorow, Ph.D., George E. Atwood, Ph.D., and Arnold Goldberg, M.D., all of whom early in the writing of the book read, critiqued, and offered suggestions for improvements of several of the chapters. Another senior member of the psychoanalytic community, Michael Eigen, Ph.D., also read and discussed material for chapters 6 and 7. He helped us to appreciate the need to deal with the issue of the phenomenology of the self and the distinction between mental and physical dimensions of self-experience. We are indebted to Dorchen Leidholdt, who helped us to appreciate and become more sensitive to radical feminist thinking, especially as it bore on the difficult process of dealing critically yet fairly with much of the often baffling psychoanalytic literature analyzed in chapter 2.

We are also grateful to the intellectual fellowship and professional camaraderie of Peter B. Zimmerman, Lic. Phil., Harry Paul, Ph.D., and Louis J. Petrillo, Psy.D., all of whom have served with us on the Board of Directors of two self-psychological organizations—the Society for the Advancement of Self Psychology (SASP) and the Training and Research Institute for Self Psychology (TRISP)—and who all read and offered helpful comments on a number of the book chapters.

Although benefiting enormously from the assistance and encouragement of a number of individuals and organizations, we are solely responsible for the views presented in this book. None of these individuals or organizations should therefore be held accountable for our ideas and the conclusions we reached in this book.

Preface

The history of our collaboration on this book and the research project that gave rise to it is filled with fortuitous coincidences. We had both devoted years to treating trauma survivors: Vietman combat veterans (RBU) and incest and rape survivors (DB). Moreover, our clinical work had been shaped by the same influences. Both of us had been moved and excited by Heniz Kohut's writings on psychoanalytic self psychology and had incorporated his clinical innovations into our therapeutic work. We had also been greatly influenced by our contacts with Robert D. Stolorow, who unstintingly shared his deep and thorough understanding of self psychology. In addition, our clinical thinking had been enriched by his ideas on psychoanalytic phenomenology and his theory of intersubjectivity.

When we met for the first time to discuss the progress of several adolescent patients we had referred for treatment to each other, neither of us was aware of the other's interest in trauma. We soon discovered, however, that we had both attempted to understand and treat trauma from a self-psychological perspective. We also found that we had run into the same problems with prevailing theories of psychic trauma and approaches to its treatment. We had become particularly dissatisfied with many of the short-term stress-oriented therapies. Together with our patients we had painfully discovered that the treatment of the shattering impact and devastating psychological aftermath of incest, rape, and combat often required long-term analytic therapy. We also discussed the difficulties we had encountered in attempting to apply Freud's classical views on trauma to our clinical work with our respective treatment populations. Freud's views were hard to put into practice because they emanated from three different theoretical models, all rooted in an obscure and antiquated metapsy-chology.

Shortly after our meeting, we agreed to begin work on the research study that forms the basis for this book. A comprehensive theory of trauma began to emerge from our discussions of the preliminary results of our research. However, many of our initial hypotheses underwent substantial revision as we learned more and more about the effects of trauma on the unconscious fantasy lives of our research subjects.

Our method of collaboration was as follows. One of us assumed responsibility for the first draft of an entire chapter, while the other critiqued it and made suggestions for revisions and additions. The exception is chapter 7, the treatment chapter, in which the therapy histories were prepared by the therapist who had treated these survivors of incest and rape (DB) and combat (RBU) trauma. Most chapters went back and forth between us many times and were shared with colleagues. Then the chapters were sent to The Analytic Press reviewers, Paul E. Stepansky, Ph.D., editor-in-chief, and Daniel H. Buie, M.D., who we called the "Boston reviewer" before learning of his identity after completing revisions on the book.

To provide the reader with a general overview of the theoretical and clinical ground covered in the book, we introduce some of the central ideas developed in each of the individual chapters. In chapter 1, we address Freud's abandonment of the seduction theory in favor of the oedipal theory of neurosis, a controversial issue most recently raised by Masson (1984). We do so by rejecting as false the traditional psychoanalytic formulation that trauma is caused by a *fantasized* event. We also reject as simplistic the idea that the event in and of itself holds the key to understanding the psychological meaning for the person experiencing it. Instead, we argue that real traumatic events shatter archaic narcissistic fantasies central to the organization of self-experience and that in this shattering and subsequent faulty (defensive and/or compensatory) attempts to restore these fantasies lies the unconscious meaning of the traumatic event.

In our effort to understand and explain the shattering and faulty attempts at restoring these "central organizing fantasies," we studied a unique research population consisting of female incest and rape trauma survivors and male combat trauma survivors. We also devel-oped and employed a new clinical research methodology, which we call the "applied psychoanalytic research technique of empathic or vicari-ous introspection." We present a total of 15 representative clinical and treatment case studies in support of our self-psychological theory of trauma and our argument for a theoretical reconceptualization and diagnostic reclassification of posttraumatic stress disorder (PTSD) as a dissociative disorder.

In chapter 2, we offer a critical review of a number of significant psychoanalytic theorists of trauma, including Freud, Greenacre, Jacobson, Krystal and Kelman, as part of an historical survey of three major psychoanalytic schools of thought on trauma—classical, neoclassical, and revisionist. We discuss two different models of trauma—psychoenergistic and pathogenic fantasy arousal—constructed at different times by Freud to explain sexual trauma. Freud's shift from the first to the second model had unfortunate consequences for the future development of psychoanalysis and a devastating impact on its treatment of female sexual trauma survivors. In their overeagerness to embrace Freud's second model, many psychoanalysts uncritically accepted the spurious notion that sexual trauma was a product of fantasized and imaginary occurrences rather than real events.

In chapter 3, we examine the tragic aftermath of incest. We begin with a brief historical review of the classical analytic literature on incest including the writings of Abraham, Bonaparte, Annie Reich, and Ferenczi. We also consider the work of Bach and Schwartz, two contemporary analysts who view trauma and fantasy in ways that are highly congruent with our theory.

Previous research demonstrates that incest is traumatic because it involves the betrayal of a vulnerable and impressionable child or adolescent by an older, usually male, family member on whom the youngster is often psychologically dependent. However, it was only when we applied our self-psychological theory to our research with incest trauma survivors that we could clearly understand why incest is so devastating to its young victims.

As our three representative clinical case studies show, the central organizing fanatasies of incest survivors are shattered while the youngsters are still undergoing formative developmental transformation during childhood and adolescence. But that fact alone does not account for the relative severity of the PTSD symptoms we found in a number of our incest trauma survivors. An important contributing factor is that sexual abuse at the hands of a family member disturbs the youngster's archaic narcissistic fantasies, which then come to dominate their subjective worlds. There is a severe "developmental arrest" (Stolorow and Lachmann, 1980) in the psychic structuralization of the incest survivor's self-experience because these central organizing fantasies are repeatedly shattered and faultily restored with each incestuous assault.

On the basis of our findings, we can explain why PTSD sometimes reaches psychotic proportions in survivors of incest. We also explore the connection between incest and so-called conversion symptoms, multiple personality, and victimization by pornography and prostitution.

Chapter 4 is devoted to rape trauma. In this chapter we show that our theory is supported by recent literature on rape. We examine the work of Nadelson and Notman, who study rape survivors from a psychoanalytic perspective, as well as the writings of Bard and Ellison, who offer a nonanalytic perspective.

Our study of female rape survivors confirms that they, like male combat trauma survivors, often suffer from severe and chronic forms of PTSD. We present our findings to dispel misconceptions about rape that continue to deprive rape trauma survivors of proper and effective treatment. Among these misconceptions is the notion originally propounded by Deutsch (1944) that rape fantasies express women's so-called normal masochistic wish to be raped.

Viewed from our self-psychological perspective, rape fantasies reflect women's experiences of growing up in a patriarchal society in which they are routinely subjected "against their will" to perverted and violent forms of sexuality. We maintain that rape fantasies resemble the reexperiencing symptoms of PTSD. In other words, they are symbolic expressions of experiences that disturbed central organizing fantasies and that generated faulty efforts to restore these fantasies.

In addition to reviewing Deutsch's writings on rape fantasies and other "masochistic" phenomena, we also consider the work of Schad-Somers, Shainess, Stoller, Bach and Schwartz, and Stolorow and Atwood, with whom we share a similar perspective. We also examine Freud's famous paper "A Child is Being Beaten" as a means of demonstrating that Freud recognized the developmental vicissitudes and narcissistic dimension of unconscious fantasy.

Chapter 5 includes a critical review of selected psychoanalytic writings on combat trauma ranging from Freud and several of his early followers, such as Abraham, Ferenczi, and Simmel, through Fisher and Kardnier, to Lifton, Horowitz, Shatan, Hendin et al., and Brende and Parsons. In this chapter, we discuss the important relationship between adolescent psychological development and young men's preparation for and participation in bloody and violent combat. We point out that in modern western society the psychological development of adolescent males usually entails tumultuous changes in the sense of self as a result of rapid psychic inflation and deflation of archaic narcissistic fantasies.

The dehumanizing process of preparing for and fighting in war subjects these adolescent male fantasies to even more accelerated forms of inflation and deflation, thus further destabilizing them. The unleashing in combat of such powerful unconscious forces creates a "narcissistic vortex" that plunges the young combatant into a swirling psychological crisis of overwhelming magnitude. For the typical teenaged American soldier, the psychological crisis of fighting in the Vietnam War resulted in dissociated states as manifested by the reexperiencing and numbing symptoms of PTSD. We present three detailed representative cases of Vietnam combat veterans suffering from PTSD to illustrate our understanding of the unconscious meaning of combat trauma.

In contrast to therapies relying on techniques for simple symptom alleviation, our approach, as outlined in chapter 6, relies on the analytic technique of analyzing selfobject transference fantasies of mirrored grandiosity or idealized merger as the means of restoring and transforming shattered and faultily restored central organizing fantasies. Our analytic therapy entails the reconstruction and working through of the unconscious meaning of psychic trauma as a means of alleviating PTSD symptoms and transforming basic character structures.

We base our approach to the analytic therapy of the trauma patient on an impressive body of psychoanalytic literature ranging from the self-psychological works of Kohut, Marian Tolpin, Anna Ornstein, Basch, and Stolorow and coworkers Atwood and Ulman, to the ego psychological and object relations work of Annie Reich, Pumpian-Mindlin, Modell, Volkan, Bach, Bloch, and Eigen. Specific emphasis is given to working therapeutically with narcissistic rage, recurrent traumatic nightmares as forms of "self-state dreams," and countertransference. Particular attention is also devoted to the therapeutic use of what Ulman and Stolorow (1985; see also Ulman, forthcoming) termed the "transference-countertransference neurosis."

In chapter 7, we illustrate our treatment approach with three detailed histories of analytic therapy with representative trauma survivors of incest, rape, and combat. These three cases (Marge, Thea, and Nick) illuminate the actual workings of our approach and highlight difficulties sometimes encountered in analytic therapy with surviviors of trauma. For example, in two of the cases (Thea and Nick), the transference-countertransference neurosis created an intersubjective configuration that led to a temporary interruption in treatment. Yet, despite the considerable psychological damage suffered by survivors of trauma, our three representative treatment cases demonstrate that notable therapeutic improvement is possible using our analytic techniques.

In the eighth and last chapter, we present a final report on our theoretical and methodological conclusions as well as clinical and treatment findings. We assess the reliability of our new research methodology and the degree to which our clinical and treatment results validate our self-psychological theory of trauma and its treatment. We focus on important characteristics found in a number of our cases. We also point out how the shattering and faulty restoration of archaic narcissistic fantasies contributes to disturbances in gender identity. Finally, we refer to current and planned research projects, the results of which will help to modify and further substantiate our theory.

CHAPTER 1

Trauma: Reality or Fantasy?
Conundrum for Psychoanalysis

> *. . . fantasy*, that vehicle of hope, healer of trauma, protector from
> reality, concealer of truth, fixer of identity, restorer of tranquility,
> enemy of fear and sadness, cleanser of the soul—Stoller, 1975, p. 55.

As Janet Malcolm (1983a,b, 1984) chronicles, a heated debate
within psychoanalysis was triggered by the publication of Jeffrey
Masson's (1984) controversial work, *The Assault on Truth: Freud's
Suppression of the Seduction Theory*. Masson raises serious questions
about Freud's personal motives for his abandonment of the seduction
theory in favor of the oedipal theory. Originally, Freud believed that
his female patients' hysterical symptoms were caused by childhood
sexual seduction (molestation and abuse) by older male relatives or
acquaintances. In other words, real occurrences caused trauma that
was manifested in hysteria.

For a variety of reasons, however, Freud questioned his original
theory. He could not believe that so many of his female patients had
actually been seduced in childhood by older males. He concluded,
instead, that his female patients had imagined or fantasized sexual
seduction—which proved to be as traumatic as if they had actually
been seduced. In other words, according to Freud's new oedipal
theory, sexual (and aggressive) fantasy caused trauma that was manifested in neurosis.

Masson argues that Freud's dramatic shift from the seduction to the

1

oedipal theory was not the result of a revolutionary scientific break-through, as Freud claimed. Instead, it stemmed from a lack of personal courage. According to Masson, Freud sought to suppress the seduction theory because he feared the consequences to his professional career from continuing to expose the truth about the widespread sexual abuse of little girls.

Masson's book and the controversey surrounding it (see, for example, Blumenthal, 1981, 1984; Malcolm, 1983a,b, 1984; Goleman, 1984; Storr, 1984; Rycroft, 1984) provide a meaningful context within which to understand the significance of our work for psychoanalysis. At the heart of the entire psychoanalytic enterprise lies a conundrum that might be formulated as follows: Does reality or fantasy cause trauma? We agree with Masson that Freud's abandonment of the seduction theory in favor of the oedipal theory (see chapter 2) represented a fateful shift in Freud's thinking, which led psychoanalysts to turn their attention away from the personal (unconscious) meanings of real occurrences in the social world of shared experiences. Instead, psychoanalysts emphasized the significance of imaginary experience fabricated by the child's supposedly overactive fantasy life. In the process, psychic conflict replaced psychic trauma as the major theoretical and clinical paradigm of psychoanalysis (see Cohen, 1980, 1981).

We join Lifton (personal communication, 1985) and others in urging psychoanalysis to return to the paradigm of psychic trauma. In this sense, our work represents a self-psychological addition to what Cohen (1980, p. 426; 1981, p. 100) called the "trauma paradigm" in psychoanalysis. We add our work to the previous studies of the survivors of war, combat, the Holocaust, Atomic bomb blasts, natural and man-made disasters, as well as sexual abuse and assault. Taken together, these studies correct the false impression within psychoanalysis that compared with the personal world of private fantasy, real occurrences in the social world of shared experience are of little import for the unconscious.

As a self-psychological addition to the psychoanalytic trauma paradigm, our work offers a possible solution to the question of whether reality or fantasy causes trauma. (See, for example, Neu, 1973, and Ostow, 1974, for a discussion of this issue.) We argue that it is neither reality nor fantasy that causes trauma but, rather, that the unconscious meaning of real occurrences *causes* trauma by shattering "central organizing fantasies" (Nurnberg and Shapiro, 1983) of self in relation to selfobject.

Our contention rests on a view of fantasies as "meaning structures" (see Atwood and Stolorow, 1984, p. 5, and Stolorow and Lachmann, 1984/5, p. 26 on "structures of meaning"), which unconsciously organize the subject's experience of self in relation to selfobject. Our conception of fantasy as a meaning structure derives from a basic psychoanalytic proposition that fantasies have unconscious meaning. (See, for example, Stoller, 1979, p. xiv.) If these meaning structures reflect archaic narcissistic fantasies, they are extremely vulnerable to traumatic shattering and faulty (defensive or compensatory) restoration.

Another way of understanding trauma, then, is that the meaning of an occurrence changes one's experience of oneself in relation to selfobjects in ways that are intolerable. In other words, the meaning of an occurrence changes a person's experience of self.

The shattering and faulty restoration of archaic narcissistic fantasies is typically manifested in the reexperiencing and numbing of the symptoms of posttraumatic stress disorder (PTSD), the current version of traumatic neurosis. Psychoanalysis has always regarded symptoms and dreams as symbolic representations of unconscious fantasy. In line with this widely accepted position, we view the reexperiencing and numbing symptoms of PTSD, and especially recurrent dreams and traumatic nightmares, as symbolic representations of the shattering and faulty restoration of fantasmagorical meaning structures.

We are, therefore, defining trauma as a real occurrence, the unconscious meaning of which so shatters central organizing fantasies that self-restitution is impossible. Our definition presumes that the traumatic shattering and faulty restoration of central organizing fantasies is symbolically expressed in symptoms such as those of PTSD.

Our definition of trauma is both psychoanalytic and psychiatric. It is analytic in underscoring unconscious meaning, fantasy, and symbolization, it is psychiatric in pointing up a diagnosable pathological syndrome with specific symptoms (see Basch, 1985, p. 33).

Our emphasis on the unconscious meaning of trauma is consistent with a "hermeneutic definition" (Rothstein, 1986), one of three broad and general psychoanalytic definitions of trauma. According to Rothstein, trauma may be defined psychoanalytically as hermeneutic, developmental, or adaptational, each category having "derivative conceptions of reconstruction and mode of therapeutic action" (p. 227). The hermeneutic definition focuses on the unconscious meaning of an occurrence and involves an insight-oriented form of analytic therapy. The developmental definition stresses the impact of an occurrence on psychological structure; the adaptational emphasizes the effect of an occurrence on psychological functioning.

Both the developmental and the adaptational definitions of trauma entail analytic therapies in which the therapist functions as a "new object" (or selfobject) with whom the patient (survivor) resumes interrupted and arrested psychological development and adaptation. Although our theory focuses on the concept of meaning and is therefore hermeneutic, our approach to treatment is decidedly developmental. It utilizes the therapist as a fantasized selfobject facilitating the restoration and transformation of shattered fantasies of self.

In focusing on the unconscious meaning of an occurrence, our definition entails what Kohut (1971, pp. 254–55, n. 3) distinguished as the "genetic approach" and the "etiological approach" in psychoanalysis. According to Kohut, "The *genetic approach* in psychoanalysis relates to the investigation of those subjective psychological experiences of the child which ushers in chronic change in the distribution and further development of the endopsychic forces and structures" (pp. 254–55, n. 3).

He related the etiological approach ". . . to the investigation of those objectively ascertainable factors which, in interaction with the child's psyche as it is constituted at a given moment, may—or may not—elicit the genetically decisive experience" (pp. 254–55, n. 3).

From an etiological perspective, we view incest, rape, and combat as "objectively ascertainable factors" that "elicit the genetically decisive experience" (Kohut, 1971, p. 255) of the shattering and faulty restoration of central organizing fantasies of self in relation selfobject.

Like Cooper (1986), we contend that psychoanalysis needs to return to Freud's original, limited definition of trauma (see also A. Freud, 1967). We disagree with him, however, about the necessity of formulating such a definition in the mechanistic and energistic terminology of classical psychoanalysis. We believe that our self-psychological definition is more in keeping with important trends in modern psychoanalytic thinking, specifically with the hermeneutic perspective within psychoanalysis. (See Ulman and Zimmermann, 1985, 1987, on psychoanalysis as a "hermeneutic science" of mental action and meaning). Moreover, our definition is also consistent with the nonmechanistic view of trauma also present in Freud's work (see chapter 2).

We do not subscribe to a relativistic definition of trauma (see, for example, Josephs and Josephs, 1986). According to such a definition, an occurrence is labeled as traumatic simply on the basis of a personal and subjective assessment. Subscribing to a relativistic definition logically leads to a position whereby any occurrence may be designated as traumatic. Such a position makes it difficult to speak of such occurrences as incest, rape, and combat as traumatic in the same sense as imagining these events is traumatic.

It makes no sense to diagnose a person as schizophrenic simply on basis of a claim to be schizophrenic. Similarly, it makes no sense to designate an occurrence as traumatic simply on the basis of a personal assessment. Designating an occurrence as traumatic is an analytic and clinical procedure appropriate only if the experience takes on a specific unconscious meaning as symbolically represented in symptoms.

On the basis of Freud's (1913, p. 159, 1916–17, p. 368) important distinction between "factual" or "material" reality and "psychic" reality, we contend that psychic reality includes the unconscious meaning of factual or material reality. The psychoanalytic method enables us to interpret or make "empathic inferences" (Atwood and Stolorow, 1984, p. 5) about the unconscious traumatic meaning of real occurrences by carefully analyzing the psychological record of these experiences as symbolically encoded in dreams, nightmares, and other symptoms. Understanding, interpreting, and working through the unconscious meaning of traumas should be a major purpose of therapy.

Our work has relevance for the treatment of a wide variety of common psychopathological conditions. Most persons experience some type of trauma at critical points in their lives; trauma is, therefore, typical of most normal psychological development. In fact, several analytic commentators (for example, Glenn, 1984; Forman, 1984) argue that character is best understood in the context of the unconscious meaning of trauma. In this regard, we believe that careful clinical exploration for possible pathological sequelae of trauma, even if not manifested in a diagnosable syndrome such as PTSD, is an important yet unfortunately often overlooked aspect of analytic therapy.

TRAUMA: THE SHATTERING AND FAULTY RESTORATION OF CENTRAL ORGANIZING FANTASIES

Our theory originates in the work of Heinz Kohut and such early collaborators as Marian Tolpin. In fact, both Kohut (1966, p. 433, no. 6; 1984, p. 23) and Tolpin (1974, p. 227) invoke the powerful image of the traumatic shattering of the self.

At the heart of our theory is the idea that trauma shatters the self. But, what is the self? Psychoanalytically and philosophically speaking, the self is a multidimensional psychological construct reflecting the subject's experience of mental being and physical existence. As a subject, a person may make self an object of conscious reflection or awareness; or, a person's self may become the object of another person's interest and attention. This is the basis for both introspection and empathy (see Kohut, 1959). However, at a basic ontological level, self is always a psychological construct reflecting the subjective experience of mental being and physical existence. In other words, as subject, a person creates self; and, according to self psychology, such a creation always occurs in the context of a relationship to selfobject.

The self has both ideational and affective dimensions that exist on conscious, preconscious, and, most important for our purposes, unconscious levels of awareness. From a self-psychological vantage point, we view the formation and development of self—the epigenesis of selfhood—in the context of the selfobject milieu. On the basis of the revolutionary psychoanalytic discoveries of Kohut and self psychology, we contend that there is no self except in relation to selfobject.

Self and selfobject remain throughout life an inseparable psychological unit. A basic theoretical tenet of Kohut's work is that the self-selfobject unit develops from archaic to mature forms. This is the crux of Kohut's finding that narcissism has an autonomous developmental lines separate from the development of object relations.

Whether viewed in a developmental or a clinical context, a selfobject is the person's experience of another person or object (animate or inanimate) as subjectively connected to and extended from self. According to Kohut and self psychology, such selfobjects are subjectively experienced by the person as performing vital psychological functions. These functions include providing an experience of being admired, praised, and valued (mirroring of grandiosity and exhibitionism), or facilitating experiences of merger with figures or objects of great strength and power (idealized merger with the omnipotent), or offering experiences of "essential alikeness" (Kohut, 1984, p. 193) as a twin (alter ego).

Kohut (1971) first conceived of psychological selfhood as a developmental process whereby "*a living self* has become the *organizing center* of the ego's *activities*" (p. 120, italics added). According to Kohut, the "living self" consisted of two components—an archaic grandiose self and an idealized parent imago—both of which underwent varying degrees of developmental transformation. Kohut (1977; Kohut and Wolf, 1978) subsequently altered his conception and spoke of selfhood in terms of the "nuclear self (core self)" or "bipolar self," which consisted of two poles of ambitions and ideals as well as a "tension arc" created by these poles. In his later conceptualization, Kohut (1977) spoke of the "self as a *supraordinated configuration* whose significance transcends that of the sum of its parts" (p. 97, italics added).

Our view of self (in relation to selfobject) as a central organizing fantasy is based on Kohut's early emphasis on the self as a center of organizing activity. (See also P. Tolpin, 1985, pp. 86–7, on the "central organizing experience of the developing or developed self.") We find support for our view in nonanalytic and analytic work in the areas of cognitive and developmental psychology. For example, the studies of Piaget (1959, 1962, 1970) as well as the work of more recent nonanalytically oriented cognitive psychologists (for example, Greenwald, 1980, and Greenwald and Pratkanis, 1984), view the subject's self as a center for organizing knowledge. Analytic work on cognition and development, such as that of Noy (1969, 1980), George Klein (1976) and Stern (1985), places the self at the center of mental activity that organizes experience.

It is because the self is the person's center of mental activity for organizing the meaning of experience (that is, knowledge) that a serious disturbance or interference in its ability to function constitutes a trauma. The person's sense of self (see Stern, 1985, on the development of a sense of subjective self) or experience of self is critical to its organizing activity. Thus, any occurrence taking on an unconscious meaning that seriously challenges or undermines this sense may be experienced as a traumatic shattering of self.

However, the full unconscious meaning of trauma is not completely captured by the shattering of self. Part of the meaning for the subject lies in the unsuccessful (faulty) attempt to restore the self as a center of organizing activity. Viewed from an ontological perspective, attempts at restoring self occur because a sense of self is necessary for psychological selfhood. A person ceases to sense selfhood without some center for organizing experience into meaning structures.

Our theoretical position is supported by Kohut's "principle of the primacy of the preservation of the self" (P. Tolpin, 1985, p. 87). Building on this principle, Kohut (1971) described "fragmentation-restoration sequences" (P. Ornstein, 1978, p. 75) as involving a

> breakdown of the archaic narcissistic positions (including the loss of the *narcissistically cathected* archaic objects), thus the fragmentation of self and archaic self-objects . . . and . . . the secondary (restitution) resurrection of the archaic self and the archaic narcissistic objects . . . [Kohut, 1971, p. 6].

Our theoretical position also finds support in the writings of Klein (1976) as well as those of Atwood and Stolorow (1984). Klein wrote that from the "first emergence of a self-schema, preservation of its identity and continuity is a prominent organismic concern" (p. 280). Atwood and Stolorow postulate as a "supraordinate motivational principle" that *"the need to maintain the organization of experience* is a central motive in the patterning of human action" (p. 35).

Kohut, Klein, and Atwood and Stolorow all recognize the need to maintain the organization and meaning of (self) experience as the primary purpose of all mental activity. We have found empirical support for this theoretical postulate in our study of trauma. We amassed from our trauma survivors abundant clinical evidence of a pattern of immediate, persistent, albeit faulty attempts at restoring central organizing fantasies that had been shattered by the unconscious meaning of incest, rape, or combat.

Thus far we have pursued a general discussion of the reasoning behind our main thesis that an occurrence is traumatic only if its unconscious meaning shatters the self. However, we have claimed as part of our thesis, that the self that is shattered and faultily restored consists of central organizing fantasies. In other words, we are asserting that the unconscious traumatic meaning of an occurrence involves the shattering and faulty restoration of what might be abstractly conceptualized as the "self-as-fantasy."

A number of prominent psychoanalytic thinkers have suggested that the subject's self is actually a fantasy formation or construction of fantasizing. This is the reasoning behind Kris's (1956) notion of the self as "personal myth," Arlow's (1969a) idea of self as "self-representations in unconscious fantasy, persistently and selectively reactivated and fused with each other" (p. 21), and Grossman's (1982, 1984) concept of the self-as-fantasy. All these conceptions have in common the notion that the self that exists psychologically is formed and constructed on the basis of unconscious fantasizing. From this perspective, development might be viewed as the epigenesis of a self created by unconscious fantasizing.

Our conception of the self-as-fantasy is an "experience-distant" theoretical construct in contrast to a more "experience-near" formulation such as central organizing fantasy. (See Kohut, 1977, p. 245, on the distinction between "experience-distant" and "experience-near" levels of theorizing.) We do not intend, however, to imply that the self can be reduced to a figment of a person's imagination with no ontological status and epistemological significance. On the contrary, the concept of the self-as-fantasy constitutes the fundamental psychic reality or subjective frame of reference from which to understand and interpret the unconscious meaning of occurrences. (See Piaget, 1959, as well as Greenwald, 1980, Greenwald and Pratkanis, 1984, on the egocentric nature of knowledge; see also, Noy, 1969, 1980, on the "self-centered" nature of the primary process organization of experience and meaning, and Klein, 1976, on the "self-schema" as the basic psychic organizer of all experience and meaning.)

We strongly dispute, therefore, Grossman's statements that the "fantasy of self-structure may not correspond to an actual structure at all" (1982, p. 933) and that "self-fantasies, conscious or unconscious,

are not direct manifestations of some elementary entity 'the self' "
(1984, p. 40). (We are indebted to Arnold Goldberg [personal communication, 1987] for alerting us to the important difference between our
self-psychological conception of the self-as-fantasy and Grossman's
identically termed but theoretically very different view.)

On a more "experience-near" level of theorizing, our conception of
the self-as-fantasy focuses on a specific domain of unconscious fantasy,
that is, archaic narcissistic fantasy. These fantasies involve the original, and hence most archaic, experiences of self in relation to selfobject. Many psychoanalytic thinkers have written about the centrality
of narcissistic fantasy in unconscious mental life (Ferenczi, 1913;
Federn, 1952; A. Reich, 1960; Tartakoff, 1966; Pumpian-Mindlin, 1969;
Bach and Schwartz, 1972; Volkan, 1973; Modell, 1975, 1976; Silverman,
Lachmann, and Milich, 1982; Bloch, 1978; Grunberger, 1979; Rothstein, 1984a, b; Eigen, 1980, 1982; Schwartz-Salant, 1982; Bach, 1985).

Several of these authors (see, for example, Tartakoff, 1966, and
Pumpian-Mindlin, 1969) had an implicit and rudimentary understanding of archaic narcissistic fantasy as an unconscious representation of
self in relation to selfobject. Tartakoff, for instance, wrote of two basic
types of narcissistic fantasy—the "active, omnipotent fantasy of being
the 'powerful one,' with grandiose features . . . and the passive fantasy
of being the 'special one,' chosen by virtue of exceptional gifts" (p.
237). However, a conceptualization of archaic narcissistic fantasy in
terms of the self-selfobject matrix was not explicitly formulated until
the appearance of the early work of Kohut, and, later, of Marian
Tolpin.

From a self-psychological perspective, we define a narcissistic fantasy as a representation of self (mental and physical) in relation to
selfobject. This representation consists of specific ideational content
and affective valence. The ideational content may concern either or
both the mental and the physical dimensions of selfhood. (See Eigen,
1986, p. 320, for a discussion of the important difference between
mental and physical self especially for understanding the distinction
between omniscience and omnipotence as two archaic forms of narcissism.)

For the purposes of the present study, we are primarily concerned
with narcissistic fantasy in its most archaic form. We have argued (see
Ulman and Brothers, 1987) that such archaic narcissistic fantasies
entail illusions *(not delusions)* of personally unique attributes and
special endowments, sense of entitlement, essential alikeness, superhuman invulnerability and invincability, magical and uncanny powers
(for example, clairvoyance, psychokinesis, and telepathy) as well as

merger or "oneness" (Silverman, Lachmann, and Milich, 1982) with supreme and almighty beings.

We distinguish narcissistic fantasy, in either its archaic or its mature form, from the classical, drive-related oedipal fantasy of sex and aggression. (See also Bach, 1985, p. 94, on the distinction between "primitive narcissistic fantasy" and "object fantasy.") Narcissistic fantasies operate simultaneously on different levels of awareness from conscious or preconscious daydream and reverie to unconscious dream. In modified form (that is, developmentally transformed), these fantasies consist of a tempered sense of one's own mental, physical, and emotional capacities as well as the abilities of others as selfobjects. Yet, even in moderate form, narcissistic fantasies always retain a measure of the illusory, magical, and uncanny.

At an archaic level, the affective valence of these fantasies is expressed in a mood characterized by euphoria, elation, and ecstasy as well as awe, astonishment, and reverence. At a more mature level of emotional development, the affective tone of these fantasies reflects satisfaction, appreciation, and admiration. (See Arlow, 1969b, p. 46, on the relation between unconscious fantasy and mood.)

Both Kohut and Tolpin have formulated a self-psychological perspective on narcissistic fantasy. However, with only a few exceptions (see, for example, Kohut and Wolf, 1978), after the 1977 publicaiton of *The Restoration of the Self*, Kohut and self psychologists more or less abandoned the general concept of unconscious fantasy and the specific notion of narcissistic fantasy. Consequently, a fully developed self-psychological conception of fantasy has yet to be formulated. Our work constitutes an effort to develop such a conception and apply it to the study of trauma.

Originally, Kohut conceived of what he later (1977, p. 177) termed the "nuclear self" or "core self" and its two major components—the archaic grandiose self and idealized parent imago—as types of narcissistic fantasy. For example, in an early article, Kohut (1966) described the "narcissistic self" in terms of the "grandiose fantasy that is its functional correlate," (p. 436) or, as a "system of infantile grandiose fantasies" (p. 437). He also referred to the "overestimation of the power and perfection of the idealized object" (p. 436) (that is, an idealization fantasy). He viewed both the fantasy of grandiosity and idealization as "phase-appropriate and adaptive" (p. 436).

In another early article, Kohut (1968) wrote of "infantile fantasies of exhibitionistic grandeur" (p. 490) and "fantasies of the grandiose self" (p. 494). In *The Analysis of the Self*, Kohut (1971) mentioned the "fantasy of an omnipotent idealized parental figure" (p. 83), "fantasies about an idealized father" (p. 83), the "fantasy of an omnipotent father," (p. 84) the "narcissistic-exhibitionistic manifestations of . . . grandiose fantasies," (p. 107) "unmodified grandiose fantasy concerning the self or . . . fantasies concerning an omnipotent archaic object" (p. 111).

Kohut (1971) was very clear in maintaining that narcissistic fantasies are *primary* psychological structures. As such, they are not to be construed as secondary and essentially defensive or compensatory in nature and function. He stated:

> The fact that the child endows the 'fantasy father' with grandiose features is, I believe, not in the main to be understood in the Adlerian sense . . . i.e., as an overcompensation meant to counteract the deprivation and to cover a defect. It is rather the fact that the *primarily existing* narcissistic idealization now has no realistic object in relation to which a gradual disillusionment can be experienced. . . . Such *fantasies*, as noted before, may be formed, consciously elaborated, and temporarily clung to in response to an external deprivation which requires the postponement of a developmental task [pp. 83–4, italics added].

However, Kohut (1968) indicated that "primarily existing" narcissistic fantasies may undergo "defensive [or compensatory] reinforcement" (p. 433, n. 6).

Kohut argued against conceptualizing narcissism as merely a developmental waystation on the road to mature and healthy object relations. He (see also M. Tolpin, 1974) thought of narcissistic fantasies as evolving from archaic to mature forms. (See Federn, 1952, and Bach, 1985, on the concept of a continuum of narcissistic fantasy ranging from healthy or normal to pathological; see also chapter 4 for a discussion of Freud's thoughts on the transformation of unconscious fantasy.) Likewise, he believed that narcissistic fantasies may be transformed and integrated as necessary and healthy parts of the personality. (See also Tartakoff, 1966, p. 248 for a critique the "renunciation hypothesis" with respect to narcissistic fantasy.)

In a discussion of David Beres' paper, "The Unconscious Fantasy," Kohut (1961) referred to "creative unconscious fantasy" (p. 315). In a later article, Kohut (1966) spoke of the degree of the "deinstinctualization" of the "grandiose fantasy" as determining the "extent of its integration into the realistic purposes of the ego" (p. 440). He also indicated that in normal development there is a *transformation* of "narcissistic constellations into more highly differentiated, new psychological configurations" (p. 445). He implied that such "new psychological configurations" are "adaptively valuable narcissistic fantasies which provide lasting support to the personality" (p. 440).

Kohut (1966) concluded, "It is evident that in these instances the early narcissistic fantasies of power and greatness had not been opposed by sudden premature experiences of *traumatic disappoint-ment* but had been gradually integrated into the ego's reality-oriented organization" (p. 440, italics added).

Marian Tolpin (1974) elaborated Kohut's idea about the transforma-tion of archaic narcissistic fantasy. She wrote of the "reshaping of the grandiose fantasy in the course of its development" (p. 213) into a "more differentiated and integrated psychological structure" (p. 226).

Kohut and Wolf (1978) implied that narcissistic fantasies are formed and undergo developmental transformation or derailment within the context of a self-selfobject matrix. They (see also A. Reich, 1960) stated:

> In view of the fact, furthermore, that the *selfobjects' response* had focused prematurely and unrealistically on *fantasied performance* or the *fantasied products of the self* but had failed to respond appropriately to the exhibitionism of the nascent nuclear self of the child as the initiator of the performance and as the shaper of products, the self, will, through-out life, be experienced as separate from its own actions and weak in comparison with them" [p. 419, italics added].

Kohut's conception of the development of narcissistic fantasy within the selfobject milieu of the child-parent unit has parallels in the earlier work of Tartakoff (1966) and Pumpian-Mindlin (1969). Tartakoff re-ferred to a "state of 'magic participation' " (p. 242) in which the "preoedipal child" introjects the " 'omnipotent' parent" and merges "magical self and other images" (p. 248). She observed that if such a "state of 'magic participation' " is "prolonged and reinforced by con-scious or unconscious maternal attitudes, *the child's fantasies of omnipotence do not undergo a modification in keeping with reality*" (p. 242, italics added). Instead, according to Tartakoff, these develop-mentally untransformed and unmodified "narcissistic fantasies" of being " 'the center of the world' " and destined for a special fate assume a dominant role in the child's, and, later the adult's, uncon-scious mental life.

In a developmental perspective similar to Tartakoff's (and presaging Kohut's), Pumpian-Mindlin (1969) observed that the growing child unconsciously attempts to retain an increasingly imperiled sense of omnipotence either by fantasizing the incorporation of a "presumed" omnipotent parental object or by the *"reverse fantasy* of being incor-porated by the omnipotent adult and thereby sharing in his omnipo-tence" (p. 217, italics added). In fact, Pumpian-Mindlin went as far as suggesting that all object relations develop as a result of unconscious narcissistic motivations.

In a refinement of Kohut's conception of the formation and development of narcissistic fantasy within the self-selfobject matrix, we view the relevant developmental context as an "intersubjective field" (see Stolorow, Brandchaft, and Atwood, 1983; Brandchaft and Stolorow, 1984; Atwood and Stolorow, 1984; Ulman and Stolorow, 1985; Ulman, forthcoming) constituted by the respective subjectivities of the child and caretakers. The concept of the intersubjective field highlights the importance of the unique personality of the caretaker(s) as well as that of the child.

We believe that the concept of the intersubjective field is consistent with and a logical extension of Kohut's own thinking. For example, he (1977) indicated that the nuclear self is formed in the developmental context of

> the specific interactions of the child and his self-objects through which, in countless repetitions, the self-objects empathically respond to certain potentialities of the child (aspects of the grandiose self which he exhibits, aspects of the idealized image he admires, different innate talents he employs to mediate creatively between ambitions and ideals), but not others [p. 100].

However, Kohut (1977) emphasized that the

> *nuclear self*, in particular, is not formed via conscious encouragement and praise and via conscious discouragement and rebuke, but by *the deeply anchored responsiveness of the self-objects*, which, in the last analysis, is *a function of the self-object's own nuclear selves* [p. 100, italics added].

We read Kohut as implying that the archaic narcissistic fantasies of the child unfold or derail within the intersubjective field constituted, in part, by the parents' (or primary caretakers') own narcissistic fantasies. This intersubjective view of narcissistic fantasy formation and development has influenced our approach to the treatment of trauma. Specifically, our approach utilizes the therapist's narcissistic countertransference fantasies as a therapeutic agent for the restoration and transformation of the survivor's shattered archaic narcissistic fantasies. (See chapters 6 and 7 for a more detailed discussion of the rationale behind our treatment approach as well as representative studies of three therapies currently in progress.)

Implicit in the writings of both Tartakoff (1966) and Pumpian-Mindlin (1969) is the notion that the formation and development of narcissistic fantasy occur through the unconscious process of internalization (respectively, "introjection" and "incorporation"). Internalization is also critical in Kohut's thinking about this topic. In his early work, Kohut (1971) viewed "transmuting internalization" (p. 83) as the basic unconscious process whereby archaic narcissistic fantasies are transformed and integrated into the personality as "adaptively valuable" and "differentiated psychological structures" (p. 165).

For example, Kohut (1971) referred to a fantasy of an omnipotent idealized parental figure that undergoes "phase-appropriate transmuting internalization" as part of normal and healthy psychological development (p. 83). According to Kohut, transmuting internalization takes place in the following self-selfobject developmental context (or, as we view it, intersubjective context):

> Under favorable circumstances (appropriately selective parental response to the child's demands for an echo to and a participation in the *narcissistic-exhibitionistic manifestation of his grandiose fantasies)* the child learns to accept his realistic limitations, *the grandiose fantasies and the crude exhibitionistic demands* are given up, and are replaced by ego-synotic goals and purposes, by pleasure in his functions and activities and by realistic self-esteem [p. 107, italics added]. . . . The gradual recognition of the realistic imperfections and limitations of the self, i.e., *the gradual dimunition of the domain and power of the grandiose fantasy*, is in general a precondition of mental health in the narcissistic sector of the personality [p. 108, italics added].

(See chapter 6 for a further account of transmuting internalization particularly in connection with a discussion of the distinction between "horizontal" and "vertical splits.")

The notion of the transformation of archaic narcissistic fantasy through a process of transmutation is implicit in the work of A. Reich (1960, p. 297), who wrote of transposing "compensatory narcissistic fantasies." It is more explicit in the works of Pumpian-Mindlin (1969, p. 213) and Bach (1985, p. 94), both of whom indicated that narcissistic fantasies may be "transmuted."

We maintain that transmuting internalization involves the transmutation of meaning. Transmuting internalization of archaic narcissistic fantasy leads to structural change based on a change in the unconscious meaning of the subject's experience of self in relation to selfobject. Instead of a sense of subjective self (see Stern, 1985) unconsciously organized primarily in terms of archaic and illusory notions of greatness, grandeur, power and perfection (as well as twinship), self-selfobject experience (or the intersubjective field) has been unconsciously organized more in accordance with tempered and moderate notions of grandiosity, omnipotence, and idealization. The extent of a person's vulnerability to traumatic shattering and faulty restoration of fragile central organizing fantasies is determined by the degree to which sense of self (in relation to selfobject) remains organized by archaic and illusory notions of personal grandeur or idealized merger with the omnipotent.

Kohut recognized that narcissistic fantasies are not always adequately transformed and integrated into the personality. Originally, he (1966, 1968) viewed these developmental failures as resulting from the repression of archaic narcissistic fantasies, which prevented them from being modified by "external influence." Such a repressed archaic narcissistic fantasy, according to Kohut (1968) continues "to disturb realistic adaptation by its recurrent intrusions into the ego" (p. 490).

Later, however, Kohut (1971) described an unconscious process whereby archaic narcissistic fantasy was split off and disavowed. According to Kohut, disavowed fantasies create a vertical split (in contrast to a repressive, horizontal split) in the psyche. Basch (1981, 1983), one of Kohut's earliest and most important collaborators, argued that disavowal involves the failure to fully acknowledge meaning (in contrast to the attempt to *deny* perceptual awareness of external phenomena). A person who disavows and splits off archaic narcissistic fantasies, which are central to the unconscious organization of the experience of self in relation to selfobject, remains unaware of the extent to which the meaning of such experience revolves around magical illusions of personal grandeur and idealized merger with the omnipotent. In vertical splits, therefore, disavowal is critical in accounting for both vulnerability to trauma and its psychologically devastating aftereffects (that is, faulty restoration).

Our self-psychological theory of trauma has much in common with "fragmentation-restoration sequences," a phrase coined by Ornstein (1978, p. 75) to describe Kohut's (1971, p. 6) ideas about self-restitution. Kohut (1966) wrote:

> Not only parental illness or death but also the parents' reactions to an illness of a young child may prematurely and *traumatically shatter* the idealized object imago [leading] later to vacilliation between the search for external omnipotent powers with which the person wants to merge [that is, compensatory reinforcement], or to *defensive reinforcement* of a grandiose self concept [p. 433, n. 6; italics added].

We have taken Kohut's allusion to compensatory and defensive reinforcement of the shattered component of the nuclear self as the basis for our view of compensatory and defensive restoration of shattered archaic narcissistic fantasies. Restoration of these fantasies involves at least two unconscious processes: (1) the elaboration of a fantasy that has been shattered, and (2) the elaboration of a relatively undisturbed and intact fantasy.

Because Kohut (1971) initially believed that the grandiose self formed at an earlier stage of development than the idealized parent imago, he linked "defensive reinforcement" with repair of the grandiose self and compensatory reinforcement with repair of the idealized parent imago. In the interest of maintaining consistency with Kohut's formulations, we employ the term "defensive restoration" when either of the two restorative processes just described involves fantasies of exhibitionistic grandiosity. We employ the term "compensatory restoration" when either process involves fantasies of idealized merger with omnipotent or alter ego (twinship) imagos.

Suppose, for instance, that the unconscious meaning of a particular occurrence shatters an archaic narcissistic fantasy of idealized merger with an omnipotent parent imago. In this case, compensatory restoration entails the elaboration of a fantasy of idealized merger, whereas defensive restoration involves the elaboration of a fantasy of exhibitionistic grandiosity. It is hypothetically possible that either compensatory or defensive restoration might prove successful in repairing a shattered fantasy. But it is questionable whether cases of successful restoration constitute traumas. We have found empirically that self-restitutive efforts following trauma are usually unsuccessful.

It is important to distinguish our formulations on defensive and compensatory restoration of shattered fantasies, which constitute primary structures, from Kohut's (1977) ideas about defensive and compensatory *structures* arising out of his conceptualization of a "bipolar self." According to Kohut, a structure is defensive "when its sole or predominant function is the covering over of the primary defect in the self. . . . [A structure is compensatory] when, rather than merely covering a defect in the self, it compensates for the defect" (p. 3) and rehabilitates the self by making up for a weakness in one area of the personality with a strength in another.

Kohut observed that a "weakness" in the grandiose self is frequently compensated by a strengthening of the idealized parent imago. However, the "reverse may also occur"; that is, a weakness in the idealized parent imago may be compensated by a strengthening of the grandiose self. In other words, according to Kohut, a weakness in one pole of the self may be compensated by a strengthening of the other pole. In this context, therefore, compensation refers to a strengthening of either pole rather than to the elaboration of fantasies of idealized merger with omnipotent parent imagos.

We find parallels for Kohut's explanation of the unconscious dynamics of "fragmentation—restoration sequences" in the work of A. Reich (1960) as well as Bach and Schwartz (1972). Reich (1960) argued that for most children trauma occurs early in life as "shattering" blows or "narcissistic injuries" to a previously unchallenged and unchecked "infantile feeling of power to subject the disobedient object world, including [one's] own body to the wishes of the infantile ego" (p. 298). According to Reich (1960), the child reacts to these narcissistic blows with intense and overwhelming "feelings of helplessness, anxiety and rage" (p. 299). (See Kohut, 1977, on "disintegration anxiety" [p. 104] and "disintegration products" [p. 114].) Reich maintained that, in addition to these "feelings of helplessness, anxiety and rage," narcissistic injuries "necessitate *continuous reparative measures*" (p. 299, italics added).

Commenting upon castration threats, Reich observed, "However, any need for *repair* or *restitution* may be condensed into fantasies about phallic intactness and greatness" (p. 299, italics added). Reich also referred to such efforts at reparation and repair as "magical restitution." Although framed in the classical analytic terms of castration and psychosexuality, Reich's observation parallels Kohut's thoughts on the "defensive reinforcement" of the "grandiose self concept." The magical and illusory nature of defensive and compensatory restoration of shattered fantasies helps to account for the faultiness of these attempts.

In an analysis of the sadomasochism of the Marque de Sade, Bach and Schwartz (1972) referred to narcissistic trauma and the "restitutional attempts that follow" (p. 474). (See chapter 3 for a further discussion of the relevance of Bach and Schwartz to our work.)

Having discussed in detail the nature and development of narcissistic fantasy, we need to explain precisely what is meant by the concept of a central organizing fantasy of self in relation to selfobject. We have taken Kohut's and Tolpin's ideas of self as a psychological center of organizing activity and applied them to narcissistic fantasy. Rather than placing self at the psychological center of organizing activity, we place narcissistic fantasy there.

We have borrowed the concept of the central organizing fantasy from the work of Nurnberg and Shapiro (1983). They suggest that "each individual develops an organized system of fantasy" (p. 494). (See Lagache, 1964, on a "phantasmatic system".) The concept of the central organizing fantasy is similar to earlier notions such as the "basic fantasy and its derivatives" (Joseph, 1959) and the "central masturbatory fantasy" (Laufer, 1976; Stoller, 1979) as well as more recent concepts such as the "central affect-laden fantasy" (Rothstein, 1984a,b).

If, on one hand, a narcissistic fantasy fails to undergo sufficient developmental transformation and therefore remains in its original archaic form, it may be spoken of as a central organizing fantasy. So constituted, a person's self is extremely vulnerable to traumatic shattering and faulty restoration. If, on the other hand, a narcissistic fantasy does undergo adequate developmental transformation as part of its integration into the mature personality organization, the self is less vulnerable—although not invulnerable—to traumatic shattering and faulty restoration.

In line with Kohut's and Tolpin's emphasis on organizing activity, we view central organizing fantasies as unconscious meaning structures that begin to take form early in life and remain active throughout life. Unlike Melaine Klein and her followers, we are not suggesting that elaborate and complex unconscious fantasies are present throughout infancy and early childhood. The Kleinian position on fantasy has been justifiably criticized by non-Kleinian psychoanalysts for adultomorphizing the unconscious of the infant and child. Recent infant research (see, for example, Stern, 1985) empirically substantiates these criticisms.

We are suggesting, however, that narcissistic fantasies as agents of unconscious organizing activity are present early in life. Narcissistic fantasies gradually assume specific ideational form and affect-laden valence with the increasing development of unconscious symbolization. This ability is evidenced by the capacity for language and verbalization occurring between the ages of 18 and 24 months (see Stern, 1985, p. 11).

We distinguish between fantasizing as unconscious organizing activity and fantasies as mental products of this activity. We emphasize, therefore, the dynamic rather than the static quality of unconscious fantasy life. From our perspective, fantasizing is a basic form of mental action. (See Schafer, 1976, 1978, for an alternative view on the nature and function of mental action; see also Wolff, 1963, pp. 323–24, on Kant's philosophical theory of the mind as a locus of mental action governed by "innate rules of the mind").

We find support for our dynamic conception of fantasizing as unconscious organizing activity both within and outside of psychoanalysis. Within psychoanalysis, we cite the work of Joseph (1959), Arlow (1969a,b), Beres and Arlow (1974), Klein (1976), Stoller (1975, 1979), Nurnberg and Shapiro (1983), and Rothstein (1984a,b).

Basing his ideas on the early work of Freud (1908), Joseph (1959) distinguished between unconscious fantasizing and fantasy. He referred to "a hierarchy of fantastic thinking," (p. 202) "levels of fantastic thought," (p. 202) "various levels of a developmental continuum of fantastic thought," (p. 202) and "fantasy activity (p. 203). According to Joseph, fantasizing is a form of thought activity that operates on various levels of consciousness with its own developmental line; fantasy is a product of such thought.

Arlow (1969a) presented clinical evidence in support of his hypothesis that "fantasy activity is a persistent and constant function" (p. 19) and "feature of mental life" that "has a special relationship to clinical phenomena involving *the psychology of the self*" (p. 5, italics added). In particular, unconscious fantasy is related to pathological "alterations in the *experience of the self*" (p. 21, italics added). Arlow suggested that the study of unconscious fantasizing and fantasy is a means of gaining "insight into primitive concepts of reality and self" (p. 14) (See Ferenczi, 1913, on the early stages in the development of a sense of self and reality.)

The fantasmagorical nature of such archaic or "primitive concepts of reality and self" constitutes an ultimate "psychic reality." Such a psychic reality is the critical subjective frame of reference for understanding and interpreting the unconscious meaning of all occurrences and experience. (See Schimek, 1975, for a similar view of Freud's concept of "psychic reality.)"

We contend that Kohut originally thought of archaic forms of narcissism (that is, fantasies of self in relation to selfobject) as an ultimate "psychic reality" or subjective frame of reference. Empathically accessible by "vicarious introspection" (Kohut, 1959, p. 209; 1971, p. 219), this fantasmagorical domain serves as a context for understanding and interpreting unconscious meanings. In this sense, fantasies of the self as grandiose, the idealized selfobject as omnipotent, or the alter ego selfobject as identical twin, constitute what Stolorow and Lachmann (1984/5) refer to as "archaic organizing principles" (p. 23).

As a central "psychic organizer" (Spitz, 1965), an archaic narcissistic fantasy consists of a specific type of mental activity. First, it is a type of "ego-centric thought" (Piaget, 1959; see also Noy, 1969; Greenwald, 1980; and Greenwald and Pratkanis, 1984) or "self-centered" cognitive process (Noy, 1980). Raw and unprocessed sensory and experiential data are constantly organized into meaning structures (knowledge).

As a type of unconscious mental organizing activity, archaic narcissistic fantasy is therefore a "structure" in the Piagetian sense. Piaget (1970) defined structures as a "system of transformation" involving "instruments of transformation" and "transformation rules or laws." According to Piaget, the basic "instruments of transformation" are assimilation (p. 63) and accommodation. Piaget defined assimilation as the "process whereby an action is actively reproduced and comes to incorporate new objects into itself" (p. 63) and accommodation as the "process whereby the schemes of assimilation themselves become modified in being applied to a diversity of objects" (p. 63).

Klein (1976) and Noy (1969, 1980) have applied Piaget's ideas to the psychoanalytic theory of the self. Klein spoke of "reversal of voice" and repression as the principle unconscious organizing principles by which "self-schema" are initially created by assimilation and subsequently altered by accommodation. Noy viewed the "self-centered" primary process as the unconscious means by which the self is created and maintained by the reciprocal processes of assimilation and accommodation.

We draw the following conclusion from the work of Piaget and others on the egocentric or self-centered nature of cognitive process and activity: Experience is mentally organized as knowledge and imbued with meaning primarily because of the epistemological principle of self-referentiality. (See the work of Stephenson, 1954, and followers such as Brown, 1980, on Q-methodology as a scientific means of empirically verifying self-referentiality.) In line with the principle of self-referentiality, we view all trauma as narcissistic. Incest, rape, and combat take on a traumatic unconscious meaning for the subject *because* they entail the shattering and faulty restoration of archaic narcissistic fantasies.

We take issue with Atwood and Stolorow's (1984) conceptualization of structures as subjective organizing principles. According to those writers, these principles emerge through the process of analysis as thematic patterns in a person's life. In Stolorow's view (personal communications 1985) such "structures of subjectivity" may be perceptually concretized as sensorimotor symbols such as fantasy. Stolorow maintains that structures of subjectivity are primary whereas fantasy is secondary. Stolorow implies, however, that our view of the primacy of fantasy, and more specifically, archaic narcissistic fantasy, is more consistent with Kohut's position.

Our self-psychological theory of trauma is at odds with many previous psychoanalytic views. These perspectives implicitly understand the relationship between trauma and fantasy in one of two interrelated ways: either trauma is the originator and reactivator of fantasy or fantasy is the originator and reactivator of trauma.

However, important parallels to our theoretical formulation exist in the work of Stoller (1975), Janoff-Bulman (1985), and Blum (1986). Stoller views (perverse) fantasy as the undoer and reverser of (sexual) trauma. In this sense, his ideas are similar to ours in that the faulty restoration of shattered fantasies is essential in determining the unconscious meaning of trauma.

Using findings from cognitive and social psychology, Janoff-Bulman

(1985) developed a theory of trauma as the shattering of a person's "assumptive world." Such shattering, she claimed, often leads to psychological upheaval as symptomatically manifested in PTSD. She indicated that the shattering of any one of three basic assumptions about self and the world may constitute a trauma. According to Janoff-Bulman, these three basic assumptions include: (1) the belief in personal invulnerability; (2) the perception of the world as meaningful and comprehensible; and (3) the view of oneself in a positive light (p. 18).

Janoff-Bulman's theory of trauma as the shattering of basic tenets of an assumptive world and the resulting psychological upheaval closely parallels our theory of trauma as the shattering and faulty restoration of fantasmagorical meaning structures.

Finally, Blum (1986) argues that unconscious fantasy is a "prexisting determinant of the meaning of trauma and that "trauma is elaborated in an altered fantasy system" (p. 16). Blum's argument closely parallels our view of the personal meaning of trauma as unconsciously determined by the shattering and faulty restoration of fantasy.

According to DSM-III (1980) the "essential feature" of PTSD "is the development of characteristic symptoms following a psychologically traumatic event that is generally outside the range of usual human experience" (p. 236). Clearly, incest, rape, and combat fall "outside the range of usual human experience."

In DSM-III, the symptoms of PTSD are grouped into three major clusters, including reexperiencing, numbing, and "other". (DSM-III-R, the newly revised version of DSM-III, was not available during the period in which we were writing this book.) According to DSM-III, reexperiencing symptoms include recurrent and intrusive recollections of the event, recurrent dreams" (and nightmares) "of the event," and "sudden acting or feeling as if the traumatic event were reoccurring, because of an association with an environmental or ideational stimulus" (reliving episodes). Numbing symptoms consist of "reduced involvement with the external world" as exhibited by "markedly diminished interest in one or more significant activities, feeling of detachment or estrangement from others, and constricted affect" (p. 238).

DSM-III includes other major PTSD symptoms such as

hyperalertness or exaggerated startle response, sleep disturbance, guilt about surviving when others have not, or about behavior required for survival, memory impairment or trouble concentrating, avoidance of activities that arouse recollection of the traumatic event, intensification of symptoms by exposure to events that symbolize or resemble the traumatic event [p. 238].

DSM-III also describes "associated features" of PTSD such as "depression and anxiety," "increased irritability" at times "associated with sporadic and unpredictable explosions of aggressive behavior, upon minimal or no provocation" and "impulsive behavior" (p. 237).

PTSD is the most recent version of what Freud originally diagnosed as traumatic neurosis. (PTSD is not, however, equivalent to trauma.) Freud distinguished traumatic neurosis from anxiety neurosis on the basis of whether the neurosis was caused by a real occurrence or by an imaginary experience. As examples of the former, he cited accidents, death of a loved one, and combat; he mentioned sexual and aggressive oedipal fantasies as instances of the latter. In other words, Freud attempted to distinguish between traumatic and anxiety neuroses on the basis of a questionable epistemological differentiation between reality and fantasy.

We find Freud's differentiation artificial. It has also been extremely detrimental for the study and treatment of sexual trauma. In the past, with only rare exceptions (for example, Ferenczi, 1949), psychoanalysts uncritically adopted Freud's clinical distinction between traumatic neurosis and anxiety neurosis. Despite female patients' numerous reports of actual sexual abuse, the resulting trauma was incorrectly attributed to fantasy rather than reality. The pathological condition was then treated as a form of anxiety rather than as traumatic neurosis, usually with disastrous consequences for these patients. In addition, the widespread and uncritical acceptance of Freud's position by psychoanalysts discouraged analytically-oriented, empirical studies of sexual trauma.

By classifying PTSD as an anxiety neurosis, the authors of DSM-III collapsed Freud's distinction between traumatic and anxiety neurosis. Logically, PTSD should have been classified as a separate diagnostic entity. We believe, however, that phenomenologically, PTSD should be reclassified according to DSM-III diagnostic criteria as a dissociative disorder. We do not believe that the reexperiencing, numbing, and other related and associated symptoms are manifestations of anxiety at least as understood by classical psychoanalysis. Rather, we see these dissociative symptoms (including depersonalization, derealization, and disembodiment) as expressions of disintegration anxiety (Kohut, 1977, pp. 104–5). Viewing the reexperiencing and numbing symptoms of PTSD as forms of depersonalization, derealization, and disembodiment is the clinical basis from which we derive our diagnostic reclassification of PTSD as a dissociative disorder. (See DSM-III, 1980, pp. 253–60 for a discussion of the nature and symptoms of dissociative disorders.)

Our self-psychological reconceptualization of PTSD as a dissociative disorder (see Ulman and Brothers, 1987; Ulman, 1987) derives primarily from Kohut's discoveries. In his early writings, Kohut (1971) wrote of the "fear of loss of the reality self" and the "fear of loss of contact with reality" as central anxieties "encountered in the analysis of narcissistic personality disorders." In the same passage, Kohut indicated that in the case of the narcissistic personality disorder the central anxiety "is not castration anxiety but the fear of the dedifferentiating intrusion of the narcissistic structures and their energies into the ego" (p. 153).

We think of the shattering and faulty restoration of archaic narcissistic fantasies as symptomatically manifested in the dissociative disturbances, including depersonalization, derealization, and disembodiment in self-experience. (See chapter 3 for our rationale for including disembodiment as a manifestation of dissociation.) Such disturbances are manifestations of disintegration anxiety from the fear of loss of the reality self and fear of loss of contact with reality.

Our view of PTSD as a dissociative disorder also grows out of Kohut's (1971, p. 185) important distinction between vertical and horizontal splits in the psyche. We do not see reexperiencing, numbing, and other symptoms of PTSD as pathological byproducts of repression and a horizontal split in the psyche. Rather, we veiw them as pathological manifestations of disavowal and a vertical split. (See chapter 6 for a further discussion of Kohut's distinction between horizontal and vertical splits.)

These dissociative symptoms give symbolic voice to the disavowed unconscious meaning of trauma. Careful analysis of these symptoms is therefore essential to understanding and interpreting unconscious traumatic meaning. We provide many clinical examples of this analytic process of decoding the symbolic meaning of PTSD symptoms, especially recurrent dreams and traumatic nightmares.

In his later work, Kohut (1977) elaborated his original ideas about "dedifferentiating of narcissistic structures," "fear of loss of the reality self," and "fear of contact with reality." He argued that a basic trauma experienced by many person's involves the fragmentation or collapse of the self resulting from the shattering of one of the major components of the "nuclear self." Paul Tolpin (1985) referred to fragmentation or collapse of the self as "disintegration-depletion experiences" (p. 87). These experiences entail "the dread of the loss of self" (Kohut, 1977, p. 105) following its "breakup" and "dissolution." The disintegration anxiety (as well as the depressing feelings of emptiness and depletion, that is, an "empty depression") and its "products" result in pathological alterations in self- (including selfobject) experience. These changes are manifested in dissociative states such as depersonalization, derealization, and disembodiment, as well as chronic narcissistic rage, directed at either the faulty self or the failing selfobject.

According to Kohut, dreams may symbolically express either attempts at disguising forbidden and unacceptable wishes or representing a disturbing state of self-fragmentation or depletion. He indicated (1977, p. 109) that recurrent traumatic nightmares may be viewed analytically as symbolically representing a subject's experience of self-dissolution. Kohut regarded such nightmares as examples of "self-state dreams" (p. 109). The disintegration anxiety or despair that accompanies the dream image of the "endangered self" (A. Reich, 1960, p. 295) interrupts sleep.

Expanding upon Kohut, Stolorow and Atwood (1982; Atwood and Stolorow, 1984) argued that dreams could be understood and interpreted as symbolically depicting both the dreamer's experience of fragmentation or depletion and the experience of emerging cohesion and wholeness. By extension, we view the dissociative symptoms of PTSD as symbolic expressions of both the shattering and the faulty restoration of central organizing fantasies.

The works of Geleerd, Hacker, and Rapaport (1945), Jacobson (1959), and Arlow (1966, 1969a) also support our self-psychological reconceptualization of PTSD as a dissociative disorder (See also Frances, Sacks, and Aronoff, 1977.) As early as 1945, Geleerd and colleagues presented substantial clinical evidence to buttress their contention that trauma can result in amnestic states. According to these authors, in these states, unconscious fantasies are "lived out" in an attempt to magically undo and reverse trauma (see also Stoller, 1975). Geleerd et al. went as far as arguing that such traumatically induced fugue states result from "splits" in the ego. They indicated that split-off parts of the ego seize hold of consciousness in the form of previously repressed fantasies.

Jacobson (1959) described states of depersonalization as consisting of extreme emotional detachment, a sense of being "outside of the self" (p. 137) and "emotional inhibition or blocking or affective emptiness" (that is, numbing) (p. 139). She viewed these states as posttraumatic manifestations originating "in a continued defensive struggle aiming at the mastery of the traumatic situation" (p. 143). Jacobson (p. 145) implied that depersonalized forms of emotional detachment or numbing are in the service of fantasies of invulnerability.

Jacobson maintained that "states of self-estrangement and depersonalization" (p. 154) always constitute attempts at solving a "narcissistic conflict." Such a conflict is created by a split in the ego between "two contradictory self-images reflecting opposing fantasies of identification" (p. 161). A solution is neurotic because it entails efforts at reaffirming and restoring the intactness of the ego by inherently faulty psychic mechanisms such as detachment, disavowal, and denial. Jacobson concluded that posttraumatic depersonalization "represents a restitutive process" whereby "the ego tries to recover and maintain intactness by opposing, detaching, and disavowing the regressed, diseased part" (p. 164). (See chapter 2 for a further discussion of Jacobson's work on trauma.)

Building on the work of Jacobson, Arlow (1966) contended that trauma results in splits in the ego as evidenced by dissociation between the "experiencing self" and the "observing self." Such ego splits are sensed by the subject as pathological alterations in self-experience and are manifested in states of depersonalization and derealization. In such dissociative states, the person is under the psychological control of unconscious fantasies which entail the denial of trauma either by detachment from self or from reality.

These fantasies and the accompanying dissociative states may be analyzed as the unconscious illusion that danger does not exist in the external world (derealization) or that it exists but is not a threat to the subject (depersonalization). Arlow (1966) translated the respective unconscious fantasies involved in derealization and depersonalization as follows: "All of this isn't real. It's just a harmless dream, or make-believe" and "This is not happening to me. I'm just an onlooker" (p. 472).

METHODOLOGY AS A MODE OF INQUIRY

We divide our discussion of the methodology of our study into two parts: the first deals with the clinical cases, and the second with the treatment cases. In each of these separate discussions, we cover the important methodological topics of design, rationale, sampling, data gathering, and analysis.

We conducted several pilot research projects yielding preliminary data that raised serious questions about the accuracy of two traditional psychoanalytic postulates about the cause of trauma. Freud's (1905; Breuer and Freud, 1893–95) seduction theory postulated that the reality of sexual abuse and attack causes trauma as symptomatically manifested in traumatic neurosis. Freud's oedipal theory postulated that the memory of fantasized sexual and aggressive experience causes trauma as symptomatically manifested in anxiety neurosis. We suspected that neither reality nor fantasy per se "causes" trauma; rather, we hypothesized that the unconscious meaning of such real occurrences as incest, rape, or combat caused trauma by shattering fantasies.

To test our hypothesis, we undertook a full-scale empirical study as a follow up to our pilot research projects. Our follow-up study was designed to enable us to examine the unconscious fantasy lives of men and women who had survived traumas prototypical for males and females in our society. The use of a research sample made up of both males and females is a particularly important feature of our study.

We decided to use incest, rape, and combat trauma for several reasons. First, these traumas are prototypical for men and women; they are also consistent with Freud's early focus on sexual trauma and subsequent attention to combat trauma. Second, studying these specific traumas provided our project with a built-in developmental frame of reference stretching from childhood through adolescence to young adulthood. We could therefore study trauma in three critical developmental periods.

And, third, these specific traumas are usually so catastrophic and massive that they typically produce florid and chronic symptoms. The analytic examination of these symptoms would provide us with invaluable information on the unconscious meaning of trauma.

In conducting our study, we employed a special set of research techniques. It would have been unrealistic and impractical to attempt to conduct the research using standard analytic methods of research investigation; these methods depend on the collection and analysis of data derived solely from a formal analysis requiring years and years of almost daily therapy. It seemed highly unrealistic to expect that we would be lucky enough to have enough survivors of incest, rape, and combat trauma in analysis at the same time. Moreover, even if we did have such a large number of survivors in treatment, we would have no way of insuring that our sample was representative of the general population of incest, rape, and combat trauma survivors.

We decided, therefore, to rely on a previously developed and tested methodology combining structured and unstructured clinical research interviewing techniques (see Kardiner and Ovesey, 1951; Hendin, 1964; Hendin, Gaylin, and Carr, 1965; Hendin, 1969, 1975, 1982; Hendin, Pollinger, Ulman, and Carr, 1981; Hendin and Siegel, 1981, Hendin and Haas, 1984; Hendin, Haas, Singer, Ellner, and Ulman, 1987; Haas, Hendin, and Singer, 1987; Gaylin, 1974). More specifically, we employed the clinical research methodology of Hendin and his coworkers (Hendin, Pollinger, Singer, and Ulman, 1981; Hendin, 1983; Hendin, Haas, Singer, Gold, Trigos, and Ulman, 1983; Hendin, Haas, Singer, Houghton, Schwartz, and Wallen, 1984; Hendin and Haas, 1984). These authors use detailed and systematic life history material and PTSD symptoms as a preliminary context for a more in-depth and unstructured psychodynamic analysis of the unconscious meaning of trauma in the lives of carefully selected research subjects. In utilizing this clinical research methodology, we sought to revitalize further the small sample, single (or "intensive") case study method as a legitimate scientific mode of inquiry (see Berg, 1947; Chassan, 1961, 1970, 1979, 1980; Bromley, 1977; Runyan, 1980, 1982).

Edelson (1984) argued that the traditional case study method of narrative histories and accounts of treatment, "in the form they are usually written," was unable to meet the "canons of eliminative inductivism" necessary to "justify provisional acceptance of a hypothesis as scientifically credible" (p. 60). Edelson may have been correct. However, like Bromley (1977) and Runyan (1980, 1982), we believe that the case study method need not meet such "canons" in order to be considered scientific. Instead, the scientific status of the case study method rests on "quasi-judicial" standards involving the presentation and evaluation of evidence in support of a particular hypothesis or thesis.

We tailored the clinical research methodology of Hendin and colleagues (Hendin, et al., 1981; Hendin, 1983; Hendin, et al., 1983; Hendin, et al., 1984; Henden and Haas, 1984) to better suit the specific requirement of our study. First, we adapted what Kohut (1959) initially referred to as the "introspective and empathic method of observation" (p. 464) and later termed "vicarious introspection" (1971, p. 219, n. 8) and the "empathic-introspective observational stance" (1977, p. 309). A psychoanalytic method of gathering and analyzing self-reported and introspective data, vicarious introspection, is, according to Kohut (1971), "defined by the position of the observer who occupies an imaginary point *inside* the psychic organization of the individual with whose introspection he empathically identifies" (p. 219, n. 8).

Using vicarious introspection, we sought to gain empathic access to the unconscious fantasy lives of our research subjects as a clinical means of gathering data related to the shattering and faulty restoration of central organizing fantasies. In other words, we used the empathic-introspective observational stance to arrive at inferences about the unconscious meaning of trauma.

To sustain our empathic immersion in the inner lives (Kohut, 1977, pp. 252, 306; see also A. Ornstein, 1983, p. 391) of our clinical research subjects, we conducted intensive and in-depth interviews that often continued for several years. In a number of instances, the interviews evolved into formal therapeutic relationships. For example, two of our representative treatment cases (Thea and Nick) were originally interviewed as clinical research subjects. Moreover, the majority of our clinical research subjects reported significant relief from symptoms of

PTSD as a result of the therapeutic nature of the interviews and the opportunity afforded them for meaningful discussion of traumatic experiences. We use the term "therapeutic interview" (see MacKinnon and Michels, 1971, pp. 6–7) to capture the therapeutic nature of the clinical research interviewing process.

We used all our therapy cases—the length of treatment for whom was a minimum of three years with frequency of one and often more sessions per week—as internal checks on conclusions derived from our clinical research interviews. However, the sustained and lengthy duration of the therapeutic interviews enabled us to gather and analyze introspective data sufficient in quantity and quality for arriving at independent and valid inferences about the unconscious meaning of trauma.

We are not implying that either the therapeutic interviews or the analytic therapies are equivalent to a formal analysis consisting of many years of daily (or almost daily) therapeutic contact. As the primary clinical tool for gathering and analyzing data, we relied in our clinical research interviewing (in contrast to our research therapy) on less intense and well-defined transference and transferencelike reactions in contrast to a full-blown transference neurosis. (See Hendin, Gaylin, and Carr, 1965, pp. 6, 44 on the use of transference with volunteer subjects in clinical research.) Our approach is consistent with the long and respected tradition in psychoanalysis known as applied psychoanalysis—the application of clinical techniques, such as dream interpretation as well as symptom and character analysis, to the study of the unconscious fantasy lives of historical and literary figures unavailable for analytic dialogue.

In contrast to traditional, nonclinical studies, we applied such analytic techniques as empathy to the direct clinical study of the unconscious fantasy lives of preselected research subjects. (See, for example, Oremland, 1984; Gedo, 1984; Muslin, 1984; Kligerman, 1984; Poland, 1984, as instances of the application of empathy to the traditional nonclinical research areas of art and literature. See also Strozier, 1982; Kohut, 1985, as instances of the application of empathy to the nonclinical research areas of history and culture.) In addition, there exists within personality research a long tradition of using projective psychological tests as well as experimental techniques as clinical means of observing the operation of unconscious fantasy (see, for example, Symonds, 1949; Sebastiano, 1977; Silverman, 1977).

We call our methodology *the applied psychoanalytic research technique of empathic or vicarious introspection*. We view our research methodology as in keeping with Kohut's application of the psychoanalytic technique of empathy to a wide variety of areas of study outside the confines of the analytic consulting room (see, for example, Kohut, 1974, 1976, 1985).

Our methodology is also consistent with the important work of Lifton on the clinical application of in-depth interviewing techniques to the study of specific research populations and problems. He (1973, p. 21) named his approach "disciplined" (1972a, p. 260) or "articulated subjectivity" (p. 1973, p. 21). He defined it as the "use of the self as investigative instrument" (1973, p. 21) for conducting "depth-psychological research interviews" (1976, p. 93).

We used the "representative case study method" (Spotts and Shontz, 1976, 1980) to insure that our three clinical subsamples were not random but were instead typical and characteristic (that is, representative) of the general population of survivors of incest, rape, and combat trauma. As established and developed by Spotts and Shontz and subsequently applied by Hendin et al. (1981, 1987), the representative case study method consists of a two-phase sampling procedure. As part of the first phase, we conducted a general survey of the separate populations of incest, rape, and combat trauma survivors. We determined the basic characteristics of the individual survivors making up each of these major groups. Based on this determination, we assembled samples *representative* of each of the three larger groups.

Our three samples consisted of 50 incest, 50 rape, and 50 Vietnam combat trauma survivors. Fifty individuals for each sample provided us with numbers sufficient for critical selection of cases for further clinical interviewing. Many of the individuals from the larger samples were diagnosed as suffering from PTSD. Diagnosis of PTSD was established with 40 of the 50 incest survivors (80%), 25 of the 50 rape survivors (50%), and 23 of the 50 combat survivors (46%).

The percentage of those Vietnam combat survivors suffering from PTSD falls within the general range established by previous research findings on the incidence of PTSD in this population (see, for example, Wilson, 1978; Egendorf, Kadushin, Laufer, Rothbart, and Sloan, 1981; Hendin and Haas, 1984; Laufer, Brett, and Gallops, 1985; Brende and Parson, 1985; Boulanger and Kadushin, 1986). Reliable figures of PTSD in incest and rape survivors are still unavailable. We suspect, however, that our findings on the incidence of PTSD in these populations will be confirmed by future research.

We then divided each of the three samples into clinical subsamples based on specific distinguishing characteristics. One of the major features was the presence of key PTSD symptoms. Another important distinguishing feature, as assessed during initial screening, was the extent to which either fantasies of grandiosity or idealization were the primary meaning structures shattered as part of trauma.

We established three individual "cells" as part of a separate typology created for each of our three clinical subsamples. These cells were based on which of the two major fantasy constellations was shattered as part of trauma. In addition to a typological cell for cases characteristic of the shattering and faulty restoration of fantasies of either grandiosity or idealization, we also established a third cell for cases in which both fantasies were equally effected.

During the second phase, we conducted intensive and indepth therapeutic interviews with each survivor from the three typological cells. For presentation in each of the separate chapters on incest, rape, and combat, we selected cases that were most *representative* of the other cases within the cell. In this way, the three clinical case studies presented in each of the separate chapters are representative of a group of cases, which, taken together, are *representative* of the larger research population under study.

From the three samples, we selected as clinical subsamples, for intensive and in-depth study, one half of the incest, rape, and Vietnam combat trauma survivors. We prepared detailed clinical reports covering pretraumatic, traumatic, and posttraumatic periods in the lives of all these survivors. These reports were the basis for the descriptions and explanations of trauma in the lives of the survivors appearing in each of our three chapters on incest, rape, and combat.

By using the representative case study method, we were able to generalize from our specific research findings to the larger population of incest, rape, and combat trauma survivors, who, we maintain, are representative of trauma survivors in general. In other words, our research findings are significant in understanding the unconscious meaning of trauma in the lives of all survivors.

We also used the representative case study method of Spotts and Shontz (1976, 1980) in selecting our three illustrative treatment studies, thus insuring that they exemplified the general population of incest, rape and combat trauma survivors. In choosing our representative treatment cases, we selected from our clinical subsamples of incest, rape and combat survivors those who best illustrated the characteristic patterns of these three groups.

Our selection of these specific cases also rested on an assessment that they would be likely to benefit from in-depth and long-term analytic therapy. Our assessment was based on a determination of relative verbal ability and intelligence as well as high motivation. Having chosen this representative group of survivors for teatment (including 10 incest, 10 rape, and 10 combat cases, for a total of 30), we then selected for presentation three cases that best illustrated the key features and themes from the treatment of the group of 30.

Selection of treatment cases on the basis of the foregoing variables (verbal ability, intelligence, and motivation) conforms with considerable clinical evidence that these variables are crucial in determining a person's capacity to benefit from analytic therapy. The use of standard psychoanalytic treatment techniques with patients suffering from severe forms of narcissistic pathology (that is, self-disordered patients) is consistent with much of the recent work of a diverse group of analytic theorists, including Kohut, Kernberg, Giovanchini, Boyer, Masterson, Volkan, Rothstein, Bach, and, most recently, Stolorow and his co-workers (see, for example, Ulman and Stolorow, 1985; Ulman and Brothers, 1987; Ulman, forthcoming).

Our three trauma patients—Marge, an incest survivor; Thea, a rape survivor; and Nick, a combat survivor—were all seen in analytic therapy for extended periods of time ranging from three to six years. The results of these currently ongoing therapies provide encouraging support for our contention that severe trauma can be analytically treated using self-psychological therapy techniques.

We measured therapeutic improvement, or "the curative effect of analysis" (Kohut, 1984), by the use of two treatment criteria. Our first criterion was clinical evidence of noticeable and prolonged dimunition of symptoms of PTSD. (See Hendin et al., 1981, 1983, and Hendin and Haas, 1984 for a discussion of this clinical method of assessing thereapeutic improvement of patients sufferng from PTSD.) In applying this criterion, we sought clinical evidence of the sustained alleviation of the dissociative symptoms of depersonalization, derealization, and disembodiment.

Our second criterion was clinical evidence of the successful working through of the (selfobject) transference neurosis or "traumatic transference neurosis" (Glover, 1955; Forman, 1984). We assessed working through in terms of the therapeutic transformation of shattered and faultily restored archaic narcissistic fantasies into a mature and healthy sense of self. We looked for evidence of the latter in the patient's sense of enhanced self-cohesion and stability as well as greater ability to cope successfully with the unavoidable crises of daily living.

Although the majority of our 30 treatment cases (20 cases, or 66%) showed marked improvement as measured by our two treatment criteria, a statistically significant minority (10, or 33%) showed only limited improvement. Yet, our overall treatment results support our claim for the therapeutic value of our self-psychological approach.

The important interrelationship between our two measures of therapeutic improvement must be highlighted. The therapeutic transformation of shattered and faultily restored archaic narcissistic fantasies is reflected in the presence of increased psychic structuralization of the survivor's "subjective world" as well as in the relative absence of disorienting and disruptive states of dissociation. (Stolorow and Lachman, 1980, p. 3; see also Atwood and Stolorow, 1984, p. 1).

A SAMPLE OF INCEST, RAPE, AND COMBAT TRAUMA SURVIVORS

We present the case synopses of Fran, Nettie and ".44 Mike" as illustrative of survivors of incest, rape, and combat trauma. (All names and other identifying personal information have, of course, been changed to protect the anonymity of all research subjects.) Each case vignette is designed to illuminate the unconscious meaning of trauma as reflected in the shattering and faulty restoration of archaic narcissistic fantasies organizing the mental lives of each of these patients. We offer more detailed and in-depth case studies of trauma survivors in chapters 3, 4, and 5.

Fran

From the time of her earliest memories until the age of 13, Fran, a 52-year-old, married, white woman from a prosperous upper middle-class background, had been involved in a sexual relationship with her father. Incest remains the focus of her life. As the founder of a large peer-support organization, Fran devotes most of her time to helping other survivors of sexual abuse.

Fran said that she welcomed the opportunity to tell her story as another way of educating the public about the prevalence and devastating impact of incest. With the utmost clinical detachment, she presented a highly detailed account of her life. Fran went to great lengths to exonerate her father for his role in initiating incest. Instead, she blamed her mother for creating an atmosphere of deprivation in which incest could thrive. (Such "mother blaming" is a form of scapegoating commonly found in incestuous families. See, for example, Russell, 1986, pp. 134–45.)

Fran described her mother as cold, remote, and harshly critical; a woman whose overriding preoccupations were keeping a spotless, well-run home and preserving the family's leadership position in their country club community. As far as Fran could tell, her mother was only too willing to allow her husband to assume an active role in Fran's early care. As an executive for a large corporation, he regularly traveled away from home on business trips. However, when he was at home, Fran recalled, he bathed, dressed, and put her to sleep.

Fran surmised that even as a child she had accepted her father's fondling as expressions of the affection and tenderness she missed from her mother. She recalled that as a little girl she had become accustomed to sexually pleasing her father. Fran described lying on his lap while he used the toilet, sucking catsup off his penis, and urinating into his mouth. Their sexual contact remained primarily oral, and even when she reached puberty, her father never attempted intercourse.

According to Fran, her father used every opportunity to have sex with her, most often when Fran's mother was away at church or at bridge parties. Occasionally, however, they would have sex while her mother, apparently unaware, busied herself in another part of the house.

It was not until Fran entered first grade that she began to worry that something was "wrong" with her relationship with her father. She remembered avoiding close friendships with other children to protect their "secret." Until that time, Fran said, she regarded her father as a combination of "Superman" and the "Wizard of Oz." Even when she observed healthy interactions between her classmates and their fathers, Fran told herself that her father had sex with her because he loved her so much.

In spite of her academic excellence, Fran earned a reputation in school as a social outcast and mischievous daredevil. Once, for example, she climbed a church steeple where she perched above a large crowd for hours. Fran said she often thought of herself as "supergirl," invulnerable to physical injury and possessing extraordinary powers.

At the age of 13, Fran told her mother about the incest. Although her mother responded with cool indifference, all sexual contact between Fran and her father came to an abrupt halt. Fran described her behavior in the next few years as "increasingly weird." Once, after only a few flying lessons, she took her father's plane on a solo ride. She spent eight hours a day practicing the piano after proclaiming her "calling" for music. At the age of 16, she became "my mother's chauffeur," driving her to and from her many social functions.

The summer before Fran entered a prestigious college, her father died of heart disease. Finding herself among students whose academic and musical talent rivaled her own and "numb with grief," Fran felt so depressed she would spend days at a time in bed. After dropping out of this college and completing her B.A. at a local school, Fran married a music student with whom she had three children.

Fran described her marriage as a tragic reenactment of her early family life. She found herself unable to experience tender feelings for her children and, like her own mother, provided them with only the most perfunctory maternal care. She reported feeling "sexually dead" and refused to have any physical contact with her husband. "I hated when he touched me," Fran said, "it reminded me of sex with my father."

Observing that she lived in a "zombielike state of detachment" (depersonalization), Fran said she was dimly aware that her husband was sexually molesting her children. Yet she took no action to stop him. "Maybe I couldn't face that I had become just like my horrible mother, who closed her eyes to my abuse," she said. However, when Fran's eldest daughter ran away from home and initiated court proceedings for placement in a foster home, Fran left her husband and sought a divorce.

After the divorce, Fran "hit bottom." She described a prolonged period in which she struggled against terrifying episodes of fragmentation and dissolution. "I couldn't pretend that I was anything more than a total failure," she said. Desperate for guidance, Fran entered therapy with three different mental health professionals but found none of them willing to explore the psychological aftereffects of her incestuous relationship.

Fran observed that a turning point in her life came when she found a number of survivors of sexual abuse with whom she could share her experiences. With them, Fran said, she discovered her "gift" for bringing consolation to others. Within a few years, Fran established herself as a key figure in the newly emerging survivors' network.

Despite the many years that have elapsed since sexual contact between Fran and her father ended, she is still plagued by symptoms of PTSD. As a result of years of emotional numbing, a major symptom of PTSD, Fran's features are devoid of expression and her voice has an odd, monotonous quality. She spoke of "having gone through the motions of my life half asleep," which probably reflects her awareness of living, more or less continuously, in dissociated states of depersonalization and derealization. In another reference to dissociative states of depersonalization, Fran mentioned feeling as if "I am watching myself from a corner of the ceiling." She noted that she feels this way most intensely when she describes her incestuous experiences to large audiences.

Fran also suffers from many of the reexperiencing symptoms of PTSD. She reported reliving experiences, during sex, when she suddenly has the eerie feeling that she is once again with her father. She reported bizarre, aggressive images that intrude into her waking thoughts such as "sticking a knife into my mother's belly." Such images undoubtedly reflect the narcissistic rage Fran felt toward her mother for failing to protect her from her father's sexual abuse.

Fran is still subject to terrifying recurrent nightmares. In one such nightmare, which originated in adolescence, Fran is driving a car, terrified that she will speed out of control and crash. Fran associated the experience of speeding out of control to a conscious childhood fantasy of aging rapidly and marrying her father. While Fran tried to console herself with the idea that she was her father's cherished favorite, she was still painfully aware that becoming her father's surrogate wife meant losing her mother completely. Without hope of ever experiencing her mother's guiding, protective presence, Fran imagined that her life would hurtle toward catastrophe.

In another version of these nightmares, Fran sees herself after the car crashes. She has survived, but to her horror, everyone around her is dead. This apparently represents a faulty effort at the defensive restoration of her shattered grandiose fantasies. Fran, by dint of her extraordinary power to survive, lives through a crash that kills everyone else. However, her effort is ultimately unsuccessful insofar as she must survive alone.

Case Summary

By the time Fran entered school, her trust, respect, and admiration for both parents had been repeatedly shaken. Again and again, her mother had rebuffed her efforts at closeness. Again and again, she had submitted to her father's bizarre sexual demands. They were, in other words, figures who constantly interfered with Fran's need to unconsciously enact a fantasy of idealized merger with omnipotent parental imagos. In addition, her parents were grossly unempathic to Fran's needs for mirroring. Her mother apparently withheld all expressions of approval; her father showered her with praise but only when she served his sexual needs.

Because profound disappointment in her parents occurred so early and frequently in Fran's life, her central organizing fantasies of grandiose exhibitionism, as well as those of idealized merger, were repeatedly shattered. As she grew up, Fran's self-experience was increasingly organized by these fantasies, which underwent ever greater defensive and compensatory elaboration. For instance, the exhibitionistic displays Fran staged during her school years, as well as her inflated estimation of her musical ability, may be understood as unconscious efforts at defensive restoration of her grandiose fantasies.

Her efforts at compensatory restoration were even more dramatic. By exonerating her father for incest, Fran attempted the compensatory restoration of her fantasies of idealized merger with a benign paternal imago. By serving as her mother's chauffeur in adolescence,

Fran unconsciously sought a closeness that would restore similar fantasies of idealized merger with a maternal imago.

Fran's unceasing efforts in behalf of other survivors and her ambitious plans to establish a world-wide network of survivors appear to reflect her attempt to work through the traumatic unconscious meaning of incest. In counseling survivors, Fran continually draws on her own experiences of incest to reassure others that they are not alone in their suffering. Because her references to her father are, therefore, in the altruistic service of helping others, Fran's incestuous relationship with her father is given new meaning. At the same time, Fran experiences her own unique power as the survivor who helps others to survive. Yet, Fran is only too aware of her continuing vulnerability to episodes of terrifying fragmentation when life proves overly challenging or stressful.

Nettie

A tall and strikingly attractive black woman of 38, Nettie was interviewed several days after she had been brutally raped. Her initial recall for the event was so disjointed and contradictory that the following account could be reconstructed only after many months of therapeutic interviewing sessions.

One morning, Nettie was followed by a young black man to the incinerator where she intended to drop a bag of garbage before leaving for work. When Nettie refused the man's crude sexual invitations, he threw her to the ground, tore off her clothes and pinned her beneath him. Fearing for her life, she did not scream or struggle.

Nettie reported that he entered her vaginally, but withdrew without ejaculating. After beating her with his fists, he ran off, leaving her naked and dazed in the hallway. Nettie could not recall how she made it back to her apartment and was unable to account for the hours that passed between the time of the rape and her phone call to the police in the late afternoon.

In the days that followed, Nettie developed dissociative symptoms warranting a diagnosis of PTSD. She felt that her experience with the police only heightened her distress. She was mortified by the skeptical and contemputous tone of their questions when she could not fill in the many gaps in her story. Fearful of retaliation by the rapist, she decided not to press charges. She said the police classified her case as "unfounded."

Describing herself as the brightest and best looking of five children growing up on a modest farm in the South, Nettie remembers her parents as relying on her to validate their drab lives. "They always showed me off to friends and neighbors," Nettie remarked. "They gave me the idea that I was God's gift to the world. I must have been living proof that they were good, respectable, and successful folks." Because they continually reminded her of their sacrifices in her behalf, such as "scrimping and saving" so that she could have fashionable clothing, Nettie remembered feeling ashamed of her desire to break away from the narrow confines of their provincial life.

Inspired by biographies of famous black figures in American history, Nettie believed that she too was destined for special accomplishment. She remembered the many hours she had spent absorbed in highly embellished daydreams[1] of "making it big" in the North. Nettie envisioned herself variously as a famous doctor, a leading scientist, and a glamorous actress. "In those days," Nettie confided, "I thought I could do anything, be anyone I set my sights on." She admitted that it had never occurred to her that she would be handicapped by her lack of specialized training.

In all her daydreams, Nettie imagined her parents, beaming with pride as she recounted her latest exploits. To her dismay, Nettie's parents expressed only alarm and anger about her "high falutin' " notions of leaving them. They warned that only "loose women" lived on their own. Her mother advised Nettie to cook and sew, as she did. Her father encouraged stereotypically feminine weakness and helplessness.

At the age of 18, in spite of her parents' warnings that she was "asking for trouble," Nettie moved to a big Northern city. As if to confirm her parents' direst predictions, within months of leaving home, she became pregnant during a brief romance with a serviceman. Nettie recalled her fierce determination to overcome this humiliating setback by "rising to the top" of a big company. She returned to the North immediately after leaving her newborn daughter with her parents to raise.

After a series of disappointing "deadend" clerical jobs and relationships with men whom she described as exploitative and abusive, Nettie was promoted to a supervisory position. Once again she imagined that it was just a matter of time before she reached a top administrative position with her firm.

Several months before her rape, Nettie, involved in yet another unhappy relationship, this time with an abusive alcoholic man, discovered that she was pregnant again. She considered her decision to end the relationship and undergo an abortion a "great accomplishment."

These daydreams may be understood as conscious versions of unconscious (narcissistic) fantasies.

Proud of her newfound competence in managing her personal life, Nettie arranged to have her daughter, now a teenager, come to live with her. "I thought we'd be sitting on top of the world," Nettie said ruefully, "but the rape made me worry if I would ever get anywhere in life." She also mentioned her serious worries about her ability to cope with the needs of her daughter.

Almost immediately after the rape, Nettie experienced dissociative states of depersonalization, characteristic of PTSD. She complained of feeling "numb and detached, a stranger to myself." She became intensely preoccupied with her bodily functioning and expressed many bizarre concerns about her reproductive organs. For instance, she worried that her uterus had "fallen" and that a "sour smelling" vaginal discharge indicated cervical cancer. Her memory and concentration were so badly impaired that she needed assistance filling out an application in the emergency room of the hospital where she was treated for shock following the rape.

Nettie also reported a number of reexperiencing symptoms, including recurrent nightmares, that combined fragmentary yet vivid images of the rape and other abusive experiences with violent men in her past. The most florid of Nettie's reexperiencing symptoms were intrusive thoughts that the rapist and other members of his family were diabolically plotting to ruin her life. She believed that they were contriving humiliating encounters designed to destroy her reputation in the community. For example, she dreaded the thought of leaving her apartment because she anticiapted being pointed out as a "prostitute and whore." On one occasion, when she saw a man looking at her on the street, she imagined that he was leering furtively because he had been informed that she was "easy prey."

Despite the seemingly psychotic quality of this and other of her symptoms, a careful examination of Nettie's life revealed no evidence of an underlying psychotic disorder. Furthermore, after several months of therapeutic interviews her delusional thinking completely abated.

Case Summary

As a pampered favorite child, Nettie's early self-experience was unconsciously organized in accordance with archaic narcissistic fantasies of her unique endowment and limitless competence. However, Nettie felt that her special status in the family was contingent on her serving selfobject needs for her parents. Her parents appear to have required Nettie to reward their sacrifices by exhibiting her special gifts only for them and never venturing beyond the confines of the farm.

Because they provided no empathic understanding of Nettie's intense need to display her beauty and intelligence to the outside world, Nettie's fantasies of grandiose exhibitionism failed to undergo normal developmental transformation. As a result, her illusion that she would effortlessly attain success was not significantly modified by her life experiences. Rather than lowering her sights after her humiliating pregnancy, abusive relationships, and career disappointments, Nettie unconsciously embellished her fantasies of special endowment.

Judging from the state of fragmentation and disintegration anxiety that she experienced immediately following her rape, it seems likely that Nettie experienced herself primarily through these archaic fantasies. Powerless to defend herself against the brazen and vicious assault, Nettie's grandiose fantasies shattered. Because these fantasies had undergone so little developmental transformation, her PTSD symptoms were extremely severe. Nettie's bizarre hypochondriacal symptoms may be understood as somatic concretizations of her experience of fragmentation and dissolution. Her amnesia for details of the rape reflects the severity of her dissociation.

The grossly unempathic treatment she received at the hands of the police immediately following the rape undoubtedly exacerbated Nettie's PTSD. She experienced their disrespectful and skeptical response to her plight as another blow to her already shattered grandiosity.

In stark contrast to her feelings of pride at having ended an abusive relationship and obtaining an abortion, Nettie appears to have experienced the rape as confirming her parents' warning that she would never achieve success and prominence on her own, but instead would become a "loose woman." Her belief that the rapist was spreading rumors that she was a "prostitute and whore" unconsciously represented this shattering confirmation.

Nettie's notion that the rapist was diabolically plotting to ruin her life revealed the unconscious traumatic meaning of the rape as well as her faulty efforts at defensive restoration. Nettie's illusion that she was the focus of such wide-scale persecution (the rapst's plot to humiliate her before the community) enabled her to view her victimization as dramatic and consequential. However, it is evident that this desperate effort at the defensive restoration of her shattered fantasy of grandiose exhibitionism proved faulty in stemming the tide of her catastrophic experiences of fragmentation and disintegration.

".44 Mike"

Mike, muscular and powerfully built, is a 40-year-old, white Vietnam combat veteran. During the course of the lengthy therapeutic interviewing procedure, Mike, disabled by PTSD, lived with his parents.

At the time of the initial interviews, he had just returned from eight years in the Alaskan wilderness, where he had worked as a trapper, hunter, and commercial fisherman. He later admitted that he had also been an occasional gunman and enforcer for a drug dealer.

In his screening interview, Mike complained of a variety of problems including extreme anxiety, depression, nightmares, insomnia, panic attacks, uncontrolled rages, and agoraphobia. As the interviews proceeded, the interviewer found sufficient clinical evidence of reexperiencing and numbing symptoms to make the diagnosis of PTSD.

In his early interview sessions, Mike boasted that he had been a brave and fearless warrior in Vietnam, revelling in the fighting and killing. He also insisted that he had been unafraid of serious wounds or of dying. Only gradually did a more accurate picture of his combat experiences emerge.

A brief review of Mike's precombat history provides a genetic context for understanding some of the unconscious traumatic meaning of combat. Sickly throughout infancy and early childhood, Mike on several occasions nearly died of pneumonia and convulsions. Because of his frail health, Mike noted, his mother "doted on me" and treated him as her favorite child. (Mike has two younger sisters and one younger brother.) He described his mother's relationship with him as that of a "lioness with her cub."

Mike indicated that his mother had continued to lavish him with special attention when he was an adolescent. Mike acknowledged that he had grown up feeling that he was entitled to special treatment. In fact, Mike revealed, his mother is still extremely devoted to caring for him.

Mike's father, a highly decorated World War II combat veteran, had been a member of the Allied Forces that invaded Europe at Normandy Beach. Throughout his childhood, Mike constantly heard stories from paternal uncles about his father's heroic exploits as a glider pilot during the war. Mike grew up determined to realize his childhood fantasies of himself as a brave soldier like his father.

Although he admired, even worshipped, his father, Mike sadly related that he was unable to establish an emotionally close relationship with him. Throughout Mike's childhood and adolescence, his father, who worked as a night watchman, was rarely at home during the day. Mike bemoaned the loss of opportunities to hear firsthand from his father about his war exploits.

During high school, Mike, an outstanding athlete and winner of varsity letters and state awards in boxing and football, was a "real he-man." Mike loved the physical violence of both these contact sports. He worked at very physically demanding jobs, which also filled him with an intense pride and sense of unlimited physical prowess. Mike unabashedly stated that as an adolescent he had been blessed with such vast and superior physical strength that he had thought of himself as invincible and invulnerable.

At the age of 19, and enjoying typical adolsecent male fantasies of exhibitionistic grandiosity, Mike welcomed being drafted into the Army. Mike explained that he was absolutely certain that he would finally realize his embellished fantasies of himself as a "lean, mean, fighting machine."

In Vietnam in the late 1960s, Mike initially served as a member of a Howitzer mobile cannon crew. Halfway through his tour, he was promoted to the rank of corporal and put in charge of his own gun crew. Mike explained that he had been given this responsible position because of his outstanding ability to carry out orders. Even in the heat of battle, he had demonstrated a rare and highly valued ability to accurately calculate complicated coordinates necessary for hitting distant enemy targets.

As a member of a mobile artillery unit, Mike often found himself in isolated jungle clearings totally surrounded by the enemy. Shortly after he arrived in Vietnam, Mike got his first "taste" of combat in just such a remote area. Trapped by the enemy on a hilltop, his unit was cut off from all escape. As Mike and his unit prepared for the enemy assault, Mike thought for the first time about dying. At a later time in the interviews, Mike grudgingly acknowledged that during the ensuing firefight he had been "scared shitless"—his cherished illusions of invincibility and invulnerability shattered.

In fact, the remainder of Mike's combat tour and postcombat life can be understood as frantic but faulty attempts at restoring his shattered fantasies of grandiosity. For instance, he described being filled with a sense of superhuman potency as he pulled the trigger of the Howitzer and unleashed its awesome and destructive firepower. Mike claimed that as the trigger man for the Howitzer, he was responsible for the death of hundreds of enemy soldiers and their suspected sympathizers. Mike also reported that he had volunteered for dangerous patrols during which he acted recklessly, apparently unconcerned about his own safety and well-being.

During truck trips through bombed out villages, Mike went into wild frenzies, mutilating the bodies of enemy soldiers and villagers killed during the artillery barrages. He fired his automatic rifle at point blank range into the bodies. He also cut off various body parts including ears, which he collected on a necklace as "souvenirs." Mike justified his violent excesses as avenging the loss of buddies.

Mike remembered wounding and capturing a teenage enemy soldier.

In an exhibitionistic display of his prowess as a warrior, he had carried the man back to the American base camp on his shoulders like a big game trophy. He remembered the exhileration he felt as he strutted triumphantly through the camp, exulting in the cheers of the other soldiers.

After returning from Vietnam, Mike was divorced twice following brief and turbulent marriages. Before going to Alaska, he worked at a succession of unskilled and semiskilled jobs such as driving a taxi cab and serving as rifle range instructor.

Mike sought refuge in the wilderness of Alaska because he felt a need to avoid social contact. (This is an example of numbing.) He claimed that in Alaska he was renowned for his skill as a trapper, hunter, and fisherman. He was especially proud of his reputation as a skilled expert with handguns, rifles, and knives.

Mike related that he had gotten his nickname, ".44 Mike," after other hunters saw him use a .44 Magnum revolver to shoot, at almost point blank range, a charging grizzly bear. Always heavily armed, Mike was also involved as a gunman and enforcer for a drug dealer in numerous acts of violence against others.

Mike reported that after he returned from the Alaskan wilderness his PTSD symptoms rendered him a virtual prisoner in his parents' home. He described a pervasive sense of paranoia, and fear, as well as hyperalertness, which made going outside and dealing with people painfully unbearable. Whenever he ventured outside his parents' home, he suffered massive panic attacks (disintegration anxiety) in which he felt totally out of control, as though unraveling (depersonalization).

Moreover, Mike found it almost impossible to concentrate on even the simplest tasks or remember familiar names and dates. Mike was painfully aware of the marked contrast between his current difficulties in concentrating and remembering and his previous ability to quickly and accurately plot complicated artillery coordinates.

In addition to the agoraphobia reflective of numbing, Mike also described dissociative states in connection with reexperiencing symptoms including traumatic nightmares, reliving episodes, and recurrent dreams. In one nightmare, Mike was engaged in a firefight with enemy soldiers but could not get his gun to shoot; in another, he was armed with only a toy M-16 rifle; in a third, Mike, caught by surprise in his foxhole, was bayoneted and shot by an enemy soldier; and, in a fourth, he fired his weapon at enemy soldiers but they kept coming at him as if untouched by his bullets.

In his associations to these nightmares, Mike spoke of the reccurring and terrifying image of himself as defenseless, helpless, and at the mercy of a clearly superior and seemingly invincible enemy. He connected this image to his first exposure to combat and the shattering of his illusion of unlimited power and invulnerability. He had tried (unsuccessfully) to restore this image of himself throughout the remainder of his combat tour by magically merging with the awesome power of the Howitzer, engaging in bold, daring, and even foolhardy behavior and acts of savagery and brutality.

Apparently, Mike's life as a rugged outdoorsman in the Alaskan wilderness and his strongarm activities were also unconsciously intended to restore his shattered grandiose fantasy. His traumatic nightmares of terrifying impotence and the disintegration anxiety that accompanied these self-state dreams attest to the faultiness of his attempts at self-restitution.

Mike also reported somnambulistic episodes in which he had quasi-hallucinatory visions of "seeing" the mutilated and bloody bodies of enemy soldiers and villagers, who had been killed during artillery barrages, about to attack him. In one of these nocturnal episodes, he became so agitated and disturbed that he swung his fist at what he imagined were the menacing bodies only to strike his bedroom wall and break his hand. He often awoke from his sleep lying on the floor with his room in a shambles, with no conscious memory of getting out of his bed or ransacking his room.

Mike related that the disturbance in his sense of reality and time (derealization) was also characteristic of his waking hours. He regularly found himself staring into space for hours, lost in reveries of combat. During some of these fuguelike states, Mike lost contact with reality and imagined that he was back in combat.

In addition to traumatic nightmares and reliving (nocturnal and waking) experiences, Mike also referred to several recurrent dreams, whose interpretation revealed much about his disturbed sense of self (depersonalization) in the context of the unconscious meaning of traumatic combat occurrences. For example, in one of these dreams:

> I've been drafted into the Army and assigned to combat duty in Vietnam. I'm on a train headed for boot camp. I've been issued my military equipment and M-16 rifle. Suddenly, I discover that I've lost my name-tagged duffel bag with my equipment as well as my rifle. I search all over the train but cannot find my stuff.

While exploring this dream, the interviewer asked Mike if he had any associations to the dream image of losing all his equipment. Mike sobbed as he related it to his disturbing sense of having lost both his mental and physical prowess in combat. Mike and the interviewer connected the loss of his equipment and rifle ("my stuff") to his sense that the traumatic shattering of his grandiose fantasies meant the loss of his masculinity, that is, the loss of a self-image as a well-equipped and potent he-man. (See chapter 8 for a discussion of traumatic disturbances in gender identity.)

They related the dream image of being unable to find "my stuff" with the failure of exhibitionistic displays of *macho* violence to defensively restore his fantasies of grandeur. A self-psychological explanation of his violence would focus on the unrelenting narcissistic rage and need for revenge that follows the shattering of an archaic narcissistic fantasy. (See chapter 5 for a further exploration this dynamic as it relates to understanding narcissistic rage as a symptom of PTSD in Vietnam combat veterans.)

Case Summary.

From his account of his early life, it seems likely that Mike went into combat unconsciously organized in accordance with archaic, exhibitionistic, and fragile fantasies of grandiosity. Apparently, Mike's mother unknowingly had overstimulated his fantasies of grandiosity, perhaps because of her own anxiety about his early physical frailty and brushes with death.

As a result of the emotionally distant relationship between Mike and his father, these fantasies failed to undergo sufficient developmental transformation. In other words, the absence of a close father-son relationship prevented Mike from unconsciously enacting a healthy fantasy of idealized merger with an omnipotent paternal imago. This unconscious fantasy enactment could have modulated and tempered his fantasies of grandiosity.

The traumatic shattering during Mike's first exposure to combat in Vietnam and subsequent faulty defensive restoration (primarily by exhibitionistic displays of violence and other *macho* grandstanding) of Mike's grandiose fantasies left him severely dissociated. He suffered from PTSD throughout the postcombat period, and his sense of self and reality were constantly disturbed and undermined by dissociative states of depersonalization and derealization.

CHAPTER 2

Psychoanalytic Schools of Thought on Trauma

In reviewing the extensive psychoanalytic literature on trauma, we distinguished three distinct schools of thought, which we call the "classical," "neoclassical," and "revisionist." The classical school consists of the works of Freud and a number of his early followers including Abraham and Deutsch. The neoclassical school includes the works of such theorists as Greenacre, Jacobson, and Krystal. It encompasses three separate yet interrelated views on trauma: developmental, narcissistic, and catastrophic. Although differing in clinical emphasis, all the neoclassists utilize Freud's experience-distant metapsychology and (second) model of trauma. The revisionist school includes the work of such theorists as Kardiner, Rado, and Kelman, whose understanding of trauma derives from a theoretical framework relatively free of metapsychological concepts.

Our self-psychological theory stems, in large part, from the neoclassical and revisionist emphasis on narcissism and disturbances in sense of self or self-experience. Our critical comments on the work of selected representatives of these three schools of thought are based on our belief that an honest discussion of problems in the psychoanalytic theory of trauma is necessary to insure its continuing vitality and relevance to problems of our times. Our remarks are meant to expose blind spots and biases of classical (and neoclassical) psychoanalytic thinking that have seriously distorted and limited its theory of trauma. More specifically, we question the psychoanalytic theory that trauma, and especially sexual trauma or "seduction," is a product of fantasy. Classical and neoclassical psychoanalytic theories proposing that sexual trauma is the result of fantasized, not actual, seduction stand in sharp contrast to Freud's (as well as other early analysts' including Abraham, Ferenczi, Simmel, and Jones) clear recognition that the trauma experienced by World War I combat soldiers resulted from actual, and not fantasized, wartime events (see chapter 5). Following Freud's theory on sexual rather than combat trauma caused many psychoanalysts to miss the important point that trauma results from actual and not fantasized events.

FREUD AND THE CLASSICAL SCHOOL

The classical school of psychoanalytic thought centers on two conceptual models of trauma developed by Freud at different stages in the evolution of his thinking. (See chapter 5 for a discussion of Freud's views on traumatic war neurosis and a third model of trauma; see also Krystal, 1978, for his previous division of Freud's thought on trauma into two conceptual models.) Freud constructed his first model of trauma during the early stages of his work. In *Studies on Hysteria* (1893–95), Freud reported the case of Katharina, a young woman who complained of unsolicited and unwanted sexual advances by an uncle. The case material reveals a pattern of abusive sexual behavior on the part of the uncle. In a footnote to the case in 1924, Freud (Breuer and Freud, 1893–95) noted that Katharina's hysterical neurosis resulted from her father's "sexual attempts" (p. 134), that is, incestuous behavior, as well as from the uncle's sexual molestation.

Freud's (1905) description of his treatment of "Dora" provides a similar example. Throughout the case, Freud referred to instances of seduction. The case material reveals that Dora's hysterical symptoms followed several rapes committed by her father's friend, "Herr K.".

In his early works, Freud argued that following trauma the mental apparatus automatically attempts to regain psychic equilibrium and homeostasis by suppressing or "strangulating" affects that threaten to overwhelm it. Despite efforts by the mental apparatus to keep them closed off, these strangulated affects press for emotional, motoric, and behavioral expression.

Influenced by Helmholtz (see Sulloway, 1983), Freud initially understood (and treated) trauma on the basis of mechanistic concepts such as psychic energy, homeostasis, and equilibrium as well as therapeutic techniques such as catharsis and abreaction. Freud theorized that real sexual trauma is explicable in terms of a psychoenergistic disequilibrium caused by the breakdown of a stimulus barrier and sudden overwhelming of the psychic apparatus by powerful affects generated by an actual occurence, that is, seduction. We refer to Freud's early theory of trauma as the "psychoenergistic" model.

Freud began constructing his second theory or model in a number of his early works, including *The Interpretation of Dreams* (1900–01), and several of his case histories, such as *Analysis of a Phobia in a Five-Year-Old Boy* ("Little Hans," 1909a) and *Notes Upon a Case of Obsessional Neurosis* (the "Rat Man," 1909b). In these works, Freud focused more explicitly than in his previous writings on "psychic reality," or unconscious meaning, as essential to understanding (and treating) trauma.

Freud further refined his second model in later writings, and especially in *From the History of an Infantile Neurosis* (the "Wolf Man," 1918), *Moses and Monotheism* (1939), and "Splitting of the Ego in the Process of Defense" (1940).

Freud's second theory, the "pathogenic fantasy arousal" model of trauma, stands in contrast to his first. This second model views trauma as a complex psychological process involving disturbing visual and auditory impressions of the primal scene (that is, parental intercourse and other adult sexual activity). These impressions are repressed and unconsciously organized in the form of pathogenic fantasies of sado-masochism and castration.

Freud argued that the traumatic meaning of specific events can be understood only in the context of earlier and latently pathogenic impressions and the unconscious (repressed) memories connected with them. According to Freud, the child is not mature enough at the time of the initial impression to organize it into a meaningful mental content. Rather, the child is overwhelmed by these perceptions and plunged into hypnoid states in which impressions are "split off".

These impressions are then unconsciously organized as affect-laden yet repressed memories. Freud contended that as a result of later occurrences, these memories are stimulated and break into consciousness, where they press for immediate emotional discharge. Unconscious defense mechanisms are then called into play in an attempt to block out these memories.

In describing the case of the Wolf Man, Freud (1918) pointed out that as a three-year-old boy the Wolf Man had been "seduced" by his older sister. Close scrutiny of the details of Freud's account reveals that the seduction involved actual sexual molestation and abuse. Today, this seduction might be described as brother-sister incest.

In applying his second model of trauma, Freud contended that the sexual contct between the Wolf Man and his sister was not in itself traumatic. Rather, it took on a traumatic meaning only when the Wolf Man witnessed the primal scene. This experience, according to Freud, overstimulated the Wolf Man, arousing and intensifying unconscious fantasies of seduction. The breakthrough into conscious awareness of these pathogenic fantasies retroactively imbues the prior seduction with its traumatic meaning and pathogenic impact. In other words, Freud argued, an early childhood seduction had a delayed impact because of the breakthrough of sexually aggressive fantasies of the primal scene.

As evidence of the traumatogenicty of these fantasies, Freud referred to a nightmare that the Wolf Man reported as reccurring during this period of his childhood. We need not describe the details of this nightmare and the Wolf Man's associations to it; suffice it to say that Freud interpreted the unconscious meaning of the nightmare in terms of the Wolf Man's identification with his mother, whom he perceived as a helpless, passive, and defenseless victim during parental intercourse.

Freud contended that in an effort to defend himself against the anxiety-provoking meaning of these fantasies (that is, that the Wolf Man, like his mother, was a helpless, passive, and defensive victim), the Wolf Man imagined himself in the earlier contact with his sister as the initiator. Freud implied that such a defensively motivated revision of the incident was reassuring and comforting to the Wolf Man and hence alleviated his anxiety.

Freud (1939, 1940) apparently used the fact that the Wolf Man was a survivor of seduction as the basis for two hypothetical examples of sexual trauma involving little boys. In *Moses and Monotheism* (1939), Freud introduced a hypothetical case of a little boy who, sharing his parents' bedroom during the early years of his life, repeatedly witnessed parental intercourse and other sexual activity. According to Freud, these experiences left unorganized impressions, which at the time created only a mild emotional disturbance. Several years later, however, the little boy, who had entered a new psychosexual phase of development, unconsciously organized these repressed memories of the primal scene into disturbing fantasmagorical images.

Under the influence of this newly organized fantasmagorical imagery, the little boy adopted a sexually aggressive stance toward his mother and engaged in compulsive masturbation. To curb his behavior, his mother threatened him with the loss of his penis at the hands of his father. Freud contended that this threat of castration generated intense and overwhelming anxiety.

According to Freud, the threat of castration took on its traumatic meaning because of repressed memories of witnessing the primal scene. The little boy remembered seeing his mother naked and imaginging that she had lost her penis. The little boy's unconscious illusion that his mother had been castrated convinced him that the loss of his own penis was a real possibility.

Freud reported that shortly after being threatened with castration, the little boy's character and behavior changed abruptly and dramatically. Previously aggressive and cocky, he became extremely passive and submissive. Freud also alluded to powerful sadomasochistic fantasies accompanying these personality changes.

In "Splitting of the Ego in the Process of Defense" (1940), Freud presented another hypothetical case of what he now implied was the prototypical form of childhood sexual trauma, that is, a little boy being seduced by an older girl. Freud insisted that the seduction was not traumatic at the time of its original occurrence, but that this experience took on unconscious traumatic meaning only at a later age when the little boy, who engaged in masturbation, was threatened with castration. The threat of castration became traumatic because the little boy had repressed memories of the earlier seduction. He vividly remembered perceiving the girl's genital area and being shocked by the absence of a penis.

Freud's two hypothetical cases suggest several problems in Freud's evolving theory of trauma. First, Freud increasingly became more concerned about the unconscious meaning of fantasy than of fact. He interpreted the unconscious meaning of trauma in terms of childhood sadomasochistic and castration fantasies rather than on the basis of the shattering impact of actual sexual assaults. Freud's dramatic shift in theoretical emphasis from the fact of seduction to oedipal fantasy (see Masson, 1984) is essential to the classical psychoanalytic theory that (sexual) trauma is a product of fantasy.

Second, in contrast to his early writings on hysteria (see, for example, Breuer and Freud, 1883–85, and Freud, 1905), Freud no longer referred to girls and women as victims of sexual abuse by older adult males. Instead, he presented actual (that is, the Wolf Man) and hypothetical cases in which little boys were sexually victimized by older girls. These cases are at odds both with Freud's own earlier work and recent empirical research (see, for example, Herman, 1981; Russell, 1986) indicating that girls are typically the victims of incest at the hands of older males. By giving the impression that seduction of little boys by older girls is typical of childhood sexual victimization, Freud's (1918, 1940) writings grossly misrepresented the truth of the nature of sexual trauma in childhood.

THE NEOCLASSICAL SCHOOL

Most of the neoclassists utilized Freud's metapsychology and a version of his second model of trauma. In addition, with a few noteworthy exceptions (see our discussion of Greenacre and Jacobson), neoclassical investigators rarely offered any actual clinical material in support of their position. Their writings tended to be extremely abstract and dogmatic with little, if any, clinical documentation.

Phyllis Greenacre: Theorist of Developmental Trauma

Greenacre (1949, 1950, 1967) advanced the view that trauma is primarily a phenomenon of development. She argued that trauma is an inevitable part of all psychological development, encompassing expectable as well as extraordinary ocurrences. Greenacre implied that the crucial question for psychoanalysis was not whether trauma occurs, but its timing, type, and intensity. She contended that the earlier, more prolonged, and more intense the trauma, the more severe and lasting will be its damaging psychological effects.

Relying heavily on the work of Fenichel, a well-known proponent of classical psychoanalytic doctrine, Greenacre modified Freud's second model of trauma. Whereas Freud believed that the child typically witnessed the primal scene during the oedipal stage of psychosexual development, Greenacre dated such observations as occurring earlier, in the preoedipal period. However, like Freud, Greenacre maintained that witnessing the primal scene constitutes for the child, the primary traumatogenic experience.

Greenacre indicated that because of the child's psychological immaturity, primal scene impressions are unconsciously organized as sadomasochistic fantasies. These pathogenic fantasies then imbue later, prepubertal sexual experiences with traumatic meaning. According to Greenacre, when young children are traumatized, they often regress to earlier stages of psychosexual development. Although she set an earlier date for primal scene observations, Greenacre agreed with Freud's contention that the unconscious traumatic meaning of later childhood and adolescent experiences are based on repressed memories of the primal scene.

In support of her views on trauma, Greenacre (1949, 1950) presented case material from her private analytic practice. For example, she (1949) described the case of a 35-year-old female nurse who as a little girl had witnessed a strange man masturbating and who had at a later time been raped. Both occurrences, according to Greenacre, took on traumatic meaning and triggered a pathological psychosexual regression primarily because of earlier disturbances stemming from witnessing the primal scene.

Greenacre (1949) argued that as a youngster, the nurse was "really a very seductive little girl, who was predisposed [to trauma] by long exposure to sexual scenes and she cooperated in the instigation of these exprieriences" (p. 202). To substantiate her assertion, Greenacre insisted that the primary trauma in the nurse's life was a preoedipal observation of the primal scene rather than her later experiences of witnessing a strange man masturbating and being raped. Greenacre even went so far as to suggest that these later occurrences need not have been traumatic because the little girl's supposed seductiveness had precipitated them.

In another treatment case, that of a 30-year-old woman, Greenacre (1949) described a series of early traumas that she claimed not only imbued a later experience with its unconscious traumatic meaning but precipitated it. The early childhood traumas included a painful and humiliating series of enemas administered by the mother, who forced her daughter to lie naked in a bathtub with her legs spread open. Greenacre argued that these experiences formed the critical psychic reality imbuing the witnessing of the primal scene with its traumatic unconscious meaning. Specifically, according to Greenacre, the little girl reported having witnessed her mother performing fellatio on her father, an impression that the child unconsciously organized in the form of pathogenic fantasies of "sex urination and mouth impregnation" (p. 212).

Greenacre asserted that these pathogenic fantasies set the stage for an episode of sexual molestation by a gas meter man when the woman was ten years old. The woman remembered asking him to lift her up to read the numbers on the gas meter, and that in "lifting her he put his hand under her dress and stimulated her genitals" (p. 207). The woman could not recall what happened after the meter man molested her. Apparently, she was so traumatized by the experience that she went into a dissociated state in which "she lost consciousnes or 'went blank' " (p. 207).

Greenacre interpreted the unconscious meaning of this traumatic occurrence in terms of castration. She insisted that the woman had unconsciously sought to "seduce" the gas meter man in the hope of seeing his genitals, apparently to reassure herself of the existence of the penis. According to Greenacre, the unconscious motivation for the little girl's seduction involved an attempt to belatedly master the trauma associated with the primal scene.

The significance of her patient's dissociation immediately following the molestation seems to have eluded Greenacre. For Greenacre, the traumatic meaning of the sexual molestation derived entirely from pathogenic fantasies stemming from earlier preoedipal traumas. As in Greenacre's previously cited case report, the patient's supposed seductiveness (flirtatiousness and coquettishness) was viewed as unconsciously intended to precipitate the molestation. Greenacre's line of reasoning contributed considerably to the classical psychoanalytic theory that (sexual) trauma is a product of fantasy.

Greenacre based her understanding of trauma on a total of four cases, only two of which she reported. She provided no rationale for her case selection. Moreover, despite an attempt (see Greenacre, 1980, 1981) to modify her highly questionable views on female psychology, Greenacre's insistence that her two female patients unconsciously induced their own sexual traumatization as a result of their seductiveness is a classic example of "blaming the victim" (Ryan, 1971).

Edith Jacobson: Theorist of Narcissistic Trauma

The second group of analytic theorists on trauma understand trauma as a narcissistic disturbance inside the ego involving conflicts between different self-representations. Traditionally, psychoanalysts have regarded this domain of the ego as the narcissistic realm. According to this group of theorists, narcissistic disturbance involves problems in the formation and maintenance of a healthy self-image as well as self-esteem regulation. In addition to Jacobson, other proponents of trauma as a narcissistic disturbance and conflict include Federn (1952), Rosen (1955), Murphy (1959), Sarlin (1962), Arlow (1966), and Bach and Schwartz (1972; Bach, 1985).

As a group, these theorists employed Freud's second model of pathogenic fantasy arousal as a conceptual framework for their work. However, they refined a number of features of this model. First, they did not conceptualize psychic conflict as occurring between a pathogenic childhood fantasy and the ego. Rather, they viewed trauma as triggering conflict within the ego itself in the area of self-representation.

For these theorists, psychic conflict occurs between a self-representation organized around a pathogenic childhood fantasy and a nontraumatic self-representation. In other words, they envisioned trauma in terms of psychic conflict occurring on a basic level of unconscious mental life, namely, the level of self-experience.

Second, these theorists modified Freud's depiction of the psychological aftermath of trauma as a breakdown of ego functions including the loss of reality testing, integration, synthesis, and so forth. They described the aftermath of trauma as involving depersonalization and derealization, concepts critical to our self-psychological theory of trauma. (See chapter 1 for a discussion of Jacobson's views on the relation between trauma and the dissociated states of depersonalization and derealization.)

Jacobson's (1949, 1959) early studies laid the foundation for a psychoanalytic understanding of trauma as narcissistic decompensation and regression. Most of the foregoing theorists based their work on Jacobson's influential studies. Jacobson's views on trauma emerged during the course of her clinical research with female political prisoners of the Nazis as well as her analysis of private practice patients.

Jacobson (1949) described the arrest, interrogation, imprisonment, and torture of these female political prisoners. She emphasized the almost complete loss of control over basic aspects of their lives as well as their prolonged humiliation and degradation. She focused on the resulting narcissistic injuries, blows to their pride and dignity that led to the widespread incidence of trauma and posttraumatic symptomatology.

Jacobson maintained that the trauma for many of these women was rooted in psychic conflict between preimprisonment self-representations and later identifications arising from their prison experiences. To varying degrees, the former self-representations were organized in accordance with healthy self-respect. The latter self-representations were organized around a painful and unacceptable sense of the self as degraded, humiliated, and worthless.

Jacobson argued that because of the inner turmoil created by this psychic conflict, these women became vulnerable to dissociative states of depersonalization involving a loss of a sense of reality about previous experiences of self. She (1959) added that "we . . . find in depersonalization a detached, intact part of the ego observing the other—emotionally or psychically dead—unacceptable part" (p. 608). She explained dissociative states as occurring because of "disidentification" (p. 598), an unconscious process leading to an altered state of awareness. According to Jacobson, in such an altered state of consciousness people experience "feelings of unreality about themselves and their environment" (p. 586) and "psychic self-estrangement . . . with feelings of being outside their self and of watching themselves think, talk, or act as though they were another person . . ." (p. 587).

Employing Freud's classical concept of compromise formation, Jacobson stated that to avoid the unendurable psychic pain that accompanies disidentification and depersonalization, the traumatized person unconsciously splits off and disowns self-representations crystalized in awareness following traumatic experiences. However, such unconscious efforts at preserving a sense of identity and avoiding pain ultimately fail, exacting a high psychological cost. The price of such failures is the splitting of the represenatation of the self that makes up the psychological nucleus of the ego. These splits create psychic fissures that seriously impair any sense of a cohesive identity.

Jacobson (1959) explained "narcissistic regression provoked . . . by trauma" (p. 606) in neoclassical terms as involving a "regressive pregenital, sadomasochistic 'primal-scene' identification with the parents" (p. 596). In other words, Jacobson argued that the women prisoners were not directly traumatized by their shattering experiences in prison, but rather were traumatized by identifying themselves with sexually aggressive fantasy images unconsciously organized around repressed memories of the primal scene. In her eagerness to substantiate further the classical psychoanalytic theory that trauma is a product of fantasy, Jacobson, like Greenacre, followed Freud in discounting the unconscious traumatic meaning of actual occurrences.

Jacobson offered several clinical vignettes from her private practice in support of the classical psychoanalytic theory of trauma. For example, she (1959) described the case of "Mrs. A.," a young mother whom she had treated. According to Jacobson's analytic reconstruction of her past, Mrs. A. had invested her young daughter with an imaginary phallus as a narcissistic compensation for her unconscious belief in her own castration. In other words, Jacobson suggested that Mrs. A.'s experience of herself as lacking a penis was so injurious to her self-esteem that she identified herself in fantasy with her phallically endowed daughter. Such a fantasized identification was unconsciously intended to maintain an illusion that she too possessed phallic qualities. In Jacobson's account, Mrs. A. can be understood as attempting magically to undo her imagined castration.

Jacobson (1959) reported that Mrs. A.'s "neurotic solution" was successful only until she saw her daughter and a little boy standing naked next to each other. Jacobson observed: "The perception of the little girl's genital in comparison with that of the boy had *destroyed the patient's phallic illusions* and inflicted a severe castration shock upon her" (p. 593, italics added). Jacobson contended that Mrs. A.'s reaction was based on "a sudden libidinal withdrawal and an immediate denial of the frightening perception, which found expression in her feeling of detachment" (p. 593). Mrs. A. had become depersonalized. Following this traumatic incident, Mrs. A. continued to suffer from dissociative states of depersonalization which were central to understanding her traumatized condition.

In another vignette, "Mr. B." suffered from depersonalization following the death of his mother when he was five years old. Although Jacobson acknowledged that the mother's death produced a severe emotional shock, she contended that the trauma surrounding the death of Mr. B.'s mother must be understood in terms of its deeper roots in the unconscious. Jacobson reconstructed Mr. B.'s reaction to his mother's death in terms of the mobilization of "wild primal-scene fantasies visualizing the mother as a victim of her passion for the father, and the father as the sexual murderer of the mother" (p. 595).

Jacobson's explanation for Mr. B.'s vulnerability to states of depersonalization is based on her belief that he repudiated (that is, unconsciously disidentified) a self-representation organized around an identification with the father, whom he fantasized to be a murderer. According to Jacobson, Mr. B. split his self-representation between pretraumatic and traumatic identifications. As a result of disidentification, Mr. B. was subject to disorganizing states of depersonalization.

Both of Jacobson's clinical vignettes reveal the strengths and weaknesses of her neoclassical theory of trauma. On one hand, Jacobson demonstrated her clear recognition of the dissociative nature of posttraumatic symptomatology. She correctly pointed out that traumatically induced depersonalization results from the disavowal of the meaning of some shattering experience that is split off from conscious awareness.

On the other hand, Jacobson's reliance on classical metapsychology and Freud's second model of trauma compelled her to view dissociative symptoms such as depersonalization as reflective only of unconscious defensive processes. Jacobson (1959) pointed out that depersonalization can be employed by the ego "to affirm and restore its intactness" (p. 591) as well as to "restore and maintain a normal level of behavior, resting on stable identifications" (p. 606).

However, rather than pursuing her important ideas on the restoration of the self, Jacobson (1959) is critical of the "opinion . . . that depersonalization represents a *restitutive* process" (p. 609, italics added). Instead, she insisted that "it must be regarded as a *defense of the ego* which tries to recover and to maintain its intactness by opposing, detaching, and disowning the regressed, diseased part" (p. 609, italics added).

By relying so heavily on the classical psychoanalytic theory of the traumatogenicity of primal scene fantasies of sadomasochism and castration as the critical factor in understanding the unconscious meaning of trauma, Jacobson obscured rather than illuminated the shattering impact of real events in the lives of those she studied and treated.

Henry Krystal: Theorist of Catastrophic Trauma

Krystal and other theorists of catastrophic trauma such as Niederland, Sterba, Tanay, and Lifton based their views on extensive clinical research with survivors of the Nazi concentration camps, the World

War II atomic bomb blasts on Nagasaki and Hiroshima, and natural disasters as well.

Krystal (1971, 1975, 1978, 1988; Krystal and Niederland, 1968; Krystal and Raskin, 1970) has advanced the psychoanalytic theory of trauma in several important respects. First, he (Krystal, 1978) made a useful distinction between "near trauma" and "catastrophic trauma." According to Krystal, in near trauma the personality is threatened but is not psychologically overwhelmed. However, the threat may trigger serious forms of psychopathology. In contrast, catastrophic trauma overwhelms the entire personality, causing the person to collapse into a state of total helplessness. Catastrophic trauma may lead to permanent psychological damage.

Second, Krystal (see also Niederland, 1968a, b) described a cluster of symptoms, the "survivor syndrome," that seemed to be almost universal among concentration camp survivors. According to Krystal (and Niederland), the survivor syndrome consists of the following symptoms: survivor guilt at having lived while others died or having lived at the expense of others; chronic anxiety as reflected in traumatic nightmares; psychological changes; psychosomatic symptoms; and disturbances in cognition. Krystal also viewed problems in handling aggression as a central symptom of the survivor syndrome. (See A. Ornstein, 1985, for a self-psychological critique of Krystal's work as well as other psychoanalytic studies of Nazi concentration camp survivors.)

Expanding on his work on the survivor syndrome, Krystal (1978) distinguished between direct and indirect (or secondary) aftereffects of trauma. The direct aftereffects include: "a general dullness, obtuseness and concomitant lowering of occupational and social functions which may last a lifetime," "episodic freezing," psychological and physical paralysis, and "pseudophobia," and the continuing capacity of memory fragments to evoke intense affects (pp. 106–8). Krystal's (and Niederland's) work on the survivor syndrome was critical to the development of the current DSM-III clinical criteria for the diagnosis of PTSD.

Krystal's work is important because it represents a serious attempt to clear up some of the confusion within psychoanalysis about the nature and treatment of trauma. He (1978, pp. 82–5) distinguished two different theoretical models of trauma that, he argued, Freud employed at different times throughout his work. Krystal called the first the "unbearable situation" model (p. 84), which he stated conceptualized trauma as a personal confrontation with overwhelming affects. More specifically, according to this model, a person's "affective responses produce an unbearable psychic state that threatens to disorganize and even destroy all psychic functions" (pp. 82–3).

Krystal called the second construct the "dynamics of pathogenesis" model (p. 84). This model depicts trauma as an emotional conflict arising from the clash between the desire to express "unacceptable" drives and the need to defend against expressing these same impulses.

Krystal maintained that Freud's different conceptualizations of trauma represented by these two models are both flawed and inconsistent. The first model presents trauma as primarily an overwhelming affective *state* resulting in psychological disorganization; the second model portrays trauma as essentially a pathological *condition* of emotional conflict between drives and defenses. These two different models of trauma are reflections of theoretical developments in Freud's overall thinking, which, if viewed together, are at odds with one another.

Krystal attempted to correct these flaws in Freud's thinking about trauma by formulating a third and alternative model. Krystal's model, which incorporated the strengths of Freud's thought, conceptualized trauma as a potential or actual state of subjective distress and disorganization involving emergency, defensive measures against overwhelming affects. His model advanced beyond Freud's in a number of important respects. First, it combined Freud's early attention to affect and affective states with his later focus on defense. Second, it emphasized the primacy of subjective states in understanding the pathogenesis of trauma. According to Krystal (1978, pp. 94, 95, 99), these states involve feelings of helplessness and hopelessness arising from a confrontation with a situation that is subjectively experienced as an unavoidable threat to life.

Krystal divided trauma as an "affective experience" (p. 91) into cognitive and expressive aspects. Affectively, trauma involves what Krystal referred to as the primary unpleasure or "UR-affects," that is, anxiety and depression. These UR-affects appear in the form of "affect storms," which Krystal defined as "endlessly violent and unbearable" sensations and feelings that "overwhelm all executive functions" (p. 92). With the loss of these executive functions, the ego succumbs in a pattern of surrender and defeat that may degenerate into "psychogenic death" (p. 94). This may involve suicide and other forms of self-destructive behavior.

The cognitive aspect of trauma is "composed of its meaning as a signal and the 'story' behind it" (p. 91). As an example of this aspect of trauma, Krystal mentioned fears that "aggressive wishes may get out of hand and magically cause great destruction" (pp. 91–2).

Krystal (pp. 81, 93) pointed out that the affective and cognitive aspects of trauma give it a different meaning depending on the phase in development at which it occurs. In the infant and young child, it has primarily an emotional meaning, with little or only secondary cognitive meaning. Krystal argued that such early forms of trauma lead in older children and adults to serious vulnerability to still further trauma. He described this form of vulnerability as the "dread of the return of (the infantile type) trauma" (p. 92).

In older persons, trauma takes on both an emotional and a cognitive meaning. In addition, in adults, unlike in infants and young children, there is the "capacity for blocking emotions and constricting cognition" (p. 100). Krystal cited "denial, depersonalization, and derealization" (p. 109) as typical ego defenses employed for the purpose of emotional numbing and cognitive blocking.

In differentiating between the affective and cognitive aspects of trauma, Krystal formulated a psychoanalytic theory of trauma as a subjective experience determined by its psychic reality or unconscious meaning. A careful examination of Krystal's later work reveals, however, that his understanding of the unconscious meaning of trauma is limited by reverting to Freud's second theory or model of trauma as a product of fantasy. For example, Krystal (1978) stated that the subjective experience or unconscious meaning of trauma can be understood as a "confirmation of a threat of castration as evidence that dangerous wishes may come true or bring punishment" (p. 90, n. 1). With this example, Krystal implied that the psychic reality or unconscious meaning of trauma can be understood in terms of the arousal of pathogenic fantasies of castration. In this sense, Krystal's interpretation of the unconscious meaning of trauma was limited by his adherence, like Greenacre's, to the classical psychoanalytic theory that trauma is a product of fantasy.

Krystal also constructed his model of trauma from the experience-distant theoretical vantage point of classical metapsychology. For example, he explained trauma as involving the loss of basic executive ego functions including reality testing and integration. Relying on an experience-distant theory of ego functions and defenses in understanding the unconscious meaning of trauma is inconsistent with Krystal's attention to subjective and experience-near factors such as affect and cognition.

THE REVISIONIST SCHOOL

The revisionist school of psychoanalytic thought on trauma originated in the work of Rado (1942) and Kardiner (1947), was further developed by Kelman (1945, 1946), and has been refined by Lifton (1967, 1973),

Horowitz (1973, 1976), and Hendin (and Haas, 1984). As a group, the revisionists broke from the tradition established by the classical and neoclassical schools of psychoanalytic thought on trauma. They abandoned Freud's experience-distant metapsychology and replaced it with a more experience-near theoretical framework. Kardiner and Rado formulated a view of trauma as a disturbance in adaptational functioning involving a pathological alteration in images of the self and the outer world. Although initially employing the adaptational approach to understanding trauma, Kelman subsequently developed an approach based on the work of Horney.

Kelman (1945, 1946) stated that trauma is caused by the loss of and the failure to revive a neurotic character structure organizing a basic sense of self. (See chapter 6 for a discussion of Kelman's views of traumatic war neurosis; see also Ulman, 1987a, for an earlier analysis of Kelman's work and its anticipation of our self-psychological theory.) Kelman viewed trauma as manifesting itself symptomatically in a recognizable syndrome of extreme personality decompensation.

According to Kelman, certain people are particularly vulnerable to trauma owing to a specific form of character pathology. These are people whose character structure is organized primarily around what Kelman (1945), following Horney, referred to as an "idealized image of the self" (p. 134). This idealized self-image includes the "need for self-control and external control" in the service of a "sense of uniqueness and need to be unqiue" as well as a personal belief in "being inviolate, invulnerable and unassailable" (p. 139). Kelman described the idealized image of the self as a "neurotic illusion of the self, which is unconsciously maintained" in order to "act as a unifying force at least giving to the individual a feeling of pseudoequilibrium" (p. 134).

Kelman claimed that for a neurotically organized person the idealized image of the self "acts as a goal in life . . . and gives his life purpose, although the goal and purpose are illusory and fictitious" (p. 134). Such a neurotic person guides himself in accordance with an idealized image and is "compulsively involved in attempting to attain this goal, acting as though he were maintaining it, and trying to force everyone around him to believe in and service that image" (p. 134). Kelman contended that the unconscious meaning of trauma may be understood as involving the neurotic individual's sense of having failed to live up to an idealized image of the self.

Suppose, for example, that a particular person's basic sense of self is organized primarily in accordance with an urgent need to feel unique, inviolate, invulnerable, and unassailable. This person has an experience in which he or she is forced to feel ordinary, plain, vulnerable, helpless, and violated. According to Kelman, such a person is likely to be traumatized by such an experience. For the neurotic person, the traumatic meaning of failing to live up to an idealized self-image is, Kelman observed, symptomatically manifested in a typical pathological syndrome. The main symptomatic features of this syndrome include fixation on the traumatic event; a generalized constriction of the level of personality functioning and narrowing of the total scope of living; inhibitory phenomena; unpremeditated explosive and violent expressions of crying or aggression; exaggerated physical irritability (that is, auditory hypersensitivity and violent startle reactions); and, repetitive traumatic nightmares (including replica dreams or dreams of retributive justice, guilt dreams, and frustration dreams).

The recurring nature of many of these symptoms, which are almost identical to those of PTSD, is viewed by Kelman as a manifestation of the persistent but unsuccessful attempt to revive an idealized image of the self. They represent the emotional reliving of trauma motivated by the unconscious intent to undo failure and defeat by magically turning them into success, victory, and glory. Kelman's description of the typical symptoms associated with the traumatic syndrome anticipated by 35 years the current DSM-III description of the reexperiencing and numbing symptoms of PTSD.

Kelman presented several clinical vignettes in support of his main thesis. For example, he (1945) described the case of a law enforcement officer who was actively involved for a number of years in "apprehending dangerous criminals under hazardous circumstances" (p. 142). During the course of his work, the officer was frequently "in life and death situations, including involvement in gun duels" but he "had never been seriously injured and always [got] his man" (p. 142).

The officer's remarkable record of achievement and success changed dramatically, however, in the course of a routine arrest. The officer was injured and failed to apprehend the suspected criminal. Kelman maintained that following this dramatic incident, the officer broke down and developed a fullblown traumatic syndrome. He became progressively incapacitated and unable to carry out his normal duties.

In treating the officer, Kelman said that he came to understand that the officer was neurotically organized around a central yet vulnerable idealized self-image. The officer experienced his failure to arrest the suspected criminal as a devastating and crippling blow to his idealized self-image. Kelman interpreted the unconscious meaning of the officer's traumatic reaction as a failure to live up to a neurotic idealized image of the self.

In formulating a revisionist psychoanalytic theory of trauma, Kelman avoided the shortcomings that, we argue, have limited both the classical and neoclassical psychoanalytic theories of trauma. For example, Kelman did not need to resort to the notion that current traumatic experience is determined in its unconscious meaning by pathogenic fantasies stemming from the primal scene and the threat of castration. Instead, he interpreted the unconscious meaning of current traumatic experience in terms of the loss of and failure to revive neurotic illusions about the self.

Kelman's Horneyan theory of trauma therefore adumbrated our self-psychological theory in the following important respects. First, his concept of the neurotically idealized self-image can be viewed as a precursor to our concept of the narcissistic central organizing fantasy (and, to be more precise, the grandiose self rather than the idealized parent imago). Second, Kelman's theory of the traumatic syndrome as the loss of and failure to revive a neurotically idealized self-image is similar to our theory of PTSD as a dissociative disorder caused by the shattering and faulty restoration of archaic narcissistic fantasies.

And, third, Kelman's analysis of the unconscious dynamics underlying the symptoms of the traumatic syndrome anticipates our self-psychological analysis of the unconscious origins of the symptoms of PTSD. He analyzed the symptoms of the traumatic syndrome as pathological manifestations of the loss of and failure to revive a neurotically idealized self image. We analyze the symptoms of PTSD as dissociative disturbances in a subjective world reflective of the shattering and faulty restoration of archaic narcissistic fantasies. Kelman's work is crucial to our formulation of a new psychoanalytic theory and model of trauma.

CONCLUSION

It is greatly to Freud's credit that especially in his early work he adopted an experience-near clinical perspective of empathic attunement. This analytic listening stance enabled him to remain empathically attuned to his female patients' subjective experience, which had been shaped by the unconscious meaning of occurrences of actual sexual assault. Unfortunately, Freud explained these experience-near empathic observations in terms of an experience-distant theoretical model of trauma, the psychoenergistic model.

We have discussed Freud's momentous leap in thought from the seduction to the oedipal theory primarily in terms of his two models of trauma (see chapter 5 for a discussion of a third model). In constructing his second model of trauma, the pathogenic fantasy arousal model, Freud discarded his earlier view on the occurrence of actual seductions in favor of a view of these happenings as purely imaginary and fantasmagorical. On the basis of the second model, Freud argued that these occurrences never actually happened but were unconsciously fantasized in the context of repressed memories of witnessing the primal scene (that is, parental intercourse and other sexual activity).

In replacing the first model of trauma with the second, Freud formulated a psychoanalytic theory that (sexual) trauma was a product of fantasy. He viewed pathogenic fantasies of sadomasochism and castration as unconsciously organized around repressed memories of witnessing the primal scene and around threats of castration for masturbating. Trauma, he contended, is a product of these fantasies rather than of occurrences of actual sexual assault.

Freud's abandonment of the seduction theory has been criticized both from within psychoanalysis (see, for example, Ferenczi, 1949, and Masson, 1984) and from outside by feminists (see, for example, Brownmiller, 1975, and Rush, 1980). Freud's critics have taken him to task for failing to uphold his original position that trauma is a product of actual childhood sexual assault. They maintained that this failure led psychoanalysis and the mental health professions to question the veridical truth of instances of sexual molestation, incest, and rape as reported by their female patients.

Analysts and other mental health professionals influenced by Freud's abandonment of his original seduction theory have viewed female patients' reports of sexual assault as being grounded in child-hood sexual fantasies rather than in fact. Analysts and therapists did recognize that female patients suffered from neurotic symptoms stemming from traumatogenic fantasies. However, they sought the determinants of the unconscious meaning of these traumatic experiences in pathogenic fantasies rather than in shattering facts.

We would like to add several objections of our own to these criticisms. We contend that in shifting from the first to the second model of trauma, Freud established within psychoanalysis and the other mental health professions a questionable theory that trauma is a product of fantasy. This psychoanalytic theory was further elaborated by a number of noted classical analysts such as Greenacre.

In fact, Greenacre added a new and bizzare twist to this theory: she maintained that instances of sexual molestation, abuse, and attack had occurred but were not in themselves traumatic. Rather, according to Greenacre, these occurrences took on traumatic meaning solely because of their unconscious connection to what she, following Freud, contended was the basic traumatic experience—that is, witnessing the primal scene. Greenacre argued that to whatever degree sexual assaults are traumatic, they are unconsciously desired and precipitated by the victim to repeat the primal scene in an effort to belatedly master this trauma.

We do not question that the experience of watching parents engaged in sexual intercourse or other sexual activity may be traumatic for a child. We do, however, reject the argument that all later devastating and catastrophic experiences are imbued with their unconscious traumatic meaning primarily because of their connection with repressed memories of the primal scene and the potential of such events to arouse pathogenic fantasies of sadomasochism and castration. Such an argument amounts to psychological reductionism. It unnecessarily reduces and limits the unconscious traumatic meaning of actual occurrences to pathogenic fantasies associated with repressed memories of witnessing the primal scene and with threats of castration.

In chapters 3, 4, and 7, we present a number of detailed case and treatment histories documenting instances of traumatic incest and rape. We present these cases, as well as cases of combat trauma (see chapters 5 and 7), in an attempt to rectify what we believe are serious shortcomings in the classical psychoanalytic theory of trauma.

We contend that the traumatogenicity of fantasy does not reside primarily in the extent to which actual occurrences stimulate and arouse poorly repressed memories (of witnessing the primal scene and being threatened with castration) and associated pathogenic fantasies. Instead, it lies in the extent to which actual occurrences shatter preexisting archaic narcissistic fantasies central to the organization and maintenance of self-experience. In other words, we contend that the unconscious traumatic meaning of an occurrence is not psychically determined or caused by the arousal of a pathogenic fantasy associated with repressed memories. On the contrary, the unconscious traumatic meaning is largely determined by the shattering and faulty restoration of central organizing fantasies of self in relation to selfobject. To bolster our position, we refer to Kelman's ideas about the loss of and failure to revive neurotically idealized self-images.

To conclude, let us return to Freud's case of the Wolf Man. The Wolf Man's recurrent childhood nightmare of seeing wolves perched in a tree outside his window may be classically understood as symbolically representing both his experience of the primal scene and the sexual contact with his sister. However, this recurrent nightmare also may be self-psychologically understood as a self-state dream symbolically depicting the Wolf Man's traumatic experience of being unable to ward off his sister's sexual abuse.

The case material seems to warrant the inference that the Wolf Man's sexual involvement with his sister traumatized him and left him unconsciously organized around faultily restored grandiose fantasies.

From our self-psychological perspective, we view the Wolf Man as unconsciously attempting to restore (defensively) central organizing fantasies of grandiosity. As part of this defensive restoration, he unconsciously elaborated an imaginary scenario in which he magically reversed his role as a passive victim of his sister's sexual abuse. Instead, he imagined himself in the active role as the initiator of sexual activity.

CHAPTER 3

Incest: The Dissolution of Childhood Fantasies

For most psychoanalysts, incest and fantasy are inextricably related concepts, linked by a history that extends back to Freud's historic discoveries of infantile sexuality and the Oedipus complex. Freud (1905) proposed that the child's sexual desires for its parents endure throughout life as unconscious fantasies and crucially affect psychological development. So powerful are these fantasies, according to Freud, that under their sway female patients often falsely claim to be victims of incest.

This connection between incest and fantasy has been brought into question by recent investigators of incest (e.g. Peters, 1976; Herman and Hirshman, 1977, 1981; Rush, 1980, deYoung, 1982, Goodwin, 1985), many of whom hold psychoanalysis responsible for the paucity of empirical research on incest conducted during the first half of this century.

Although we do not accept the classical psychoanalytic view that incest trauma is caused by pathological fantasies rather than by actual events, the relationship between incest and fantasy also figures importantly in our theory. We argue that incest is traumatic because the unconscious meaning of incestuous experiences shatters central organizing fantasies of self in relation to selfobject that cannot be fully restored.

Since incest usually occurs within severely disturbed family environments (Maisch, 1972; Meiselman, 1978; Justice and Justice, 1979; deYoung, 1982), the child victim, even before the onset of sexual contact, is likely to suffer arrests in development that interfere with the healthy transformation of narcissistic fantasies. During the course of development, these fantasies, which are unconsciously intensified, tend to dominate more and more of the child's subjective world. Overt sexual contact with an adult member of the family shatters these fragile and vulnerable fantasies, leading to faulty efforts at defensive and compensatory restoration.

As a result of the shattering and faulty restoration of these fantasies, the child victim often suffers from the characteristic dissociative symptoms of PTSD. Narcissistic rage directed at self or others as disillusioning selfobjects often accompanies the shattering of these fantasies.

In incest, unlike other traumas occurring later in life, the shattering and faulty restoration of narcissistic fantasies is likely to be repeated over and over. Because these repeated traumatizations tend to occur early in life, profoundly disrupting crucial periods of development, incest often results in very severe forms of PTSD, which, at times, assume psychotic proportions.

Before presenting three representative case studies to illustrate our theory, we examine current literature supporting our position that reactions to incest meet the *DSM*-III (1980) diagnostic criteria for PTSD. Next, we present a brief historical review of the classical analytic literature on incest in an attempt to demonstrate that the roots of our theory lie in Freud's original discoveries about trauma.

With the exception of Ferenczi, whose writings reflect his belief in the devastating effects of actual sexual traumas in childhood, Freud's early followers tended to support Freud's shift in focus from trauma to fantasy (see chapter 2). In spite of their efforts to present their clinical data as consistent with Freud's theoretical position, we contend that reinterpretation of their case histories from a self-psychological perspective yields support for our theory. Following our reexamination of case histories on incest by Abraham, Bonaparte and Annie Reich, as well as a discussion of Ferenczi's position on sexual abuse, we examine the writings of Bach and Schwartz, present-day psychoanalysts whose understanding of trauma and narcissistic fantasy is similar to our own.

INCEST AND POSTTRAUMATIC STRESS DISORDER

Aside from the "pro-incest" researchers whose work supports such groups as The Childhood Sensuality Circle, The Rene Guyon Society, and The North American Man/Boy Love Association (Demott, 1980), a consensus exists among most recent investigators that incest results in acute and chronic symptoms of severe psychic trauma. Russell (1986), in an interview study of 930 women, of whom 16% disclosed that they were incest survivors, found severe traumatization regardless of the relative involved. Incest with stepfathers, for example, was found to be just as traumatic as incest with biological fathers. Despite the popular notion that brother–sister incest is harmless, Russell found severe traumatization among survivors of sibling incest.

In addition to depression (Kaufman, Peck, and Tagiuri, 1954; Weiner, 1962; De Francis, 1969; Katz and Mazur, 1979;) guilt, shame, and trust disturbances (Butler, 1978; Forward and Buck, 1978; Brothers, 1982) a wide spectrum of sexual problems (Sloane and Karpinsky, 1942; Meiselman, 1978; Justice and Justice, 1979, Becker, 1980) and prostitution (Weinberg, 1955; Weber, 1979), many of these researchers have found severe disturbances in self experience that are readily translatable into the diagnostic criteria of PTSD.

For example, a number of researchers have observed phenomena resembling reexperiencing symptoms among incest survivors. Maisch (1972) reported that over 70% of the daughters in his study showed some sort of personality disturbance. Of particular interest were those subjects he described as suffering from traumatic neurosis. According to Maisch, the neurotic symptoms represent attempts to relive the traumatic experience. Moreover, Maisch noted the similarity of those reactions to those of combat soldiers. Tsai and Wagner (1978) document episodes of reliving among participants in their therapy group for abused women, and deYoung (1982) found that 48% of the 80 incest victims in her study reported reliving the trauma of their incest experiences.

Many investigators have also observed signs of numbing among incest survivors. Forward and Buck (1978) emphasize the survivor's fundamental lack of self-confidence and self-respect. Survivors in their study described feelings of self-loathing so extreme they believed they were undeserving of emotional, physical, or material satisfaction. Justice and Justice (1979) observe that "perhaps the most pervasive long-term consequences of incest are the effects it may have on the daughter's self-image" (p. 182). They describe a sense of worthlessness that haunts the lives of survivors as well as painful feelings of being "uniquely different" that accompany social isolation, a hallmark of numbing.

Silver, Boon, and Stones (1983) have also found evidence that incest trauma results in another reexperiencing symptom, the vulnerability to recurrent, intrusive, and disruptive ruminations about the incest. They relate such patterns to the survivor's efforts to "make sense" of incest. Their study of 77 adult women who were child-victims of father–daughter incest provides a high degree of confirmation for our theory.

Adopting a view of incest that derives in large part from cognitive psychology, Silver et al. (1983) emphasize meaning as an important factor in incestuous victimization. According to these authors, incest often disrupts the survivor's perception of living in an orderly and meaningful world (see Frankel, 1963, for a discussion of meaning as a primary motivation; Lerner, 1970, 1980, on "Just World Theory"). Silver et al. found that 80% of the victims in their study attempted to make sense of their victimization by asking such questions as "Why me?" or attempting to examine the character of their fathers in an effort to explain their behavior. Other subjects attempted to make sense of their sexual victimization by sympathizing with the thwarted sexual needs of their fathers or regarding their fathers as mentally ill. Results of their study showed that the more active the search for meaning, the more the respondents reported recurrent, intrusive and disruptive ruminations about their incest experiences.

The survivors' experience of the world as no longer orderly and meaningful is consistent with our theory insofar as it reflects the subjective disorganization resulting from a shattering and faulty restoration of central organizing fantasies. The "search for meaning" may be understood, in part, as an attempt by incest survivors to ward off terrifying experiences of fragmentation and disintegration.

Recently a number of researchers have undertaken studies to determine if victims of various forms of trauma suffer from PTSD. In a clinical study of 26 adult women who had experienced incest as children, Donaldson and Gardner (1985) report that 25 met DSM-III (1980) diagnostic criteria for delayed or chronic PTSD. Pynoos and Eth (1984) suggest that DSM-III criteria for PTSD as validated for adults can be directly applied to children. They cite Lifton and Olson (1976) and Terr (1979) to support their contention that "common traumatic elements can be found across all age groups" (p. 37).

In a study of 40 children who had witnessed homicide of a parent, Pynoos and Eth found symptoms that coalesced into patterns consistent with a diagnosis of PTSD. Particularly relevant to our theory was their finding that children attempt to reverse traumatic helplessness and anxiety through the use of fantasy. Comparing these fantasies to what Lifton (1982) has referred to as "inner plans of action," they note, "these fantasies may seek to alter the precipitating events, to undo the violent act, to reverse the lethal consequences or to minimize future risks" (Pynoos and Eth, 1984, p. 41). As the authors point out, the reactions of these children correspond to the defense mechanism identified by Anna Freud (1936) as "denial in fantasy." From our theoretical perspective, these are efforts to restore traumatically shattered narcissistic fantasies.

The authors found that these restitutive fantasies varied according to the age of the child involved. For example, preschoolers were found to have fantasies of possessing "superhero powers protecting them from attack" (in Kohution terms, grandiose fantasies) and to imagine that certain adults also possessed such powers (idealized merger fantasies). School-age children were found to have fantasies of performing actions that would have averted the trauma. Pynoos and Eth (1984) note, "These wishful inner plans of action may reflect the magical invulnerability of this age group" (p. 44). We would say that the narcissistic fantasies among children in this age group are relatively untransformed and retain their archaic character. Pynoos and Eth found behavioral enactments of traumatic experiences to be common in adolescence.

It is interesting to note that these efforts to restore shattered narcissistic fantasies, which are conscious preoccupations of traumatized children, closely resemble the restorative efforts we empathically infer to occur on an unconscious level among adult victims.

CLASSICAL ROOTS OF A
SELF-PSYCHOLOGICAL THEORY

Facing a skeptical and, quite probably, hostile audience at the Society for Psychiatry and Neurology in Vienna on April 21, 1896, Freud said: "Sexual experience in childhood consisting in stimulation of the genitals, coitus-like acts, and so on, must therefore be recognized, in the last analysis, as being the traumas which lead to a hysterical reaction to events at puberty and to the development of hysterical symptoms" (Masson, 1984, p. 267).

A little more than one year later, in a letter to Wilhelm Fliess, Freud (September 21, 1897, quoted in Masson, 1984) wrote: "I no longer believe in my neurotica [theory of neurosis]." Freud explained that if his original theory were true, the fathers of most of his hysterical patients would be guilty of incest, a possibility, given the high incidence of hysteria, he apparently found hard to accept. Instead, he suggested that since truth and fiction cannot be distinguished on an unconscious level, children predisposed to hysteria by hereditary factors elaborate sexual fantasies which "invariably seize upon the theme of the parents" (Masson, 1984, p. 108).

In a 1906 paper, "My Views on the Part Played by Sexuality in the Aetiology of the Neuroses," Freud elaborated these ideas. He came to view hysteria as a neurotic expression of the unconscious psychic conflict between highly disturbing fantasies of incestuous seduction arising from primal scene observations and defenses against the enactment of these fantasies. By replacing "accidental influences" (traumatic sexual experiences) with "constitutional factors" (the tendency to elaborate incestuous fantasies) as primary in the aetiology of neurosis, Freud shifted the focus of psychoanalysis from psychic trauma and traumatic neurosis to psychic conflict and psychoneurosis (see chapters 1 and 2).

This shift in focus, which underlies Freud's abandonment of the seduction theory of neurosis, had profound implications for the subsequent investigation of incest. Although an extensive body of literature accumulated in support of Freud's formulations concerning the centrality of the Oedipus complex in the pathogenesis of neurotic symptoms, few studies (see, for example, Shengold, 1980; Cohen, 1981; Eisnitz, 1984/5; Williams, 1987) of the effects of overt incestuous relations have been conducted by analytically oriented investigators.

Two positions, equally detrimental to future empirical investigations of incest, were advanced. First, despite Freud's original observations, some analysts presumed that actual instances of incest were relatively rare. In fact, recent surveys indicate that 5% to 15% of the population is involved in incest (see Woodbury and Schwartz, 1977) and that 1% to 5% of women in the general population have experienced incest with a father or stepfather (Goodwin, McCarty, and DiVasto, 1981). Moreover, these analysts contended that because incest fantasies are universal, it would be virtually impossible to distinguish clinically between *real* events and *imaginary* experiences. In this instance, the analysts fell victim to what might be termed the "Archimedean fallacy" of clinical objectivity, which rests on a "one-reality model" (see Ulman and Zimmermann, 1985, 1987). Assuming that there are correct and incorrect views of reality and that the clinician possesses the "true" view, whereas the patient possesses the "false" view, these analysts failed to recognize the "material reality" of sexual trauma and to understand its "psychic reality" or unconscious meaning.

Second, these analysts maintained that in rare instances of documented incest, the child, under the psychological domination of incest fantasies, was eager for actual contact with older relatives and therefore provoked sexual liaisons. This latter position was largely responsible for "blaming the victim" (Ryan, 1971), an attitude that pervades subsequent studies of sexual traumatization.

Despite these unfortunate consequences of Freud's shift away from a theory emphasizing the reality of trauma, his monumental clinical discoveries about the unconscious traumatic meaning of hysterical symptoms paved the way for our understanding of the unconscious traumatic meaning of the dissociative symptoms of PTSD. For example, bodily symptoms having no physiological basis, which Freud characterized as "conversions," may be understood as symptoms of reexperiencing, a major diagnostic category of PTSD. Our study reveals that the unconscious traumatic meaning of these symptoms involves the shattering and faulty restoration of narcissistic fantasies. (See the case of Jean, this chapter, for a more detailed discussion of this point.)

Sexual Trauma as "Unconsciously Desired"

A number of Freud's early followers elaborated the role of pathological fantasy among child victims of sexual trauma. Karl Abraham was one of the first to pick up this theme. He did not deny that children were frequently involved in sexual abuse and incest. However, in his paper, "The Experiencing of Sexual Trauma as a Form of Sexual Activity," he claimed that "in a great number of cases, the trauma was desired by the child unconsciously" (Abraham, 1907a, p. 48). Presenting case material intended to demonstrate that certain children "respond more readily to seduction than others," Abraham concluded that such children possess an "abnormal psycho-sexual constitution," which leads them to be sexually provocative towards adults.

He even went so far as to argue that children who failed to report sexual experiences with adults kept silent because of their guilt in desiring the encounter. He wrote:

> When the child yields to the trauma it is because its libido is striving to obtain sexual fore-pleasure or satisfaction pleasure. This fact of a pleasure gain is the secret which the child guards anxiously. It alone explains its sense of guilt and the psychological events which follow upon a sexual trauma [p. 53].

By taking the implications that followed from Freud's second theory of trauma to their logical conclusion, Abraham turned Freud's first theory on its head: pathology is not consequent upon sexual trauma, trauma is a consequence of the child's pathological makeup!

Abraham's efforts to understand the relationship between childhood sexual trauma and psychosis were also greatly influenced by his adherence to Freud's second theory of the aetiology of trauma. Although Abraham (1907b) noted that sexual traumas were as prevalent in the early histories of persons who later became psychotic as in the histories of those who became hysterics, he denied their aetiological significance. "Experiences of a sexual nature," he argued, "are not the cause of illness, but merely determine its symptoms. They are not the cause of delusions and hallucinations," he added, "they merely give them their particular content" (p. 19).

By employing Freud's method of dream interpretation as a means of discovering how sexual traumas determined the content of psychotic productions, Abraham focused on the unconscious meanings of sexual trauma. As a result, his case illustrations, which beautifully illuminate his patient's experience, lend themselves to reinterpretation from a self-psychological perspective.

In one case, Abraham (1907b) vividly described the reactions of a woman whose violent and alcoholic uncle raped her in a barn on several occasions during her childhood and threatened to burn down their house if she told anyone. Shortly after the rapes, according to Abraham, the woman became depressed, shy, and withdrawn. She had nightly visions in which she saw the barn on fire and had terrifying dreams that contained "reminiscences of the attack." As she grew older, the woman suffered from auditory hallucinations.

For example, during a difficult period in the woman's life, she heard the voice of another uncle who had died some years earlier. Speaking from "heaven," this uncle, whom the woman had liked and had identified with because of his unhappy life, forbade her to commit suicide and prophesied that she would outlive her siblings, inherit the farm, marry, and have children. Later in life, in the course of a severe suicidal depression, she heard the voice of the "bad" uncle coming from hell and advising her to kill herself.

From Abraham's description of the patient's symptoms, she appears to have suffered from numbing and reexperiencing, suggesting a possible diagnosis of PTSD (of psychotic proportions). His interpretations of the content of her visions and nightmares reflect his interest in their unconscious meaning. However, they are also determined by his efforts to affirm Freud's second theory of sexual trauma. He explained the woman's vision of the barn on fire as "doubly determined": first, the uncle had raped her in a barn and second, he had threatened to burn down her house if she told anyone. Then, in an obvious attempt to adapt these insights to Freud's second theory, Abraham stated that "the wish for sexual satisfaction is hidden behind the feeling of anxiety" (p. 14). However, his suggestion that the woman actually desired the rapes is not supported by clinical evidence.

Abraham's understanding of the woman's auditory hallucinations closely parallels the inferences we draw from this case based on our theory. Applying Freud's method of dream interpretation to hallucinations, Abraham asserted that the woman's hallucinations of the "good" uncle contained "a clear wish fulfillment" reflecting the woman's acceptance of life. Her hallucination of the "bad" uncle, Abraham believed, signaled her abandonment of hope.

Although we do not have enough information about this woman's early experience to identify the specific fantasies shattered by her incestuous experiences, it seems likely that they involved merger with idealized figures. We base this inference on her hallucinations. It is possible, for example, that her hallucination of the good uncle's voice reflected a desperate effort to restore a merger fantasy, whereas hearing the bad uncle's voice suggests the failure of such an effort.

Suicide may have represented the women's attempt to relieve the intolerable "disintegration anxiety" resulting from her failure to restore her fantasies. She may also have anticipated reunion, in death, with the good uncle as a means of achieving an idealized merger. Thus, it appears that Abraham's case reflected the traumatic shattering of fantasies of idealized merger and faulty efforts at compensatory restoration. The severity of the woman's PTSD lent a psychotic character to her pathology.

A Case of Brother–Sister Incest

Marie Bonaparte (1953), another of Freud's disciples, presented cases of brother–sister incest in which she attempted to demonstrate the positive effect of such relationships on the woman's later sexual functioning. In presenting her findings, Bonaparte referred to Freud's (1905) contention that the woman, being, like the child, more "infantile, passive and malleable [than the man] . . . freely retains the stamp she is given" (Bonaparte, 1953, p. 116). She argued that the woman is therefore greatly influenced by her first sexual experience. A good first experience with a brother, according to Bonaparte, may insure the woman's sexual normality. "The father . . . following our civilized code, must not erotically initiate his daughter," she writes. "The brother, though by parental injunction he must not do so either, nevertheless frequently does and often with beneficial results, thus applying a corrective to the sister's oedipal frustration" (p. 136).

Despite this contention, Bonaparte presents one case in which brother–sister incest resulted in the sister's "complete retreat from sexuality." The incestuous relationship between Bonaparte's patient and her brother, which did not include intercourse, ended when it was discovered (presumably by their father) and the brother was punished. Noting that every lover the women chose thereafter bore a striking resemblance to her brother, Bonaparte asserts that the obligation the woman felt to "succor" her brother became a "most obdurate repetition-compulsion." She felt compelled to demand money from her rich lovers to give to indigent people.

Bonaparte's case may be interpreted as supporting our theoretical position that incestuous experiences are traumatic because of their unconscious meaning for the survivor. For Bonaparte's patient, her brother's punishment, as well as the sexual activity itself, may have shattered an archaic narcissistic fantasy of merger with her brother. We understand the behavior that Bonaparte characterizes as motivated by "repetition-compulsion" as a form of exhibitionistic enactment intended to restore a shattered fantasy. By obtaining money from her lovers, Bonaparte's patient may have enacted a fantasy of her own grandiosity as a means of defensive restoration.

Such inferences, however, must be regarded as highly speculative. Only a prolonged, empathic immersion in the patient's (or research subject's) subjective world lead to valid inferences about unconscious and fantasmagoric organizing activity. We have no experiential data about the organization of the woman's subjective world prior to the incest. Such data is necessary to establish the extent to which her self experience had been organized in accordance with the unconscious meaning of narcissistic fantasies.

The "Tom Thumb" Fantasy

Annie Reich did not openly challenge Freud's theoretical position on the pathogenesis of oedipal fantasies underlying sexual trauma. However, in a 1932 case history of brother–sister incest, Reich demonstrated her understanding of the devastating psychological impact of sexual abuse and the central role played by archaic narcissistic fantasies in such traumas.

In this case history, Reich (1932) described her treatment of Herta, a 20-year-old, working-class girl who had been involved since the age of 16 in an incestuous relationship with her brother. From Reich's careful description of Herta's presenting symptoms, which included severe anxiety, reexperiencing, numbing, sleep disturbances, and guilt feelings, a diagnosis of PTSD seems warranted.

According to Reich, Herta's early life was marked by disruptions and deprivation. Beside being beaten, scolded and severely chastised for masturbation, Herta was subjected to many abusive sexual experiences, including incestuous sexual contacts with an uncle before the age of four. The second of three children born out of wedlock, she had been raised by foster parents until the age of two, when she was placed in the care of a "hard, coldhearted, intolerant" grandmother and finally, at the age of four, was reunited with her parents.

Reich explained that Herta was ignored and ridiculed by her mother, who seemed grossly unempathic to Herta's changing needs. Herta was beaten by her father when she tried to protect her mother from his drunken assaults. Despite this heartless treatment, Reich poignantly described Herta's efforts to assume a caregiving role vis-à-vis her parents.

As she grew older, Herta outwardly appeared to comply with her mother's restrictive demands for submissive obedience and renunciation of her sexuality. However, she was described by Reich as dominating and sadistic in her relationships with her younger brothers and possessive, tyrannical, and pathologically jealous in her incestuous relationship with her brother. An "hysterical attack" during her hospitalization for a kidney ailment following the death of a child she had had by her brother led her to enter treatment with Reich.

Reich summarized her understanding of the case in terms of libidinal drive theory as involving "a simple genital father relation, completely in accord with the usual hysterical structure, superimposed over a deeper oral disturbance of the relation to the mother" (Reich, 1932, p. 21). However, her detailed analysis of one of the patient's childhood fantasies reveals Reich's grasp of the narcissistic issues in the case.

In Herta's fantasy, she had a nut that housed a tiny elf, Tom Thumb, who magically fulfilled her every command. The patient, according to Reich, enthralled her younger brothers with stories of living with them in a wonderful castle supplied with innumerable delicacies by Tom Thumb. At night they would all sleep in a plush, windowless bedroom where the boys would be allowed to engage in sex play and mutual masturbation with Herta.

Reich believed that one function of the Tom Thumb fantasy was to overcome Herta's fear that "sexual intercourse was dangerous and frightening", a fear that derived from the girl's many traumatic sexual experiences. Even more significantly, Reich understood the unconscious defensive meaning of the Tom Thumb fantasy. Reich (1932) wrote: "The possession of this magic spirit had made her more powerful than all the others, and the blind devotion of her admirers [her brothers] compensated for the love the adults had never bestowed upon her" (p. 12). In addition, according to Reich, since Herta consciously wished to be a boy, Tom Thumb symbolized a penis, the possession of which enabled her to overcome her experience of herself as a "second-class citizen," subservient to men.

Reich's interpretation of this fantasy corresponds very closely to our self-psychological understanding. Herta's early mirroring and idealizing needs seem to have been largely neglected. As a result, her archaic narcissistic fantasies failed to undergo developmental transformation. Her Tom Thumb fantasy of possessing unlimited power appears to be a conscious manifestation of an unconscious fantasy of grandiosity. Her efforts to provide caregiving functions for her parents and her belief that "she would be a movie star; all men would lie at her feet" (p. 13) may be other expressions of this fantasy.

At the same time, since her power was derived from a male spirit, the more conscious form of this basically unconscious fantasy also entails merger with an idealized paternal figure. Her efforts to elaborate a fantasy of merger with an idealized maternal figure are apparent in her admiration of her mother for "bearing her father's brutality with calm unconcern" (p. 15).

Reich was also cognizant of the fragility of these archaic fantasies. She noted that Herta's Tom Thumb fantasy was "disrupted repeatedly" by her mother when she treated Herta as a powerless female. Her fragile fantasy of idealized merger with her mother was also threatened when she discovered that her mother had committed adultery. Because Herta's mother had continually warned her of the dangers of sexual behavior and had broken up a relationship between Herta and a boyfriend, Herta was shocked by her mother's hypocrisy.

From the vantage point of our theory, the unconscious traumatic meaning of Herta's relationship with her brother appears to reside in her shattering disillusionment with a fantasy of grandiosity when her relationship with her brother fell short of her imaginary relationship with Tom Thumb. She became enraged when he failed to meet her every whim and prove his unswerving devotion. In other words, she could not exert total control over her brother as she had imagined she controlled Tom Thumb.

At the same time, her pregnancy with her brother's child and the child's subsequent death appear to have shattered a fantasy of idealized merger with her mother. Perhaps wishing to do as her mother did, not as she said, Herta engaged in the incestuous sexual relationship. Her pregnancy concretely represented her fantasy of idealized merger with her mother. However, the death of the child destroyed this illusion. As Reich observed, the news of the child's death caused a storm of conflicting emotions in Herta. She later said, "If my mother had been at my side, everything would have turned out differently" (p. 3). Overwhelmed with disintegration anxiety at the shattering of her fantasies, Herta said, "Now I am going to die, too, and my brother will be free to love someone else" (p. 3).

When Reich terminated the analysis for unspecified reasons at the end of two years, she felt that the goals of treatment had not been reached. "We did not succeed in resolving either the sexual fixation on the father or the oral relation to the mother" (p. 21). It is tempting to speculate that if Reich had been guided by her insights into the meaning of Herta's Tom Thumb fantasy instead of by her beliefs in the centrality of oedipal drives, the analysis might have been more successful.

A Return to the "Seduction Theory"

As Masson (1984) has pointed out, Ferenczi was the only analyst among Freud's "inner circle" to question Freud's ambivalence about sexual trauma as the source of neurosis. In a paper he read before the 1932 International Psychoanalytic Congress in Wiesbaden, originally titled, "The Sexual Passions of Adults and their Influence on the Character Development and Sexual Development of the Child," Ferenczi described the devastating effect of sexual abuse on children. The title under which this paper was published in 1949 in the *International Journal of Psycho-Analysis*, "Confusion of Tongues Between Adults and the Child: The Language of Tenderness and the Language of Sexual Passion," refers to the adult's gross misunderstanding about the child's presumed wish for actual sexual relations. The child, according to Ferenczi, has no such desire.

Disappointing results with patients who claimed to have been sexually abused as children led Ferenczi to "place stronger emphasis on traumatic factors which have been undeservedly neglected of late in the pathogenesis of the neuroses" (quoted in Masson, 1984, pp. 283–84). Basing his rejection of the psychoneurotic theory of childhood seduction (that is, that seduction is a fantasy, not a reality) on the fact that many of his adult patients confessed to having had sex with children, Ferenczi (1949; see also Masson, 1984) noted that children were victims of incest and sexual abuse far more frequently than was generally acknowledged.

Ferenczi understood incestuous "seduction" as occurring because the adult with a "pathological disposition" confuses the playful behavior of the child emulating the same-sexed parent with the wishes of a sexually mature person and engages in sexual acts with the child "without consideration of the consequences." Ferenczi, moreover, fully appreciated that the consequences were likely to be extremely harmful. In empathic attunement with the child's probable reaction, Ferenczi speculated that its first impulse would be to cry out, "No, no, I don't want this, it is too strong for me, that hurts me" (quoted in Masson, 1984, p. 289). Explaining that sexually abused children typically do not react in this manner because they are "paralyzed by tremendous fear," Ferenczi observed, "The children feel physically and morally helpless; their personality is still too insufficiently consolidated for them to be able to protest even if only in thought. The overwhelming power and authority of the adult renders them silent" (quoted in Masson, 1984, p. 289).

In addition to Ferenzci's finding that child victims may keep the incestuous abuse secret because of overwhelming fear of the abusive parent, our empirical findings suggest that they may keep silent as part of an unconscious attempt to restore a traumatically shattered fantasy of idealized merger with a parent. For the same reason, the child may assume responsibility for provoking the incestuous relationship and claim to find it pleasurable.

That Ferenczi intuitively grasped the narcissistic implications of incest trauma is evidenced in his use of the "metaphor of fragmentation" to describe the child's reactions. Because of the child's urgent need to maintain its "tender, trusting relationship with the adult" and to "undo the trauma," he or she institutes the defense first discovered by Ferenczi, which he called "identification with the aggressor." By means of this defense, according to Ferenczi, the child "introjects" the guilt it believes the parent should feel. Describing the consequences of the child's identification with the aggressor, Ferenczi says, "The child feels extremely confused, in fact already split, innocent and guilty at the same time, indeed the testimony of his own senses has been destroyed" (quoted in Masson, 1984, p. 280). He went on to note that as the child experiences additional traumas, it suffers more and more psychological splits in personality organization until reaching a state of profound confusion or fragmentation.

Ferenczi also pointed out that the abused child often serves what we would view as selfobject functions for the sexually abusive as well as the nonparticipating parent. Our empirical research confirms his assertion that because of their strong desire to maintain loving connections in the family, children can easily be turned into lifelong nurses or caretakers for their own parents.

TRAUMA AND SADOMASOCHISTIC "RESTITUTION"

Bach and Schwartz, two analysts strongly influenced by Kohut's work, take a position on trauma that is similar to our own. In a 1972 paper, they view a dream of the Marquis de Sade and a series of his perverse sadomasochistic fantasies as "attempts to cope with narcissistic decompensation" (Bach and Schwartz, 1972, p. 473). They contend that the construction of a "delusional grandiose self" and a "delusionally idealized selfobject" represent restitutional attempts following the traumatic dissolution of ties to childhood selfobjects.

"In the context of de Sade's psychosis, his narcissistic pathology, and the struggle to master his narcissistic rage," they write, "we view the masochistic fantasies as attempts to restitute delusionally idealized selfobjects, and the sadistic fantasies as efforts to animate a delusional grandiose self." They understand the sadomasochistic sexualization of his fantasies as attempts to "deny experiences of self-fragmentation, bodily disruption and 'death of the self' " (p. 474).

Our most significant point of disagreement with Bach and Schwartz is that we do not distinguish delusional grandiose-exhibitionistic, omnipotent, and merger fantasies from other forms of unconscious fantasy organization. From a nonempathic point of view outside the person's subjective frame of reference, all fantasies may be viewed as delusions. We contend that neither the content nor the quality of the fantasies (i.e., whether or not they are delusional) determines if trauma will result in psychosis. Rather, it is the extent to which archaic narcissistic fantasies have undergone developmental transformation prior to the traumatic experience that influences the severity of the resulting PTSD and the likelihood that it will assume psychotic proportions.

REPRESENTATIVE CASES

Sybil/Carrie

Her delicate good looks, soft voice, and poised, dignified bearing made Sybil, a black 21-year-old mother of three, seem more like a celebrity in a public relations appearance than an incest survivor in a therapeutic interview. Almost proudly proclaiming her similarity to the famous case of multiple personality, she asked that her true identity be disguised with the cover name "Sybil" so that she might avoid "getting into trouble." Asked to describe her different "personalities," Sybil said, "Sometimes I feel like somebody's social worker and sometimes I act so mean to people."

With each succeeding interview, the story of Sybil's incestuous involvement with her father grew more bizarre and convoluted. She appeared to relish providing the interviewer with graphic accounts of episodes that increasingly resembled scenes in a gothic novel. Curiously, however, Sybil described the early stages of her sexual relationship with her father, beginning when she was three or four years old, as intensely pleasurable. She denied having any feelings of fear or repugnance.

The third child in a family of five children (she has two older brothers and a younger brother and sister), Sybil remembered feeling that her father had selected her to "take to bed" because she was the most worthy of his attention. She believed that her talent for singing and dancing made her superior to her siblings. Sybil said that her father's sexual relations with her, like the toys and clothing he bought her, merely confirmed her idea that she was destined to become a famous star and to escape from the bleak, dreary world in which the family lived.

In spite of her father's violent temper, which he periodically unleashed against everyone in the family, and her growing realization that he was involved in drug dealing and other criminal activities, Sybil looked up to him as supremely powerful and clever. She remembered feeling that he would reward her for gratifying his sexual desires by seeing to it that her fantasies of fame and fortune were actualized.

In contrast, Sybil saw her mother as incompetent and powerless. She described her as "nervous and scared," a woman who had been bullied by her own mother and then terrorized by her sadistic husband. In an early interview, Sybil excused her mother's failure to provide her with affection and protection by stressing the hardships she continually faced. She spoke of the many times her mother had been forced to relocate the family when her husband's criminal activities necessitated his hiding from the police or underworld figures.

In later interviews, however, Sybil portrayed her mother as an enemy, who maliciously spread stories of Sybil's sexual relationship with her father throughout the neighborhood in order to humiliate her. She railed against her for doing nothing to stop her father's abusiveness even though according to Sybil, she knew of everything that was going on in the family. Sybil wept as she recalled speaking to her mother at the age of seven about her abhorrence at having to perform fellatio for her father. "She cried," Sybil said, "but then she acted as if I had never told her about it."

When Sybil was seven, her father was convicted and imprisoned for raping a child. After he was released, the physical abusiveness, which had always been present in their relationship, became more extreme and frequent. Sybil described how he would handcuff her to her bed, beat her with an extension cord, and then have sex with her. Sex, at these times, she said, degenerated to only the most brutal and painful penetration. Sybil stressed that by this time sex with her father had lost all illusion of fantasy and pleasure and had become a nightmarish experience.

By the time she reached puberty, her father had begun to stage group sexual encounters involving her siblings and a young woman whom he had married while still married to Sybil's mother. Violent beatings were a common feature of these episodes.

As Sybil's attitude toward her father changed from worshipful obedience to terrified submission, her experience of herself also changed. No longer the exuberant little entertainer, Sybil remembered herself during her grade school years as a quiet, lonely, fearful child. She was afraid of the dark, phobic about large dogs, and plagued by nightmares. In a common nightmare of this period, Sybil saw her father running toward her. As he came close, she saw that his face was distorted into an "evil" grimace. She remembered waking in terror. She also remembered having uncontrolled crying spells and even thought of killing herself without forming any specific plan.

Although Sybil changed schools frequently, she remembered school as a place where she could proudly exhibit her quickness to learn and her capacity for diligent study. Increasingly, however, Sybil found it difficult to concentrate. "I was always wondering what was going to happen when I got home." Sometimes her father would beat her for being just a few minutes late. She remembered the intense feelings of shame and humiliation she had experienced as she repeatedly invented excuses for her cuts and bruises. Because of her father's tyrannical monopolization of her afterschool life, Sybil became a "loner" in school.

It was during this period that Sybil first decided she had a "split personality." She reported that her reaction to a negative comment or criticism was to "become a bad person." Eventually, Sybil began to call herself "Carrie" at these times. Although she could not say what had led her to select this name, it is probable that she chose the name of the character in the motion picture "Carrie" who possessed destructive psychokinetic powers. Angry and spiteful, she experienced herself at these times as completely different from the sad, passive, compliant girl she called "Sybil."

When she was 14, Sybil became pregnant with her father's child. To explain her pregnancy to relatives and friends, Sybil told them that she had been sexually involved with a young man who had been killed. Shortly after giving birth to a baby girl, Sybil developed a kidney disorder requiring hospitalization. Her emotional state was so precarious at this time (she was suicidally depressed) that she was assigned a social worker who specialized in working with adolescent mothers.

A few days later, her father's second wife was admitted to the hospital with gunshot wounds she said had been inflicted by him. She subsequently pressed charges against him. With the support and encouragement of her social worker, Sybil testified against her father, who was convicted of assault. However, she did not reveal that she had also been raped and impregnated by him.

For a brief period following her father's second imprisonment, Sybil appeared to make considerable gains in her life. While continuing treatment with her social worker, whom she experienced as selflessly devoted to the care of others, she decided to return to high school for night classes. In addition to caring for her daughter, Sybil worked part time in a fast-food restaurant. She developed a close relationship with the manager of the store, and she and her daughter lived with him.

Sybil's gains proved to be shortlived, however. A year and a half after her daughter was born, Sybil became pregnant again. Increasingly troubled about not having revealed the truth about the paternity of her first child and believing that she had let down her therapist as well as herself by becoming pregnant again, Sybil left treatment. Soon after, she quit her job, dropped out of school, and went on welfare.

Sybil's reasons for leaving school just prior to her anticipated graduation were confused and contradictory. She blamed her mother for spreading "lies" about her to her classmates, which interfered with her ability to focus on her schoolwork. However, Sybil also suggested that she could not tolerate receiving poor grades in school. Her difficulties with memory and concentration apparently had worsened, with a pattern of increasing dependence on alcohol and marijuana. Sybil explained that she had used alcohol for as long as she could remember. She said that her father had given her beer daily when she was a child. Smoking "pot" and drinking beer were common and acceptable among the grade-school children in the neighborhoods where Sybil grew up.

Sybil gave birth to a third child, a son, within a year of her second daughter's birth. Later, in spite of her belief as a Baptist that abortion is a "sin," Sybil decided to terminate a fourth pregnancy. She was separated from her boyfriend, she explained, and was finding it very difficult to care for her three children in the squalid room she shared with them in her mother's apartment. She felt that the additional burden of another infant would be unbearable.

With the money she received from the damages awarded her after a car accident, Sybil found an apartment with her three children. However, after learning of letters written by her father, threatening to kill her as soon as he was released from prison, Sybil became fearful that he would find it too easy to locate her where she was. Terrified by her father's threats, filled with self-contempt at her failure to make more of herself, and overwhelmed by the burden of raising three young children alone, Sybil felt desperate and helpless. She walked in front of an oncoming car with the thought of killing herself, but stepped aside at the last moment, explaining, "My children needed me." Shortly after this suicidal gesture, Sybil requested the presence of one of the authors (D.B.) for a meeting with her social worker at which Sybil intended to reveal the truth about the paternity of her first child. Sybil said she was ready to "go public" with the story of her incestuous relationship and asked that the meeting be tape recorded. Expecting her revelation to have a momentous impact on the world, Sybil declared herself ready to appear on national television and be interviewed in the newspapers. Other victims hearing her story, she explained, would be inspired to get help.

Sybil was expansive and exuberant during most of the interview. She spoke of her unstinting generosity in sharing the money she had received from her accident with her mother and siblings and how much they all depended on her. She described an unsuccessful scheme, which she had masterminded for her siblings, to use their father's gun to kill him. With undisguised pride, she boasted that she had inherited her craftiness and charisma from her father.

When she mentioned her mother, Sybil's mood abruptly changed. She burst into tears as she spoke of her mother's stinginess toward her compared with her generosity with others in the family. She also cried when she related a conversation in which her mother warned her to stay away from her mother's new boyfriend. Sybil felt that in so doing, her mother had implied that Sybil had seduced her father and stolen him from her.

After making plans to resume treatment with her social worker, Sybil also enlisted her support in her efforts to prevent her father from being released from the low security facility where he was awaiting parole. She hoped to have him placed permanently in a facility for the criminally insane.

In spite of her bravado, Sybil acknowledged that she was still troubled by a range of symptoms associated with PTSD. Intrusive thoughts and images related to her traumatic sexual experiences were a constant source of distress. They occurred most frequently when something she saw or heard reminded her of her father. For example, while she was living with her mother in an apartment where her father had raped her, merely looking at the site of some sexual episode could bring back the entire scene.

Much of this intrusive mentation had a decidedly psychotic and paranoid quality. For example, after seeing a man whose strange smile reminded her of her father's, she heard her father's voice calling her by a secret name. She often felt that strangers were ridiculing her because they knew about her sexual involvement with her father. At times, the very sight of her daughter's face triggered a flood of painful memories over which she had no control.

Sybil's sleep was often interrupted by recurring nightmares. She said that dream sequences appearing to reproduce actual events occur amid other dream images. In one such recurring scene, she saw her father choking her with an extension cord from an air conditioner and then beating her with it. When this event actually took place, Sybil recalled thinking she was about to die.

The following is Sybil's account of a recent version of another recurring nightmare:

> I go into an elevator. My mother's building has 21 floors but I am pressing to go to the 14th floor. The elevator is going slow and picking up speed. It goes past the roof and bursts out of the roof. I am laying on the floor of the elevator. I can't reach out to anybody. I can hear people speaking but I can't talk to them.

The feeling Sybil associated with this dream, both as she experienced it and after she awakened, was suffocating panic. She confirmed that the dream symbolized her sense of being out of control of her life. She was particularly disturbed by her own violent rages that seemed to her so like her father's. Sybil reported feeling at these times that he was somehow "inside me." Having become pregnant with her father's child at 14, Sybil believe that this was when she abandoned all hope of becoming a famous star who would share the limelight with her father. Her sense of being alone with agonizing feelings of shame, guilt, rage and terror have always pervaded her subjective world.

"Bugging out" was Sybil's term for reliving experiences usually precipitated by sexual activity or heated arguments. When she lived with her boyfriend, Sybil often would cry uncontrollably during sex because "my boyfriend became my father." Sybil also reported that she would run out of the apartment in a state of confusion and panic when quarrels with her boyfriend deteriorated into physical violence. "I would find myself in the hall," she said, "not really sure what had happened." In recalling these incidents, Sybil said that she probably imagined that she was being beaten by her father.

Sybil also reported a sensory "flashback" whenever her arm "falls asleep." The sensation recalls her experience of being handcuffed to her bed. "I see the whip swinging and I see him tearing off my clothes," she said, "His face has that evil little smile on it—like a 'psychy' look—like he knows what he's doing and he don't know what he's doing." According to Sybil, her father's "craziness" was even more terrifying than the beatings and violent sex to which she was subjected.

Sybil's paranoidal withdrawal was occasionally interrupted by violent outbursts, which she usually directed at her father's child. Ashamed, Sybil reported having pushed her daughter's stroller into the street in the hope that she would be hit by an oncoming car. She also spoke of administering severe punishments to his child, such as holding her hand against a hot stove, ostensibly to teach her not to play with the stove knobs.

Symptoms of numbing, another common feature of PTSD, were very prevalent in Sybil's life. She reported feeling "stiff inside" and needing to be "quiet to myself." Sybil claimed to spend days at a time in silence. At such times, she felt utterly helpless to rouse herself from a leaden apathy. Because of her periodic listlessness as well as her belief that she would be attacked by neighborhood gangs who "hate me because of the lies my mother tells," Sybil spent a great deal of time indoors with her children. She was also fearful that if she went out too frequently, she would be discovered by men whom she believes her father has hired to watch her.

Sybil also suffered from a number of the secondary symptoms of PTSD, such as hyperalertness, difficulties with memory and concentration, and sleep disturbances. She attempted to justify the continual state of hyperalertness in which she lived as necessitated by a host of vague dangers. She believed, for example, that people, influenced by her mother, wished to hurt her for having participated in an incestuous relationship.

Sybil was particularly distressed by her frequent difficulties with memory and concentration. She poignantly described her unsuccessful efforts to prepare for an examination to obtain her high school equivalency diploma. "I used to be such a wonderful student," she said, "and now so many thoughts fly into my head about my father, I can't even read."

Sybil also experienced difficulty falling asleep. She explained her reliance on alcohol and marijuana as motivated, in part, by their usefulness as sedatives.

Case Summary

A child of the inner city, Sybil was subjected, almost from birth, to a series of traumatic experiences against which she had little protection. The chaos of her early environment is reflected in the extreme disorganization of her subjective world. Insufficiently mirrored by her overburdened mother, Sybil could not attain a sense of self-cohesiveness, much less a sense of herself as unique and valuable.

It can be inferred that as a result, Sybil's fantasies of grandiose exhibitionism failed to undergo developmental transformation. In conscious daydreams reflective of these unconscious fantasies, Sybil saw herself as a budding star, superior in every way to her siblings, against whom she had to compete for her mother's limited attention. Unconsciously, she substituted acclaim by an imagined public for deficient maternal mirroring. Deprived of the sustaining warmth of her mother's prideful acceptance, Sybil also appears to have intensified an unconscious fantasy of idealized merger with her father, whose violent temper and criminal activities she initially construed as evidence of his malevolence and cunning.

So pervasive and dominating were these untransformed and unintegrated narcissistic fantasies that Sybil's entire personality seems to have been organized around a psychotically dissociative sense of self. Her self-references, for example, often had the quality of confabulation. Thus, when Sybil spoke about having sung and danced as a child, she sounded as if she were recounting memories of actually having been on stage. Her illusion that her actions would have enormous impact on the world also reflects the extremely archaic nature of her untransformed grandiose-exhibitionistic fantasies. Sybil's request for a news conference to announce that her child had been a product of her incestuous relationship with her father is another expression of these fantasies. From a classical psychoanalytic viewpoint, such behavior would be considered symptomatic of megalomania. We prefer to avoid this sort of diagnostic categorization because it connotes a constitutional "weakness" or predisposition to psychosis. Instead, we view her behavior as a consequence of severe and repeated trauma.

Sybil's perceptions of her father were as exaggerated as those of herself, reflecting the untransformed nature of her fantasies of idealized merger. She believed him to be completely immune to the dangers inherent in his various criminal activities. Initially, Sybil's incestuous experiences with her father promoted these illusions. As her archaic merger fantasy was actualized by their sexual relationship, Sybil came to believe that her grandiose fantasies would be realized. The strength of these fantasies enabled her to disavow feelings of fear and repugnance arising out of their sexual contact.

Considering the limitless power she ascribed to her father, his arrest when she was seven must have come as a shocking blow. Not only were her fantasies of idealized merger with an omnipotent paternal imago profoundly shaken, but her illusions about her grand destiny were also thrown into doubt. Desperately needing to buttress her endangered fantasies when her father was released from prison, Sybil unconsciously attempted even further elaboration. She came to view her father as an evil genius whose cruelty and immorality reflected demonic strength. To the extent that Sybil entertained a fantasy of idealized merger with her father, she also experienced herself as evil, destructive, and enormously powerful.

However, on discovering that she was just another victim of her father's sadistic sexuality and not his special little star, Sybil found it increasingly difficult to sustain this fantasy. As her nightmare image of her father's face suggests, she began to perceive him as "crazy," a demented villain who inflicted unforgivable torture on those closest to him. In addition, she felt more and more hopeless about her chances for fame and glory.

It appears that the ultimate shattering of her fantasy of idealized merger with her father as well as the destruction of her fantasy of grandiose exhibitionism coincided with her conception of her father's child. All her illusions that her father would insure her success were dashed by this mortifying occurrence. She also realized that the burden of caring for a baby ruined her chances of becoming a famous performer. The shattering of these fantasies filled Sybil with narcissistic rage directed both at herself and her selfobject father. By the time of her hospitalization following the birth of her child, she had not only thought of killing herself, she had also devised a bizarre but unsuccessful plan to kill her father.

Remarkably, in spite of her repeated traumatizations, Sybil's unconscious efforts at self-restitution proved indomitable. Her idealization of the social worker who treated her during this period, involving an illusion of the woman's perfect goodness, attests to the vigor with which she unconsciously attempted to restore her shattered fantasies. Apparently, however, in order to maintain this fantasy of idealized merger with her therapist, Sybil disavowed those aspects of herself which she perceived as evil or shameful. Consequently, she found it impossible to reveal that her daughter had been conceived through incest.

Because her selfobject transference fantasy had never been examined during the course of treatment, Sybil discontinued treatment when she became pregnant with her second child. For Sybil, the pregnancy was clear evidence of her debased sexuality and, therefore, disturbed her experience within the transference of sharing in the therapist's fantasied chastity and perfection. Without this sustaining self–selfobject fantasy relationship, Sybil plunged into despair and was overcome once again with severe symptoms of PTSD, some assuming psychotic proportion. For example, she experienced auditory hallucinations of her father's voice and persecutory delusions, including a belief that she was in danger from neighborhood gangs bent on punishing her for her incestuous relationship.

The unconscious traumatic meaning of Sybil's incestuous experiences illuminates the relationship between PTSD and psychosis. Because Sybil's personality was dominated to such a great extent by relatively untransformed and unintegrated archaic narcissistic fantasies, their shattering subjected her to severely dissociated states of depersonalization and derealization. It is precisely these terrifying subjective states and their symptomatic expression that lie at the heart of PTSD. In other words, we argue that the symptoms of PTSD are likely to assume psychotic proportion depending on: (1) the degree to which archaic narcissistic fantasies remain untransformed and unintegrated at the time of the trauma; and (2) the extent to which they dominate the personality as a result of unconscious embellishment over the course of development.

Sybil's faulty efforts to restore her fantasies also took on a psychotic character. One can infer, for example, that hallucinating her father's voice was an attempt at the compensatory restoration of her shattered fantasy of idealized merger with him. Her experience of having a dual personality vividly illustrates the depth of her experiences of depersonalization and derealization as well as the faulty nature of her restorative efforts.

Because of developmental arrests in the structuralization of her subjective world (Stolorow and Lachmann, 1980; Atwood and Stolorow, 1984), Sybil appears to have found it difficult to integrate affectively disparate experiences of herself and others. Thus, she experienced herself either as evil and destructive, as she perceived her father, or pure and good, as she perceived her therapist, depending on which of these powerful selfobjects dominated her fantasy life. With the traumatic shattering of her fantasies and the loss of a cohesive sense of herself, Sybil's vulnerability to states of depersonalization and derealization became even more pronounced. The formation of these polarized experiences of herself as good or evil into two separate personalities may be understood as an effort to stem the tide of fragmentation. In other words, her experience of herself as all good or all evil enabled her to fend off overwhelming feelings of disintegration anxiety.

Although these efforts were never completely successful—that is to say, the evil, destructive Carrie was never totally isolated from the meek, chaste, virtuous Sybil—they made possible some compensatory restoration of her fantasy of idealized merger as well as some defensive restoration of her fantasy of grandiose exhibitionism. Behaving as saintly Sybil, she could enact a fantasy of merger with an idealized maternal selfobject; experiencing herself as evil Carrie, she could sustain a fantasy of merger with her father based on their shared malevolence.

At the same time, as someone capable of experiencing herself in duality, Sybil imagined that she belonged to a select group of people who were so special that books and movies celebrated their lives. No ordinary person, Sybil believed, could be capable of such extremes of goodness and evil. Thus, for Sybil, the meaning of having a dual personality also promoted her efforts at the defensive restoration of her fantasy of grandiose exhibitionism.

Sybil's decision to participate in the study on which this book is based heralded another attempt at self-restitution. By vividly describing the details of her victimization, Sybil found a way to perform before a potential audience. It is encouraging to speculate that Sybil's reunion with her therapist would recreate an intersubjective context in which to resume the developmental process whereby her archaic narcissistic fantasies would become transformed into healthy ambitions, goals, and ideals.

Jean

Seated opposite the interviewer so that only her well-sculpted profile was visible, Jean, a 36-year-old white woman, seemed to be protecting a vulnerable part of herself. Yet she expressed her determination to overcome all "blocks" to revealing the harrowing details of her traumatic life. At times, especially in her early interviews, Jean struggled to accomplish this self-imposed goal, ignoring her evident discomfort.

Over a year of interviews, Jean related to the interviewer with earnest, almost childlike trust that seemed curiously incongruous with her gruff, somewhat awkward manner and her tall, angular, "androgynous" appearance. Adopting the rule of "collaborator," Jean committed herself to a lengthy series of interviews. She also provided written descriptions of her incestuous experiences, as well as drawings and short stories she had written on the theme of incest.

Jean described herself as a "healer" (she used herbs, gems, and rituals), a writer, a private investigator, and a social theorist. She explained her participation in this study as motivated both by her desire to learn more about the psychological effects of her own incestuous relationships and her wish to call further public attention to the problem of sexual abuse.

During her early interviews, Jean complained that her childhood memories were sparse and hazy. As time passed, however, and Jean adopted an increasingly collaborative role in the interview process, she produced more vivid and complete recollections of her early life. In fact, her zeal in complying with the interviewer's request for detailed information seemed at times to obscure rather than facilitate the analytic reconstruction of her childhood. Despite her apparent determination to recapture all her traumatic experiences, during her final interview Jean still expressed exasperation over her inability to fill in some remaining gaps in her memory for specific incestuous assaults.

Jean's memories of her early childhood were filled with scenes of violence. Her father suffered from alcoholism and the aftermath of tubercular meningitis, which rendered him alternately childlike and subject to violent outbursts. For example, he often had violent physical fights with Jean's mother. Jean remembered one particularly brutal fight in which she saw her mother stab her father in the eye with a knife. He required emergency surgery, which left him with a glass eye.

When Jean was four years old, her mother divorced her father and married a man with two teenaged sons. She then moved with Jean and her two older daughters to a bungalow in a beach resort next to her new husband's clothing store. Because her mother subsequently gave birth to five children (three boys and two girls) Jean said, "Role reversal came early." She remembered that she was expected to look after the younger children and do the lion's share of the housework and cooking while her mother helped out in the store. Asked why she had been given these responsibilities instead of her two older sisters, Jean responded with obvious pride that she was more intelligent, reliable, and competent than either of them. She particularly enjoyed the role of "little mother." "By the time I was five," she bragged, "I had a kid."

Jean prefaced her description of her mother by noting that they shared many physical similarities, particularly their tall, lean bodies and strong-looking features. She portrayed her mother as a cold, moody, taciturn woman, who cruelly exacted submissive obedience from her children. Because, Jean said, she rarely spoke, her harshly punitive disciplinary measures took them by surprise. Jean remembered that she had often heard the screams of her siblings coming from the basement of the bungalow where her mother took them for beatings with a belt or cat o'nine tails.

Jean believed that because she relieved her mother of more and more of the domestic chores, freeing the mother to indulge in periodic drinking binges and gambling sprees, she alone was spared the sadistic "punishments." "My mother and I were allies," Jean explained. "She often sent me out on 'spy missions' to find out what the other kids were up to."

"We were kept in silence," Jean observed, comparing the atmosphere of the bungalow to that of a concentration camp. As in a concentration camp, the children were afforded no privacy. They all slept in one bedroom while her stepfather had an adjoining bedroom to himself and her mother slept on a couch in the living room. As a child, Jean said, she never questioned these peculiar sleeping arrangements.

Jean's first incestuous experience occurred when she was ten years old. It was with her mother's brother, a serviceman, who was stationed nearby. Jean remembered looking forward to his frequent visits. "I liked him a lot," she said. "I guess he was a kind of father figure." One night while they were driving home from an army base, where he had taken Jean on a tour, he stopped at a motel, explaining that it was too late to go home. After putting her in his bed, he asked if he could have oral sex with her. When Jean protested, he said, "That's what I do with my wife." Jean remembered becoming upset because she knew he was not married. Jean said he masturbated her but neither asked her to touch him nor attempted intercourse.

Jean said that she could only surmise that she was shocked and distressed by the molestation, because her memory of the immediate aftermath of this experience remained hazy. However, she did remember "feeling sorry for my mother," because she now realized "what she had to put up with all the time." Jean also recalled that following this incident she had experienced a growing repugnance for her body. She reported walking out of art class, which previously had been her favorite subject, because the teacher insisted she draw a self-portrait that included her body. Jean contended that she was "flatchested" because "I made up my mind then that I would not grow breasts and look like a woman."

Shortly after being molested by her uncle, she was frequently criticized for mumbling. "I couldn't tell anyone, she explained, "that I was training myself to transmit thoughts nonverbally." Jean summed up her behavior during this period as an attempt "to exist purely as a spirit."

Jean also remembered feeling that she could not tell anyone what her uncle had done. "Because my mother was so fond of her brother," she explained, "I didn't think she would believe me." It never occurred to Jean to tell her stepfather because, as she noted, he virtually ignored her existence at this time. Jean regarded her stepfather as a coarse, ill-tempered, forbidding man, in whose presence she felt tense and uncomfortable.

Around the age of 12, Jean had to substitute for her mother in the store. She recalled feeling so afraid of her stepfather that she obeyed him automatically. When he commanded her to masturbate him in the bathroom one day, Jean said she did what he asked without question. He then took her into the basement of the shop, where he told her to undress and then placed her on a table. "With one hand he pushed me back and held me down," Jean said. "He spread my legs open and pushed as he tried to break into me."

From that day on, Jean said, her stepfather turned the bungalow into "a little whorehouse." He removed the door between the two bedrooms and every night would take Jean or one of her older sisters into his room to have sex with him. Jean said that she was required to engage in all forms of sexual activity, including oral and anal sex.

Jean poignantly recalled hoping that her mother would realize what was happening and intervene. "I guess her life was so miserable, she couldn't pay attention to what was happening to me," she said. Jean remembered imagining that since her mother had been "kept pregnant" by her stepfather, they were both "courageous martyrs" bound up in a "sexual tyranny." Asked why she had not told her mother about the incest, Jean replied, "Maybe I was too afraid to find out that she wouldn't or couldn't do anything to stop it."

Jean characterized her reaction to the relentless sexual assault as "disconnecting completely from my body." Repeating to herself, "This is not really happening," Jean prided herself on her ability to keep her features perfectly composed during the incestuous rapes, thus betraying no visible sign of her anguish. She also recalled a bedtime ritual that involved slowing her breathing down to a deathlike stillness in order to reassure herself of her "perfect control" over her body.

Often during the day, Jean said, she "listened to the silence," convinced that she possessed extrasensory powers to detect danger. She mentioned walking between rows of bungalows with her eyes closed in order to test her paranormal ability to sense any threats to her safety. Jean also described bizarre daydreams that occupied a great deal of her waking thoughts. In all of these daydreams, Jean envisioned herself being bound and tortured without ever displaying fear or pain.

Jean recalled her shocked disbelief when David, a stepbrother, joined in raping the girls. He forced Jean and her sisters to use drugs and pose nude for pornographic photographs, which he then sold to his friends. For as long as Jean could remember, she had been in love with David and imagined that he had similar feelings for her. In spite of her fierce efforts to pretend that sex with David was different from the rapes by her stepfather, Jean said she soon became despondent over his callous disregard for her wish to be treated as a lover.

Jean's adolescent years consisted of drab, joyless days and terror-filled nights of waiting to be sexually attacked. She had no friends, she said, because she experienced herself more as an adult than as a child. She liked to think that she needed no one and that she could do things perfectly without having to be taught. The one diversion she was permitted from her heavy burden of domestic chores was drawing. However, when her mother praised the artwork of a younger sister, Jean said, "I just gave it up."

Jean described her mother's suicide attempt when she was 15 as a final blow. She had stayed home from school that day with a cold, and her mother had sent her to the store to deliver (she later learned) the suicide note. When she returned home, she found that her mother had drawn the shades and locked the doors. Alarmed, Jean entered the house through a basement window and found her mother sprawled on the floor with a bullet wound in her abdomen.

In an essay describing her immediate reaction, Jean wrote, "The bullet that pierced my mother's stomach and seven other organs also shattered the existence of any delusion I was living in." Jean explained her "delusion" as a belief that she and her mother would always be together no matter how horrible their existence. She added, "I felt abandoned and betrayed by her."

Ignored by everyone except the policemen who questioned her for hours, Jean struggled with conflicting feelings of grief over her near loss as well as narcissistic rage at being abandoned and betrayed. She desperately wanted to escape, but her concern for her younger siblings kept her from running away from home. However, in spite of her fear that her siblings would be separated, Jean planned to leave and report her stepfather to child abuse authorities in the event of her mother's death.

Jean said she was overwhelmed by a strange mixture of relief and despair when she first saw her mother following her recovery from the bullet wound. As her mother walked through the front door, Jean fainted. "After that," she said, "I thought I would enter a world of insanity." She experienced peculiar sensations and perceptions, which she said were similar to later reactions to drugs. For example, accompanying her stepfather on a business trip, Jean had the strange sensation that the hotel was swaying.

Jean also reported having had premonitions of her mother's suicide attempt. She described repeated "visions" of her mother slitting her throat months earlier. She referred to a similar experience at the age of 17, when her biological father suddenly reappeared on their doorstep. According to Jean, her premonition of his return anticipated the actual event in precise detail. In spite of her mother's scathing criticism of him as a worthless, violent alcoholic, Jean had envisioned him as a gentle, loving man who would some day "rescue" her. She vividly recalled her disillusionment and contempt when she discovered that he had sought her out in the hope that she would cook, clean, and take care of him.

Afraid that she was "going crazy," Jean confided in a teacher about her reactions to her mother's suicide attempt. With the teacher's support and encouragement, Jean graduated with her class and made plans to leave home to attend a junior college. Before leaving for college, Jean decided to confront her mother with details of her incestuous relationships, hoping that her mother would protect the younger siblings who were still living at home. After receiving assurances from Jean's older sisters that they had not been sexually abused, her mother accused her of lying. Disillusioned of any hope of establishing trusting and caring relationships with her mother and sisters, Jean left home.

Immediately upon entering college, Jean began to experiment with a variety of drugs. She preferred L.S.D., she said, because it helped her reach a state of pain-free detachment combined with a sense of her perfection and oneness with all things. After finding that she required three or four "hits" a day to reach this state, Jean consulted a psychiatrist at the college. She became extremely depressed on the tranquilizers he prescribed and several times nearly died of suicidal overdoses. In spite of her acute distress, Jean managed to complete her two-year college program. Jean then moved to a large metropolitan area, where she got her own apartment and studied criminology at an urban college. Ironically, during this period, she supported herself by illegal drug dealing.

After graduating with a bachelor's degree, Jean toured Europe for six months. Traveling alone from country to country, she seldom spoke to anyone. She camped out in a small tent and spent a great deal of time visiting zoos. On returning to the United States, Jean "went underground," supporting herself by drug dealing and occasional prostitution. Comparing her aimless drifting to her mother's present life as an itinerant gambler, loan shark, and prostitute, Jean sadly noted many similarities.

During this period, Jean entered into a series of pathological sadomasochistic sexual relationships with both men and women. She was extremely proud of her bisexuality. Acknowledging that in these relationships it was she who frequently introduced the sadomasochistic elements, including bondage and beatings with whips and riding crops, Jean said that she "acted out adolescent fantasies."

Jean also described her involvement with a charismatic male "psychic" who made and sold pornographic movies of their sadomasochistic encounters. Usually assuming the masochistic position ("I was not cut out to be a sadist"), Jean said she often participated in these sadomasochistic "scenes," some lasting days at a time, in a dazed, detached state. "I somehow leave my body," she said, "and concentrate on not being hurt." Afterwards, Jean said, her memory for what had occurred was extremely vague and only the pain and marks on her body reminded her of her experience.

Jean derived enormous satisfaction from separating her emotional experience from her bodily sensations of pain. She said, "The aches and pains reinforced my sense of being special. Marks and bruises were the ways I measured my self-esteem."

Several years ago, Jean studied for a Master's degree in criminal justice as preparation for a career with the police department. However, after passing all the entrance examinations, she decided against joining the police department. Instead, she claimed to have established herself as a private investigator connected with the police force. She spoke of enjoying the special privileges afforded by this status such as being allowed to provide photographs of suspected rapists, evidence that, she said, would not be admissible if obtained by a member of the department. Jean purported to have contributed her "psychic powers" to the investigation of baffling criminal cases. She said she entered into trance states in which she provided detectives with such information as license plate numbers and locations of hideouts.

One morning about five years ago, Jean woke up with a high fever and intense pain and swelling in her joints. Her symptoms, which affected her entire body, became so severe that she required crutches or a wheelchair. The doctors she consulted, although unable to find any somatic causes, tried a wide variety of conventional forms of medical treatment, all without success. In desperation, Jean induced hypnoticlike trances in which she reexperienced intense somatic sensations of sexual encounters with her stepfather or stepbrother, often involving the same part of her body. For example, the memory of being raped by her stepfather while her thighs were pressed against her chest was associated with intense pains in her hips and thighs. Jean reported that after each of these trance episodes her symptoms vanished, only to be replaced some time later by another physical symptom requiring a repetition of the process.

With the recovery of these painful memories of her incestuous experiences, Jean resolved to devote all her energies to preventing

sexual abuse and helping survivors. In addition, Jean became obsessed
with various forms of healing. For several years she operated a health
food restaurant and store, where she purports to have achieved remarkable success in curing a wide range of physical ailments through
her use of herbs and gems. She noted that, without any instruction,
she instinctively "knew" how to heal.

Following Jean's first incestuous experience with her uncle at the
age of ten, early signs of PTSD are apparent in her history. For
example, Jean's illusion of "existing purely as a spirit" suggests that
after the abuse she experienced states of dissociation including disembodiment.[1]

Jean's experiences of disembodiment appear to have become more
frequent and pronounced during the period of sexual abuse by her
stepfather. The somatic delusion of "disconnecting" from her body
may reflect both the traumatic shattering and faulty attempt at
defensive restoration of her grandiose fantasy of herself as impervious
to injury and immune to abuse. Jean's belief in her uncanny power of
"disconnecting" from her body confirmed her conviction that she was
endowed with extraordinary and paranormal psychic powers.

Early signs of reexperiencing are also evident in Jean's recurrent
daydreams of being tortured. These daydreams bear very close resemblance to several recurrent nightmares she had later in adolescence.
In one such repetitive nightmare, she is in a school building or factory.
In a stairway, she discovers a girl who has been raped or beaten. She
wants to assist the girl, but her mother and sisters restrain her, saying
there is no point in helping. In another recurring nightmare, Jean is
being savagely beaten by her sisters while her mother watches.

Associating to the first nightmare, Jean identified herself with the
girl who was beaten and raped. Choking back tears, she noted that
her mother's indifference to the victim in the nightmare expressed her
feeling that her mother had never acted to save her from the brutal
rapes. She connected the second nightmare to her incestuous experiences with her stepbrother. She recalled wondering how her mother
could "sit by" as these assaults continued.

Jean also stressed that in these nightmare she had neither displayed

---

[1]We view states of disconnection or detachment from body as manifestations of disembodiment and as symptomatic of PTSD. Although disembodiment is not officially
recognized as a symptom of PTSD, we consider it, along with the more familiar
symptoms of alienation and estrangement, to fall within the *DSM*-III diagnostic category of numbing. Our view of disembodiment is consistent with and buttresses our
argument that all major reexperiencing and numbing symptoms are manifestations of
dissociation. This, we contend, warrants clinically reconceptualizing and diagnostically
reclassifying PTSD as a dissociative rather than an anxiety disorder.

fear nor experienced pain. "Like I rose above all pain and fear," she observed.

Jean's associations to the starkly graphic manifest content of these two nightmares suggest that the unconscious meaning of her incestuous experiences is to be found in the shattering and faulty restoration of archaic narcissistic fantasies. We infer that for Jean the unconscious traumatic meaning of incest involved: (1) the shattering of her fantasized merger with an idealized, all-protective maternal selfobject; and (2) faulty efforts at defensive restoration via elaborate fantasies of grandiosity.

Her efforts at defensive restoration are symbolically represented in her images of herself as silently enduring all abuse without showing fear or experiencing pain. Jean apparently imagined that her stoic endurance represented a magic triumph over tormentors and onlookers alike.

Jean's involvement later in life in sadomasochistic sexual encounters may be understood as yet another form of reexperiencing in which she relived the traumatic sexual abuse. Jean's belief in her paranormal ability to "disconnect" from her body is an important aspect of these scenarios and points to underlying fantasies of grand triumph.

Jean's life was still noticeably affected by a wide range of PTSD symptoms. Her mysterious physical ailments, which closely resembled those described in classical psychoanalytic literature as hysterical "conversion symptoms," may be viewed as phenomena related to reexperiencing. Her crippling pains and swollen joints, which appear to have had no identifiable physical basis, may have conveyed somatically encoded messages, hinting at the unconscious traumatic meaning of her incestuous experiences.

Because Jean seemed to have undergone these experiences in deeply dissociated states, she had only vague recollections of these episodes. With the appearance of each symptom, however, Jean somatically reexperienced a specific traumatic episode by means of painful physical sensations. For example, because of certain pains in her hip joints, she could walk only by thrusting her pelvis forward in a manner that imitated sexual intercourse. During a deeply dissociated state, Jean recaptured a memory of the first time her body responded to genital stimulation with involuntary thrusting motions of her pelvis. After she reexperienced the physical sensation of this early childhood episode of sexual abuse and described accompanying terrifying images and emotions to the interviewer, the symptom abated.

Symptoms of numbing were also prominent features of Jean's life. The hypnoticlike trances accompanying her somatic delusion of disconnection from her own body (that is, disembodiment), which once enabled her to endure sexually and physically abusive attacks, took on important functions in her life, quelling disintegration anxiety and states of fragmentation. Whenever Jean was under stress, she entered into these dissociated states of disembodiment.

Jean periodically "goes into isolation," another aspect of numbing. After phoning people to say she would be out of town for a while and stocking her house with food, Jean would retreat to her bed and sleep and rest for days at a time. Coming out of these cocoonlike states, Jean reported feeling "regressed" and childlike. Callers had noted that her telephone voice at these times sounded like that of a young child. She often spent several days lying in bed, decorating the area around her with colorful drawings until she felt ready to resume her normal busy schedule. These self-enforced periods of isolation were reflective of alienation and estrangement.

Until a recent attempt to give up all addictions, Jean utilized a variety of drugs to enhance her state of detachment and disembodiment. Amphetamines and marijuana were her most frequent "drugs of choice." She also reported suffering from many secondary symptoms of PTSD, such as hyperalertness, startle reactions, and sleep disturbances.

Case Summary

From Jean's account of the "concentration camp" atmosphere of her early years and her repeated exposure to violent battles between her parents, we surmise that these frightening and disillusioning experiences led to derailments in the developmental transformation of her fantasies of idealized merger with omnipotent parental selfobjects.

Because these violent scenes were initiated by both parents, Jean apparently could not maintain a healthy idealization of either one. However, following her parents' divorce, Jean's mother became the sole focus of her efforts to fortify her threatened fantasies. Much as she related to the interviewer as a helpful collaborator, Jean, as a young child, appears to have become her mother's trusted helper and ally. We infer that this behavior was reflective of an unconscious fantasy of idealized merger with her mother, the transformation of which was seriously impeded by developmental arrests in the structuralization of her self experience. As part of this fantasy, Jean imagined herself as a fully mature adult or a "wise child" (Bach, 1985), who possesses special knowledge and competence without having to be taught.

Jean's unconscious fantasies of herself as magically merged with an idealized maternal imago were repeatedly shattered by her devastating experiences of incest. Alone and unprotected during each of these terrifying assaults, her plight totally ignored by her mother, Jean's sense of herself was massively disturbed. In a desperate but unsuccessful effort at compensatory restoration, Jean elaborated her fantasies of idealized merger. These unconscious fantasies were reflected in conscious reveries involving a powerful and mystical union between Jean and her mother, which empowered both of them with superhuman endurance and an extraordinary capacity to triumph over their male aggressors. They were both, in Jean's words, "courageous martyrs united by sexual tyranny."

At the same time, Jean appears to have unconsciously attempted defensive restoration involving fantasies of herself as grandiose and omnipotent. For example, her somatic delusion of disembodiment and her illusion of possessing such uncanny powers as mental telepathy (imagining she could transmit thoughts nonverbally) apparently helped Jean to experience herself as "disconnected." She imagined that she had risen above her subjugated and debased body. As her daydreams of torture and her recurrent nightmares clearly show, by stoically enduring all forms of abuse without showing pain or distress, Jean imagined she had triumphed over her tormentors.

The manifest dream imagery and her associations to her two most prominent recurrent nightmares are highly revealing of the unconscious traumatic meaning of incest for Jean. Symbolically represented in these nightmares are images of the initial shattering of her fantasy of mystical oneness with her mother. These are contained in the nightmare images of Jean's mother passively standing by as Jean is unmercifully beaten and tortured as well as in the image of her restraining Jean from coming to the aid of the rape victim.

The significance of her mother's suicide attempt is closely connected to the unconscious meaning of Jean's traumatic experiences. At the time of the suicide attempt, Jean was desperately fending off disintegration anxiety brought on by the repeated shattering of her fantasy of idealized merger with her mother and her unsuccessful efforts at defensive and compensatory restoration. Experiencing the suicide attempt as yet another form of abandonment and betrayal, Jean was subject to a delayed traumatic reaction to the incest resulting in a fullblown case of PTSD that reached psychotic proportions.

Another manifestation of this delayed traumatic reaction was her consuming feelings of narcissistic rage toward her mother. In one interview, for example, Jean confessed to having experienced an almost irresistible impulse to strangle her mother as she lay comatose in her hospital bed. It is also probable that Jean's own crippling psychosomatic symptoms were, in part, expressions of narcissistic rage directed at her self for failing to live up to her grandiose fantasies.

That, to a great extent, Jean's subjective world remains organized by fantasies of merger with an idealized maternal imago was evidenced by her transference relationship with the interviewer. Her belief in her magical healing powers and her gifts as a psychic and clairvoyant attest to the continuing presence of grandiose fantasies of herself. Although she no longer participates in sadomasochistic enactments and pornography, elements of sadomasochism in her present relationships suggest her continuing need to experience herself as immune to psychic pain. Jean's pride in her bisexuality suggests her need to transcend what she perceives as humiliating limitations on her sexuality that derive from having been born female. Even her florid somatic symptoms distinguish her from other victims and serve as her "claim to fame" in the growing community of incest survivors.

In spite of all of these indications of the enormous impact that incest trauma has had on her life, Jean has, against all odds, managed to develop herself as a self-proclaimed "Renaissance woman" devoted to the betterment of society and the elimination of all forms of sexual abuse. She has been extremely resourceful in finding creative solutions to her longings for experiences of idealized merger. For example, she has developed an association with the police department, which she views as a powerful organization offering protection and support to victims. Without minimizing her important achievements, we can understand Jean's present life as dominated by archaic narcissistic fantasies, repeatedly shattered and unconsciously elaborated by defensive and compensatory restoration.

Rosa

Rosa, a 34-year-old white woman, needed little prompting to engage herself fully in the interview process. Highly verbal, she responded to questions with fluent monologues that often sparkled with sardonic wit. At times, however, despite her apparent determination to maintain a casual, almost flippant tone, an edge of cynicism could be detected in her remarks. Although she was somewhat overweight, Rosa's dark, almond-shaped eyes, full lips, and olive complexion suggested the image of a striking beauty.

As a member of a woman's group, Rosa volunteered to be interviewed for this study. Stating that her incestuous experiences with her stepfather had affected every aspect of her life, Rosa stressed her determination to do her utmost to help other women similarly victimized by men. During her initial interview, Rosa adopted a rather maternal stance toward the interviewer, commenting on the worthiness of the project and emphasizing her willingness to discuss even the most intimate details of her life. She suggested that, to a large extent, she had overcome the ill effects of numerous traumatic experiences, pointing to her success as an executive for a large manufacturing company and her happiness in her recent marriage as evidence of her healthy adjustment.

At the outset of the second interview, however, Rosa confessed to having painted too bright a picture of her present functioning. "I'm afraid I misled you," she said. "I presented myself as strong and 'together,' but I'm really very shaky." She said that all too often she found the stresses of her job overwhelming and the tensions in her marriage intolerable. "I can't seem to keep a lid on my anxiety," she said. "The only thing that ever helped on that score was heroin." She complained of difficulty in falling asleep, feeling "terribly insecure about my body" and her inability to control her weight.

Rosa and her sister Marie, four years younger, grew up in a large city. With the exception of her mother, who was born in this country, all of her adult relatives came from Italy. Her father, whom Rosa described as an ineffectual alcoholic, worked for an Italian shipping company with her uncles. Despite Rosa's memory of her mother as a chronically depressed woman who accepted her husband's long absences at sea and his excessive drinking with resignation, she recalled her early childhood with nostalgia. She described growing up among a large group of noisy, lively, loving relatives who tended to dramatize their emotions and turn ordinary events into "soap opera."

Some time around Rosa's eighth birthday, one of her uncles introduced the family to Gino, a co-worker who had recently arrived from Italy. According to Rosa, he was so charming and handsome that her mother fell in love with him "at first sight." Impetuously deciding to end her marriage, Rosa's mother ran off with Gino, taking Marie with her and leaving Rosa in the care of her grandmother. Rosa recalled that, in spite of her father's tearful distress, she enjoyed the time her mother was away. She loved the extra attention she received as the women in the family "fussed over the 'poor child'."

When her mother returned several weeks later, she announced her intention to marry Gino and asked her husband for a divorce. Rosa's father refused to consider ending the marriage on the grounds that since her mother and Gino had not had sex, no adultery had taken place. A few months later, Rosa's mother again left home with Gino, this time without Marie. At last, her father agreed to a divorce, and Rosa's mother and Gino were quickly married. The following year, Rosa's mother gave birth to a son.

Rosa recalled that for the following year or two, she felt contented and secure living with her mother and new stepfather. She attended a

local Catholic school, where she was a good student and had many
friends. The most difficult times for Rosa were the days she spent
visiting her father. Because his alcoholism had worsened she and her
sister "ended up taking care of him." Rosa said she felt very sorry for
her father but distant and detached from him. She recalled her
difficulty in accepting that the disheveled, teary-eyed, mumbling
drunkard she visited was the glamorous seaman who, in countless
daydreams, whisked her off on exciting adventures. Gino, in contrast,
seemed to embody all the qualities she had once attributed to her
father. He was handsome and distinguished looking; Rosa felt proud
to be seen in his company. She envisioned her family's rise to prominence in their community with Gino at the head of the household. She
had little doubt that she would achieve a position of great importance
and respectability by virtue of being Gino's stepdaughter. In addition,
Gino seemed to invite closeness and to offer her all the warmth,
attention, and security she missed in her relationships with both
biological parents.

As she entered puberty, Rosa noticed radical changes in Gino's
affectionate response to her. At first he began to kiss her on the lips.
"I hated it when he stuck his tongue into my mouth," Rosa said, "I
felt invaded." Next he began to fondle her breasts, and then her
buttocks and genitals.

Rosa recalled her desperate struggle to rationalize Gino's sexual
advances as indications of his "special" feelings for her. She became
more alarmed when he began to grab her roughly in the hallway of
their apartment just out of her mother's sight. Soon he began to come
into her bedroom at night, and she was often startled into wakeful-
nesses by his caresses.

Although he never attempted to have intercourse with her, Rosa
grew increasingly frightened of him. At the same time, Rosa reported,
Gino became physically abusive toward her and her mother, and family
arguments frequently degenerated into violent scenes. He insisted
that Rosa spend time alone with him and expressed resentment about
her interest in boys her own age. Rosa said that she began to despise
Gino for destroying her illusion of having the perfect stepfather. All of
her optimism about their glorious future dissolved, and Rosa was
plunged into a state of disillusionment and confusion.

Yet Rosa remembered that she never seriously considered telling
her mother about his sexual molestation, even when he ignored her
efforts to resist him. "I felt I had to keep my mother from finding
out," Rosa said. "After what she went through with my father, I didn't
want her to know that Gino was a bastard, too."

In response to questions about her fear of "hurting" her mother with the truth about Gino, Rosa indicated that she experienced her mother as weak and helpless, a woman whose only defense against exploitation and abuse was denial. Rosa explained that her mother tried to close her eyes to anything unpleasant but when forced to confront a disturbing situation, would give way to helpless despair. Her characteristic gesture was to throw up her hands and ask, "What can we do?" Even more distressing for Rosa than her mother's reluctance to face the painful realities of life was her failure to validate Rosa's negative feelings or to offer comfort and support during her troubled moments. Rosa felt that if she did not show her mother a smiling face, she would not be seen at all.

Rosa described her life at home during her early teen years as all but unbearable. In spite of her growing sense of repugnance toward Gino, she tolerated his kisses and caresses because she was terrified that if she resisted he would carry out a threat to leave her mother and take her half-brother with him. Tormented by guilt and shame, Rosa began to feel that the image she presented to the world of a "nice, well-brought up Catholic girl" was "phony." "I felt I was always acting," Rosa said. "Whether I was at home or at school, I couldn't be sure when I was being 'real'." Rosa said that avoidance was her only defense against the storm of angry, frightened, and confused feelings Gino stirred in her.

Rosa recalled an incident during this period that, she said, heralded her "rebellion" and metamorphosis. Her mother had fallen ill on the day of a family party and suggested that Rosa go with Gino. Reluctant to ride alone with him in the car for fear that "he would be all over me," Rosa and a friend let the air out of the tires. Rosa said she hoped that by the time Gino inflated them it would be too late to go to the party. As soon as Gino discovered the flat tires, he suspected that Rosa was responsible. Although she refused to confess to deflating the tires, Gino beat her severely. From that day on, Rosa spent most of her time away from home in the company of older adolescents, who introduced her to a world of cigarettes, beer, and parties. With the destruction of her fantasy of becoming the respected daughter of a distinguished man, Rosa embraced the image of herself as a defiant rebel. She exchanged her Catholic school uniform for tight-fitting jeans and heavy makeup.

At the age of 13, Rosa's life changed dramatically. She reported a traumatic incident that began when she agreed to meet a boyfriend in a bar. A man approached her saying that he would take her to a party where her boyfriend was waiting for her. "I thought I could take care of myself," Rosa said to explain why she accompanied the stranger.

Finding herself in a hotel room with the man, Rosa remembered saying, "Hey, there's no party here." The man threw her on the bed and sexually attacked her. Rosa said that although she felt certain he would kill her, she thought of a plan to escape. "I conned him by saying I would run away with him," Rosa recalled. She persuaded him to allow her to phone friends who would bring clothing and money to the hotel. When her friends came, she managed to communicate that she was trapped. They told the desk clerk that she was only 13. When he came to the room to investigate, Rosa escaped with her friends.

Trembling with shock and fear, yet proud of her clever escape, Rosa told her mother what had happened to her. Rosa described her incredulity and profound disappointment when her mother, instead of offering her comfort and support, refused to believe that she had been attacked. "She chose to believe that I had invented a 'good story' to explain why I had stayed out all night," Rosa recalled.

Devastated by her mother's totally unempathic response and feeling agitated and confused, Rosa ran away. "I had no idea where I was going," Rosa said. "I just got on the subway and got off at the last stop." Feeling dazed and disoriented "like I was in some kind of trance," Rosa walked the streets for hours until a man "picked me up." After living with him for several weeks, during which time he provided her with food and clothing, Rosa reported that "he sold me to a pimp." "In many ways," Rosa said, "life as a child prostitute was a replay of life with my stepfather." She recalled feeling "wonderful" at first, explaining that she was her pimp's favorite since she was younger and prettier than his other girls. She also experienced a sense of relief at no longer having to pretend to be a "good girl."

Soon, however, the pimp's interest in her began to flag, and he no longer treated her to the most expensive clothes and jewelry. Although he began to beat her savagely whenever she displeased him, Rosa said she remained devoted to him. Even after he locked her in a closet for days at a time and threatened to kill her, Rosa said, "I couldn't leave him." She explained that he threatened to report her to the police and have her sent to prison if she tried to run away. More compelling than his threats for Rosa was the ecstasy she experienced during their lovemaking. At these times, she imagined that they were perfectly matched; no man had more sexual power, no woman more allure. As if addicted to this ecstatic experience, Rosa believed she could not exist without it. Even his cruelty took on a perverse attraction, and Rosa stoically endured his brutal attacks.

"I guess he never understood that I was just a kid," she said. Nevertheless, she described a sense of shocked disbelief at the indifference of people who ignored her plight. "Nobody helped," she said. "Nobody paid any attention to my black eyes and swollen lips."

In all the time she spent with her pimp, Rosa could not recall ever wishing to return home. However, she reported sending money and notes to her sister Marie "so they knew I was alive." After three years, Rosa's parents managed to track her down with the help of the police. Rosa said that back with her family she felt extremely alienated and estranged. "No one asked me about what I had been through," she said. "My mother obviously did not want to know I was a prostitute."

Certain that she could not live up to her parents' expectation that she resume her former pattern of life, Rosa ran away on three occasions, each time returning to life as a prostitute. Finally she was brought to juvenile court and sentenced to an institution for delinquent girls run by Catholic nuns. Although Rosa welcomed the opportunity to "pick up the pieces of my life," she described the starkly punitive atmosphere as oppressive. Instead of offering her hope for change, Rosa explained, the nuns seemed to confirm her worst fears about herself. In their disapproving eyes, Rosa felt she could never find a reflection of her old fantasy of attaining success and respectability. Consumed with self-loathing, she believed she had been irreparably damaged by her experiences of incest and prostitution.

After a short time, Rosa found herself longing to be back "on the street," where she felt supremely confident of her desirability and her wiles as an experienced "hooker." She said that she quickly established herself as the leader of a group of girls and planned a successful escape. After stopping a car and offering to pay for a ride back to the city by having sex with the driver and his friends, Rosa said, "I was back into prostitution by the time I got back to the city." Without the glamour and security provided by her pimp, Rosa soon experienced her life as intolerably sordid and dangerous.

Filled with despair at the hopeless position she found herself in, Rosa turned to drugs as the only means of escape she could find. After experimenting with L.S.D. and suffering from "bad trips" that included flashbacks and hallucinations, Rosa began to use heroin. She quickly became addicted and supported her extremely expensive habit by drug dealing and petty crimes. She claimed that heroin was "a way out of prostitution," but she soon became involved in the dangerous, violent world of the addict. Living with a succession of abusive male addicts who involved her in drug dealing and burglary, Rosa learned to mix barbiturates and heroin as a way of cutting the expense of her habit. However, she found it difficult to control her intake of these drugs and began to suffer from overdoses. "I lived on the fine line between death and pain," she said. Despite the dangers inherent in heroin addiction, Rosa spoke of yearning for the experience of herself as soothed and oblivious to her anguish and pain.

Arrested several times for drug dealing, Rosa served time at a detention center for women. Finally, with the help of a young Legal Aid lawyer who befriended her after finding her overdosed in the hallway of his apartment building, Rosa entered into several drug abuse programs. Rosa said that none of the programs proved effective, and she would "shoot up" the day she left.

Desperate to end her addiction, Rosa called on her mother for help. "At last, she came through for me," Rosa said. Noting that her mother seemed magically changed, suddenly appearing beautiful, good, and wise, Rosa imagined that she could accomplish anything with her support. After going from therapist to therapist and program to program with no success, Rosa finally heard that the Synanon program in California offered a chance for recovery. Accompanied by her mother, Rosa entered the program and eventually left, feeling that she had freed herself from heroin.

Although Rosa remembered feeling "lost and shaky" after returning to the city, she went back to school and obtained a high school equivalency diploma while supporting herself by working as a waitress. Within months of meeting a teenaged youth five years younger than she, Rosa married him because "I wanted to live the adolescence I had never known." In the presence of this handsome young man, Rosa imagined herself cleansed of all her sordid sexual experiences, miraculously rejuvenated into the pure-hearted schoolgirl at the threshold of successful womanhood.

Once again, however, Rosa found herself involved in an intensely abusive relationship. She described her first husband at various times as "an incredibly needy boy," a "borderline-illiterate," and an "alcoholic wife-beater." "It was the same old story," she said, "Love and violence and sex always go together." This time, however, in spite of her overwhelming sense of despondency, self-contempt, and disenchantment, Rosa managed to end the relationship quickly. Nevertheless, even after their divorce, Rosa often helped him out of scrapes and lent him money.

When he was killed in a drunk-driving accident, Rosa felt both relieved and guilty at having left him. She had a similar reaction when she learned of her father's death. She related that while she was recovering from her drug addiction, she experienced a sense of closeness to her father and a fuller appreciation for his predicament. Despite not having heard from him since she had run away from home, she decided to write to him in Italy, where he had relocated. They corresponded for several years and visited each other a number of times. News of her father's death shocked Rosa, and she flew to Italy for his funeral. On discovering that he had killed himself with an overdose of pills and alcohol, Rosa said she was overcome with grief and remorse at not having been with him to prevent this tragedy.

Afraid that she would be unable to quell the tormenting pain and anxiety she experienced following these losses without resorting to drugs, Rosa entered psychotherapy with a male psychiatrist whom she admired as brilliant and compassionate, more than equal to the challenge she presented as a "difficult" patient. She felt that she made considerable gains during the course of treatment. She established herself in a career as a high level executive and married a man whom she experienced as very different from any of the other men in her life, describing him as "a gentle fellow who really cares for me." Another important development in Rosa's life during this period was her involvement in a women's group. Among these women, many of whom had undergone similar sexual traumas, Rosa believes that she discovered successfully restored versions of herself. She distinguished herself in this group as a woman who could speak out publicly for causes in which she believed. She has appeared on radio and television and has debated women's issues before large audiences.

In spite of these significant accomplishments, Rosa's life has been disrupted by a wide spectrum of PTSD symptoms. Intrusive thoughts related to her incestuous experiences with her father are a dominant feature of the groups of symptoms that fall into the category of reexperiencing. She noted that these thoughts were particularly prevalent when she was under stress or exposed to stimuli associated with incest. When, for example, her work with the women's group involved child pornography or violence against children, Rosa said she was often flooded with vivid memories of sexual experiences with her stepfather. She noted that such memories were also likely to occur in settings physically similar to those in which she was abused. She mentioned a dread of certain hallways because she anticipated that images of being molested in the hallway of their apartment would flash through her mind.

In spite of having had many abusive sexual experiences, Rosa said, it was her stepfather who "haunts my bedroom." Thoughts and images of her stepfather were particularly frequent for Rosa when she was having sex with her second husband. Because her sleep was so frequently interrupted by her stepfather's intrusions into her bedroom, Rosa admitted that she still sleeps with a light.

In addition to her difficulty in falling asleep at night, Rosa said she was frequently wakened by nightmares. She recounted the following nightmare, which originated in her childhood and recurred nightly for many years:

> I am sleeping and I hear 'bong, drag' like a pirate walking with a peg leg. I say, 'Oh, no, he's coming' and I hide under the sheets. A man comes in and rips off the sheets. He says, 'This is your last chance. I'm going to race you to your mother's room and if you get there first, you're free, and if you don't . . .' He doesn't finish, but I race to the front door and run in place while he comes closer and closer. Finally, I yell, 'Mom!' and wake up.

Over the years, Rosa observed, the content of this nightmare varied somewhat. At times the setting has been a subway tunnel and at other times a crowded street. However, the invariant elements are a chase, a crippled man, and crying out for help at the last moment. Rosa wept as she associated to the images in nightmare. She connected the peg-legged man to her experiences of men as both damaged (alcoholic and abusive) and damaging, particularly insofar as they use sexuality as a weapon. She explained that in the dream she did not cry out for help until it was almost too late, because she was afraid to find out that her mother would not protect her.

Following one of her initial interviews, Rosa reported another recurrent nightmare:

> I killed my stepfather. I was stuffing him in a box. I chopped him up but couldn't get his head in and I was pushing it and pushing it. I covered it with a wet towel like a shroud and then hid it under a stairwell. All of a sudden I realized I had to get to my mother and sister before they found him. I was panic stricken. I make up stories to tell my mother.

In reviewing this nightmare, Rosa associated the towel in which she wrapped her stepfather's head to the Shroud of Turin, which, she said, always fascinated her. Her further associations revealed her childhood fantasy of her stepfather as a Christ-like savior who would protect and provide for her and her mother. Killing him in the dream, Rosa acknowledged, represented the destruction of her illusion that he was a kind, loving protector. It is noteworthy that even in this nightmare, Rosa attempted to keep the truth about Gino from her mother.

Rosa also complained of a variety of PTSD numbing symptoms, including estrangement and alienation. Although the sense of "deadness and unreality" that had plagued her adolescence diminished somewhat for her, she reported that she still felt "that I am always acting." During a period in which she was experiencing severe strains in her second marriage, Rosa said, "I really thought I was losing it, that everything was a lie. I sometimes feel that I cannot believe in my own reality." She also complained of feelings of extreme worthlessness and alienation from others. "I feel that my experiences as an incest victim and prostitute make me different from everyone else." She observed that she was extremely sensitive to suggestions that she was inferior to others. A recent remark by a colleague at work insinuating that Rosa had grown up "on the other side of the tracks" came as a "total blow" and made her feel hopeless about ever belonging to the world of "respectable people."

Rosa continued to suffer from difficulties with memory and concentration. She complained that it was difficult for her to keep the sequence of events in the proper order and occasionally felt confused about whether or not she had completed a task. At times, she said, irrelevant thoughts "pop into my head" when she needed to think clearly about a problem at work. She said she often found herself ruminating about embarrassing or shameful moments in her life.

Case Summary

Rosa's experience of growing up in a large and loving extended family appears to have offset, to some extent, the inadequacies of her "weak and helpless" mother and her alcoholic father. Yet, for all of her relatives' warmth and liveliness, Rosa's childhood experiences of mirroring and idealized merger were not sufficient to promote the developmental transformation of her archaic narcissistic fantasies. Rosa's lifelong struggle with debilitating anxiety and her involvements with abusive men suggest that her longings for calming and soothing selfobject experiences of idealized merger with omnipotent parental imagos were especially thwarted.

Her blissful memories of the early stages of her relationship with her stepfather, in which he figured as a Christ-like savior, appear to reflect the archaic nature of these untransformed fantasies. It is also possible to understand Rosa's caregiving behavior toward her parents as an unconscious attempt to function as their selfobjects and thereby experience these selfobject functions vicariously. By nursing her father through his hangovers and shielding her mother from her incestuous involvement with her stepfather, Rosa performed the very selfobject functions of calming, soothing, and safeguarding for her parents that she urgently needed them to perform for her.

In order to protect her fantasies during her latency years, Rosa struggled to preserve her stepfather as an omnipotent paternal imago by rationalizing his abusiveness as evidence of his love for her. When she reached adolescence, however, she could no longer deny that his sexual advances violated her trust. With the destruction of her cherished fantasy of idealized merger with Gino, her disillusionment was devastating. She was overwhelmed with narcissistic rage toward herself, her stepfather and everyone around her for participating in a deception that she was part of a nice, conventional Catholic family.

Rosa's effort at defensive restoration following the traumatic shattering of her fantasy of idealized merger seems to have involved the elaboration of her fantasies of grandiose exhibitionism. This was manifested in an exhibitionistic adolescent stance of invulnerable self-sufficiency. At 13, Rosa experienced herself as perfectly able to live without adult supervision. In the company of an adolescent gang, she imagined herself to be streetwise, tough, and well protected.

It is probable that she experienced the sexual attack in early adolescence as a terrible blow to her illusion of perfect self-sufficiency and invulnerability. Following the attack, at a time when Rosa was most desperate for comfort and protection, her mother again demonstrated her own fraility and neediness by denying that Rosa had been attacked. Her failure to empathize with Rosa's obvious suffering thwarted Rosa's efforts to idealize her. With her central fantasies shattered once again, Rosa was thrown into a fugue-like dissociative state. Only by remaining in this "trance" could she distance herself from the terror of fragmentation. While it is difficult to determine how long she continued in this deeply dissociated state, it seems probable that she suffered from severe episodes of depersonalization and derealization throughout most of the period of her prostitution.

Prostitution appeared to offer Rosa a number of opportunities to restore her shattered fantasies. As a "woman of the streets," Rosa temporarily achieved defensive restoration through the unconscious elaboration of her grandiose-exhibitionistic fantasies. No longer a helpless victim who was forced to submit to her stepfather's sexual demands, Rosa now imagined herself as an irresistible seductress who could command a high price for her sexual services.

Rosa's involvement with her pimp appears to represent an unconscious effort at the compensatory restoration of her fantasies of idealized merger with an omnipotent paternal imago. Just as she had previously attempted to preserve her stepfather's idealizability, Rosa clung fiercely to this relationship even when she was most exploited and abused. Enslaved as much by her illusion that her sexual relationship with this brutal figure would provide her with ecstatic merger experiences as by her fear that he would kill her if she tried to leave him, Rosa felt utterly trapped.

Heroin brought Rosa all that she previously had sought in fantasies of oneness with powerful men—without the risk of traumatic disillusionment. Not only was a sense of calmness, serenity, and freedom from disintegration anxiety reliably available with heroin, but, because it was self-administered, Rosa's illusion of perfect self-sufficiency was enhanced. These reasons as well as her physiological addiction made it extremely difficult for Rosa to give up heroin. It is probable that her mother's support during her treatment at Synanon was critical in facilitating her recovery. At long last, Rosa found in her mother's acceptance of her serious problem evidence of her fantasized omnipotence. Merged with her in fantasy, Rosa found an ideal selfobject substitute for heroin.

Rosa has been extremely effective in securing opportunities to resume the transformation of her archaic narcissistic fantasies. Her involvement with a woman's organization has been particularly beneficial in this respect. By joining with others like herself to promote women's issues, Rosa has found an empathic milieu in which to wage her personal struggle to erase the scars of her victimization.

CONCLUSION

We have presented three representative cases of incest illustrating our theory of the shattering and faulty restoration of archaic narcissistic fantasies in the lives of incest survivors. In all three cases, these fantasies were found to have undergone relatively little developmental transformation, which made the victims vulnerable to repeated shattering as a result of incest. The lengths to which survivors of incest will go to effect the defensive and compensatory restoration of their shattered fantasies was poignantly dramatized in these cases.

Sybil's fantasies of grandiose exhibitionism fostered by her early incestuous experiences with her father were shattered when his brutality and violence destroyed her illusion of becoming a famous performer. Her unconscious efforts at defensive restoration involved illusions of her tremendous impact on the world while her efforts at compensatory restoration turned her father into an "evil genius." Her experience of herself as having a dual personality was understood as an unconscious attempt, albeit unsuccessful, to promote both defensive and compensatory restoration of her shattered fantasies.

In Jean's case, the unconscious traumatic meaning of incest involved the shattering a fantasy of merger with an idealized maternal imago by her mother's failure to protect her from abuse. Her unconscious efforts at compensatory restoration of this fantasy revolved around illusions of a mystical bond with her mother, endowing them both with superhuman powers of endurance. Her efforts at defensive restoration via the elaboration of fantasies of grandiosity involved her magical ability to "detach" from her body (disembodiment) and a belief in her psychic and healing powers.

Rosa's fantasy of idealized merger with an omnipotent paternal imago was shattered by her stepfather's incestuous molestation. The sexual attack in early adolescence foiled her attempt at defensive restoration of this fantasy via the elaboration of fantasies of her grandiose self-sufficiency and invulnerability. In her desperation, Rosa's faulty efforts at restoration led her to prostitution and heroin addiction.

All three survivors were found to suffer from the dissociative symptoms of PTSD. In the cases of Sybil and Jean, the severity of depersonalization and derealization reached psychotic proportions. We conclude that the more one's subjective world is dominated by central organizing fantasies whose transformation has been impeded by developmental arrests, the more vulnerable one is to psychotic manifestations of PTSD.

CHAPTER 4

Rape: Violation of the "Heroine"

R ape, according to Bard and Ellison (1974) is the "ultimate violation of self (short of homicide)" (p. 71). Hundreds of studies documenting the catastrophic psychological impact of rape published since 1971 attest to the validity of their statement. Yet only within the last 20 years have mental health professionals recognized rape as a devastating trauma. Before the burgeoning women's movement of the early 1970s focused public attention on rape as a political and social reality inhibiting the freedom of women and exaggerating their dependence on men, the injurious psychological effects of rape were largely ignored.

Many feminist writers (e.g. Brownmiller, 1975; Morrison, 1980; Rush, 1982) blame psychoanalysis for the neglect and social condemnation of rape survivors. They cite traditional psychoanalytic concepts, such as penis envy and feminine masochism, as well as psychoanalytic formulations about so-called rape fantasies as instrumental in perpetuating the myth that women secretly wish to be raped.

Because the psychoanalytic literature supporting a view of rape as victim-precipitated has been so thoroughly criticized by other writers (see, for example, Brownmiller, 1975; Rush, 1980) we will forego a similar critique. We will, however, discuss some of the literature on rape fantasies later in this chapter in the hope that our theoretical perspective can provide a new way of understanding this psychological phenomenon.

In contrast to the voluminous psychoanalytic literature on combat veterans, holocaust survivors, community disaster victims, and surgical patients, there have been few empirical psychoanalytic studies of rape. In their absence, old ideas about rape have persisted. Our therapeutic interviews have yielded data in support of a theory of rape trauma that challenges these outdated formulations.

In line with our general theory, we contend that rape is an act of sexual violence, the unconscious traumatic meaning of which shatters central organizing fantasies of self in relation to selfobject. Attempts at the defensive or compensatory restoration of these fantasies by means of unconscious elaboration are inevitably faulty. The shattering and faulty restoration of these fantasies wreaks psychological havoc in the lives of survivors and finds expression in the dissociative reexperiencing and numbing symptoms of PTSD. Rape trauma frequently leads to intense feelings of narcissistic rage, which the survivor may direct at herself or at others experienced as failing selfobjects.

According to our theory, it is possible (although highly unlikely) that a rape might not be experienced as a shattering trauma. We hold that in the developmental histories of most people, developmental arrests (Stolorow and Lachmann, 1980) interfere with the complete transformation of archaic narcissistic fantasies that normally organize self experience. To the extent that these fantasies retain their original meanings (and undergo further unconscious intensification in the course of development) they are vulnerable to shattering by traumas such as rape.

As Hilberman (1977) observes, the rape survivor "experiences not only overwhelming fear for her very existence, but an equally overwhelming sense of helplessness which few other events in one's life can parallel" (p. ix). Because archaic narcissistic fantasies so often entail illusions of omnipotent invincibility and impenetrability as a well as union with all-mighty beings, rape, as Hilberman describes it, is likely to destroy such illusions. It stands to reason that the more the event lends itself to an experience of terror and helplessness, the greater the likelihood of its being imbued with traumatic meaning, even if a woman's archaic narcissistic fantasies have successfully undergone developmental transformation. Conversely, a rape that does not have such shattering import might not be experienced as traumatic, even if a woman's narcissistic fantasies are highly archaic and untransformed.

Support for our position is to be found in studies showing that certain forms of rape are more likely to result in severe traumatization than others. Brothers (1982) found that rape by strangers tended to result in more severe reactions among survivors than rapes by known assailants. Burgess and Holmstrom (1980) reported that a higher percentage of survivors in their study who had not recovered after five years had experienced a stranger ("blitz") rape.

Explaining the more devastating impact of the "blitz" rape, Burgess and Holmstrom note: "She had not done anything to deserve the attack, could not have done anything to prevent it, and the random meaninglessness of the experience proved extremely difficult for the woman to accept" (p. 28). They argue that the survivor of a rape by a known assailant ("confidence rape") is better able to integrate the experience because she can find a rational explanation for what happened to her.

We understand the more devastating impact of the blitz rape as resulting from the shocking suddenness of the attack. From the vantage point of our self-psychological theory of psychic trauma, we hypothesize that these survivors are particularly likely to experience overwhelming feelings of bewilderment, helplessness, and utter terror because the unconscious traumatic meaning of the rape shatters archaic narcissistic fantasies that cannot be adequately restored.

We attempt here to demonstrate the ways in which our theory of psychic trauma is supported by current research on rape and is congruent with efforts by contemporary psychoanalysts to conceptualize the psychological effects of rape. As representative of the recent literature on rape, we have selected the work of Nadelson and Notman (1976, 1979, 1982; Notman and Nadelson, 1976), two rare researchers who study rape from a psychoanalytic perspective, and that of Bard and Ellison (1974), whose writings about rape have influenced much of the nonanalytic research. We also examine the literature on "rape trauma syndrome" (Burgess and Holmstrom, 1974) recognized since 1980 as a form of PTSD, in order to show how this syndrome accords with our view of the dissociative nature of PTSD.

We then turn to some of the psychoanalytic literature on so-called rape fantasies. In their interpretations of rape fantasies as well as other masochistic phenomena, psychoanalysts reveal a great deal about their views on the role of psychic trauma in psychogenesis. We contrast Deutsch's (1944) view of rape fantasies and other "masochistic" phenomena with more recent interpretations by Schad-Somers (1982), Shainess (1984), Stoller (1975, 1979), Bach and Schwartz (1972), and Atwood and Stolorow (1984), whose thinking in this area more closely approximates our own. Next we review Freud's famous 1919 paper, "A Child is Being Beaten," to highlight aspects of Freud's understanding that anticipates our formulations not only on masochistic fantasy in particular, but on unconscious fantasy in general.

Finally, we present three representative case histories in support of our theory.

PSYCHOANALYTIC CONSIDERATIONS OF RAPE

Although Nadelson and Notman (1979, 1982; Notman and Nadelson, 1976) couch their understanding of reactions to rape in the terminology of ego psychology, they view rape in ways that are generally consonant with our theory. To begin with, they fully recognize that rape is a "trauma-inducing crisis" comparable in impact to community disasters, surgical procedures, and combat. They observe that, in contrast to other trauma survivors, rape survivors are likely to be blamed for causing their own traumas. "Unlike the soldier who braves an attack in a battle and is praised and decorated," they note, "the rape victim is awarded no medal (1976, p. 408). They argue that societal attitudes that blame the victim contribute to the severe psychological distress following rape by interfering with efforts at restitution and reinforcing guilt and low self-esteem.

Our research findings confirm the crucial importance of reactions to the rape survivor by significant others. There are few times in a woman's life when the need to experience others as empathic selfobjects is greater than during the first weeks and months after she has been raped. Since the unconscious traumatic meaning of the rape resides in the shattering of fantasies that organize self experience, the survivors's sense of cohesive selfhood is often profoundly disturbed. The mirroring or idealizing selfobject functioning of empathic others at such a time may avert or lessen disintegration experiences and reduce the likelihood of severe dissociative symptoms of PTSD. Critical or rejecting responses, on the other hand, may itensify such reactions. (See, for example, the case of Nettie in chapter one and the case of Tina, this chapter).

Notman and Nadelson (1976) also agree with our contention that the unconscious traumatic meaning of a rape depends on the psychological makeup of the survivor. They observe that the individual's character structure, developmental history, and coping mechanisms affect her vulnerability.

Finally, Nadelson and Notman understand that rape affects the individual's fantasy life. They note: "The event itself may evoke pre-existing conscious or unconscious fantasies which contribute to the response" (p. 410). Although they distinguish between these fantasies and so-called rape fantasies, they do not examine their unconscious narcissistic meanings.

"THE VIOLATION OF SELF"

Bard and Ellison, with backgrounds in social psychology and social personality theory, respectively, rather than psychoanalysis, adopt a view of rape that is even more congruent with our theoretical understanding. Basing their conceptualization of rape on the modern crisis theory of Erich Lindemann, Bard and Ellison (1974) have attempted to understand the experience of rape as a violation of the self.

They note that a crisis such as rape disrupts the defenses that operate to protect the self against the vicissitudes of life. As a result, the person in crisis may develop nightmares, compulsions, phobias, disturbed eating and sleeping patterns, work inhibitions, and attention and concentration difficulties—that is, many of the symptoms associated with PTSD. In addition, such persons often "regress" to states of helplessness and dependency that characterize earlier stages of development.

Bard and Ellison compare the impact of rape with that of other crimes against the person in order of the severity of the stress involved. Burglary, the least severely stressful, is nevertheless experienced as a crisis-inducing violation of the self because home and possessions are symbolic extensions of the self. Armed robbery is seen as a more complex violation of the self because, in the encounter, the victim experiences a coercive deprivation of independence and autonomy and surrenders control under the threat of violence. Injury in addition to the robbery is a visible reminder of helplessness. Injury to the body or "envelope of the self" severes as concrete of the forced surrender of autonomy.

Rape is by far more traumatic than any of these crimes. As Bard and Ellison note: "The victim is not only deprived of autonomy and control, experiencing manipulation and often injury to the envelope of the self, but also intrusion of inner space, the most sacred and private repository of the self." (p. 71).

From our theoretical perspective, the degree of stressfulness is determined by the unconscious meaning of the crime for the victim. The more violently a person is deprived of autonomy and the more severely injured, the greater is the likelihood that the event will take on unconscious traumatic meaning that reflects the shattering and faulty restoration of archaic narcissistic fantasies.

RAPE TRAUMA SYNDROME AND PTSD

Before 1980, rape survivors, unlike combat veterans, were rarely diagnosed as suffering from a trauma syndrome. However, in the 1980 edition of the *DSM* III, the American Psychiatric Association included rape as one of the stressors likely to produce PTSD. Today, despite the difficulties of using this diagnosis in court cases (see Rowland, 1985) there is a growing recognition among clinicians that PTSD is an appropriate diagnosis for many rape survivors.

Rape trauma syndrome, a condition first identified by Burgess and Holmstrom (1974) in their pioneering study of rape survivors, appears to be a form of PTSD. It is described as a two-phase process consisting of an acute phase lasting from a few days to a few weeks, and a longer reorganization phase. According to Burgess and Holmstrom, victims in the acute phase suffer from shock, dismay, agitation, and gross anxiety. These symptoms are described in *DSM* III (1980) as "associated features of PTSD." From the standpoint of our theory of trauma, we view these symptoms as expressions of the disorganization of self experience caused by the shattering of archaic narcissistic fantasies and their faulty restoration. They may be seen as precursors of the more familiar dissociative symptoms of PTSD such as reexperiencing and numbing.

Certain survivors in the acute phase, however, may appear cool and complacent (Burgess and Holmstrom, 1973). The bland affect and attitude of apparent indifference to the rape exhibited by these survivors, may, in fact, be manifestations of "numbing." It is also possible that survivors appearing calm and unperturbed immediately after a rape may experience a delayed reaction to the trauma and manifest more florid symptoms at a later time.

Peters (1976) noted that severe psychological symptoms may first appear weeks or months after a rape. *DSM* III (1980) recognizes a "delayed" subtype of PTSD in which the onset of symptoms occurs at least six months after the trauma. Our empirical study of rape survivors also indicates that the dissociative symptoms of PTSD may first be experienced months after a rape. (See, for example, the case of Violet, this chapter.) For other victims, an attitude of indifference may reflect unconscious efforts to restore shattered fantasies. (See, for example, the case of Maggie, this chapter.)

Most of the symptoms associated with the second, or "reorganization," phase of rape trauma syndrome may be categorized as either reexperiencing or numbing symptoms, the two major categories of PTSD. (See Katz and Mazur, 1979, for a summary of these research findings.)

Of the reexperiencing symptoms associated with the reorganization phase, "flashbacks" are commonly reported. It is often difficult to determine from reading these accounts whether the term "flashback" refers to intrusive thoughts of the attack or reliving experiences, described in *DSM* III (1980) as "sudden acting or feeling as if the traumatic event were recurring, because of an association with an environmental or ideational stimulus" (p. 238). Becker (1982), for example, appears to use the term to describe reliving experiences. She finds that of all the psychological disturbances experienced by rape survivors, flashbacks have the most disruptive effect on sexuality following rape. She noted that flashbacks often occurred during sex when a specific touch or position reminded the woman of the rape.

A number of rape survivors in our study also reported sensory flashbacks or reliving experiences during sex. (See, for example, the case of Tina, this chapter.) The confusion of past event with current experience that characterizes these symptoms suggests a state of extreme dissociation. In fact, it is our contention that all the reexperiencing and numbing symptoms of PTSD following rape reflect severe states of depersonalization and derealization. With the shattering of archaic narcissistic fantasies that had, before the rape, lent coherence and stability to self experience, survivors experience a terrifying loss of familiarity with themselves and a lack of conviction about the existence and reality of external objects. In this "twilight zone," survivors are subject to recurrent traumatic nightmares, intrusive recollections of the event, and reliving experiences (reexperiencing symptoms), on one hand, and diminished interest in customary activities, feelings of detachment and estrangement, and constriction of affect (numbing symptoms), on the other.

RAPE FANTASIES

According to Deutsch (1944, Vols. I and II), rape fantasies are variants of the "seduction fantasies" of hysterical women. She argues that these fantasies provide incontrovertible proof of feminine masochism. They reflect the girl's renunciation of her aggressive strivings in response to her father's seductive "bribe" that he will reward her with love and tenderness if she does so.

Deutsch's allegiance to Freud's drive theory is evident in her belief that the aggressive forces which have been renounced must find an outlet. This is accomplished by endowing the passive state of being loved with an unconscious masochistic meaning. Underlying this developmental scenario is Deutsch's belief in the female's innate predisposition to masochism resulting from the biological inferiority of her sexual organs.

She elaborated on Freud's (1924) assertion that penis envy lies at the root of female masochism. Whereas Freud emphasized the little girl's *perception* of the penis as superior to the inconspicuous clitoris, for Deutsch it *is* a superior organ. After noting that the "anatomic structure, tumescent character, innervation and erectibility make the clitoris an organ comparable to the penis," she asserts, "the comparison must naturally prove unfavorable to the clitoris because this organ lacks the forward thrusting, penetrating qualities of the penis (Vol. I, p. 228).

She postulated that because the inadequacy of the clitoris induces the little girl to give up masturbation, she lacks an erogenous zone in the phallic stage of development. In addition, according to Deutsch, the girl lacks a passive organ, the vagina, until it is "awakened" by an act of rape. Deutsch states:

> The "undiscovered" vagina is—in normal, favorable instances—eroti-cized by an act of rape. By "rape" I do not refer here to that puberal fantasy in which the young girl realistically desires and fears the sexual act as rape. That fantasy is only a psychologic preparation for a real, milder but dynamically identical process. This process manifests itself in man's aggressive penetration on the one hand, and in the "overpow-ering" of the vagina and its transformation into an erogenous zone on the other [Vol. I, p. 79].

Because rape and intercourse are synonymous for Deutsch, and both are necessary components of female sexuality, it follows that rape fantasies must express the woman's normal masochistic wish to be raped. These fantasies, Deutsch claims, may take on the appear-ance of events that actually transpired. "Even the most experienced judges," she asserts, "are misled in trials of innocent men accused of rape by hysterical women" (Vol. I, p. 254).

Deutsch's conclusions about the tendency of women to fabricate stories of rape may be understood as a reflection of her belief in the domination of the psychological world of women by pathogenic oedipal fantasies and her minimization of the traumatic meaning of actual occurrences. Her allegiance to these theoretical biases prevented her from understanding that rape fantasies may symbolically represent actual traumatic occurrences.

A number of Deutsch's contemporaries took exception to the biolog-ical determinism underlying her conceptualization of feminine maso-chism. Some (Adler, 1927; Horney, 1924, 1926, 1933) argued that masochism among women has cultural rather than biological origins and is a neurotic rather than a normal aspect of female personality. Horney, for example, argued that the real possibility of rape may give rise to the rape fantasy.

Today, the idea that masochism among women has its roots in the patriarchal organization of society is widely accepted. Schad-Somers (1982), for example, contends that throughout history women have acquiesed in attempts by men to "subjugate and crush" their sexuality. She suggests that a sadomasochistic arrangement between men and women was developed and institutionalized because of a "fundamental sense of human dependency implanted in infancy" (p. 95). She argues that women adopt a masochistic stance in order not to be abandoned.

Shainess (1984) also views social and cultural factors as the primary causes of masochism in women. Male dominance and female subordination, according to Shainess, are maintained in myriad ways, from differential childrearing practices and the messages about male power continually relayed by the media to the very laws that govern the country. Growing up in a male-dominated society, she states, causes women to develop masochistic feelings and a masochistic "style" by which they communicate these feelings.

Rape fantasies, from Shainess' perspective, are perfect expressions of the masochistic woman's self-punishing, guilt-ridden, fearful, self-abnegating style. She observes that performing passively, almost lifelessly, in the sexual act is at the heart of most masochistic fantasies. This passivity, Shainess explains, is the result of feelings of fear and guilt that pervade the masochistic woman's self experience. Guilty about her sexual desires and fearing the disapproval of forbidding authority figures (i.e., her parents), the masochistic woman circumvents disapproval by "concocting a fantasy that robs her of her own volition" (p. 94). In being forced to submit to rape, Shainess observes, the woman represents herself as a passive victim. Thus, the rape fantasy represents the woman's experience of herself in society as impotent and vulnerable.

Shainess also notes that rape fantasies are frequently reported by women who have been victims of sexually violent behavior within their own families. Their fantasies symbolically represent the violence and abuse they actually experienced. Both of Shainess's explanations for the prevalence of rape fantasies among women depend on a belief in the importance of actual experience in shaping psychological development: (1) they reflect the woman's experience of growing up in a male-dominated society in which women are commonly portrayed as victims of violent male sexuality, and (2) they represent past experiences of actual sexual abuse.

Stoller also describes sadomasochism and other "perversions" as fantasies that revive traumatic childhood experiences of victimization. According to Stoller (1975), the meaning of perversion and perverse fantasy is to be found in the transformation of these humiliating experiences into triumphant victories. "In perversions," he observes, "trauma becomes triumph" (p. 59). Stoller (1979) contends that the exact details of perverse enactments are "meant to reproduce and repair the precise traumas and frustrations—debasements—of childhood" (p. 13). (Compare Stoller's view of perverse enactment with our understanding of recurrent nightmares, chapter one.)

Stoller's attempt to understand rape fantasies reflects his overall theoretical position on perversion. Because a woman is the author of the rape fantasy and therefore controls the fantasmic events, he explains, she achieves a sense of power. The fantasy, he maintains, enables the woman to surmount "the illusion of danger" and thereby experience herself as omnipotent and invulnerable. In contrast to Deutsch, Stoller clearly understands that rape fantasies do not indicate a woman's secret wish to be raped. He states, "Most women who dress in response to fantasies of being raped would be shocked if actually assaulted" (p. 19).

Like Stoller, Bach and Schwartz (1972) appreciate the restorative function of sadomasochistic fantasies. They interpret sadistic and masochistic fantasies recounted by the Marquis de Sade as functioning to stave off narcissistic decompensation. (See chapter 3 for a more detailed discussion of their work.) Similarly, Atwood and Stolorow (1984) understand sadomasochistic experiences as "enactments" that function to concretize and hence maintain the organization of experience.

Atwood and Stolorow wrote:

> In persons with deficits in psychological structure formation, masochistic experiences can serve to restore or sustain a damaged, menaced or disintegrating sense of self through the stimulation afforded by pain and skin eroticism, through exhibitionistic displays of suffering to a real or imagined audience, through mergings with omnipotent object images and by actualizing an archaic grandiose self [p. 95].

Our understanding of rape fantasies and other masochistic experiences shares much with the work of Schad-Somers, Shainess, Stoller, Bach and Schwartz, as well as Atwood and Stolorow. From our theoretical perspective, rape fantasies are not expressions of a normal component of feminine personality, nor do they reflect a woman's secret wish to be raped. Rather, we understand rape fantasies as symbolic expressions of experiences that disturbed or shattered unconscious fantasies of archaic narcissism and as faulty efforts to restore such fantasies.

We agree with such writers as Schad-Somers and Shainess that masochistic phenomena, including rape fantasies, may be the outgrowth of experiences of growing up in a society in which male power and female subordination are blatantly manifested. For example, pornographic images of women as humiliated victims are likely to interfere with a little girl's normal fantasies of grandiose exhibitionism. Similarly, images of men as brutal victimizers may interfere with normal fantasies of idealized merger with omnipotent paternal imagos. In this respect, rape fantasies are similar to recurrent traumatic nightmares and other reexperiencing symptoms of PTSD.

Our clinical experience with rape survivors does not support Shainess's contention that rape fantasies reflect actual experiences of sexual violence. Rape survivors are more likely to report recurrent traumatic nightmares as part of PTSD.

At the same time, like Stoller, Bach and Schwartz, and Atwood and Stolorow, we recognize the restorative significance of these fantasies. In other words, rape fantasies may be thought of as classic instances of *sexualized restoration* of archaic narcissistic fantasies. For example, a woman's fantasy of being raped may symbolically represent an unconscious attempt at sexually restoring a vital sense of merger undermined by disillusioning experiences with idealized men. Or, to take another example, a woman's rape fantasy may involve a scenario of a man losing control of himself in the face of overpowering sexual attraction. This may unconsciously represent an attempt at sexually restoring a fantasy of grandiosity challenged by experiences of rejection by men.

"A CHILD IS BEING BEATEN"

Freud's (1919a) essay "A Child is Being Beaten" is often cited as illustrating his drive-oriented conceptualization of feminine masochism. A careful reading of this essay, however, reveals that Freud also appreciated the narcissistic dimension of masochistic fantasy.

A child being beaten is, according to Freud, a pleasurable fantasy, often accompanying masturbation. He discovered that this fantasy undergoes three phases of transformation during the course of a girl's development. In the first phase, the girl's father is beating a hated sibling. In the second phase, which is unconscious and may only be reconstructed during analysis, the girl herself is being beaten by her father. And in the last phase, the fantasy involves another child, usually a boy, being beaten by a father substitute.

Freud hypothesized that the transformation of this fantasy from phase one to phase two is a direct expression of the girl's sense of guilt over her incestuous wishes and reflects the conversion of the girl's sadism into masochism. Freud wrote: "The phantasy of the period of the incestuous love had said, 'He (my father) loves only me, and not the other child, for he is beating it.' The sense of guilt can discover no punishment more severe than the reversal of this triumph: 'No, he does not love you, for he is beating you' " (p. 189).

Since the erotic component of this fantasy was not a direct genital experience but was transmitted through a beating, Freud theorized that this component represented a regression to the anal-sadistic level. Thus, the masochistic experience in the beating fantasy was simultaneously a punishment and an erotic pleasure at the anal-sadistic level.

Freud's reliance on "experience-distant" (Kohut, 1977, p. 245) energistic notions related to his drive theory, as well as his emphasis on the centrality of the Oedipus complex in pathogenesis, is evident in his theoretical reconstruction of this fantasy. Almost obscured by these formulations, however, is Freud's alternative explanation, which, in its emphasis on the transformation of narcissistic fantasy, foreshadows our own understanding.

In describing the transformation of the beating fantasy, Freud suggests a developmental progression from an explicitly "sadistic" scenario to one in which the sadism is disguised. This conceptualization of developmental transformation of fantasies is fundamental to our theory. We also contend that fantasies are transformed in the course of healthy development from archaic and magical to forms that are more tempered.

In addition, Freud suggests that a conscious fantasy may have an unconscious origin. This, too, is consistent with our view. For example, we maintain that conscious fantasies of rape may reflect the shattering of unconscious fantasies of grandiosity or idealized merger.

Even more significantly, Freud offered an explanation of the beating fantasy that underscores his awareness of the vulnerability of the child's archaic narcissistic fantasies to shattering experiences with its parents. Freud (1919a) stated:

> One soon learns that being beaten, even if it does not hurt very much, signifies a deprivation of love and a humiliation. And many children who believed themselves securely enthroned in the unshakeable affection of their parents have, by a single blow, been cast down from all the heavens of their *imaginary omnipotence* [p. 187, italics added].

Freud's understanding that, to a child, a beating may represent a narcissistic injury inflicted by a parent is evident. He even goes so far as to question whether the fantasy of the first phase ought to be described as purely "sexual," insofar as it is "powerfully reinforced by the child's egoistic interests" (p. 187). Clearly, Freud appreciated the narcissistic as well as the oedipal dimension of this fantasy.

From our theoretical perspective, the beating fantasy, much like so-called rape fantasies, symbolically encodes actual experiences that disturbed or shattered the child's archaic narcissistic fantasies as well as faulty efforts at restoration. That is to say, the girl's unconscious fantasy of being beaten by her father may reflect an actual experience whose unconscious meaning disturbed or shattered fantasies of grandiose exhibitionism or idealized merger with omnipotent imagos.

If, as Freud suggested, the first fantasy may be translated as "my father loves only me," it may symbolize the defensive restoration of a fantasy involving the child's unique and unrivaled place in her father's affection. This conscious fantasy may also reflect efforts to restore an unconscious fantasy of idealized merger with omnipotent parental imagos after disillusioning experiences with them. As our study of survivors of childhood incest revealed (see chapter three), children often willingly accept sexual abuse as the price they have to pay for urgently needed selfobject experiences of merger with idealized imagos.

REPRESENTATIVE CASES

Violet

Despite strenuous efforts to maintain her composure, Violet, a tall, pretty, white woman of 29, who had been raped four months before her first interview, showed signs of acute distress. She was dressed in bright colors and heavily made up; her features remained set in a taut smile even as her eyes filled with tears. When questioned about her obvious attempts to disguise her painful feelings, Violet said, "I can't seem to get over the rape, but I'm sure no one wants to hear about it anymore." She explained that relatives and friends continually complimented her on "handling it so beautifully."

As she described her unsuccessful efforts to "put the rape in the past and be happy," Violet finally broke into sobs. Her preoccupation with the traumatic episode, she said, made it increasingly difficult for her to care for her six-month-old son. Violet spoke of "having a crush" on the infant and of her longing to care for him in a relaxed, confident way instead of feeling tense and anxious when she was with him.

Recently, she confided, she had been horrified to find herself erupting in uncontrolled rages at the slightest provocation, noting "even my husband's chewing can drive me crazy." Violet also observed that the rape "magnified the dark side of life" and that she often ruminated about nuclear war and other disasters. She said she tried to avoid such thoughts because "I'm afraid that thinking about terrible things will make them happen."

These and a host of other seriously disturbing reactions to the rape led Violet to seek help at a rape crisis center. She said she met with a counselor only a few times because the woman had insisted that she describe the rape in explicit detail and seemed surprised at her lack of anger at the rapist. Violet acknowledged that she had experienced the counselor's insistent questioning as invasions of her privacy. "I know she meant to help," Violet said, "but I couldn't stand the feeling that I was letting her down by not opening myself up to her."

After failing to keep her second appointment in the extended series of therapeutic interviews, Violet phoned to say that she had become so preoccupied with thoughts about the rape she had gotten lost. Panic stricken on finding herself in an unfamiliar part of the city, Violet said she had wandered the streets in a "stupor" until she was approached by a female police officer. While waiting in the station house until the officer could accompany her home, Violet said, she felt as if she had been "enveloped in a warm blanket." According to Violet, the officer seemed strong and calm, "like she knew what she was doing," and for the first time since the rape, Violet said, she felt safe. At the officer's invitation, Violet telephoned several times to let her know how she was faring and each time reexperienced a calming sense of security.

Following this incident, complaining of acute anxiety each time she ventured out on her own, Violet requested that the interviews be delayed for two months. In response to questions about her reaction to the first interview, Violet denied that she had experienced it as invasive. "You didn't press me for all the gory details like my mother or the counselor," Violet said. She said she felt relieved to talk about the rape with someone who is "an authority on the subject." Violet kept all of her remaining interview appointments. Her detailed account of her life and her traumatic experience provided ample life history data for empathic inferences about the unconscious meaning of the rape.

The eldest of three children, (she has a brother one year younger and a sister three years younger), Violet remembered herself as an extremely well-behaved, quiet child who always "kept things to myself." She portrayed her mother as a domineering, intrusive woman "with a loud voice and an opinion about everything." She was, according to Violet, given to presenting herself as a self-sacrificing martyr. "She complained about everything in her life—except me," Violet said. "She thought I was a 'perfect child' who could do no wrong." Violet explained that she developed the idea that it was her "job" to make up for all her mother's sacrifices by being charming, happy, and obedient. She noted that she was continually held as a shining example to her siblings, who were "wild, outgoing kids."

Violet said that her mother assumed that Violet shared all her thoughts, feelings, and opinions and seemed shocked and hurt when Violet disagreed with her. As a result, Violet learned to keep discrepant thoughts to herself. "I didn't dare open my mouth because I knew I could destroy her. Then she would totally ignore me."

As she talked about her early life, Violet recalled her childhood fascination with the fairy tale "The Sleeping Beauty." "From the first time I heard the story," Violet said, "I imagined that I *was* the princess." She spoke of feeling terrified when the bad fairy cursed the princess with death in the event that she pricked her finger while spinning. She also remembered her enormous relief when the good fairy changed the curse from death to sleep for 100 years. Violet mentioned that she particularly loved the ending of the story because the princess was awakened from her long sleep by the kiss of a handsome prince.

Violet acknowledged that the many correspondences between her experiences in growing up and the details of this fairy tale were "amazing." For example, Violet confided that, like the princess, she was terrified that sharp objects might pierce her skin. "I was deathly afraid of doctors," she said, "because they give injections." She explained that she had learned to "blot out" her mother's intrusive presence by pretending to be asleep. "I never complained at bedtime," Violet recalled, "alone in my bed, I became the Sleeping Beauty on her silken couch."

Violet also noted that the ending of the story held special delight for her because of her secret wish to be "rescued from my mother's clutches by a handsome man."

Violet described her father, in contrast to her mother, as quiet and unassuming. She said she loved his gentle manner and secretly believed that she resembled him more that she did her mother. Violet also believed she inherited his artistic talent. At her mother's insistence, Violet's father had not pursued a career as a fine artist but had gone into business as a building contractor. Because of his poor business skills, his company was forced into bankruptcy when Violet was an adolescent.

Following her father's business failure, Violet's mother returned to work as a secretary and, according to Violet, complained incessantly about this additional burden. She was openly contemptuous of her husband's failure in business, criticizing him in front of the children as an incompetent dreamer. Violet remembered sympathizing with her father at these times and feeling that she shared in his humiliation. She imagined that they both secretly regarded her mother as a "witch." At the same time, she recalled a sense of disillusionment with her father for "not daring to defend himself." Violet said she had often wished that her father would "shut my mother up."

For Violet, her mother's return to work provided a welcome relief from her relentless surveillance. "Suddenly, I blossomed," she said. Always shy and retiring, Violet now became one of the most popular girls in her high school. Proudly, Violet said, "I wasn't one of the cheerleaders. I hung out with the druggies and hippies." Violet said that although she experimented with marijuana, she never used it heavily. "I thought I was really something then," Violet said. "There wasn't a boy I couldn't get. Everyone wanted to be my friend." Violet also established a reputation as the "resident artist" of the high school.

Emboldened by her social success in high school and the recognition she had gained for her artwork among teachers and fellow students, Violet decided to leave her home in the suburbs to attend art school in the city. Ignoring her mother's pained expression and warnings that she would never amount to anything as an artist, Violet envisioned herself as an adventurous bohemian whose work would be widely acclaimed and whose company would be sought after. She remembered thinking that her father would be "thrilled" if she achieved success as an artist.

During her first semester, Violet felt that she was "sitting on top of the world." She said she thoroughly enjoyed the feeling that she was "in charge" of her life. In contrast to the social whirl of her high school days, Violet immersed herself in her studies and limited her social activities. Although many young men asked her out, Violet dated infrequently.

At the beginning of her second semester, Violet became intensely attracted to one of her instructors, a man 20 years her senior. "Craig was Prince Charming," Violet said. "I couldn't believe it when he showed an interest in me." Violet described the exhilaration she experienced when he began to wait for her after class so that they could spend time together. "I was so flattered," Violet said. Not only did Violet find Craig extremely attractive, she admired and respected him for having established a reputation as a first-rate artist. They soon became lovers, and, Violet said, she "walked on a cloud." "I thought that being Craig's girlfriend automatically made me a super-star, too," Violet said. "Craig was my mother and father and lover. He took an interest in every detail of my life."

Gradually, however, Violet's experience of being a special and gifted "superstar" diminished. Craig became very critical of her work as well as her personality. "He had something nasty to say about everything I did," she said, explaining that she tolerated his insults because she did not want to lose him.

When Craig announced that he had fallen in love with another student, Violet was devastated. "I had never been rejected before," she said, "and I just couldn't get over it." Violet spoke of mourning the loss of the glamorous image she had cherished of the two of them. "We were like a prince and princess," she said. "We had looks, talent and each other." With his rejection, Craig suddenly seemed to her like "a dirty old man."

Violet remembered that without the excitement of her relationship with Craig she lost interest in her artwork as well as her optimism in the future. Before graduating from art school, she married a man she had met while she was involved with Craig. "I didn't even like Phil when I first met him," Violet remarked, "but when he reentered my life, I saw him with a halo." Violet abandoned her efforts to pursue a career as a painter and instead helped Phil run his typesetting business.

Violet described her marriage in terms that closely resembled her account of her relationship with her mother. "He worships me," she said, "but he has no idea who I really am." Whenever she became sad or angry, Violet explained, Phil would remind her that he married her because she seemed so happy. Because Phil suffered from colitis, Violet worried that expressing negative feelings would aggravate his condition. Almost proudly she announced, "It's my duty to be happy."

Violet related that her mother was pleased by her decision to marry Phil and to give up her "crazy ideas" about becoming an artist. She soon began to pressure Violet to start a family. Violet envisioned the birth of her son as "a Christmas present for my mother." During her difficult pregnancy, Violet suffered her discomfort in silence. "Above all," she said, "I didn't want to sound like my mother—complaining, complaining, complaining."

Violet was raped only two months after her baby was born. Her recall for the events surrounding the episode was almost photographic in detail. She began by describing the hours before the rape, recalling that she had decided to take her husband's sweaters to the dry cleaners and that she had left careful instructions with her husband for the care of the baby. She described in detail the appearance of the tall, heavyset black man who followed her into the store. He asked the proprietor some questions about mending the cuffs of a pair of leather pants and then abruptly walked out.

As she left the store, Violet recalled having "a funny feeling" that prompted her to look for the man as she walked home. Immediately after she entered the building where she and her husband lived in a converted loft, the man rushed in. The elevator was waiting, but Violet, feeling frightened, decided to run back outside. The man lunged, grabbed her, and covered her mouth with his hand as he dragged her toward the elevator.

At that moment, Violet saw a man standing outside the building. Struggling with the attacker, she sought desperately to attract the man's attention. Finally, he seemed to respond and walked toward the door. To Violet's horror, she realized that this man was an accomplice who had been standing guard in front of the building. "I was never so disappointed in my life," she said.

When the first man pulled her into the elevator and began tearing off her clothes, Violet recalled thinking that she was about to die. "I begged him not to hurt me," she said. "I told him I had just had a baby so that maybe he would feel sorry for me and not kill me."

The rapist pinned her down with his body and Violet believed it would be futile to struggle. He entered her vaginally and she recalled that "it was all over quickly." With great difficulty Violet described her disgust and sense of humiliation when he told her that he would not ejaculate inside her, "as if he was doing me a big favor."

After ejaculating on the floor, the man warned her not to call the police. Violet said she lay on the floor of the elevator, "frozen with terror" for some time after the attacker left, and then made her way upstairs to her loft. Violet notified the police and was taken to a nearby hospital, where she was treated for shock. Although she spent many hours poring over photographs at a police station, Violet was unable to identify the rapist; she believes that both men are still free and she expressed apprehension about her safety.

Violet said that after some discussion with Phil about notifying friends and relatives about the rape, they entered into a "conspiracy of silence." "I didn't want people to picture me being raped," she said. "I knew I would feel humiliated." They did, however, decide to inform tenants in the building in order to arrange for the installation of a better security system. Violet spoke of feeling "furious" with neighbors who asked if she had also been beaten. She suspected that they thought the rape "wasn't such a big deal" by itself.

At first, Violet hid her distress very well, believing that it was necessary to shield Phil and the baby. However, Phil made her angry when he said, "Boy, you're having a strange reaction! Are you sure you didn't know the guy?" Violet exclaimed, "How could he even joke that I wanted this nightmare to happen!"

Two and a half months after the rape, Violet found herself obsessed with thoughts about her ordeal. Finding it impossible to ignore images of the rape that frequently intruded into her waking thoughts, she decided to confide in relatives and friends in the hope that talking about the rape would free her from these obsessive ruminations.

Instead of feeling relieved, Violet found that telling people made her feel worse.

"I always thought that people would be there if I really needed them," she said. "But they weren't. They seemed to say 'This is not the nicest thing to talk about so let's forget it.' Only my mother wanted to talk about it," Violet continued. However, Violet felt she could not comply with her mother's insensitive demand for a "blow by blow" description of the rape. Violet went on to say that she didn't want to tell people how to respond. "I wanted them to know without being told," she said. "It felt so humiliating to ask for help."

Within three months of the rape, Violet experienced all of the classic symptoms of PTSD. Most distressing were the intrusive images of the rape that frequently flashed into her mind. She described her exquisite sensitivity to any stimuli associated with rape. For example, she found herself overwhelmed by vivid images of her rape at a newsstand where pornographic magazines with covers depicting violent, sadomasochistic scenes were sold. Even hearing jokes that were remotely associated with rape brought on a "kaleidoscope" of similarly disturbing images, Violet added. Violet's intense feelings of fearfulness and repugnance in response to her own intrusive thoughts suggest that she experienced these symptoms as a form of mental rape.

Violet also reported flashbacks associated with tactile stimuli. When, for example, a man accidentally brushed against her on the street, she said, "A shock of pain went through my body and I again felt the terror of the rape." Violet confided that since the rape she had been unable to have sex with her husband. "Even touching and kissing makes me feel like I am being attacked," she said. Any kind of physical contact now seems unbearable, because she feels as if the boundaries of her body have lost their firmness and capacity to protect her against intrusions and violations. "I feel like I don't want to be a woman any more. I used to have long hair but I cut it all off. I have the urge to walk around in men's clothing."

Violet is also troubled by three recurrent nightmares that "play over and over like a movie in my mind." She described them as follows:
In the first:

I am in the loft, in a back room. The rapist comes in through the back door and locks it. I can't stop him from coming throught the apartment. I know the baby is in the front room, so I can't escape.

In the second:

Someone is holding my baby on a windowsill and I say, "Don't do that because the baby will fall." The baby falls and I see it down in the courtyard, dead.

In the third:

I am out on a road somewhere and there are two rapists; I have the baby in a knapsack. By luck it turns out the baby isn't there any more. I wonder what happened to the baby.

Violet reported waking from these nightmares "bathed in sweat" and sometimes screaming out loud. An examination of her associations to the central images in the nightmares suggests the unconscious traumatic meaning of the rape.

The baby in Violet's nightmares appears to symbolize helpless vulnerability to invasion and violation. Thus, for Violet, being raped was like being reduced to helpless infancy and stripped of every means of self-protection. Violet acknowledged that, in this respect, the rape repeated her early childhood experience of being "invaded" by her mother's intrusiveness. As she described her sense of profound humiliation during the physical assault and rape, Violet suddenly blurted out, "I can't stand being near my mother. I can't stand it when she touches me or even looks at me." Apparently, her efforts to conceal her narcissistic rage at her mother for disturbing her fantasies of inviolability suddenly failed.

Violet's associations to "the baby in the knapsack" revealed that this image symbolized her pregnancy. Describing her bouts of morning sickness and acute discomfort that lasted for the entire nine months, Violet spoke of feeling "invaded by an alien creature." Although the unconscious meanings for her of being pregnant were not as devastating as being raped, Violet does appear to have experienced her pregnancy as yet another violation of her bodily integrity.

The nightmares also hint at Violet's unconscious efforts at defensive restoration. In the first two nightmares, the baby is in danger of harm or has been harmed. In the third nightmare, however, the baby has been spared; it has magically disappeared. We interpret the magically disappearing baby as a symbolic representation of Violet's unconscious effort to defensively restore fantasies of herself as inviolate and impregnable. Yet the appearance of this dream image as part of a terrifying nightmare suggests that this defensive effort has failed to restore Violet's shattered fantasies.

Of the numbing symptoms Violet described, her sense of alienation and estrangement was particularly prominent. She reported isolating herself increasingly as the strain of hiding her distress from friends and relatives grew. In addition to her outbursts of rage, Violet described her preoccupation with a number of violent daydreams. In one daydream, Violet imagines herself carrying a gun and shooting men who make obscene gestures or comments. In another daydream, Violet encounters Craig, her old boyfriend, on the street and says to him, "You are the rapist!" Violet said that the intrusive images of the rape as well as these violent daydreams had seriously interfered with her ability to concentrate. She reported finding even the simplest household task exhausting.

Case Summary

Like the princess in the fairy tale who lived in dread of pricking her skin, Violet, in her inner life, appears to have been dominated by the terrifying threat of intrusion, penetration, and violation. It seems likely that Violet experienced her mother's blatant disregard for her individuality as grossly violating her psychological boundaries. Her intense dread of such physical intrusions as injections seems to reflect her fear of psychological invasion.

As she grew up with this ever-present threat to her psychological integrity, the developmental transformation of Violet's childhood grandiose fantasies was impeded. Although she acted the part of a docile, obedient child, in Violet's fantasies she was protected against all forms of psychological and physical intrusion by an enchanted spell of inviolability.

From Violet's description of her mother's distress in response to signs of her differentiated functioning, it seems probable that Violet entertained a notion that her independent thoughts and feelings, as well as any expression of rage at her mother's intrusiveness, were imbued with destructive potential. Violet's worry about destroying her mother with a discrepent idea may also reflect another aspect of her grandiose fantasies—a belief in the omnipotence of her thoughts.

Violet's disillusionment with her father for failing to protect her against her mother's intrusiveness, suggests that she was deprived of an idealizable paternal imago with whom to merge in fantasy. Lacking this opportunity for healthy compensation, Violet's grandiose exhibitionistic fantasies may well have undergone further unconscious embellishment. By high school, Violet appears to have lived the role of "suburban princess."

In spite of her disappointment with her father, Violet's wish to be rescued by a Prince Charming remained very strong. Craig, her art instructor, seems to have possessed all the requisite princely attributes to revive Violet's fantasies of idealized merger. Violet's intense distress following Craig's rejection attests to the severe impact this had on her unconscious fantasy life. Not only did the breakup deprive Violet of the soothing and calming effects of idealized merger, but Craig's replacing her with another student apparently disturbed Violet's grandiose fantasies of herself as unique and irresistible.

Violet's marriage so close on the heels of this disturbing experience appears to have provided her, on an unconscious level, with an opportunity to recreate the fantasies that had dominated her relationship with her mother. Once again, Violet's compliant behavior (acting the perfect wife as she had previously played the perfect daughter) hid a grandiose fantasy of inviolability and impenetrability.

Experiencing herself as exposed, penetrated, and violated by the rape, Violet found that her illusions of inviolability and impenetrability were completely shattered. Her daydream in which she calls Craig the rapist suggests that the rape also revived her sense of profound disillusionment and rage toward the male figures with whom she had unconsciously attempted to merge in fantasy. The rape, like Craig's rejection, stripped Violet of her most cherished illusions; she felt exploited, humiliated, and exquisitely vulnerable to intrusion.

Violet's restitutive efforts appear to involve the compensatory restoration of her fantasies of idealized merger as well as the defensive restoration of her grandiose-exhibitionistic fantasies. Her wish to remain in contact with the police officer whose presence had offered her a sense of safety and calm indicates her continued longing for idealized mergers with omnipotent imagos. Her unconscious efforts to restore her fantasy of inviolability appear to involve an illusion of possessing unlimited powers for retribution. Such efforts are reflected in her conscious fantasy of shooting men who make obscene gestures. Violet's remark that she avoids thinking about nuclear war for fear that it will occur suggests a belief in the omnipotence of her thoughts, another reflection of the defensive restoration of her shattered grandiose fantasies.

The violence of her daydreams, as well as her preoccupation with nuclear catastrophe, also reveal her intense feelings of narcissistic rage toward her violators and disappointing protectors alike. Her fears of the destruction that would follow the expression of her rage seem to contribute to her painful sense of anxiety and vulnerability.

Thus far, Violet's efforts at self restitution have done little to diminish the acute symptoms of PTSD from which she suffers. However, with proper treatment, her archaic narcissistic fantasies, which were brutally shattered by the rape, might resume transformation. Relief from the debilitating symptoms of PTSD would be among the chief benefits of such a therapy, which entails the reconstruction and working through of the traumatic unconscious meanings of the rape. (See chapter 6 for a detailed account of this therapeutic process and chapter 7 for clinical examples.)

Tina

Eighteen-year-old Tina looked like a little girl dressed up to pass for one of the tough, swaggering adolescents at the service agency where she was interviewed. The black leather jacket and pants she wore, and the heavy metal spiked chains that circled her neck, wrist, and hips, seemed to emphasize the smallness of her petite frame. Her huge eyes, exaggeratedly outlined in black pencil, stared from a tiny, pale face, contributing to her waif-like air. Although she relied on street slang punctuated by obscenities, Tina's vivid descriptions and shrewd observations suggested her intelligence and sensitivity.

Gradually, after participating in a number of the many in-depth therapeutic interviews that stretched over a period of many months, Tina abandoned her disdainful pose of hardened cynicism. She revealed that from the time of her rape three months earlier until the day of her first interview, an overwhelming sense of terror had prevented her from venturing out on her own. She expressed the hope that her participation in the interviews would speed her recovery from the rape trauma. "I want to understand what happened," she said, adding that she also felt confused about many other aspects of her life.

Tina confided that she had grown up suspecting some "mystery" in her background. As a child she had lived in a crowded, working-class neighborhood with her mother, maternal grandmother, and older brother, Tony. Tina said she had been told that her father had moved to California when she was a baby, following her parents' divorce.

In response to her insistent questioning, her mother had described her father as a "handsome charmer" who had ruined his life and theirs with his gambling and drinking. Despite her mother's assurances that the family was "better off without him," Tina said she lived in hope that one day he would return. She often gazed at a torn photograph she believed to be of him and imagined that he had become wealthy and successful. She often fell asleep imagining the wonderful moment of his return. In her daydreams, her father showered her with presents and said that his happiness had been marred by his longing for his little girl.

Tina began her account of her relationship with her mother by observing, "She never should have had any kids." Explaining that her mother was still a teenager at the time of Tina's birth, she added, "She just couldn't deal with having babies, so she tried to ignore us."

Tina mentioned that in her earliest memory she sees herself sitting in a highchair, screaming in frustration and hunger, ignored by her mother who is playing cards with friends in the next room. Elaborating this memory, Tina speculated that she had probably thrown pieces of meat on the floor because her mother had not cut them small enough for her to chew.

"Life got a lot better when I was five," Tina said, noting that her grandmother came to live with them then. She said that this strong, stern, domineering, yet kindhearted woman treated her mother and her as if they were both her children. Tina spoke of her unbounded admiration for her grandmother's strength and courage. "I wanted to be just like her when I grew up," she said, "so proud and tough that nobody could boss me around." Tina recalled her sadness on learning that her grandfather had died when her mother was a little girl. "The women in my family never had it easy. They didn't have men to help them out," she remarked.

Tina expressed concern about her mother's promiscuity and irresponsibility and complained about the "steady stream" of men who had disrupted their lives. "I guess I always thought of my mother more as a sister than as a parent," Tina said. She noted that she and her mother related to one another as "equals" who shared clothing, advice on boyfriends, and even slept in the same bed for "comfort." She said she often wished her mother would "act her age" instead of dressing, speaking, and behaving like a teenager.

At times, Tina commented, she felt more evenly matched in her competition with her mother than with her brother. Tina spoke of her frustration at never "winning" in her struggles with Tony. She remarked that although Tony was only a year older than she, he treated her as if she were a baby. As they grew up, he excluded her from games with his friends, teased her unmercifully and, adopting the role of punishing father, would beat her for misbehaving if she were left in his care. Nevertheless, Tina said she admired Tony's "macho" stance and treasured memories of being protected by him against bullies. "I just never counted for much in his life," she said sadly.

When Tina was 15, her grandmother moved away to help another of her daughters care for her newborn child. After she left, Tina said she felt "lost and frightened." She described changing from a "good girl" to a "tramp" in a matter of months.

Never a diligent student, Tina cut classes at school to "hang out" with the girlfriends of boys who belonged to a motorcycle gang. Tina remembered her longing to be recognized as one of the "Angels." She recalled looking up to "their women" as tougher and better looking than the other girls at school. But even more importantly, according to Tina, they were protected by the fearsome Angels, who exerted almost total control over their lives. To Tina, the Angels seemed more like powerful fathers than boyfriends.

Tina soon became sexually involved with a number of the boys in the gang and, at the age of 16, became pregnant. Tina noted that she had wanted to keep the baby. "Maybe, I thought, my grandmother would come back to help take care of it," she said. "If only she hadn't gone away, I would never have slept around."

At her boyfriend's insistence, Tina underwent an abortion. "I cried and cried for two weeks," Tina remembered. "I thought I was beginning to lead my mother's life and that I would go from boyfriend to boyfriend and abortion to abortion." Tina noted that her mother was unusually supportive during this period. Having had many abortions herself, Tina explained, "my mother knew the ropes."

Another unfortunate consequence of her grandmother's absence was that her mother drank more heavily. During one drinking episode, she told Tina the "truth" about her birth. After separating from her husband shortly after Tony's birth, Tina's mother said she became pregnant with Tina as a result of a rape by a visiting relative of one of their neighbors.

Tina's mother described the rapist as a "gorgeous blond" from Northern Italy who spoke little English. According to Tina, her mother seemed pleased to discover that he had watched her for many days before the attack. Her mother had decided to carry to term in the hope of effecting a reconciliation with her husband by convincing him that Tina was his child. In spite of this ploy, the marriage broke up when Tina was eight months old.

Tina said she felt as if she had been "kicked in the head" by this disclosure. "I really freaked out," she remembered, "I thought 'now I'll be depressed for the rest of my life'." Tina said that the most painful aspect of the revelation was her realization that the man she had always believed to be her father would never return. Tina described a sense of "doom" at the thought of giving up her cherished reunion fantasy.

Before long, Tina said, she became obsessed by a need for more information about the rapist. She mentioned pressing her mother for details about the rape each time her mother got drunk. With some embarrassment, Tina admitted creating an heroic vision of the rapist in her mind as well as a romantic scenario of the rape. In her imaginary version of the episode, the rapist had fallen madly in love with her mother. Because he could not communicate his passion for her in English, he had forced her to submit to his lovemaking.

Several months before her 18th birthday, Tina became sexually involved with Rob, the leader of the Angels, and moved in with him. Tina said she knew she was envied by the other girls and imagined she was tougher and prettier than all of them. Tina said that Rob, who was divorced and the father of a little girl, seemed like the paternal figure she had always wished for. She indicated that although she sometimes resented his overly controlling and demeaning manner, she loved being ordered around like "his little girl." Tina was less tolerant of his continuing involvement with his ex-wife and his demands that Tina serve as a babysitter for his child. When she protested, Rob's response was often a smack across her face or a vicious verbal assault.

He would fly into a jealous rage if other men paid attention to her, particularly if he had been drinking. During one of these rages, Tina said, he threatened her with a knife. Shortly before she was raped, Tina gave Rob's telephone number to one of her male friends. Rob became so enraged when the friend phoned that he beat Tina severely. Upset and shaken, Tina returned home to live with her mother. However, when her mother told her she deserved the beating for provoking Rob, Tina "knew then that I didn't have a mother, so I went back to Rob. Where else could I go?"

Tina's relationship with Rob had deteriorated steadily by the time of the rape. She had begun to spend more time with her brother and his girlfriend because Rob "permitted" these outings. On the night of the rape, Tina had gone ice skating with her brother and his girlfriend.

In order to free her brother to accompany his girlfriend home, Tina decided to travel alone to Rob's apartment by subway. Tina described staring in fascination at a muscular blond man seated opposite her on the subway car, imagining him as the embodiment of her fantasy father (the man who had raped her mother). During the subway ride, she invented a conversation in which she told him she was his daughter. In her reverie, the man was overjoyed by her announcement and asked Tina to live with him in his palatial villa in Italy.

When Tina got off at her subway stop, she noticed that the man also left the train. Becoming suspicious that he was following her, Tina crossed to the opposite side of the street as she walked toward Rob's apartment. The man also crossed and continued following a short distance behind her.

At last, Tina wheeled around and asked if he was following her. Without answering, the man grabbed Tina, held a knife to her neck and forced her into an alleyway. He said that if Tina did as he instructed he would not hurt her, but if she refused, he would kill her.

Although Tina was "scared shitless," she instantly developed a plan to lure him to Rob's apartment by suggesting they would be more comfortable in her bed. Every time she spoke, however, the man smacked her across the face and screamed at her to be quiet. He instructed her to perform fellatio while he twisted her hair in his hand. He then threw Tina against the wall of the alleyway, repeatedly banging her head. Throwing her on the ground, he entered her vaginally. After he ejaculated, he gently helped her to her feet, asked solicitously how she was, and apologized for hurting her. After warning her not to attract any attention, he ran off.

Sobbing uncontrollably, Tina ran to Rob's apartment. Tina hoped that when Rob saw her torn and soiled clothing and bleeding cuts he would comfort and console her. At the apartment, however, she found Rob and his ex-wife, Judy, in the midst of an intense and violent fight. Both had been drinking, and despite her obvious distress barely noticed her.

Furious at being ignored, Tina screamed at Rob and Judy. "Before I knew it," Tina said, "I was in the middle of another battle." At one point, Tina said, Rob smacked Tina and threw her on a bed and then resumed his fight with Judy. Tina phoned the police to end the fight. It was only during the course of the investigation of the domestic violence that Tina reported the rape. Tina said that she believed it would be futile to press charges against the rapist and never followed through on a police officer's recommendation that she do so.

When Rob learned what had happened, he accused her of provoking the attack and told her that he found her "disgusting." Although he later apologized for these remarks, Tina said she had never felt so hurt and disappointed. Nevertheless, Tina said, she began to believe that Rob's criticism was justified. "Maybe I did lead him [the rapist] on by staring at him," Tina said.

Tina's worries about her complicity in the rape led to doubts about every aspect of her life. Describing her sense of helpless dependence on Rob, Tina said, "I couldn't make the simplest decision on my own— not even what to eat for dinner." Because leaving the apartment alone now terrified Tina, she stayed indoors for weeks following the rape.

"I began to believe that nothing good would ever happen to me again," Tina said. She felt she was repeating her mother's life. "My mother was raped and I was raped," Tina said. "She never made anything of herself, and neither can I." Tina poignantly described a wish to pray to God for relief from her paralyzing sense of hopeless despair, but, she explained, "The rape made me feel too dirty to talk to God."

After the rape, Tina became seriously troubled by a wide range of PTSD symptoms. Most notable among her reexperiencing symptoms are the following two nightmares that have recurred with terrifying frequency since her rape:

There are two men. One of them has a knife and one of them has a gun.
The man drops the knife. I pick it up and stab him but it doesn't hurt
him at all. He says, 'Now I'm really going to hurt you.'

I an covered with blood and I have a knife in my hand. I think I have just
killed the rapist. I don't feel glad; I feel frightened and lonely.

Tina's recurrent nightmares dramatically convey the traumatic
shattering of her fantasies of idealized merger that had been her only
protection against an experience of herself as completely impotent and
ineffectual. The two men in the first nightmare, according to Tina,
represent her two "fathers" (her mother's ex-husband and the rapist/
father). Tina's inability to hurt the man she stabbed is a striking
representation of her sense of impotence. Killing the rapist in the
second dream reflects the destruction of her idealized image of her
rapist/father and her cherished fantasy that he would magically appear
to provide her with legitimacy and protection. At the same time, this
image of vengeful retribution might be viewed as an unconscious
attempt at defensive restoration of a grandiose fantasy. Yet her
feelings of fear and loneliness in the nightmare reveal the faultiness of
this restorative effort.

Both of Tina's nightmares clearly reflect her narcissistic rage toward paternal figures, who first disappoint her longings for idealized
merger and then become abusive exploiters. Other associations to
being "covered with blood" revealed her deep sense of guilt and shame.
She said the grim reality of her terrifying experiences had destroyed
her illusions that her mother's rape had been a romantic interlude.
Consequently, Tina's narcissistic rage was also directed toward herself
and expressed in suicidal ruminations. "I have to face facts," she said,
"I never should have been born. My whole life is a freaky mistake."

Reliving experiences that occurred during Rob's attempts to have
sex are another distressing feature of Tina's PTSD. "I always feel like
I'm about to be raped when Rob wants sex," Tina said. She described
one episode in which she suddenly began to struggle, hit, and scratch
Rob during sex. "I just lost it," she reported, "like Rob *was* the
rapist."

Tina vividly described a variety of numbing symptoms, including
feelings of alienation and estrangement. She mentioned her fears
about going outside of Rob's apartment on her own and spoke of
"closing myself off" to people since the rape. Feeling "dead inside"
was her way of conveying the constriction of her affective experience.
Tina also attempted to describe states of depersonalization involving a

loss of a sense of familiarity with herself. "I don't remember who I used to be," she said.

Tina mentioned dropping out of the 12th grade only a few months before graduation (she had had to repeat two grades). "There was no way I could concentrate on schoolwork," she said, "even if I wasn't afraid to travel to school myself."

Case Summary

From neglected baby in the high chair to victim of a brutal rape, Tina's experiences have led her to expect little from life beyond impotent rage, shame, and disillusionment. As one of her nightmare images so vividly depicts, even with a knife in her hand, Tina experiences herself as incapable of having an impact on others and exerting control over her destiny. She feels doomed to repeat her mother's empty, childlike, dissolute existence.

Only her narcissistic fantasies of idealized merger with omnipotent images have enabled Tina to experience compensatory grandiosity. Caught up in such fantasies, her unbearably painful feelings of powerlessness, incompetence, and worthlessness magically disappear, and Tina experiences herself as sharing the idealized attributes of powerful others.

Tragically, however, the figures around whom Tina has unconsciously attempted to weave these fantasies have repeatedly proved disappointing and unreliable. Although Tina's grandmother appears to have been the most readily idealizable figure of her childhood, Tina could not sustain a fantasy of idealized merger after her abrupt departure. With the loss of her grandmother, Tina apparently turned her efforts at idealization and merger toward male figures whom she fantasized as omnipotent. Her brother, her boyfriends in the motorcycle gang, and even Rob, the gang leader, all proved to be disillusioning as idealizable protectors with whom to merge in fantasy. Unable to nurture and sustain narcissistic fantasies of idealized merger around these men, Tina employed her rich imagination to concoct elaborate daydreams of her "fantasy fathers."

Before her mother's disclosure that Tina had been fathered by a rapist, Tina lived in the hope that her favorite conscious fantasy would come true and that she would be reunited with the man she then believed to be her father. Her daydream of sharing his wealth and success appears to reflect an unconscious fantasy of merger with his idealized attributes. After learning that she was not his daughter and that her fantasies of a joyous reunion were doomed illusions, Tina appears to have recast her mother's rapist into the fantasy role of long-lost father. Not only did this fantasy afford Tina the opportunity, on an unconscious level, for idealized merger, it also appears to have intensified her untransformed fantasies of grandiosity. Born of passion and romance, Tina could imagine that her life was very special.

The brutal and degrading circumstances of her own rape completely destroyed Tina's notion of rape as a romantic act of passion. In the space of one hour, all of the fantastic illusions that had organized her experience of herself and others were shattered. No longer able to keep alive her narcissistic fantasy of idealized merger with her father/rapist, Tina felt overwhelmed by rage and humiliation. Without this glamorous bond, Tina apparently experienced herself as inconsequential and utterly powerless. She imagined that without her fantasy father's comfort and protection, her life would be a meaningless repetition of her mother's.

From the wholesale manner in which Tina adopted the dress style, speech patterns, and exhibitionistic posturing of the Angels, it is reasonable to suspect that she had attempted, through her relationships with members of the motorcycle gang, to enact an unconscious fantasy involving idealized merger with omnipotent paternal imagos. However, judging from the severity of the PTSD symptoms from which she suffers, this compensatory restorative effort has been unsuccessful. As her nightmare suggests, instead of deriving a sense of her own power and competence from these men, Tina seems to experience herself as threatened by their coarseness and violence.

The unconscious traumatic meaning of Tina's rape appears to be contained in its cruel confirmation of the dread that accompanied her archaic narcissistic fantasies. This terrifying experience dramatically convinced Tina that the powerful idealized fathers of her fantasy world do not exist and that she is doomed to a life of impotent rage and disillusionment.

Maggie

"You've probably heard all about my troubles with men," Maggie, a single black woman of 21, said. "Isn't that why you want me for your study?" Without waiting for an answer, Maggie described in a loud, shrill voice that could be heard throughout the health center where she was being interviewed, her sexual history, which included two abortions, bouts of venereal disease, and a rape two years earlier.

As if determined to keep all eyes on her, Maggie was dressed in a clashing array of reds, pinks, and orange and adorned with every conceivable form of jewelry, including feather earrings that hung to her shoulders. Constantly in motion, Maggie gestured expansively and, at times, leapt to her feet to make a point. Her broad, expressive features registered a wide range of emotions that shifted from moment to moment. Throughout the interviews, Maggie took every opportunity to congratulate herself on her superior intelligence, her attractiveness to men, and her accomplishments. Although she worked for a small dress company, she proclaimed herself a "great" fashion designer.

Maggie asked many questions about the research project and displayed an unusually extensive familiarity with the literature on rape. When questioned about her store of information, she said in a pleased but offhand way, "Oh, I've read a little here and there." Surprisingly, Maggie minimized the negative effects of the rape, vehemently denying that many of the symptoms of PTSD from which she still suffered had been caused by the rape. "I made up my mind to overcome that business," she insisted angrily. It was only toward the end of the data-gathering process, consisting of a lengthy series of therapeutic interviews, that Maggie finally admitted that her two-year "slump" was the result of her shattering rape.

In spite of her assertion that she was "not your typical rape victim," Maggie seemed eager to participate in the interviews. She acknowledged that she enjoyed talking about herself and all the "no-good men" in her life. She reported growing up with her mother, father, and older sister, Betty, in a predominantly black neighborhood in which most families were poor but embraced such middle-class values as obtaining a good education. She explained that because her father's alcoholism had made it hard for him to hold down jobs (he held a variety of blue-collar jobs), her mother had been "the backbone of the family" and the main wage earner. "I know she went back to nursing when I was a baby," Maggie remarked, "but I don't know who took care of Betty and me. I don't remember anyone teaching me the important things like who to avoid, who to hit back, and who to get things from."

Maggie remembered her mother as a "kind" person, but "hard to get close to." Although Maggie said she could not recall "a word of criticism" from her mother, she could not remember ever having been praised or admired by her either. She went on to describe her mother as always seeming harried and preoccupied. The only time Maggie could count on her undivided attention was when she was sick. "Isn't it weird," she asked, "to remember the chicken pox as the best time of your life?"

"I didn't need my mother to tell me how wonderful I was," Maggie claimed, "I always knew." According to Maggie, her superiority resides primarily in her ability to "size up" other people and "to get what

I want from them." She also claimed to have an amazing faculty for predicting the outcome of events and situations. She recalled that as a child she usually knew in advance who the winner of a game or contest would be. "When we played hide-and-seek and I was 'it'," she said, "the other kids never had a chance because I knew where they were hiding."

Maggie reflected that her mother's distracted air probably resulted from the vigilance required to keep her husband from "flying off the handle" during his drinking binges. "I always think of her with a finger across her lips, warning us not to wake Pa. We all tiptoed around like he was a sleeping tiger."

Maggie said she could not recall a time when she was not afraid of her father. He was explosively violent when he was drinking and sullen, watchful, and restrictive between his drinking binges. At times, Maggie remembered, he would allow no laughing in his presence. If she or Betty violated one of his innumerable household rules, he often lectured them for hours or beat them severely. Nevertheless, Maggie recalled being awed by the total control he exercised over the entire family. Betty reminds her that she often assumed the role of tyrannical leader with playmates, imitating her father's threatening mannerisms. Maggie said she was certain that her father did not acknowledge her efforts to emulate him. "He never showed pride or joy or affection for me," Maggie said. "All I ever got from him were scoldings and beatings."

Maggie noted that her father was particularly concerned with the chastity and purity of his wife and daughters. He would often threaten to kill his wife if he found her cheating on him, Maggie recalled. She reported an incident in which she was playing outside with some boys and girls and her father appeared brandishing a metal pipe. He accused the boys of "feeling up" his daughter. Maggie said she almost "died of embarrassment" when neighbors had to call the police to restrain him. Because of incidents such as this, she and Betty were taunted by the neighborhood children, who called their father "the bogeyman."

Maggie believed that her father's "strangeness" "rubbed off" on her. Although she agreed with the neighbors' assessment of her father as "the local weirdo," she often defended him bitterly against their derisive jeers. As a result, Maggie herself became the target of much of their abuse. "It didn't bother me," Maggie claimed, "Those know-nothings were just jealous of my brain." Maggie explained that she much preferred reading alone in her room to "hanging out." She found it difficult to "tolerate" her "intellectual inferiors" and found her own company was far "more rewarding."

With her insatiable appetite for books and delight in learning,

Maggie became an honor student in grade school and was accepted into a prestigious high school for "gifted" children. Maggie blamed her father for causing her to drop out of this school and having to graduate from the local high school. She said that although her father approved of her studiousness, he regarded school as a potentially corrupting influence. Once, she remembered, he tore up a book she was reading for an English class because he interpreted certain passages as extolling the value of drugs. He also believed that the school was "racist" and that school administrators discriminated against black students. Maggie said that after her father showed up drunk for a parent–teacher conference and accused her teacher of instructing the students in "indecent sexual practices," she felt too embarrassed to return to school.

Although she was almost two years younger than Betty, Maggie reported that she was always the more dominant of the pair. "I was smarter, quicker and more imaginative," Maggie said. She recalled how she would entertain Betty for hours with fantastic stories about their future lives. In these stories, her father was always dead either because he had succumbed to a terrible illness or because he had been killed in some ghastly fashion. Maggie would either find or steal a great deal of money and build a sumptuous house for her mother and Betty. She said her fondest wish was to provide her mother with luxury and ease. "I guess I hoped that if she didn't have to work so hard she'd spend more time with us," Maggie said.

Maggie reported that her sister was the first to rebel against her father's moralistic strictures by becoming pregnant at the age of 17 and insisting on keeping the baby. Maggie said her father became so enraged with Betty that she worried that he would kill her. When he told Betty that she could no longer live in the same house with him, Maggie's mother strongly objected. She wanted Betty to keep the child and bring it up in their household.

After many bitter and violent scenes, Maggie's mother told her husband that she was through with him and that she never wanted to see him again. Maggie remembered feeling terrified when her father said he would leave but would return when they were asleep and "mow them down" with a machine gun. She said she felt very proud of her mother for her courage in standing up to her husband and for her cool bravado in the face of this threat. Although Maggie's father returned many times, threatening them at first and later pleading for a reconciliation, Maggie's mother remained firm in her decision to end the marriage.

Immediately after their father left home, Maggie said, Betty and she were overjoyed with the prospect of living without his gloomy, forbidding presence. However, it soon became apparent that their mother was becoming increasingly depressed. Finally, she was no longer able to go to work but lay in bed moaning and weeping. When she stopped eating and lost a great deal of weight, Maggie and Betty had no choice but to have her hospitalized. After several hospitalizations Maggie could no longer recognize her mother. "She became old and feeble in one year's time," Maggie said.

Maggie spoke of her despondency as she witnessed her mother's collapse and deterioration. She had imagined that her mother would be relieved to be rid of her husband and content to have Maggie assume the role of provider. Above all, Maggie said, she could not bear the sense of helplessness she experienced at the failure of all her attempts to lift her mother from her depression.

Welfare checks and food stamps barely covered their expenses, and they were forced to move to a dangerous neighborhood where the rent was low. Maggie, her mother, Betty, and Betty's baby all lived in a dilapidated, one-bedroom apartment. Maggie said she welcomed the opportunity to demonstrate her cleverness in supporting the family. She believed that with her special "know how" they would soon be living a life of ease and luxury.

Maggie said, "I did a little of this and a little of that to earn money while I finished high school." She confided that her money-earning activities included shoplifting, drug dealing, and prostitution.

Maggie said that she was "too smart" to get involved with a pimp. "I did alright on my own," she bragged. "I could always spot the rich johns a mile away." Taking money from rich men to help her destitute mother and sister elated her. "I felt just like Robin Hood in those days," she said. She reluctantly admitted that her cleverness had not prevented her from contracting gonorrhea and "crabs," nor from becoming pregnant twice. "I thought I wouldn't get pregnant if I really didn't want to, so I didn't use the pill," she explained. "Maybe a lot of what I did was illegal," Maggie said, "but I didn't hurt anybody." She said that she hoped that if she could only provide her mother with a beautiful place to live she would "snap out of her depression."

One evening Maggie picked up an older white man who "fell in love with me." He bought Maggie presents and took her to fancy nightclubs and restaurants. He had a small dress company and encouraged her to capitalize on her flair for dressing in a flashy creative way. With his support, she decided to attend a two-year college to learn fashion designing. When she graduated, he hired her as an assistant designer in his business. Maggie said, "I thought all men were garbage until I met Sam. But now I think he's the only exception."

At the time of her rape, Maggie had just begun her fashion training.

"I thought I would be rich and famous in no time," Maggie said, "and I still think I will be." As she was walking home one rainy night, Maggie slipped and badly cut her chin. Unable to stop the bleeding, she went to a nearby hospital emergency room for suturing. The doctor who sutured her chin was a good-looking young resident from the West Indies. Maggie enjoyed his compliments and his ability to engage in witty flirtatious repartee. He spoke earnestly about his "mission" to help blacks obtain higher quality medical treatment. She gladly accepted his invitation to have dinner the following night.

When he picked her up for their date, he told her that his plans had changed and that he had ordered food to be delivered to his apartment. He told her that another couple, friends of his, would be joining them. Maggie said she felt suspicious about this change in plans but decided to accompany him "against my better judgment." In his apartment, he began to insult her, calling her a "whore" and a "slut." When Maggie tried to make her way out of the apartment, he threw her on his bed, smacking her face and head, and opening the cut on her chin, which bled profusely. Then he raped and sodomized her.

Maggie described her initial reaction as "astonishment." She could not believe that her assessment of the doctor's character had been so faulty. During the initial interviews, Maggie said that all she felt during the rape and immediately afterward was "wild fury." "As soon as he let me go I began to beat and scratch him," she said. According to Maggie, he had to use all his strength to free himself from her battering assault and get her out of the apartment. Venting her rage at the rapist, she declared, "He is unnecessary. He should just die. And to think he was telling me how humanitarian he was!"

Eventually, Maggie admitted that her feelings of rage had been secondary to terror for her life, as well as an overwhelming and humiliating sense of her own gullibility and short-sightedness.

Acknowledging her painful reactions to the rape, she confided, was very frightening. "I have to keep my mind on my strengths and forget my weaknesses," she said. "If I lose my confidence, I lose everything." Maggie reiterated that she was different from "your typical rape victim." To admit that she suffered on account of the rape would throw doubt on her self-proclaimed uniqueness.

Maggie said that immediately after the rape, she planned "my revenge." She notified the police and pressed charges against the doctor and filed a formal complaint against him with the hospital authorities. To her enormous satisfaction, Maggie succeeded in getting him suspended from his residency, and he returned to the West Indies.

According to Maggie, her response to the rape was "to go out there and use men for my own purposes." Within weeks after the traumatic episode, she had begun to date a number of wealthy, married men. She bragged about her ability to get them to spend a great deal of money on her and of her collection of expensive gifts. "As soon as they start to fall for me," Maggie said, "I treat them like dirt." She claimed that the only way to get even with men was to act like a man.

In spite of her attempts to minimize her distress, Maggie appeared to be suffering from symptoms of chronic PTSD directly related to her shattering rape. Asked about intrusive or recurring thoughts, Maggie admitted that for months after the rape she could not stop herself from obsessively ruminating about why she had allowed herself to be "conned" by the doctor. "I always trusted with my eyes open before," she said. "How could I have been so stupid?" Maggie's confidence in her own judgment had been badly shaken. "All I ever really trusted was my own great mind," she said, "my ability to think clearly and to make the right choices. If I made the wrong decision this time, maybe I could make other bad choices."

She also admitted having nightmares. Although none involved direct and undisguised repetitions of the rape, they appeared to symbolize the traumatic experience. One of these nightmares was about two knights dueling with heavy metal poles:

> Somehow, I become one of the knights. I see that my armor is rusted and crumbling. I start to scream that the duel must be called off, but the other knight keeps thrusting with his pole. I realize that he will easily pierce my armor and kill me.

At this point, Maggie said she would wake up feeling so terrified she could not get back to sleep. As Maggie freely associated to this nightmare, she became aware that it only thinly disguised the rape. In particular, Maggie was struck by the terrifying image of her crumbling armor. The rape, she finally admitted, forced her to confront her own flaws and inadequacies. Most painful was the obvious limit to her uncanny power to "read" people and situations.

Maggie said that her experience with her father should have taught her that there are no knights in shining armor. "All men are pigs," she repeated, again expressing astonishment at having been deceived by the rapist.

The nightmare also contains evidence of Maggie's desperate but faulty efforts at defensive restoration. Her association to the image of the knight revealed her childhood fascination with stories about King Arthur and Robin Hood. She associated her childhood fascination with adolescent fantasies of herself as a "knight in shining armor" coming to the rescue of her mother and older sister.

By "acting like a man" to "get even with men" (that is, having numerous sexual relationships with married men), Maggie attempted to disavow her sense of flawed and vulnerable femininity. This disavowal may be understood as defensive restoration of a shattered fantasy of herself as a fearless knight. Only in this way, Maggie apparently imagined, could she win her mother's love and admiration.

Maggie has also been plagued since the rape by episodes of intense depersonalization and derealization. She spoke of feeling like "the audience at my own performance." She said that such experiences were particularly common during sex. Aside from her numerous sexual involvements, Maggie admitted that she had severely curtailed other social relationships since the rape. The only women she had regular contact with were her mother and sister. Asked why she had no friendships with women, Maggie replied, "There are so many sick, weak ones out there. I just have no use for them."

Maggie also spoke of being hyperalert and of having to "keep my guard up" even more since the rape. She described her compulsion to check and recheck every situation for signs of danger. Maggie has enrolled in a variety of martial arts courses including karate and judo. "I will never be raped again," Maggie said. "I will fight to my death before that could happen."

Maggie also confided that since the rape she had begun to use cocaine regularly. "If a guy can't provide me with coke, I drop him," she said. Cocaine helps Maggie to feel supremely confident, potent, and in total control of her relationships with men.

Case Summary

Despite Maggie's claim that as a child she had needed no one to tell her how "wonderful" she was, the extensive domination of her personality by unconscious fantasies of grandiose exhibitionism suggests failures in mirroring. Neither her remote mother nor her abusive father seem to have enabled Maggie to develop a firm and accurate sense of herself. Maggie's flamboyant manner, attention-riveting attire, and extravagant claims about her talent and intelligence may be interpreted as exhibitionistic displays by which she unconsciously enacted grandiose fantasies that did not undergo sufficient developmental transformation. Maggie's claims about her infallible talent for "sizing up" people and her uncanny powers of prediction reflect a belief that she possesses paranormal gifts of clairvoyance and prescience, another manifestation of these grandiose fantasies.

While Maggie apparently felt awed by her father's tyrannical control over the family and even emulated his imperious manner, his forbidding sullenness and hostile attacks interfered with Maggie's unconscious efforts to merge in fantasy with his idealized attributes. It seems likely, instead, that her grandiose fantasies underwent further unconscious embellishment. The tales she spun for her sister in which she figured as a kind of Robin Hood, bountifully providing for her mother and sister and substituting for her impotent father, reflect this unconscious intensification of fantasy. It is also probable that Maggie imagined that by "rescuing" her mother from her bondage to her tyrant husband she would be rewarded with the admiration and attention she so sorely craved.

On an unconscious level, the breakup of her parents' marriage may have provided Maggie with the context in which to enact grandiose-exhibitionistic fantasies of herself as a "knight in shining armor," rescuing her "mother in distress." It is likely that her mother's decompensation during this period seriously threatened Maggie's fantasies. When her mother needed to be hospitalized, the failure of her rescue efforts must have been inescapable.

Maggie's response was characteristic insofar as she sought, unconsciously, to stave off this threat to her grandiosity with even more elaborate enactments. In her fantasies, Maggie imagined herself a fearless Robin Hood figure who could shoplift, deal in drugs, and engage in prostitution with impunity because her gains would benefit her mother and sister. While unconsciously enacting these fantasies, Maggie experienced herself as superior to those who lived in accordance with prevailing moral norms.

Imagining that she possessed uncanny powers of clairvoyance and prescience, she maintained an experience of herself as grandiose. It is also in keeping with her illusions of supreme control over her life that she did not use birth control in the belief that she would not become pregnant unless she so wished.

Like the crumbling armor in her recurrent traumatic nightmare, Maggie's fantasies of grandiosity eroded under the brutal assault of the rape. She was forced to confront the realization that her terrifying experience was the result of an humiliating defect in her defensive armamentarium. Having mistakenly placed her trust in the rapist, she could no longer entertain her grandiose fantasies of clairvoyance and prescience.

Because Maggie's subjective world was organized so completely in accordance with fantasies of self-sufficiency based on her possession of a "great brain," the unconscious meaning of the rape shattered these fantasies and left her vulnerable to experiences of fragmentation and disintegration. Having played the part of rescuer and provider for so long, she now had no one to turn to for comfort and support. Maggie's desperate response was to disavow the meaning of the rape and deny the severity of the trauma. Viewing the symptoms of PTSD as totally unrelated to her rape was part of Maggie's unconscious effort at defensive restoration of her fantasies.

As if to prove that she had not been incapacitated by the trauma, Maggie counterphobically engaged in sexual behavior immediately following the rape. By extracting expensive gifts from wealthy men in exchange for sex, Maggie may also have unconsciously attempted to restore her Robin Hood fantasy. Revenge offered Maggie another avenue for restoration of her shattered fantasies. By displaying courage and intelligence in forcing the dismissal of the resident, as well as through her exploitative relationships with men, Maggie imagined herself magically triumphant over those who had overpowered and humiliated her.

The continuing "slump" Maggie described attests to the faultiness of her restitutive efforts. It is ironic and tragic that these attempts at self-restitution, such as her denial of the connection between the rape and her PTSD symptoms, prevented Maggie from seeking the therapeutic help necessary for recovery from the rape trauma.

CONCLUSION

We have presented three representative case studies of rape in support of our self-psychological theory of psychic trauma. Developmental arrests in the structuralization of the subjective worlds of our three subjects seriously interfered with the transformation of these fantasies. As they grew up, the self–experience of all three victims was increasingly organized in accordance with these fantasies, whose content became embellished.

As a result of the shattering and faulty restoration of their fantasies, all three subjects were thrown into nightmare worlds of terror and despair. Exploration of the dissociative symptoms of PTSD led to inferences about the unconscious meaning of rape trauma and to conjectures about characteristic defensive and compensatory modes of self-restitution.

At the time of her rape, Violet's self experience was organized primarily around unconscious fantasies of herself as impenetrable and inviolable. In the context of maternal overintrusiveness and in the absence of a counterbalancing paternal presence, Violet's childhood fantasies failed to undergo adequate developmental transformation. The breakup of an adolescent romance with a man about whom Violet had unconsciously woven a fantasy of idealized merger heightened fantasies of impenetrability and inviolability.

The unconscious traumatic meaning of Violet's rape appears to reside in her experience of having been violently exposed, penetrated, and violated. Her recurrent traumatic nightmare in which rapists intrude into her loft captures her sense of utter vulnerability to intrusion. Her faulty efforts at compensatory restoration centered on illusions of herself as merged in fantasy with omnipotently endowed figures, such as the female police officer. They also involved grandiose fantasies of retribution reflected in her daydreams of shooting men who made obscene remarks to her in the street.

Tina's self-experience was organized in accordance with narcissistic fantasies of idealized merger with imaginary omnipotent fathers. Tina constantly struggled with painful feelings of impotence, inadequacy, and incompetence. Because of the emotional impoverishment of her family life, her healthy needs for mirroring and idealization were largely unfulfilled. Tina experienced herself as in control of her life and destiny only when she was caught up in unconscious fantasies of idealized merger.

Before the rape, Tina had intensified a fantasy of idealized merger with the man who had fathered her by raping her mother. This fantasy rested precariously on a naively romantic scenario involving a passionate encounter between her mother and the rapist. The brutal and degrading nature of Tina's own rape shattered her fantasies of idealized merger, irreparably destroying her romatic illusions.

Overwhelmed by experiences of fragmentation and disintegration, Tina's dissociative symptoms of PTSD reached such severe levels that for weeks after the rape she was unable to leave home alone. As her recurrent traumatic nightmare of stabbing a man without hurting him suggests, she once again experienced herself as completely impotent and incompetent. Tina's faulty efforts at compensatory restoration consisted, in part, of exhibitionistic enactments of fantasized mergers with motorcycle gang members, whom she imagined to be omnipotent protectors.

Maggie grew up with an aloof, preoccupied mother and a violent, alcoholic father. Because of what may be inferred as grossly unempathic parenting, Maggie's childhood fantasies of grandiose exhibitionism did not undergo sufficient developmental transformation. As a result, Maggie unconsciously wove narcissistic fantasies of herself as omniscient and prescient.

Maggie's illusion of possessing these uncanny powers was destroyed because the man who raped her had "conned" her into accompanying him to his apartment. With the shattering and faulty restoration of her grandiose fantasies, she was plagued with feelings of intolerable humiliation and terrifying experiences of fragmentation and disintegration. These were symbolically represented by recurrent traumatic nightmares of dueling while wearing crumbling armor.

Maggie's denial that her PTSD symptoms were products of her rape, as well as her exhibitionistic promiscuity, seems to reflect her faulty efforts at the defensive restoration of her shattered fantasy world.

Until their shattering rapes, all three women had lived, to varying degrees, as heroines in their private fantasy worlds, endowed with wonderous personal abilities or magically united with fabulous heroes. Despite their courageous efforts, none has found it possible to reenter this enchanted realm. Instead each woman is burdened by an excruciating sense of defeat and disillusionment.

CHAPTER 5

Combat: The Vicissitudes of "Rambo" Fantasies in Adolescence

Earlier we presented six representative case studies of incest and rape trauma as part of a self-psychological reformulation of Freud's original but abandoned or renunciated (Masson, 1984) seduction theory. Our findings support the "factual" or "material" reality (Freud, 1913, p. 159, 1916–17, p. 368) of sexual trauma and counter Freud's shift to an exclusive focus on the "psychical reality" (Freud, 1916–17, p. 368) of these traumatic experiences. Our case studies also evidence the validity of our central argument, namely that the "psychical reality" or unconscious meaning of (sexual) trauma as symptomatically expressed in PTSD resides in the shattering and faulty restoration of central organizing fantasies.

Freud's de-emphasis of the "material reality" of sexual trauma in favor of its "psychical reality" represented a shift in emphasis from real occurrences to unconscious fantasy and conflict as determinants of psychopathology. This move constituted perhaps the decisive step in the creation of "psychoanalysis as a theory of meaning" (Basch, 1981, p. 166). However, it also led Freud to a false distinction between anxiety and traumatic neurosis (see chapter 1).

According to this distinction, anxiety neurosis does not result from an unconscious conflict. The conflict is created by the clash between pathogenic oedipal fantasies pressing for access to conscious awareness and countervailing ego mechanisms defending against their expression. Traumatic neurosis results from real occurrences, such as accidents or combat.

Unlike the sexual traumas, the "material reality" of traumatic combat experiences was never questioned by Freud and most of his earlier followers. Rather, it was only a question of interpreting the unconscious meaning behind the "psychical reality" of these traumatic experiences. Freud (1916–1917, 1919, 1920), and several of his colleagues hinted at the idea of traumatic disturbance of sense of self as the basis for war neurosis.

In this chapter, we pursue these early hints at viewing war neurosis as a narcissistic trauma. We also present three representative case studies of PTSD in Vietnam combat veterans. Together with our six representative case studies of sexual trauma, these cases serve as the clinical basis for our comprehensive self-psychological theory of traumatogenesis. We envision this as our contribution to the establishment of a "trauma paradigm" (Cohen, 1980, 1981) within psychoanalysis.

Our theory calls into question Freud's distinction between anxiety and traumatic neurosis that has prevailed within psychoanalysis (see chapter one). We contend that sexual and combat traumas are equally catastrophic and play equal roles in creating dissociative disturbances in the development of a healthy feminine and masculine sense of self. In assigning equal weight to the catastrophic traumas experienced by females and males, our self-psychological theory of trauma attests to both the "material" and the "psychical" realities of these occurrences.

ADOLESCENT NARCISSISM AND THE TRAUMA OF COMBAT

PTSD in Vietnam combat veterans falls squarely within the purview of our self-psychological theory of trauma. However, unique features about the etiology and manifestation of the disorder in this particular population require further comment. The trauma of combat in Vietnam was not strictly limited to males. For example, nurses and other female medical and support personnel often found themselves in rear areas that were suddenly transformed into frontline combat zones. Here these women experienced firsthand the horrors of battle. Nonetheless, combat is still a peculiarly male trauma with serious repercussions for the healthy development of a masculine sense of self. In other words, fighting in a war has traditionally been a formative part of the adolescent male's "rite of passage" from boyhood to manhood.

Adolescence often stretches from the early teens to the early twenties. By studying the dissociative symptoms of PTSD associated with combat in the Vietnam war, where the average age of the American soldier was 19½, we were able to trace the narcissistic vicissitudes of common adolescent male fantasies. Several major studies (see, for example, A. Freud, 1958; Jacobson, 1961; Blos, 1962, 1963, 1967; Wolf et al., 1972) emphasize the vicissitudes of narcissism or the development of a sense of self as a critical focus in the psychoanalytic theory of adolescence.

For example, Blos (1962) writes:

> The *nature and function of the self* have been presented here because it appears that *the concept of the self* is becoming an investigative and conceptual tool of increasing moment for the study of adolescence. . . . The extensive explanation of defense during the adolescent period seems to be giving way to an *investigation of the self* in its genetic and pathologic aspects, and the study of psychic organization and psychic restructuring is complimenting the concentration on instinctual conflict as the paramount feature of the adolescent process [p. 197, italics added].

We also know from these same studies that the development of a sense of self during adolescence is often perilous because of the resurgence of archaic forms of narcissism. For instance, Jacobson (1961) refers to "narcissistic inflation" (p. 171) and the "intensification of narcissism in adolescence" (p. 172) as involving "expanding, highly narcissistic, sexual and aggressive strivings" (p. 173). She warns that "regressive-archaic fears of annihilation may at times even threaten" the adolescent "with fears of loss of self" (p. 174). Blos (1962) observes that the development of "self as an effectively organized entity depends on the relinquishment of infantile megalomania and magic powers" (p. 192).

In a number of instances these authors describe the appearance or reappearance of what we refer to as archaic narcissistic fantasies. Anna Freud (1958) mentions the "defense by the withdrawal of libido to the self" consisting of the appearance of "ideas of grandeur," "fantasies of unlimited power over human beings," "major achievements and championships in one or more fields," and Christ-like "fantasies of saving the world" (p. 272). Blos (1962) describes the revival of the "omnipotent relation which the child experienced when self- and object-representation merged in a state of ideal grandeur" (p. 193). He (1967) also refers to the activation of "uniqueness fantasies and grandiose self-expectations once realized through identification with the omnipotent mother" (p. 171).

However, the otherwise important insights of these authors into the vicissitudes of adolescent narcissism are limited by their respective adherence to the classical psychoanalytic "fixation/regression and defense" model of narcissism. The use of this model leads to a view of the upsurge of archaic forms of narcissism as the basis for a pathological defense against the development of an adult sense of self. For example, this model is behind such statements as the following: The "re-establishment of primitive narcissistic types of object relatedness and identifications . . . may bring" the adolescent "to the point of refusions with objects" (Jacobson, 1961, p. 180). Blos, speaking of typical adolescent forms of "narcissistic isolation" (1963, p. 176) and "narcissistic defense" (1967, p. 180), observes that "regressed ego states are identifiable also in the well-known adolescent idolization and adoration of famous men and women" (1967, p. 175). He refers to these as "quasi-merger" states (p. 175).

The early self-psychological work of Kohut enabled psychoanalysis to view the adolescent development of sense of self in terms of the autonomous development line of narcissism from archaic to mature forms. For example, Wolf et al. (1972) point out that "the importance of the vicissitudes of the transformations of narcissism for the internalization of stable structures is of particular relevance for understanding the adolescent process" (p. 267). According to these authors, such vicissitudes in the developmental transformation of narcissism involve the transmutation of "the lost perfection of parental images . . . into the felt perfection of now internal standards and ideals. . . . If such a new ideal is set up . . . the self will have been transformed in a crucial dimension. . . . This is the change we deem to be characteristic of adolescence" (p. 267).

However, like Anna Freud, Jacobson, and Blos, Wolf et al. are cognizant of the difficulties in the transformational vicissitudes of narcissism during adolescence. They argue that "in the case of defects in the original consolidation of the self in early childhood, the loosening of structure implicit in these adolescent changes—i.e., the final separation from the parents as archaic self-objects—may threaten the cohesiveness of the personality as a whole" (Wolf et al., 1972, p. 267). Wolf et al. describe such a "narcissistic peril in development" (p. 267) as characterized by "frequent oscillations in self-esteem, caused by alternating fusions with archaic ideal images, accompanied by hypomanic excitement and disappointments in them, leading to depressive affects and narcissistic rage" (p. 268).

According to these authors, such "narcissistic perils in development" also entail the reactivation of the "archaic grandiosities" which "threaten the adolescent with increased exhibitionistic pressures. . . . The impossibility of fulfilling grandiose expectations leads to a propensity for shame" (p. 268).

Clearly, an adolescent boy's preparation for war and participation in combat raises the normal "narcissistic perils in development" to extremely dangerous heights. A number of authors (see, for example, Simmel, 1944; Shatan, 1977; Wilson, 1980) have commented on the importance of adolescence in understanding the impact of war.

As early as 1944, Simmel implied that because most combatants of both World Wars I and II were still adolescents, the development and functioning of the superego took on particular significance for understanding the soldier's reaction to combat. Simmel observes that there was an "increase of juvenile delinquency during [World War I], because it is just in adolescence that the mental system receives the last touch in cementing the superego" (p. 231). Simmel goes on to link the ability of the young soldier's "military ego" to withstand the "narcissistic traumata" of combat to the degree of superego development and functioning: "It depends upon the degree of maturity of the soldier's superego, if and to what degree his ego can withstand *narcissistic injuries* without *disintegration* of its mental system" (p. 235, italics added).

Elaborating this point, Simmel (1944) contends:

> The ego is no longer afraid of the power of fate represented by the external enemy, threatening it with annihilation, but instead has become afraid of the threats of its own superego—of its strictness, of its *collapse;* the latter would render *the ego directionless* when its instinctual drives clash with the demands of reality [p. 239, italics added].

Although couched in the terminology of Freud's structural theory, Simmel's formulation of the psychodynamics of the adolescent soldier's unconscious reaction to combat is important to our argument for two reasons. First, he focuses on adolescent psychological development as critical to understanding the soldier in combat. He abumbrates the self-psychological work of Wolf et al. (1972), who stress the importance of psychic structure building or the loss of previous psychic structures as critical to the adolescent developmental process. In other words, he provides a developmental context for understanding traumatic war neurosis. This line of thinking is consistent with our emphasis on the unconscious meaning of the trauma of combat as caused by the shattering and faulty restoration of adolescent male narcissistic fantasies.

Second, he is sensitive to the fragility of adolescent psychic structures and their vulnerability to the trauma of combat as evidenced by their "disintegration" and "collapse." This sensitivity enables Simmel to formulate an early version of a theory of war neurosis as a narcissistic trauma.

More than 30 years after Simmel's work, Shatan (1977) returned to the topic of the adolescent superego in combat. He saw it as critical to understanding the psychological metamorphosis undergone by the young recruit as he is transformed into a combat soldier. Basic training, or boot camp, "transmutes the character" of the raw recruit, Shatan contends, because the "fluidity and instability of the adolescent superego makes conscripts especially vulnerable to the will and example" of officers and drill instructors (D.I.s), who preach with a fanatical zeal the cult of masculine violence (p. 604). Shatan observes: "Part of the *regressive solution* is to model oneself after the officer or D.I. and identify with him (identification with the aggressor); this facilitates indiscriminate—and apparently remorseless killing" (p. 604). We argue that the "regressive solution" referred to by Shatan entails an unhealthy inflation of unstable and volatile adolescent male narcissistic fantasies of invulnerability, invincibility, and impenetrability, as well as of superhuman strength and power. Such unhealthy inflation helps to account for the extreme vulnerability of these archaic narcissistic fantasies.

Finally, Wilson (1977, 1978, 1980) pays special attention to adolescence in understanding the psychological meaning of combat in Vietnam for young American soldiers. Wilson's "conceptual schema" is derived from Erickson's (1968) epigenetic theory of psychosocial crises and Lifton's (1973) psychoformative model. Wilson found among Vietnam combat veterans who participated in a series of in-depth research interviews a common meaning to their traumatic combat experiences with important individual variations. According to Wilson, this underlying meaning is organized around Erikson's fifth psychosocial crisis, which involves identity versus role confusion. Wilson (1977, Part 1) points out that this Eriksonian psychosocial crisis entails the "need to form a more stable and enduring personality structure and *sense of self* in order to assume the various roles of adulthood and to meet adequately the demands that accompany them" (p. 6, italics added).

Under normal civilian conditions, the adolescent is provided with what Wilson calls a "psychosocial moratorium" (p. 7). Such a moratorium allows the adolescent "to consolidate a firm and enduring ego-identity," or an "awareness that there is a *self-sameness and continuity* to the ego's synthesizing methods, the style of one's individuality, and this style coincides with the sameness and continuity of one's meaning for significant others in the immediate community" (p. 7, italics added).

The adolescent combat soldier fighting in Vietnam had no "psychosocial moratorium," and, hence no opportunity to develop a cohesive and stable adult sense of self. Instead, he was engulfed in what Wilson (1977) refers to as a "psychological time warp" (p. 21) in which he underwent "psychosocial acceleration" (p. 22). This led to "massive psychoformative decentring" (p. 3) involving the "disintegration" of "self-structures" (p. 19): *"Disintegration* then is a psychoformative mode of inconsistency in the *self-structure* which has no coherency or images to counterbalance the feelings and images of being *broken apart* into a *fragmented* identity" (p. 19, italics added).

Employing an ego psychological framework, Wilson arrives at conclusions remarkably consistent with those we have reached using our self psychological framework. He concludes that combat in Vietnam plunged the adolescent American soldier into a "psychological time warp." In such a "warp," the young man underwent "psychosocial acceleration" involving "massive psychosocial decentring" as evidenced by the "disintegration" of "self-structures." This conclusion is consistent with Wolf et al.'s assertion about the "narcissistic peril in development" during adolescence. It is also consistent with what we believe is a psychologically devastating "narcissistic vortex" generated by the combination of boot camp and combat. This narcissistic vortex is created by the almost simultaneous yet countervailing intense inflation and then rapid deflation of already unstable and volatile adolescent male narcissistic fantasies. We present our three representative case studies of PTSD in Vietnam combat veterans to illustrate the shattering impact of this narcissistic vortex.

REVIEW OF THE LITERATURE

Freud's abandonment or renunciation (Masson, 1984) of the seduction theory led psychoanalysis to grossly underestimate the seriousness of sexual traumas. This unfortunate record of neglect is evidence in the relatively meager psychoanalytic literature on the topic.

Such is not the case, however, with the topic of traumatic war neurosis, subsequently referred to as combat neurosis and, currently, PTSD, on which there is an enormous body of psychoanalytic literature. It dates back to Freud and several of his early collaborators (including Abraham, Ferenczi, Simmel, and Jones); continues with the work of Kardiner, Rado, Kelman, Lidz, Greenson, Fisher, and others; and culminates in the more recent work of Lifton, Shatan, Horowitz, Hendin et al., and Brende and Parson.

Our review of this literature is not intended, however, as a comprehensive and systematic historical survey of this vast body of work.

There are already a number of excellent reviews that serve this purpose (see, for example, Horowitz, 1976; Hendin and Haas, 1984; Brende and Parson, 1985). Rather, our review is designed as an interpretive and critical commentary on selected works supporting our central argument, namely that combat entails a traumatic disturbance of sense of self as manifested in severe and chronic dissociative symptoms (reexperiencing and numbing) of PTSD.

Purely for heuristic purposes, we divide our commentary into two parts: the first deals with the literature on combat as a traumatic disturbance of sense of self; and the second with the literature on the dissociative nature of this traumatic disturbance. Whenever possible, we also highlight aspects of those works which point toward our self psychological theory of PTSD as traumatic shattering and faulty restoration of fantasies of self in relation to selfobject. In other words, we devote special attention to those investigators who stress that the unconscious meaning of trauma is caused by *both* the fragmentation and the faulty restoration of a core sense of self.

In the course of our interpretive and critical commentary, we also discuss limitations in the work of various authors resulting from their adherence to the classical psychoanalytic "fixation/regression and defense" model of narcissism. This model limits understanding of the role of adolescent narcissism in the development of sense of self especially as the latter relates to traumatic neurosis.

War Neurosis and the "Incapacity to Tolerate Narcissistic Injury"

Despite having written before the emergence of psychoanalytic self psychology, Zetzel (1965, 1973) anticipated our theory in many important respects. Because her work so clearly adumbrates our self psychological theory and serves, therefore, as an excellent standard by which to measure the work of others, we begin our literature review with a brief discussion of it.

In a 1965 article on depression, Zetzel compares the underlying character structures and the specific *narcissistic vulnerabilities* of depressives and "war neurotics." She states:

> Indeed the character structure of several was comparable to that of many *war neurotics* before the traumatic experience. Although potentially vulnerable to trauma or significant *narcissistic injury, they were not seriously disturbed or in any sense borderline.* . . . When more disturbed, ['war neurotics'] have typically been seen first in a state of decompensation which bore evidence to *serious incapacity to tolerate narcissistic injury* [p. 263, italics added].

Zetzel's statements are consistent with our position in two important respects. She did not find "war neurotics" to be "seriously disturbed or in any sense borderline." However, she did find that they were especially vulnerable to trauma because of a particular characterological flaw or structural defect, to which she refers as the "incapacity to tolerate narcissistic injury."

Our theory also accounts for the absence of serious underlying psychopathology and the presence of a "serious incapacity to tolerate narcissistic injury." We find that both are due to typical developmental failures and arrests in the necessary transformation of archaic forms of narcissism into a cohesive, firm, and stable sense of self. Such developmental failures and arrests are typical and therefore "normal." They are not indicative of serious underlying psychopathology characteristically attributed to borderline conditions. However, given the catastrophic nature of the fighting in Vietnam, these developmental failures and arrests left young American combat soldiers vulnerable to the traumatic shattering and faulty restoration of their adolescent male fantasies. This assertion is supported by the finding that statistically significant percentages of those soldiers seeing "heavy" combat in Vietnam suffer from the symptoms of PTSD as well as related psychosocial disturbances, including divorce, unemployment, crime, and substance abuse (see, for example, Wilson, 1978; Egendorf et al., 1981; Hendin and Haas, 1984; Laufer et al., 1985; Boulanger and Kadushin, 1986).

Commenting on the war neurotic's "incapacity to tolerate narcissistic injury," Zetzel (1973) notes that "these individuals suffered more severe disruption from *the threat to their narcissistic images of themselves* than they did from a direct threat to their lives" (p. 141, italics added). Earlier Zetzel (1965) had referred to this "narcissistic image" as based on "an underlying conviction of relative omnipotence" (p. 248). She (1973) describes the threat to the narcissistic image as the "inner psychological threat to the image of oneself as strong, brave, courageous, able to stand up to and resist any stress or danger" (p. 141).

Discussing the posttraumatic state of these "war neurotics," Zetzel (1965) points out: "While they can no longer deny feelings of inadequacy and fear, they cannot accept and integrate the recollection of traumatic experience. Since they are neither so strong nor so brave as they had previously believed, they can no longer maintain their narcissistic ideals . . ." (p. 248). Zetzel (1973) later adds: "Although they usually recovered quickly from their acute anxiety, *they were unable to reconstitute their previous self-image. The self-image had been in effect shattered* (p. 142, italics added). The latter statement captures our idea of the shattering and faulty restoration of archaic narcissistic fantasies.

Zetzel (1965) also explains why these "war neurotics" were unable to "reconstitute" their "shattered" "narcissistic images." She observes:

> Characteristically they are also unable to accept the proposition that strength and bravery of the order they had assumed is not realistically attainable. . . . [They attempt to maintain their] pretraumatic self-image"by an unconscious process of retrospective enhancement. . . . *Relative developmental failure* precludes the acceptance of realistic limitations [p. 248, italics added].

The implication of Zetzel's last statement is that "relative developmental failure" accounts for both the shattering and the failure of attempted retrospective enhancement of narcissistic self-images. This is consistent with one of our major findings. We found that typical, and therefore normal, developmental failures and arrests in the successful transformation of archaic narcissism into a mature sense of self account for vulnerability to combat trauma. This vulnerability is reflected in the shattering and faulty restoration of central organizing fantasies of self in relation to selfobject.

Traumatic Disturbance of Sense of Self

In 1918, Freud and several of his earliest and most important collaborators (including Abraham, Ferenczi, Simmel, and Jones) gathered for a special psychoanalytic symposium on traumatic war neurosis. They discussed their clinical experience with psychiatric casualties of World War I and speculated about the origins and course of traumatic war neurosis. Referring to the published results of this symposium, two commentators observe that "it was noticed that a potent factor in the onset of the disease [that is, traumatic war neurosis] was *a loss of a feeling of invulnerability. This may be viewed as a severe blow to narcissism*" (Balson and Dempster, 1980, p. 168, italics added). We equate the "severe blow to narcissism" and resulting "loss of a feeling of invulnerability" with the shattering and faulty restoration of archaic narcissistic fantasies.

Speaking about Freud's contribution to this symposium, Eissler (1986) points out that "Freud found the roots of war neurosis in an ego conflict: the old, peacetime ego defending itself against the new, warlike one. . . . [Although Freud] did not use the concept of identity . . . his differentiation [ego conflict] laid the foundations for the psychoanalysis of identity . . ." (p. 331). We agree with Eissler's assessment of the importance of Freud's "differentiation." However, consistent with Freud's (1940) later writings, we view it not as an ego conflict but as a "splitting of the ego" (p. 276).

Prior to making this critical point about the split between the "old peaceful ego" and its "parasitic double," the "new warlike one," (Freud, 1919b, p. 209), Freud (1916–17) had introduced the little discussed concept of the "self-preservative instincts" (pp. 414–15, 429). Freud viewed the "self-preservative instincts" as different from the sexual instincts. The sexual instincts included narcissism in both its original and normal form, as well as its later and so-called pathological form. According to Freud, normal narcissism consisted solely in the early ego's erotic involvement with the body (primary narcissism), whereas pathological narcissism consisted in the adult ego's overin-volvement with itself as an erotic object (secondary narcissism). Freud viewed the self-preservative instincts, in contrast to narcissism, as a form of "ego-interest" in position, status, and well-being (pp. 414–15). We believe that Freud's distinction between the sexual and the self-preservative instincts represents an early attempt at accounting for the autonomous developmental line of narcissism, or sense of self.

Freud's subsequent idea about the split between the "old peaceful ego" and its "parasitic double," the "new warlike one," makes sense only in reference to the operation of the self-preservative instincts. The split leads to traumatic war neurosis because the self-preservative instincts require that the ego maintain its integrity and cohesion. In support of our interpretation of Freud's position, we cite Simmel (1944), who quotes Freud as stating that the ego "in all its conflicts can have no other aim, than to maintain itself" (p. 227).

We envision a straight line of thought running from the Freudian "self-preservative instincts," through Simmel's postulate of the ego's need to maintain its own coherence as a psychological entity (p. 228) and Kardiner and Spiegel's (1947) "end of self-preservation" (p. 313) to Kohut's (1984) "principle of the primacy of self preservation" (p. 184; see also P. Tolpin, 1985, p. 87) and Atwood and Stolorow's (1984) "superordinate motivational principle," that is, "the need to maintain the organization of experience," as a "central motive in the patterning of human action" (p. 35). Kohut (1977) himself points to this particular line of thought. He connects his "self-state dreams" with Freud's "dreams of traumatic neuroses" (p. 109). In both, according to Kohut, the "healthy sectors of the patient's psyche are reacting with anxiety to a *disturbing change in the condition of the self*—manic overstimu-lation or a serious depressive drop in self-esteem—or to *the threat of the dissolution of the self*" (p. 109, italics added).

The imperative to preserve the self at all costs as a superordinate psychological center organizing personal experience and imbuing it with unconscious meaning is a basic premise behind the thinking of Freud, Simmel, Kardiner, Kohut, and Atwood and Stolorow. It is also a basic premise of our self psychological theory of trauma. The connection between Freud's thinking and our own is apparent in the following observation by Freud (1916–17): "It may happen, too, that a person is brought so completely to stop by *a traumatic event which shatters the foundations of his life* that he abandons all interest in the present and future and remains permanently absorbed in mental concentration upon the past" (p. 276, italics added).

Abraham, Ferenczi, and Simmel also have made important contributions to the psychoanalytic theory of war neurosis as a narcissistic trauma. For example, Abraham (1921) contends:

> Many of the neurotically disposed persons, up to the moment when the trauma upsets them, have supported themselves only through *an illusion connected with their narcissism, namely, through the belief in their immortality and invulnerability.* . . . The effect of an explosion, a wound, or things of a like nature suddenly destroys this belief. *The narcissistic security gives way to a feeling of powerlessness and neurosis sets in* [pp. 25–6, italics added].

In a similar vein, Ferenczi (1916–1917) writes, that in the case of war neurosis "we are dealing . . . with an ego-injury, *an injury to self-love, to narcissism*" (p. 141, italics added). Ferenczi points out, however, that "it is not absolutely necessary to suppose that the self-love of all these war neurotics was so greatly exaggerated as this. A corresponding severe trauma can, in so-called normal people, have an equally *shattering* effect upon their self-confidence . . ." (p. 137, italics added). In this passage, Ferenczi argues that, given enough combat stress, all soldiers are narcissistically vulnerable to trauma. In a statement remarkably in keeping with our self psychological theory of trauma, Ferenczi (1930) observes that "the immediate effect of a trauma which cannot be dealt with at once is *fragmentation*" (p. 230, italics added).

The importance of the study of Futterman and Pumpian-Mindlin (1951) lies in its serving as a body of work linking Abraham's (1921) idea of the loss of the illusions of immortality and invulnerability to our concept of the shattering and faulty restoration of archaic narcissistic fantasies. Among a patient group of World War II veterans, Futterman and Pumpian-Mindlin account for the vulnerability to combat neurosis on the basis of the shattering of an "illusion of inviolability. . . . These individuals, who could not live for any length of time with their anxieties, entered service with the feeling that nothing could happen to them. We found in them the 'illusion of inviolability' that made them particularly vulnerable to even minor wounds, *which shattered their illusion"* (p. 406, italics added).

In his contribution to the 1918 psychoanalytic symposium on war neurosis, Simmel (1921) stated: "The *unconscious meaning of the symptoms of the war neurotics* . . . is for the most part of *a non-sexual nature*, there being exhibited in them all those war-produced affects of terror, anxiety, rage, etc. associated with ideas corresponding with the actual occurrences of the war" (p. 32, italics added). In this statement Simmel appears to be hinting at Freud's distinction between anxiety neurosis, based on fantasy, and traumatic neurosis, based on reality. At this point, Simmel does not explicate the "non-sexual nature" of the "unconscious meaning of the symptoms of the war neurotics."

Simmel does return, however, to Freud's critical concept of the conflict between the "old peaceful ego" and its "parasitic double," the "new warlike one." Consistent with Freud's later thinking on this matter, Simmel views the division within the ego not as a conflict but as "splitting of the personality" (p. 33). He also introduces two other important concepts: the "complete breakdown of the ego" (p.43) as a result of traumatic combat experiences, and, the posttraumatic process of "neurotic healing" (p. 33) or "self-healing" (p.37) as reflected in recurrent traumatic nightmares. These concepts represent Simmel's initial attempt to formulate, in classical psychoanalytic terms, a version of our self-psychological theory of the traumatic shattering and faulty restoration of central organizing fantasies as underlying the symptoms of PTSD.

However, it was not until his 1944 piece, "War Neurosis," that Simmel expanded on his earlier statement about the "non-sexual nature" of the "unconscious meaning of the symptoms of the war neurotics." In this piece, Simmel discusses "narcissistic traumata" (p. 237) and "narcissistic conflicts" (p. 227) constituted by the ego's "struggle for its psychological maintenance" and "inner coherence" (p. 240) as the basis for war neurosis. Anticipating the later work of Zetzel (1965, 1973) as well as others, Simmel suggests that the critical unconscious meaning of the trauma of war resides not in the threat of physical existence but in the threat to psychological being. The latter threat arises from the "narcissistic injuries" and "narcissistic woundings" (p. 235) suffered by the "military ego"(p. 237) of the combat soldier.

We previously referred to Simmel in our analysis of the vicissitudes of narcissism during adolescence as a basis for understanding the unconscious meaning of combat trauma. We noted that he saw the "degree of maturity of the soldier's superego" as critical in determining "if and to what degree his ego can withstand narcissistic injuries without disintegration of its mental system" (p. 235). Simmel argues that the *"narcissistic equilibrium"* of those combat soldiers suffering from traumatic war neurosis "broke down under the flood of affects—particularly those of anxiety and rage" (p. 233, italics added).

Simmel hints at Kohut's (1972) later distinction between aggression and narcissistic rage. Simmel (1944) maintains that the rage leading to the "breakdown" of the soldier's "narcissistic equilibrium" arises from blows to his self-esteem suffered at the hands of his superiors (pp. 237–8). He explains that "as soon as the superior *hurts the soldier's self-esteem and inflicts narcissistic injuries upon his ego,* this superior also assumes the role of the hated father" (pp. 237–8, italics added). On the basis of this unconscious equation, the "soldier is tempted to kill his superior, instead of the enemy of his country" (p. 238). (The unusually high number of "fraggings," that is, the killing of American field officers by their own troops, during the Vietnam war is a sad confirmation of the accuracy of Simmel's observation. For a discussion of fraggings, see Moskos, Jr., 1975; De Fazio, 1978; Boulanger and Kadushin, 1986, p. 23.)

The soldier's temptation to kill his own superior officer in a fit of narcissistic rage accounts, Simmel maintains, for the conflict between the soldier's "military ego" and his superego. This potentially ego-disintegrating conflict is further intensified, according to Simmel, because the "war neurotic can bring about a transformation of affects, if he can turn anxiety into rage and aggressive action" (p. 243). The latter serves as a way for his ego to "find its way back to reality" (p. 243). Our representative case studies of Vietnam combat veterans illustrate that narcissistic rage is not simply a disintegration product (Kohut, 1977, p. 121) of the shattering of archaic narcissistic fantasies. As implied by Simmel, it is also indicative of the faulty effort at self-restitution.

At this point, it is necessary to mention that Simmel relies on the classical psychoanalytic "fixation/regression and defense" model of narcissism. This limits his otherwise brilliant analysis of war neurosis as a narcissistic trauma. His use of this model defines narcissism as a pathological state in adults.

This view is reflected, for example, in Simmel's (1944) assertion that: "The more the soldier's ego had previously *regressed to a state of narcissistic infantility,* the less was a concrete offense necessary to affect the military ego as trauma" (p. 236, italics added). According to Simmel, "soldiers are *mentally predisposed to narcissistic traumata* if, before entering the military service, they still have been carrying in their unconscious the *residues of an unresolved Oedipus complex"* (p. 237, italics added). The predisposition to "narcissistic traumata," based on "residues of an unresolved Oedipus complex," is evident in a "tendency" to rely on a pathological narcissistic defense. Simmel contends that "this 'military ego' has a tendency to employ a defense reaction—essential in psychoses—to 'break with reality' and *to withdraw all instinctual cathexes from the outside world and take refuge in narcissistic conditions"* (p. 233, italics added).

Views on narcissism similar to those of Simmel have led to the erroneous idea that only those combat soldiers with underlying and serious character pathology are vulnerable to trauma and breakdown. We present our three representative case studies of PTSD in Vietnam combat veterans in support of our contention that if subjected to enough stress, most persons are vulnerable to trauma, as evidenced in fragmentation and disintegration. We contend that the degree of developmental transformation of central organizing fantasies of self in relation to selfobject determines in each individual soldier the amount of combat stress necessary to precipitate traumatic fragmentation and disintegration.

Later (see chapter 6), in the discussion of our analytic approach to trauma treatment, we return to Simmel's work. More specifically, we discuss his ideas on the war neurotic's attempt at "self-cure" and the therapist's need to help the "soldier to liquidate the war psychologically—i.e., to *retransform* his 'war ego' into a 'peace ego' " (Simmel, 1944, p. 247, italics added).

The pioneering work of Kardiner (Kardiner and Spiegel, 1947) has been extremely influential in the psychoanalytic study of combat trauma. However, we want to focus on a little discussed aspect of his work, namely, his formulation of a view of combat neurosis as a traumatic disturbance of sense of self. Kardiner sees combat trauma as a "break in a previously well-integrated pattern of adaptation" (p. 179). This break in adaptation involves a "primary pathological process and a secondary restitutive effort" (p. 179). The primary pathologic process consists of the overwhelming of the soldier's ego by fear of annihilation, resulting in the destruction of "illusions of invulnerability" (pp. 183–5). Such overwhelming fear, accompanied by the loss of self-protective illusions of invulnerability leads, according to Kardiner, to the fragmentation and disintegration of the ego and its "action systems" (p. 218). Kardiner refers to this as the "traumatized ego" (p. 190).

The "secondary restitutive effort" is reflected in the soldier's attempt to restore a previous sense of self through a variety of "defense, substitutive and compensatory efforts" (p. 310). Such attempts include a "series of protective inhibitions and a process of *'narcissistic' with-drawal* from the world" (p. 292, italics added). All efforts at restitution ultimately fail, Kardiner insists, because the soldier "carries the traumatic situation within him at all times and cannot rid himself of it" (p. 189). They also fail because the "comeback" is attempted "on the basis of the now reduced personality with only partial return of normal (pretraumatic) personality" (p. 186–7).

Viewed in terms of the "primary pathologic process and secondary restitutive effort," combat trauma constitutes for Kardiner a failure to preserve the self. In revising Freud's instinctual theory of the "self-preservative instincts" to be consistent with his adaptational theory, Kardiner argues:

> Instincts do not occur in pure culture; they are all clothed in action. What we do observe are functioning units in the interest of a drive. These functioning units are either effectual or ineffectual in attaining *the goal of "self-preservation."* There are only a *series of highly coordinated activities toward the end of self-preservation* [p. 313, italics added].

Kardiner concludes that "what we see in the traumatic neurosis is the failure of these units" (p. 313). In other words, traumatic neurosis is the failure to preserve the self as a set of functioning units and activities.

We see in Kardiner's work his anticipation of many important features of our self-psychological theory. He views traumatic neurosis as the failure to preserve the self. Such a failure is reflected in a "primary pathologic process and secondary restitutive effort." His views parallel our self-psychological conception of PTSD as the shattering and faulty restoration of central organizing fantasies of self in relation to selfobject.

However, Kardiner, like Simmel, succumbs to a limited classical psychoanalytic conception of narcissism. We indicated that Kardiner, in discussing the unsuccessful restitutive effort, embraces the idea of the pathological narcissistic defense by withdrawal from the object world. In fact, Kardiner declares that "if we were to use the criteria of the libido theory all we could say about the traumatic neurosis is that it represents *a fixation on the narcissistic phase of development and a regression to that stage*" (p. 313, italics added). Thus, although significantly advancing the psychoanalytic theory of traumatic neurosis, Kardiner is constrained by a classical psychoanalytic conception of narcissism. This prevents him from recognizing that the trauma of combat constitutes a disturbance in the development of sense of self as reflected in the transformation of archaic into mature forms of narcissism.

The investigation of PTSD in Vietnam combat veterans has resulted in published reports on almost all aspects of the disorder. (However, well-documented and longitudinal studies demonstrating successful treatment of the underlying disorder rather than its symptoms are still rare.) The work of three major figures has blazed the path followed by others. They are Robert J. Lifton (1972a, b, 1973, 1975, 1976; Lifton and Olson, 1976), Chaim Shatan (1973, 1977, 1985) and Mardi Horowitz (1969, 1973, 1974, 1975, 1976; Horowitz and Becker, 1972; Horowitz, Wilner, Kaltreider, and Alvarez, 1980). Later we discuss the details of Lifton's and Shatan's work. However, before proceeding, we first want to allude briefly to Horowitz's work. (We return again to Horowitz in the discussion of our self-psychological approach to treatment in chapter 6.)

In a 1975 article co-authored with George Solomon, Horowitz touches on the topic of archaic narcissism. In discussing what they correctly predicted would be a national outbreak of delayed forms of stress response syndromes (that is, PTSD) in returning Vietnam combat veterans, they (1975) argue that many of these veterans were particularly vulnerable to "narcissistic injury" to their self-image (p. 74). Horowitz and Solomon indicate that these veterans had attempted to compensate for their narcissistic injuries with secret "grandiose fantasies" intensified by the use of powerful, mind-blowing hallucinogenic drugs. Once back in the States, where these drugs were far more expensive and difficult to obtain, these veterans found it increasingly difficult to shore up damaged self-esteem with grandiose fantasies (p. 74). This was a major factor in the emergence of delayed stress response syndromes.

There can be no denying the accuracy of Horowitz and Solomon's prediction about the outbreak of delayed stress response syndrome (PTSD) in a large number of the veterans returning from the Vietnam war. And their focus on "narcissistic injury" and grandiose fantasies is in line with our self-psychological theory. However, the implicit view of narcissism adopted by Horowitz and Solomon falls within the classical psychoanalytic "fixation/regression and defense" model.

Horowitz helped to promote the erroneous idea that those soldiers with particular underlying narcissistic character disorders were more vulnerable than others to combat trauma. This was evident by the regression to narcissistic points of developmental fixation. Horowitz's work failed, therefore, to advance the more accurate idea that in the context of the hallucinatory and surreal nature of combat in Vietnam, all soldiers were, relatively speaking, equally vulnerable to narcissistic trauma. Such trauma resulted in the failure to complete the developmental process of transforming adolescent narcissism into a mature sense of self.

Lifton developed a clinical research methodology, "articulated" or "disciplined subjectivity" (1973) as a guide for conducting his "depth-psychological research interviews" (1976). Lifton's "articulated" or "disciplined subjectivity" and use of "depth-psychological research interviews" parallels our methodology of the applied psychoanalytic technique of vicarious interpretation (see chapter 1).

In addition to his clinical research methodology, Lifton also constructed a theoretical model to assist him in gathering and analyzing his basically unstructured research data. Lifton (1973) refers to his theoretical framework as the "psychoformative model" (p. 424). Lifton uses this model to trace the "evolution of inner forms and . . . the specifically human mental process of inwardly re-creating all that is perceived or encountered" (p. 424). He emphasizes that his model focuses on the "formative symbolic process" and "symbolization rather than any particular symbol" (p. 424).

We see important connections between the focus of Lifton's model and that of our self-psychological theory. We equate the "formative symbolic process" with central organizing fantasies of self in relation to selfobject. These are the fantasmagorical meaning structures that organize experience and imbue it with personal signficance.

Through the use of his psychoformative model, Lifton (1973) was able to understand the "disintegrative experiences in Vietnam" (p. 285). These experiences are characterized by the psychological clash of the "John Wayne thing" and the "Gook syndrome" with "death immersion" or "death imprint" (p. 187). Beginning in boot camp and continuing in combat, the "John Wayne thing" consists, according to Lifton, of the "death of the civilian self and its rebirth as a new military self" (p. 187). In this instance, Lifton invokes an idea similar to the Freudian (1919) conflict between the "old peaceful ego" and its "parasitic double," the "new warlike one" (p. 209).

As part of his "death" and "rebirth," the adolescent male recruit undergoes a metamorphosis and assumes a new identity as a warrior. According to Lifton, this warrior identity is based on "violence-prone-super-maleness" and "hyperaggressive, numbed, omnipotent maleness" (pp. 242, 245, 250, 255). As a warrior, the soldier fantasizes himself as an invulnerable and impenetrable "killing machine."

The "Gook syndrome," which also begins in boot camp and continues in combat, involves the dehumanization of all Asians—civilian noncombatants and combatants alike. They become "tainted" with death. This is in marked contrast to the "immortalizing grandeur of a soldier's own group" (Lifton, 1972b, p. 66.) We view both the "John Wayne thing" and the "Gook syndrome" as indicative of the unhealthy inflation of archaic narcissistic fantasies of self in relation to selfobject.

At the same time that the American soldier experiences the intense emotional high generated by the inflation of volatile and unstable adolescent male fantasies, he is also subject to the countervailing experience of "death immersion" or "death imprint." Lifton (1975) defines this experience in terms of the "impact of death"and the "loss of a sense of invulnerability" (p. 182). According to Lifton, such a dramatic and sudden "loss of a sense of invulnerability" precipitates a crisis in personal meaning. Lifton and Olson (1976) characterize such a crisis as the "loss of vitality, the depression, and despair of human beings no longer able to give inner form to their lives" (p. 17). Lifton (1976) concludes that "one comes to feel *the self disintegrating* at moments when one's inner forms and images become inadequate representations of the self-world relationship and inadequate basis for action" (p. 38, italics added).

We view the experience of "death immersion" and "death imprint" as reflective of the sudden and dramatic deflation of just recently inflated archaic narcissistic fantasies. In the mind of the soldier, the "John Wayne thing" and the "Gook syndrome" clash violently with "death immersion," creating what we have referred to as a psychologically devastating narcissistic vortex. We equate Lifton's crisis in personal meaning with faulty efforts at restoring shattered archaic narcissistic fantasies.

We conclude our interpretive commentary on combat neurosis or PTSD as narcissistic trauma with a brief discussion of the work of Parson and Brende. In their earlier individual works (see, for example, Parson, 1981, 1984a, b; Brende, 1982, 1983; Brende and Benedict, 1980; Brende and McCann, 1984) and their more recent collaborative work (see Brende and Parson, 1985), both Parson and Brende have utilized self psychology in illuminating the traumatic disturbance in sense of self that they see as the core of PTSD.

In discussing "post-Vietnam traumatic states" (Parson, 1981, p. 18), Parson, for example, remarks: "For a large number of Vietnam veterans, the issues of *narcissistic vulnerability and narcissistic rage* represent core intrapsychic and interpersonal problems of significant import" (p. 21, italics added). In this context, Brende and Parson respectively describe combat in Vietnam in terms of the "fragmentation experience on the self" (Brende, 1983, p. 198) and the "fragmentation of the self" (Parson, 1984, p. 12). Both see such a fragmentation experience leading to PTSD as a disorder characterized by severe self pathology.

According to Parson (1981), "fragmentation of the self" results in "splits in self-concepts" with "self-units" behaving "autonomously, creating chaos, internal disorganization, confusional states, identity fragmentation . . . and psychosocial disorders" (p. 15). We have described the "fragmentation of the self" as the shattering and faulty restoration of central organizing fantasies of self in relation to selfobject. In line with our position, Parson suggests that the Vietnam combat veteran suffering from the dissociative symptoms of PTSD can be helped "to restore what has been lost" (1981, p. 34) as a means of aiding the " *'shattered' self* in its recovery from trauma" (1984, p. 12, italics added).

In describing the Vietnam combat veteran's reaction to the "fragmentation experience on the self," Brende (1983) uses concepts similar to our own. For instance, he speaks about the Vietnam combat veteran's "defensive reactivation of an omnipotent grandiose self," (p. 213) "defensive idealization of aggression," (p. 212) and "counterdependent or omnipotent survival behavior" (p. 212) other "omnipotent, narcissistic traits" (p. 208) including "devaluation of fear and helplessness" (p. 212). According to Brende and McCann (1984) all of these "traits" are part of an "omnipotent aggressive defense in opposition to the hidden victim introject" (p. 64). It can be inferred from Brende's writings that such an "omnipotent aggressive defense" is based on the "experience of pleasure in killing when it was associated with *invincability and omnipotent fantasies* (pp. 61–2, italics added).

Traumatic War Neurosis or PTSD as a Dissociative Disorder

The origins of the idea that traumatic war neurosis, or PTSD, is a dissociative disorder can be found in Freud's writings. We have already described his conception of traumatic combat neurosis as a split between the "old peaceful ego" and its "parasitic double," the "new warlike one." In two short essays published just prior to and after his death, Freud elaborated the thesis that trauma entails dissociative splits in the ego, or "self."

In "A Disturbance of Memory on the Acropolis" (1936), he introduced "depersonalization" and "derealization" as the two unconscious ego mechanisms of defense involved in dissociative ego splits. According to Freud, these phenomena "are to be observed in two forms: the subject feels either that a piece of reality or that *a piece of his own self* is strange to him. . . . "In the latter case we speak of 'depersonalization'; derealizations and depersonalizations are intimately connected" (p. 245, italics added).

These passages reveal that Freud conceived of both depersonalization and derealization as pathological disturbances in the subjective sense of self (Stern, 1985) and experience of reality. We link Freud's view to our self-psychological conception of PTSD as a dissociative disorder caused by the shattering and faulty restoration of archaic narcissistic fantasies.

In his 1936 essay, Freud asserts: "Depersonalization leads us on to the extraordinary condition of 'double conscience' (= dual consciousness) which is more correctly described as 'split personality' (p. 245). In a posthumously published essay, Freud (1940) links such dissociative disturbances or splits in personality to trauma. He states: "We can assign in general and somewhat vague terms the conditions under which this comes about, by saying that it occurs under the influence of *a psychical trauma*" (p. 275, italics added).

Stating later in the same essay that "psychical trauma" causes a "splitting in the ego," Freud notes that "the *synthetic function of the ego* though it is of such extraordinary importance, is subject to particular conditions and *is liable to a whole number of disturbances*" (p. 276, italics added). We see similarities between the Freudian "synthetic function of the ego" and the self psychological concept of central organizing fantasies. The latter, like the synthetic function of the ego, although of "extraordinary importance," are "liable to a whole number of disturbances" such as their traumatic shattering and faulty restoration. Such disturbances in the experience of self (mental and physical) are reflected in dissociative states of depersonalization, derealization, and disembodiment exemplified by the reexperiencing and numbing symptoms of PTSD.

On the basis of extensive clinical experience with psychiatric casualties of World War II, Fisher (1945, 1947) published two articles in which he advanced his theory of combat neurosis as a traumatic alteration of personal identity. According to Fisher (1945) it consists of a temporary "break with reality" marked by fugue states including "hallucinations and delusions" (pp. 464–5). Such temporary fuguelike breaks with reality (in contrast to psychotic breaks) involve the enactment of unconscious fantasies intended to defend against and compensate for the traumatic alteration of personal identity (p.450). Fisher suggests that "in the fugue the patient indulges in acts or *fantasies* which are in conflict with his superego and *the function of the fugue is to permit the carrying out of these acts or fantasies* (p. 459, italics added). The enactment of these fantasies represents a faulty effort at the "restoration of personal identity" (p. 440).

As evidence of this unconscious process, Fisher offers a number of clinical examples. For instance, he reports the case of a young soldier suffering from combat neurosis, who, in his fugue states, fantasizes himself as a hero in battle. Under hypnosis, however, this soldier revealed that he had been so terrified during battle that he "blacked out" (pp. 441–6). Apparently, this constituted a traumatic blow to his masculine pride because he felt that "blacking out" was a sign of cowardliness. In the midst of fuguelike or dissociative episodes, in which he relived this traumatic experience, he fantasized being a fearless warrior, thus attempting unconsciously to defend himself against the disturbing memory of cowardliness.

Fisher's work, as exemplified by the preceding clinical vignette, represents a precursor to our self-psychological theory of PTSD as a dissociative disorder involving the shattering and faulty restoration of archaic narcissistic fantasies. In fact, Fisher (1945) addresses the need for a theory like ours. He thinks it likely that "fugues can no longer be considered as simple hysterical conversions; *they would appear to represent a more serious type of disorder* (p. 465, italics added). He does not believe, however, that "fugues are explicable in terms of the usual concepts of ego and superego; that ultimately *other operational principles* will have to be utilized when we know more about fugues (p. 466, italics added). We believe that our self-psychological theory of traumatic shattering and faulty restoration illuminates these "other operational principles."

By now a vast literature has emerged about PTSD as well as related psychiatric and psychosocial disorders in Vietnam combat veterans. A number of recent studies (see for example, Alacorn et al., 1982; Hendin et al., 1984; Burstein, 1985; Milman and Davis, 1985; Kline and Rausch, 1985; Blank, 1985) have reported on PTSD reliving symptoms in Vietnam combat veterans. (One of the authors [RBU] has been actively involved in this research. See, for example, the research reported in Hendin et al., 1984, pp. 169–70, involving this author's treatment of a Vietnam combat veteran subject to PTSD reliving episodes.) We believe that reliving episodes is particularly consistent with our self psychological theory of PTSD as a dissociative disorder. Our theory is also supported by Jaffe (1968), who described the Nazi Holocaust "survivor syndrome" as a "traumatically acquired personality change" (p. 310) involving "hypnoid dissociative states," (p. 310) "reccurring hysteri-form twilight states," (p. 311) and "dissociative reactions, during which traumatic experiences emerge" (p. 311).

The work of Blank (1985) is a synthesis of the ideas of Jaffe and Fisher. In describing "unconscious flashbacks" (reliving experiences) in Vietnam combat veterans suffering from PTSD, he speculates that either *"archaic levels of ego development* are activated, and infantile traumas from the time of first good–bad object differentiation are evoked, or that *healthy psychic structures* previously adequate for such differentiation in ordinary living are undermined" (p. 307, italics added). Blank, Jr. concludes: "There is in these cases an acting-out of complex unconscious conflicts, *fantasies*, and impulses. There is a seeking for abreaction and perhaps also an element of repetition *in search of mastery*" (p. 304, italics added).

We include Blank's ideas about the traumatic activation of archaic psychic levels and the undermining of "healthy psychic structures" in our theory of the shattering of archaic narcissistic fantasies. In this context, we view the "acting out of . . . fantasies" and "repetition in search of mastery" as faulty efforts to restore shattered fantasmagorical meaning structures.

In addition to the studies of Blank and others, the works of Shatan (1977, 1985) as well as Brende (1983; Brende and Benedict, 1980) and Parson (1984) are particularly relevant to our commentary on literature on PTSD as a dissociative disorder. In Zetzel's (1965) discussion of the "narcissistic injury" leading to both depression and war neurosis, she observes that it may result in "primitive responses impairing the perception of reality" (pp. 252–3). Shatan's (1972) work on the "post-Vietnam syndrome" represents an elaboration and substantiation of Zetzel's important observation.

Shatan (1977) argues that the adolescent combat soldier in Vietnam underwent a virtual "transfiguration" of personality (p. 601). According to Shatan (1985), this transfiguration is based on the "penetrating of the membrane between two realities," that is, the sense of reality organized in accordance with peaceful civilian experiences and that organized on the basis of traumatic combat experiences (p. 14). He quotes a Vietnam combat medic as recalling that "in an ambush he had 'to permit . . . old reality to slide away . . . through a membrane' " (p. 14).

Shatan's ideas about the transfiguration of the soldier's civilian reality into a new, combat reality is similar to Freud's notion of a "new warlike" ego serving as a "parasitic double" for the "old peaceful ego." Shatan's notion also resembles Simmel's (1944) "splitting of the personality" in the form of the new "military ego," Kardiner's (Kardiner and Spiegel, 1947) "traumatized ego," and Lifton's reborn warrior. For example, Shatan echoes Kardiner, who spoke about the combat soldier's inability to escape from the trauma because he carries it "within him at all times" (p. 189). Shatan (1985) observes that "the emotional context of catastrophe persists after the trauma seems over. And this wounded ego has to cope with *the traumatic sense of reality*" (p. 12, italics added). Or, coming closer to our own self-psychological theory of traumatic shattering, Shatan points out: "Massive psychic trauma clothes survivors with a perforated, tattered, sometimes even *shattered ego* (p. 12, italics added).

Echoing Zetzel (1965) Shatan (1985) notes that after "penetrating the 'membrane' between the realities, perceptions of events is utterly changed" (p. 14). According to Shatan: "The individual adopts the paranoid stance and mentality of survival in combat. . . . Styles of action, affect and cognition are transformed. Even when the stress ends, a return to the status quo is unlikely. Each survivor's inner world is still permeated with traumatic reality" (p. 14).

Adopting a clinical perspective consistent with the empathic-introspective observational stance (Kohut, 1977, p. 309), Shatan (1985) writes:

> The new overriding mentality is paranoid only in the eyes of outsiders, outsiders who have never . . . needed to kick an adversary in the face to live. A flash of combat may alter someone's life forever. Haunting experiences are woven into the tapestry of these lives: from the vantage point of the other reality there is no deficit in thinking, and no inappropriate behavior [p. 14].

The psychologically disruptive "clash" between two opposed "reality perception systems" leads, Shatan maintains, to "perceptual dissonance" involving selective dissociation of "vast territories of experience" (p. 14). In Shatan's theoretical schema, "perceptual dissonance" and selective dissociation account for the severe and chronic disturbance in subjectivity manifested in pathological "breakthroughs (flashbacks)" and "breakdowns (syndromes)" (p. 17). Coming to a position similar to our own, Shatan concludes that as a result of such dissociative disturbances in perception and subjectivity, the soldier's postcombat "adaptive lifestyle is 'dedicated' to defending *the delicate organization of the survivor's self*" (p. 17, italics added).

Finally, in terms similar to our theory, both Brende and Parson characterize PTSD in Vietnam combat veterans as a dissociative disorder. For instance, Brende (1983) notes that: "Vietnam veterans exhibited aggressively protective behavior that resulted from *splitting off or dissociating the unacceptable self-experiences of vulnerability and fear*" (p. 211, italics added). Or, to take another example, Parson (1984) maintains that "combat stress pathology forms an 'autonomous' *split-off* mental organization of its own that, at primitive psychic levels, participate in the general personality of the individual, but in non-integrated, non-ego coordinated fashion (hence, the *split-off, dissociated phenomena* of flashbacks and other incursive, automatic ideas and feelings)" (p. 15, italics added).

REPRESENTATIVE CASES

Chuck (alias "Sharky")

Chuck is an extremely tall, large, muscular man in his mid-thirties. Despite his pleasant, almost babyish face, he usually appeared for his interviews with a haunted expression in his eyes. He often stared off into space as if lost in reverie. He drank large quantities of coffee and chain smoked throughout the therapeutic interviews, which, with several extended breaks, stretched over two years.

Chuck seemed quite intelligent and verbal, yet guarded during the early interviews. While his account of his combat tour was sketchy and vague, he did report several particularly upsetting incidents. In talking about these episodes, he sometimes broke into laughter or sobbed, quickly regained his composure, and then resumed his account as if unaware of his emotional outburst.

Chuck described his life before combat as follows. He and a younger sister, both of whom had been adopted as infants, grew up in an upper middle class family in a suburban neighborhood outside a large north-eastern city. Chuck's father was a successful hospital administrator; his mother was a housewife, who was very active as a volunteer in community and church charities. Chuck declared that although an outside observer might see his family as ideal, it was far from ideal to him.

Because as a child he was painfully self-conscious and physically awkward, Chuck remembers finding it difficult to relate to his peers. He described his parents as extremely controlling and insensitive to his needs and feelings. He was constantly "jerked" about from one place and organization to another. For example, he was forced to join a church youth group, the Boy Scouts, and other local youth organizations, without being asked if he wanted to participate in these groups. In a poignant description of his sense of impotence and lack of control over even his physical movements, Chuck recalled feeling as if he were a "puppet with my parents as the puppeteers pulling my strings."

Chuck reported that his childhood miseries worsened during early adolescence. He matured physically very early and was much taller and bigger than his peers. He noted that his physical size and strength made him feel powerful and special in relation to his pals. However, it also created considerable problems for Chuck.

Unaware of the extent of his superior strength, Chuck seriously hurt several other boys during fist fights. "Feeling my oats," as Chuck described it, he also became unruly in class and disrespectful towards his teachers. With hindsight he realized that "I had become too big for my own britches." However, at the time he lacked this self-awareness and had little control over himself and his actions.

School authorities apparently lost patience with Chuck, expelled him, and brought juvenile charges against him. The juvenile court ruled that he be enrolled in either a private school or a state facility for disturbed adolescents. For reasons that he still does not understand, Chuck's parents had him institutionalized in the state facility.

Miserable at this institution, Chuck ran away and returned home, only to have his parents bring him back. He immediately ran away again, vowing to maintain his freedom.

Forsaking his parents and home, Chuck hitchhiked to Florida, where he adopted an alias, "Sharky." From the ages of 13 to 16, Chuck assumed the identity of and created a lifestyle for himself based on his fantasy of Sharky. Chuck imagined Sharky as much older, more streetwise and savvy than himself, "a guy who knew how to take care of himself and get what he wanted." Chuck explained that by posing as a mature and sophisticated young adult in his mid-twenties, he managed to get a variety of jobs, rent his own apartment with a roommate, and establish friendships with older men and relationships with older women. In fact, Chuck exclaimed that his masquerade as Sharky was so successful that he was promoted to assistant manager of the sporting goods department of a large retail store.

Chuck expressed great sorrow at losing the opportunity to continue to live out his fantasy as Sharky. He explained that just at the height of his fantasy existence, he was arrested and jailed when his roommate was "busted" for possession and distribution of drugs. In the course of running a routine background check on their prisoner, the authorities discovered that Sharky was actually a runaway juvenile named Chuck. Following Chuck's confirmation of this fact, the Florida authorities dropped all charges against him and returned him to the custody of his parents.

In spite of finding home and school boring, especially in comparison to three exciting years as Sharky, Chuck said that he managed to resume a typical teenage existence. He made some new friends, dated, and joined the high school marching band as a tuba player. However, during his senior year, Chuck was suspended after he was caught with alcohol on a school bus en route to a football game.

Despondent and fearing that he would never graduate from school, Chuck enlisted in the Army. He tried out for the Army marching band but failed his audition. As his second choice, he was assigned to an airborne ranger unit, where he received special training as a paratrooper. Chuck underwent basic and advanced infantry training during the summer months of 1967; he received paratrooper training from September through October of the same year.

Initially Chuck was disappointed about failing to get into the Army marching band; however, his training as a member of an elite airborne ranger unit more than compensated for his disappointment. Chuck described the first time he parachuted from a plane. He remembered feeling that he could literally fly; he fantasized about himself as Superman, possessing superhuman strength and powers. His Superman fantasies were fueled by the special treatment he received from the other recruits, who were awed by his status as an airborne ranger. Chuck said that he had not felt so "full of myself" since his days as Sharky.

Under the sway of his highly inflated adolescent male fantasies of grandiose omnipotence, Chuck arrived in Vietnam at the end of 1967. He remained there until the middle of 1969, after spending his first year with an airborne ranger unit seeing action in the dense and mountainous jungles of South Vietnam's Central Highlands. Chuck explained that he served in Vietnam for more than the usual 12 months because he extended his "in country" tour of duty in order to receive an early discharge from the service. After being withdrawn from active combat during his extended tour, he was promoted to the rank of sergeant and reassigned as a medical records clerk at an enemy POW hospital camp.

Chuck was exposed to the horrors of combat almost immediately upon arriving in Vietnam. While he was awaiting assignment to his field unit, enemy forces broke through the perimeter of the staging area and launched a surprise attack against the American forces. Enemy soldiers ran through the staging area, shooting startled American soldiers as they tried to duck for cover. The enemy forces also blew up several large ammunition dumps, sending massive shock waves and shrapnel through the area. Chuck described the scene as one of chaos and pandemonium.

Although the enemy forces were eventually repulsed, they blew up key structures, wounding and killing many American soldiers who had just arrived in Vietnam. Chuck still has vivid memories of staring, dazed and shocked, at the wounded and dying as they screamed for help. Sighing, he said that he could not believe what had happened. It was as if he were having a bad dream or nightmare. All at once, he felt his Superman fantasy slipping away. It was replaced by painful feelings of being exposed, vulnerable, and defenseless.

Having barely survived his first encounter with the enemy, Chuck received his permanent combat unit assignment and went into the field or "bush." Once again, Chuck was immediately thrust into the middle of the fighting. The first night that he was in the field, Chuck and his unit engaged the enemy in a firefight during a patrol into the mountainous jungles of the Central Highlands. Caught in an ambush, Chuck and his patrol were pinned down and surrounded on top of a hill. Outnumbered and facing certain death, Chuck's platoon leader radioed for artillery and air support. Chuck said that he remembers "as if it happened yesterday" lying on the ground as the artillery shells and bombs exploded and napalm burned all around him. Chuck was convinced that either he would be blown to bits or incinerated.

Chuck reported that "I flipped out" under this intense gunfire and bombing. Describing himself as having "gone mad," he felt capable of superhuman feats "just like Superman." He started firing madly in the direction of the enemy. He imagined that the bullets fired from his M-16 automatic rifle were actually going through tree trunks and blowing off the heads of enemy soldiers. Chuck claims that during this particular firefight he killed three enemy soldiers. He was overwhelmed by a "crazed feeling of power."

During a night "OP" (outpost), Chuck and several comrades set up an ambush with Claymore mines, fragmentation grenades, and trip flares. They climbed up trees to positions well above the killing range of the explosives. Hidden safely in their treetop perches, they waited in the dark for enemy soldiers to set off the explosives.

After several hours of waiting, Chuck noted that the ground below was suddenly illuminated by the light of the trip flares. In the glare of this light, Chuck saw the startled and shocked expressions on the faces of the enemy soldiers. Looking directly into their terror-stricken faces, Chuck slammed down the plunger of the detonator box. Chuck described in graphic and gory detail watching spellbound as the powerful explosion blew the bodies of the enemy soldiers to bits. He said it was as if the explosion had occurred in slow motion. He saw heads and other body parts flying through the air in a bloody and swirling mess.

The shock waves from the explosion knocked Chuck and his comrades out of their treetop perches. In a macabre scene, Chuck and his comrades lay on the ground laughing deliriously in a "fever-pitched frenzy." Chuck was overcome with a strangely exhilarating feeling of unlimited power over the life and death of others.

In another horrifying incident, Chuck witnessed one soldier from his unit accidentally kill a comrade. Chuck explained that his squad was bivouacked for the night in enemy territory. Each foxhole held four men; to protect against surprise enemy attack each man took a turn standing watch throughout the night. As often happened, one of the men fell asleep during his turn at guard duty. Another man in the foxhole made a sudden noise as he turned in his sleep. Awaking and mistakenly thinking that an enemy soldier had slipped into the foxhole, the guard opened fire, killing his own comrade.

Chuck had been sleeping next to this man and was awakened from his sleep by the sight and sound of bullets ripping through the man's chest. The gunfire alerted enemy soldiers to the American position, and they opened fire on Chuck's squad. During the firefight, a soldier squatting next to Chuck threw a fragmentation grenade at the enemy. Unfortunately, it hit a tree, bounced back at the soldier, and exploded in his face.

In still another bizarre incident, Chuck, who was serving as a radio operator, suddenly lost radio contact with a squad out on patrol. Without success, he desperately and repeatedly tried to reestablish radio contact with the squad. He said the mysterious disappearance of the squad was "eerie and spooky." It was as if they had been plucked from the face of the earth by some supernatural and deadly force.

Chuck reported that this series of events eroded any lingering sense of Superman invulnerability and invincibility. He felt completely at the mercy of malevolent forces over which he had no control. He connected this feeling with his early childhood sense of being a puppet whose strings were pulled by parental puppeteers with little regard for his need to control his own movements.

Chuck was further traumatized by viewing a picture of an American soldier who had been captured, tortured, decapitated, and castrated. Taken by one of the American soldiers who discovered the body, the picture showed this man with his severed head under his own arm and his penis stuffed into his mouth. As a result of viewing this horrifying picture, Chuck said he began having a recurrent nightmare (which continues in the postcombat period) in which he dreamed of himself as the mutilated American soldier.

At about this time, Chuck completed his required tour in Vietnam. Despite his fears and increasing disorientation, he chose to extend his "in country" tour of duty in order to receive an early service discharge. He was aware at the time of extending that those soldiers with previous time in the field who opted for an "in country" tour of duty extension were routinely reassigned to so-called safe positions in the rear.

After returning to Vietnam from a 30-day leave in the States, during which he met and dated his future wife, Chuck began his new assignment as a medical records clerk at the enemy POW hospital camp. The hospital camp housed, treated, and interrogated enemy soldiers who had been wounded and captured. Stationed at the camp during the height of the 1968 enemy TET Offensive, Chuck gradually became suspicious of the American record-keeping system. Chuck explained that the military command in Saigon was under intense pressure from both Washington and the American press to account for the enemy offensive at a time when the command claimed that North Vietnam and the Viet Cong were collapsing and near defeat.

This was the charged atmosphere in which Chuck became convinced of an elaborate plot on the part of American military officials in charge of the enemy POW hospital camp. Chuck claimed that he had discovered that intelligence information gathered from captured and wounded enemy soldiers was being systematically falsified. Instead of accurately reflecting the numbers of enemy forces pouring into the South from the North, the intelligence information grossly underestimated true enemy troop strength.

Convinced that he had uncovered a plot, Chuck confided in a trusted superior about his discovery. However, after no investigation was initiated, Chuck became even more alarmed, now believing that his superior was a conspirator in the plot. Chuck was fearful for his life and felt that "I had bitten off more than I could chew."

In this paranoid and agitated state, Chuck believed that the plotters had tried to assassinate him by putting slivers of glass in his water. Fearing that he would die from internal bleeding, Chuck rushed to the hospital emergency room. No evidence of any glass or bleeding was found.

Despite the absence of any signs of foul play, Chuck clung to his belief in a conspiratorial plot. He adamantly insisted that it had been secretely devised and was overseen by the highest echelons of the Saigon military command. He warned his doctors that the military command was deceiving the American government, press, and people about the Tet Offensive. In view of the dispute between CBS News and General Westmoreland over the issue of deliberate deception about TET, it is hard to assess the accuracy of Chuck's suspicions.

Apparently concerned that Chuck was psychotically paranoid and delusional, his doctors requested a psychiatric consultation. Chuck was found unfit for further active duty and completed his military tour of duty in the States, receiving an honorable discharge from the Army. Chuck reported that the CBS News report on deception surrounding TET only confirmed what he already knew. He remains convinced that his life was in jeopardy as a result of inadvertently uncovering and disclosing "top secret" information about the plot.

Upon discharge from the Army in mid-1970, Chuck returned home and resumed dating his girlfriend; they were married in 1972. According to Chuck, he and his wife had serious emotional problems from the beginning of their marriage. He described his wife as a shy and timid woman who had extreme difficulty in talking about her feelings.

The marriage deteriorated over the next several years despite the births of their two children. Throughout the two-year therapeutic interviewing period, Chuck reported constant difficulty in his marriage. The marriage was marred by violent arguments and an ever widening emotional gulf between Chuck and his wife.

Chuck explained that the arguments with his wife centered on her complaints about his failure to find regular work. Chuck's employment difficulties forced the family to subsist on his wife's meager salary as a legal secretary. They were also forced to borrow money from their parents. Chuck acknowledged that there was a rational and justifiable basis for his wife's complaints, but he deeply resented her failure to understand that he was haunted night and day by Vietnam. Plagued by his memories, he found it extremely difficult to hold a regular job.

Rather than offering him compassionate understanding, Chuck felt that his wife saw him as a "lazy bum and good-for-nothing," who refused to work and support his family. This was an enormous source of shame and humiliation to Chuck. Apparently, these constant blows to his masculine pride left him feeling impotent and filled with narcissistic rage. Although he insisted that he never physically abused his wife or children, Chuck admitted that he often dreamed of killing all three of them and then himself. Chuck's dreams seemed indicative of an intense homicidal and suicidal rage that he found hard to control.

Chuck also reported that he had difficulties relating to co-workers, from whom he felt alienated and estranged. Chuck acknowledged that he had problems concentrating on his work tasks as well as remembering job assignments. In spite of these difficulties, which seriously interfered with his job performance, Chuck insisted that he possessed highly unusual talents and extraordinary skills. Chuck reported that he lost his temper and flew into wild (narcissistic) rages because his gifts were neither appreciated nor acknowledged by his co-workers or bosses. He also spent hours on the job lost in daydreams of blowing up everything and everybody at work.

During one such episode, he claimed to be rigged with explosives and threatened to blow up himself along with others. After subduing and searching him, security personnel discovered that the bomb and detonator were fakes. Chuck observed that this incident captured the desperation and impotent rage that had so consumed him throughout the postcombat period.

Chuck also reported a pattern of serious substance abuse. For varying lengths of time in the postcombat period, Chuck was addicted to a number of drugs and alcohol. He remarked, "Only when I'm high on drugs or booze do I have any peace of mind and tranquility."

Despite a clear pattern of psychiatric problems obviously related to combat in Vietnam, Chuck lamented that prior to his participation in the therapeutic interviews, he never had the chance to discuss with a clinician his traumatic war experiences. It was no surprise therefore that despite manifesting all the classic symptoms of PTSD, he had never been diagnosed as suffering from the dissociative disorder.

Chuck's obsession with combat is one of his reexperiencing symptoms. He is flooded throughout the day with intrusive and flashing images of heads and bodies being blown apart, and bloody masses flying through the air. He is also subject to reliving episodes in which he becomes dissociated and reexperiences traumatic incidents from combat. On several occasions these episodes, usually lasting for several minutes, occurred during the interviews. They seem to have been triggered by discussion of a particularly disturbing incident. During these reliving episodes, Chuck's eyes would glaze over as he muttered to himself, thrashed about wildly, and then yelled out in a blood-curdling scream.

Chuck also suffers from recurrent traumatic nightmares in which he sees himself as the captured and mutilated American soldier. Chuck said that he always awakes screaming from this nightmare. In another thematically similar nightmare, Chuck views himself from within the dream as lying dead in a field:

> I'm dressed in green camouflage fatigues, wearing a combat helmet, and I'm covered with maggots feeding off my rotting flesh.

Chuck has a "sick and hollow" feeling in the nightmare as he stares at his own decomposing corpse. He also associated the image of the maggots eating his flesh with the rage that "eats away at my insides."

In a third recurrent nightmare, he dreams of the incident in which he blew up the enemy soldiers. However, in the nightmare version:

> I cannot push down the detonator plunger to set off the explosives. As I'm struggling to push it down, I see in the light of the trip flare the faces of the enemy soldiers who are lunging menacingly at me.

Chuck and the interviewer connected this nightmare with the frustration and impotent rage that consume him.

Chuck reported a full range of numbing symptoms, including a loss of interest in music and playing his tuba. He also spoke of diminishing enjoyment of sex and being with other people, including his wife, children, parents, and sister. Alienated and estranged from other people, such as co-workers, he lamented his lack of feeling for and connection to them. Chuck resented other people because they were always "testing me to see how far they can push me before I lose my temper and strike out at them."

Finally, Chuck's postcombat history is replete with such other symptoms of PTSD as hyperalertness, startle reaction, sleep disturbance, survivor guilt, problems with concentration and memory, and avoidance of reminders of traumatic combat occurrences, as well as intensification of all these symptoms if exposed to stimuli symbolically connected in Chuck's mind to these events.

Case Summary

An examination of Chuck's early childhood and adolescence points to serious problems in the development of a normal sense of self. It is difficult to determine how much being adopted contributed to these problems. However, his early childhood memory of feeling like a puppet whose strings were pulled by callous parental puppeteers reveals a troubled child who felt powerless to control even his own physical movements. The image of the impotent and hapless puppet and overcontrolling puppeteers conveys Chuck's sense that he functioned as a selfobject for his parents. Chuck's memory may also be understood as a screen memory behind which is the painful recollection of unfulfilled childhood fantasies of exhibitionistic grandiosity.

Chuck's problems worsened during early adolescence. Apparently, once freed from the control of his parental puppeteers, Chuck attempted to defend against his early sense of impotence with a grand show of physical prowess. His inability to appreciate his own strength and to control himself forced school authorities to expel him. His parents' bewildering decision to send him to a state institution left him feeling once again like a puppet on strings.

We may empathically infer that in running away from the state institution and leading the life of Sharky, Chuck was exhibitionistically living out his adolescent fantasies of grandiosity. It appears that the unconscious intent of these fantasies was to defend against a disturbing sense of powerlessness and impotence. Chuck's success in living out this adolescent version of an archaic narcissistic fantasy attests to its unconscious organizing power in his subjective world. As Sharky, Chuck was no longer an impotent puppet who could not control his own physical movements or whereabouts. His life as Sharky was a living testament to his fantasies of grandiose exhibitionism.

Chuck's experiences in boot camp as a recruit for the elite rangers were fertile soil, so to speak, for the intensification of another version of his adolescent fantasies of grandiosity. Receiving training as a paratrooper and learning to fly through the air as a parachutist fueled the embellishment of a highly inflated fantasy of himself as Superman. Chuck had psychologically reorganized himself around a fantasy of himself as Superman, which replaced his previous fantasy of himself as Sharky.

Once in combat, however, Chuck's central yet fragile organizing fantasies shattered. We see signs of this shattering and resulting state of fragmentation in Chuck's panic reaction to witnessing the enemy attack on his base camp as well as his mad frenzy during his first firefight. There is further evidence of this empathic inference in Chuck's bizarre reaction to blowing up the enemy soldiers and his paranoid fears of being assassinated as the discoverer of the plot. Chuck's nightmare of himself as the captured and mutilated American soldier confirms this impression. Chuck's nightmare symbolically depicts in graphic dream imagery his sense of himself as once again impotent (castrated) and mad (beheaded).

Chuck's combat history also reveals unconscious efforts at the defensive yet faulty restoration of these central organizing fantasies. For instance, we see Chuck desperately attempting to restore his adolescent fantasies of grandiosity in his conviction that bullets fired from his M-16 automatic rifle were actually going through tree trunks and blowing off the heads of enemy soldiers. Another example is Chuck's delusional belief that he was an incredibly important and powerful person because he had uncovered and exposed the secret plot.

Evidence of the traumatic shattering and faulty restoration of Chuck's fantasies of himself abounds in his postcombat history of dissociative PTSD symptoms, disturbed and volatile marital and work relations as well as drug and alcohol abuse. During this period, we see in Chuck's conviction of unparalleled skill and unmatched competence, despite an employment history of repeated failure, his desperate attempt to defensively restore these shattered grandiose fantasies. His narcissistic rage, which fueled homicidal and suicidal dreams as well as daydreams of blowing up everything and everybody, were symptomatic not only of the traumatic shattering of his adolescent fantasies during combat but also of the defensive and faulty restoration of these fantasies during the postcombat period. The extent of Chuck's impotent rage is symbolized in his recurrent traumatic nightmare of being unable to push down the detonator plunger.

Chuck was haunted throughout the postcombat period by the nightmare of himself as the captured and mutilated American soldier. This nightmare portrayed his painful sense of continued impotence and madness. As his nightmare image of a decomposing corpse reveals, the traumatic loss of and inability to restore his fantasies of grandiosity left Chuck extremely anxious that he was disintegrating. The maggots consuming his rotting flesh seem to portray symbolically Chuck's gnawing feeling that his own rage was eating him up.

Chuck's case clearly illustrates our central thesis that PTSD is a dissociative disorder. Evidence of depersonalization and derealization is apparent in Chuck's reliving experiences and recurrent traumatic nightmares. During reliving episodes, several of which occurred during interview sessions, Chuck experienced a radical alteration of consciousness in which he fell into a deeply dissociated state. In this state, he relived several of his most traumatic combat experiences. In two of his nightmares, he dreams of himself as an observer staring at himself, as either the captured and mutilated American soldier or the rotting corpse. This subjective split of the dreamer between a "participating self"and "observing self" is an example from unconscious dream life of what Arlow (see chapter one) argues is a dissociated state of depersonalization.

Chuck's case also illustrates that the symptoms of PTSD can, because of the depth of dissociation, reach psychotic proportions. Examples are Chuck's paranoid and delusional state while he was stationed at the enemy POW camp. The extent to which a latent psychotic process was present in Chuck's case prior to combat is hard to determine. However, it is clear that the shattering and faulty restoration of Chuck's central organizing fantasies precipitated a traumatic psychosis or PTSD with psychotic features. (See chapter three and the cases of Sybil and Jean for similar examples.)

Alexander

Alexander (or Al, as he prefers to be called) is a black Vietnam combat veteran in his late 30s. Of medium height and slender build, he has an air befitting the ancient historical figure whose name he bears. At the beginning of the interviews, which continued intermittently for several years, he was involved in an uncontested divorce initiated by his wife, to whom he had been married for 12 years. He had no children from this marriage. However, he did have a son born out of wedlock from a previous marriage.

A second lieutenant in the Marines during the early years of the war in Vietnam, Al had worked during the postcombat period as a marketing executive for a fabric company doing business in a well-known garment center. From the early 1970s to the time of the interviews, Al had been involved in the criminal underworld. Half-jokingly, he referred to himself as a "black Al Capone"; he boasted of masterminding and carrying out many illegal acts.

During the course of the interviews, Al periodically complained of rapidly fluctuating mood swings, alternating from maniclike highs to depressive lows. Although these pronounced mood swings suggested the possible presence of a major mood disorder, Al exhibited no clinical signs of a psychotic thought process. On the contrary, he described in vivid detail all aspects of his life including his combat tour in Vietnam. Moreover, during many interviews he became appropriately emotional as he discussed his numerous traumatic combat experiences.

Al presented the following account of his childhood and adolescence. An only child until he was 11, when a younger half-brother was born, Al was born and raised in a large multiracial city in the midwest. Al reported that his father was one of the first black officers in the city corrections force. Al also announced with obvious pride that his father had been an extremely important figure in the city government and an influential member of the local black community. Yet he lamented that as a young boy growing up he had not spent much time with his father, whom he greatly admired and revered. In addition, he bitterly complained about his father's strict disciplinary measures at home, which further estranged father and son.

In spite of their emotionally distant relationship, Al still has vivid and pleasant memories of accompanying his father to informal meetings with local community leaders and political dignitaries. Al boasted that as a child he had always assumed that he would grow up to follow in his father's footsteps and take over his prominent position in the community. Al remembered that as "my father's son" everybody in his neighborhood had treated him with special consideration.

Al described his mother, who was a teacher in the local public school system, as so fond of him that she doted on and overprotected him. For instance, he recalls that his mother objected to his rather infrequent outings with his father. She feared that some of his father's acquaintances were unsavory characters who might have a bad influence on her young and impressionable son.

According to Al, his mother had insisted that he avoid all contact with kids from the street, associate only with the "right" people, behave himself at home, "mind my manners" in public, get a proper education, and become a successful professional. She also had tried to convince him that being polite and respectful towards others would assure him of success. In hindsight, Al complained that his mother had so pampered and spoiled him that he did not develop the emotional coping skills necessary for success as an adult. However, as a child and adolescent, Al had been convinced that he was destined for great success.

Al said that as a young boy he had been very popular with his peers. He always assumed a key leadership position in any group he joined. For example, he was a leader in the Scouts and Army cadets. If for any reason he could not be a group leader, he simply dropped out of the group and joined another where he could lead. He unabashedly remarked that he always believed that he was entitled to lead and command. In this regard, he revealed a cherished childhood and adolescent fantasy in which he imagined himself as a highly decorated war hero and great military leader.

Al mentioned that he was surprised by his parents' divorce when he was ten years old. He admitted that he had been so absorbed in his daily affairs that he did not notice the obvious warning signs of trouble including bickering and fighting. He also claimed that he was not terribly upset by their initial separation and later divorce.

Following the breakup of his parents' marriage, Al and his mother lived for a short time with his maternal grandmother. His mother subsequently remarried and Al spent the remainder of his childhood and adolescence growing up in his stepfather's home.

Perhaps as a result of his parents' divorce, Al had difficulties in school as a teenager. He was truant, disruptive, and disrespectful. Defiantly refusing to study, he received poor grades. He also "palled around" with delinquent youngsters and got into minor scrapes with the law. This pattern of delinquent behavior continued for several years in junior high school. When Al entered high school, however, his mother and biological father "straightened me out." Cutting off all contact with his delinquent acquaintances, he renewed old friendships and resumed working at his studies. He also became very active in school athletics and the student government.

In a "remarkable turnaround," as he put it, he graduated high school as a star athlete with varsity letters in football, baseball, and track as well as honors as the president of the senior class. Al commented that on graduating high school, he felt that he had already realized some of his most cherished childhood fantasies of great success as a powerful and admired leader.

In spite of his remarkable turnaround, Al's high school grade point average and class standing were mediocre. However, his biological father "made some calls and pulled some strings," and Al was accepted as a student by a major state university. While in college, Al led a relatively normal and uneventful life. He dated, had one serious romance, and graduated with a B.S. degree in business administration. Immediately after graduation, Al enlisted in the Marines with the clear intention of realizing his boyhood fantasy of proving himself a warrior and military leader.

Al completed Marine boot camp in the summer of 1966 and was accepted for Marine Officers Candidate School. During the course of his successful training as a Marine officer, Al said, he felt "ten feet tall" and "like an eagle soaring through the sky." In 1966, he emphasized, he was one of only a few black candidates for officer training, which further inflated his already heightened fantasies of grandiosity.

Al received his commission as a second lieutenant and was sent to Europe, where he served as an administrative assistant to a company commander. After only six months in Europe, Al received orders for combat duty in South Vietnam. Al said he had looked forward to fighting in the war in Vietnam as a means of distinguishing himself, receiving medals, and being promoted. In fact, he was convinced then that it was only a matter of time until he would be one of the first black officers to be put in charge of an entire company.

During his combat tour in Vietnam, at a battalion base camp, Al participated in the interrogation of enemy POWs. He acknowledged using extreme force and methods of torture on the POWs, which, he confessed, was sexually arousing. Al's vivid description of the interrogations and torture revealed that they were also narcissistically stimulating.

Although Al spent much of his time in the rear, he occcasionally accompanied the battalion commander to the battlefield to coordinate and oversee combat operations. He also participated in three major "search-and-destroy" missions. He was disappointed that during the first and second of these missions he remained on the periphery of the battle and therefore did not "see heavy action."

Although he missed the heaviest combat, two close black comrades, both of whom Al greatly admired as savvy and seasoned veterans of the war, were seriously wounded. He was terribly shaken by the wounding of his comrades. Al had convinced himself that soldiers like his buddies, who were experienced in the field and "knew the ropes," were safe; only those soldiers who failed to take proper precautions were in real danger of being wounded or killed.

Al declared that the wounding of his two pals "shattered" his belief in his own invulnerability and left him, for the first time since his arrival in Vietnam, fearful for his life. Now, in a dramatic reversal of his illusions of immortality, he was convinced that he and his comrades were "marked" for death. They had been hit, he said, and now it was his turn. At this point in his tour he suffered from a recurrent nightmare in which he lay mortally wounded on the field of battle.

The traumatic loss of the reassuring presence of his two comrades, both of whom Al apparently imagined as providing a desperately needed selfobject experience of merger in fantasy with omnipotent imagos, left him extremely vulnerable. In addition, during the third mission, Al found himself in the thick of the fighting. He recalled watching, horrified, as more and more of his comrades fell in battle.

Al reluctantly and ashamedly admitted that during this third search-and-destroy mission, he "flipped out." Suddenly leaping up from his protected position, and dangerously exposing himself to enemy fire, he shouted obscenities at the enemy and wildly fired his M-16 automatic rifle. A soldier standing next to Al, realizing that he had gone berserk and was about to charge the enemy stronghold single-handedly, held him back.

When Al regained his composure, he was overwhelmed with the thought that he had acted so foolheartedly because he wanted to die in a blaze of glory. Apparently, by inviting his own demise, Al attempted to escape from the intolerable feeling that he must passively await his death. Perhaps, Al's reckless action may be viewed as an exhibitionistic enactment of his adolescent fantasies of grandiosity.

Following this incident, Al became active in a group of militant black soldiers, or "brothers," as he called them. These soldiers had organized to protest what they claimed were the military's racist attitudes. Al insisted that these racist attitudes were reflected in a practice of placing far more black and Hispanic than white soldiers in the most dangerous and risky frontline positions.

Al's battalion commander tried unsuccessfully to dissuade him from continued participation in this protest group, warning him that his involvement would seriously jeopardize his chances for promotion. It also created considerable friction between Al and fellow white officers, a number of whom shunned Al for what they deemed behavior unbecoming an officer. Becoming ever more tense and anxious, Al consulted a base camp military psychiatrist, who prescribed tranquilizers and recommended that Al "toe the line."

Al confided that his primary motivation in participating in the black militant protests stemmed from tremendous fears of going back into battle. He hoped that his high visibility as a protestor would spare him further combat duty in the field. In addition, he spoke of his involvement in the protests as an attempt to salvage some of his pride and dignity, which he felt he had lost as a result of his cowardly fears.

In spite of the use of tranquilizers, Al experienced narcissistic rage and a growing sense of fragmentation, as evidenced in anxiety about "falling apart" (disintegrating). Al described the following incident as an example of his volatility and explosiveness: During a routine inspection at the base camp, a soldier refused to comply with one of his orders. He became enraged at what he felt was an intolerable affront to his authority. He went berserk and jumped into the gun turret of a nearby "APC" (armoured personnel carrier). He was subdued, however, before he could open fire on the soldier and others standing nearby. He was ordered to consult again with the base camp psychiatrist, who increased the dosage of his tranquilizers and placed him on limited duty until he calmed down.

Although Al continued to suffer from considerable anxiety and tension, he nonetheless reported back to regular duty with his battalion. He described functioning at a marginal level until he saw his battalion commander killed during a routine inspection of an area supposedly clear of enemy soldiers. He sobbed as he recalled standing over his commander's body and staring with disbelief and horror at the blood pouring out of a large bullet hole in the front of the commander's forehead. He still cannot forget the twisted and bizarre expression on his commander's face.

Al confessed that he was highly ambivalent about his commander's death. On one hand, he had hoped that the death of his commander would free him from accompanying the commander on his often dangerous trips to the front. On the other hand, his commander's sudden and totally unexpected death had left him feeling even more acutely vulnerable to certain death. He explained that he had concocted a fantasy that his commander was invincible and immortal. He imagined that if he stayed close to him he too would be safe. Losing his two comrades and his commander had shattered any lingering fantasy of magical safety through physical proximity to those imagined to be indestructible and immortal.

His fantasies shattered, Al was on the verge of psychological collapse. He made a final desperate attempt to control his situation: he tried to kill himself. He had been ordered to lead a fourth search-and-destroy mission. Unable, however, to bear any more pain, he secretly went to a deserted area and swallowed an entire bottle of the tranquilizers. Although he was not found for several hours, he was miraculously revived.

Following his recuperation at a military field hospital, Al was ordered to undergo a court martial proceeding. He explained that the Marines had formal regulations governing the conduct of officers in a combat zone. According to Al, these regulations strictly prohibited any form of unauthorized withdrawal from battle including the attempt to take one's own life.

Al said he was fortunate, however, and, with the help of his biological father, arranged to forego a formal court martial and receive an honorable discharge in exchange for a loss of his commission and demotion to the rank of sergeant. Yet, despite this break, Al was still very ashamed of the suicide attempt and of "being busted down to a sergeant." Instead of living out his fantasy of a triumphant homecoming as a war hero, Al sadly reported, he returned home as a disgraced and dishonored coward.

After his discharge from the service and his return to civilian life, Al's biological father used his contacts in the business world to get Al a good position as a junior sales executive with a successful fabric company. Al related that he was extremely grateful for the opportunity to "start over" and thus offset all the painful memories and feelings associated with Vietnam. Filled with a renewed spirit of enthusiasm and determination to live up to his fantasies of great success, Al threw himself into work and went back to school. He began a course of study at night to earn a Master's degree in sales and marketing.

During the immediate postcombat period, Al also resumed his relationship with his former college sweetheart. After they had a son out of wedlock, Al's girlfriend began to pressure him to get married. Al resisted her pressure because, he said, he felt getting married would interfere with his career ambitions. He had just received his graduate business degree and had been promoted to a top management position with his company. He broke up with his girlfriend in 1970 and has subsequently lost all contact with her and his son. He expressed no remorse over failing to maintain any contact with his son.

One year after the breakup of this relationship, Al became involved with another woman, whom he subsequently married. (He has no explanation for his sudden and dramatic change of mind concerning marriage.) Al described his marriage as marred from the beginning by turmoil and violence. During his marriage, he gradually became dependent on alcohol and cocaine. He said he used both drugs in an unsuccessful attempt to block out memories, images, and feelings connected with Vietnam.

Al was unable to escape through drugs from an unrelenting sense of shame and humiliation associated with personal defeat in Vietnam. He said he grew increasingly irritable and volatile at home. He often flew into unprovoked and violent rages in which he became dissociated and relived traumatic combat experiences. During these dissociated reliving episodes, Al imagined that his wife was a threatening enemy soldier. Mistakenly thinking he was protecting himself, he physically attacked her, almost killing her several times. On other occasions in a drug-induced high he became verbally and physically abusive. Al's wife finally left him in order to protect her own life.

In spite of Al's serious domestic difficulties, he was able for a brief time to function at work. However, shortly after the breakup of his marriage, he became dissociated at work and underwent a combat reliving experience. Imagining himself back in Vietnam, Al went berserk and, shouting madly, broke up office furniture as he fired an entire clip from a revolver he had hidden in his desk drawer. His terrified co-workers called the police, who managed to disarm and restrain Al before he hurt anyone. Following his arrest, Al appeared in court but was given a suspended sentence and put on probation.

Discouraged and disillusioned after being fired from his job, he turned to his drug contacts as a means of gaining entrée into the criminal underworld. Al boasted of his meteoric rise as a career criminal. He had quickly become involved in lucrative drug deals, extortion, racketeering, and illegal financial transactions. Al declared triumphantly that he had found his life as a "big time" criminal exciting and exhilarating. He bragged about his close association with notorious underworld figures.

According to Al, he eventually rose to an exhalted position in the underworld in which he amassed large sums of money and controlled numerous criminal underlings. He bought an expensive apartment in an exclusive building, fancy clothes and jewelry, a chauffeur-driven limousine, among other luxuries. Fantasizing himself once more as the black Al Capone, he claimed to have controlled a vast criminal empire. As the head of this empire, he often took his entourage on expensive trips to Europe, where he and his party stayed at the best hotels and resorts. They were, in Al's words, treated like royalty.

Apparently, his newly acquired "success" as a criminal had rekindled Al's fantasies of greatness and merger with idealized figures. Al said that during his overseas junkets he felt euphoric and even fantasized himself as an important and powerful "world leader" capable of great feats. Al recalled that during these states of elation he felt invincible. Convinced of his own immortality, he taunted and provoked others in a grand exhibition of his fearlessness.

Al acknowledged, however, that he always fell from these Olympian heights of grandeur into the depths of misery and despair. In these deflated and empty moods, Al withdrew into himself. Lying in bed literally for weeks, he refused to have any contact with other people or the outside world.

Al said that his depressive episodes were exacerbated by the sudden and unexpected deaths of both his biological father and mother. Al's increasingly deep depressions and prolonged isolation made it difficult for him to maintain effective control of his criminal empire. Seeing it crumbling before him and with it his grand and exalted position as a "mob kingpin," Al plunged into an even worse mood of disillusionment and deeper depression.

Finally, after drifting about, living on a meager income, and becoming suicidal again, Al sought psychiatric help. He received both psychotropic drug therapy and psychotherapy. Neither helped.

Al reported that at this time he began suffering again an almost nightly recurrence of the traumatic nightmare of lying mortally wounded and dying on the battlefield. This was the state of mind in which Al made a second suicide attempt by swallowing medication. Miraculously, he survived once again.

Al claimed that his preoccupation with death and dying had precipitated his suicide attempt. Just as in Vietnam, Al apparently preferred taking his own life to passively awaiting a slow and agonizing death. Al explained that he dreaded the thought of withering away in anonymity at a state psychiatric facility. Paradoxically, he convinced himself that by killing himself he would magically regain control over his life.

Al's wife left him and, lacking funds, he was forced to move out of his expensive apartment. He moved from the city to a rural area to be near the psychiatric facility where he was receiving outpatient treatment. During this period, he lived for over a year with a black nurse whom he met at the hospital.

Al characterized this relationship as similar to others in the postcombat period. It was marked by Al's constant suspiciousness, distrustfulness, threats, and verbal and physical abuse. In fact, Al said, this relationship was the most turbulent of the postcombat period. Still desperately attempting to restore his imperiled sense of grandiosity, he had far less patience and tolerance for even minor slights and rebuffs. Any failure by his girlfriend to attend quickly to his urgent need for mirroring triggered an immediate outburst of narcissistic rage.

Al reported a dream apparently triggered by what he had experienced as an intolerable and enraging slight at the hands of the interviewer's waiting room receptionist. According to Al, the receptionist had failed to answer promptly and courteously what he felt was a simple question. He said he was barely able to restrain himself from leaping at and physically attacking her. In the dream version of the incident:

> I'm screaming at the receptionist and threatening to blow off her head with a revolver. You [the interviewer] step between me and the receptionist and manage to calm and control me.

Al associated the dream with the waiting room incident; he spoke of the interviewer as a calming presence and controlling influence in his otherwise turbulent and chaotic life.

Al exhibited a clear pattern of PTSD symptoms both during and following his combat tour in Vietnam. While still in Vietnam, he received emergency psychiatric treatment due to a state of impending fragmentation, as evidenced in disintegration anxiety and narcissistic rage reactions. In addition, after his two comrades were seriously wounded, he began suffering from a recurrent traumatic nightmare of being mortally wounded. All these symptoms appear to be part of the acute phase of PTSD.

After Al returned from the war to civilian life, he continued to exhibit symptoms of the disorder, indicating that it had become chronic. He was haunted by intensely painful memories, images, and feelings of Vietnam. He suffered from all major forms of reexperiencing, including intrusive and repetitive recollections, recurrent traumatic nightmares, and reliving episodes. Al ruminated, for example, about POW interrogations, several instances in which he "flipped out" and went crazy, and staring at the frozen expression on his commander's face. He also was consumed by the searing shame and humiliation associated in his mind with his suicide attempt and resulting loss of commission and demotion in rank.

In addition to the continuation in the postcombat period of his nightmare of being mortally wounded, Al has two different versions of "flipping out" during the third search-and-destroy mission. The first version repeats the experience more or less exactly as it occurred. Al feels ashamed and embarrassed of himself in this version. In the second version:

> I jump up from my protected position in a foxhole and lead my entire battalion in a victorious assault against the enemy. All my men immediately follow my lead and cheer me as we charge the enemy. I'm exhilarated by the cheers of my men and the excitement of the charge.

In associating to this dream, Al spoke of his longing for a chance to recapture lost glory as well as to restore a measure of self-respect and pride.

Al suffers from a full range of reexperiencing symptoms as well as numbing symptoms. Al believes he ruined his marriage and lost his job as a result of the reliving episode at work. Forsaking legitimate employment, he turned instead to a life of crime. As a self-proclaimed "rising star" in the criminal underworld with close connections to important mob figures, Al temporarily restored and briefly lived out antisocial versions of his fantasies of grandeur and idealized merger.

Al remained alienated and estranged from people throughout this period of his life. He described himself as brutal, vicious, and callous as he extorted money from his victims. He confessed that he was not troubled by the pain and suffering he inflicted on others. On the contrary, these violent acts made him feel godlike, as he had as a POW interrogator in Vietnam. Apparently, antisocial violence was in the service of temporarily and partially restoring shattered fantasies of exhibitionistic grandiosity.

Al's life in the postcombat period was also marked by all of the secondary symptoms of PTSD. These include hyperalertness, startle reaction, insomnia, and survivor guilt, as well as difficulties with short-term memory and concentration. His symptoms are intensified following sudden exposure to stimuli in the environment symbolically connected with traumatic combat experiences.

Al's dramatic mood swings—alternating between manic states of euphoria, in which he fantasizes himself as a powerful world leader, and depressive states of emptiness, in which he secludes himself for weeks at a time—as well as his explosive and violent outbursts are characteristics of both PTSD and a bipolar manic–depressive disorder. (The additional DSM-III (1980) axes I and II diagnoses of substance abuse and antisocial personality disorder, along with the diagnosis of bipolar manic-depressive disorder, neither conflict with nor rule out PTSD as the primary axis I diagnosis.)

Case Summary

Al's subjective world was unconsciously organized throughout late adolescence in accordance with deeply rooted childhood fantasies of personal grandeur and entitlement. These fantasies were fostered by both his father's exalted position in the corrections system and the local community and his mother's lavishing attention on him. These central organizing fantasies are manifest in Al's urgent need to assume key leadership positions in all his peer groups. From a very early age, he concocted fantasies of himself as a war hero and great military figure and, perhaps, even a world leader. The power and appeal of these fantasies made it virtually impossible for him to tolerate anything less than the top leadership position of any group.

Apparently Al's father kept his distance from his young son. This interfered with Al's need to form a close and secure relationship with a father whom he worshipped from afar. The inability to form such a relationship thwarted a vital selfobject experience of merging in fantasy with an idealized paternal imago. The absence of the experience of an idealized merger disrupted the "transmuting internalization" (Kohut, 1971) of the vital capacity for self-soothing and self-control.

Al's early childhood was marked by the presence of archaic and untransformed narcissistic fantasies of grandiosity and the absence of a critical selfobject experience of merging in fantasy with an idealized and omnipotent paternal imago. This combination left Al with serious psychological vulnerabilities. In other words, Al's childhood fantasies of his own grandiosity and the omnipotence of significant others did not undergo adequate transformation and thus failed to be integrated into a healthy, mature, and stable sense of self.

Warning signs of some of Al's early psychological vulnerability were present in his disturbed and delinquent behavior during junior high school, especially following his parents' separation and divorce. However, this was a relatively brief and uncharacteristic episode in Al's early life and therefore not necessarily indicative of later serious problems. In fact, Al's dramatic turnaround in high school and graduation from college points in the opposite direction. It seems clear that Al had a relatively good chance of achieving professional and personal success had he not been traumatized by his experiences in Vietnam.

Following his graduation from college, Al immediately entered the military, apparently determined to live out exhibitionistically his fantasies of going to war and returning victoriously as a hero and great military leader. Against great odds, Al's considerable intelligence and personal strengths earned him a commission as an officer in the Marines at a time when very few blacks had achieved such rank and status in the military. In 1966, as one of the few black commissioned officers in the Marines, Al reported for duty in Europe completely captivated by his own archaic narcissistic fantasies.

Al's description of himself during the early part of his tour in Vietnam seems to confirm our empathic inference about the considerable unconscious organizing power of these fantasies. As the first assistant to a battalion commander and a POW interrogator, Al was exhibitionistically living out his fantasies of grandeur and entitlement. In addition, his relationship with the battalion commander and with his two more seasoned comrades seemed to rekindle old but previously dormant fantasies of idealized merger with omnipotent paternal imagos.

However, the traumatically shattering loss of his two comrades, with whom he had apparently merged in fantasy, seriously disturbed Al's sense of invulnerability and immortality. Shaken by these losses, Al became obssessed with the terrifying thought that he had been "marked" for certain death. The traumatic shattering of his fantasies of idealized merger with omnipotent paternal imagos and his preoccupation with his own death are symbolically depicted in his recurrent nightmare of lying alone, mortally wounded on the battlefield.

Still defensively clinging to fantasies of himself as a heroic military leader, Al found it increasingly difficult to tolerate the mounting dread of his own demise. Unable to bear this agonizing and deflating dread, Al deluded himself into believing that dying in a blaze of glory would attest to his great courage, thereby enshrining his name in the military annals as a great leader. In his wild actions during the first search-and-destroy mission, Al exhibitionistically enacted this fantasy of immortalizing himself. Failing in this suicidal gesture to defend his cherished fantasies of grandeur against his own self-doubt, Al sought to preserve them by joining the black militants and participating in their protests. This may be viewed as Al's unconscious effort at compensatory restoration of his shattered fantasies of grandiosity through merger in fantasy with idealized and omnipotent imagos.

The faultiness of all Al's unconscious efforts at restoring his fantasies is apparent in the necessity for frontline emergency psychiatric treatment for the symptoms of the acute phase of PTSD. Witnessing the bloody death of his battalion commander apparently pushed Al over the edge. Al made the first of two suicide attempts in a state of utter despair and disillusionment. In stark contrast to his grand and exhibitionistic fantasy scenarios, Al returned home from the war defeated and humiliated.

In spite of being traumatized by combat in Vietnam, Al tried in the immediate postcombat period to resume a normal life. And for a short time it appeared that he might succeed. He had a job that promised considerable career advancement, and he was earning an advanced degree in business.

However, the dissociative symptoms of PTSD and, in particular, rageful and violent reliving episodes destroyed Al's chances for both professional and personal success. Al was bitter and disillusioned by the loss of his promising job. Rather than seeking legitimate employment, he turned to the underworld and a life of crime.

Perhaps his previous delinquent behavior in school and sadistic behavior as a POW interrogator in Vietnam presaged Al's subsequent antisocial lifestyle. His life as an underworld figure who committed violent criminal acts and associated with high ranking mobsters reflects his estrangement and alienation from conventional society. It is also reflective of defensive and exhibitionistic yet faulty efforts at restoring shattered fantasies of grandiosity.

The faultiness of Al's unconscious efforts at both defensive and compensatory restoration is apparent in his disturbed and erratic behavior at home as well as in his sudden and violent mood swings. Neither his life as a self-proclaimed rising star in the mob nor alcohol and cocaine could offset the disorganizing effects of his PTSD symptoms. The deaths of his father and mother left Al totally bereft.

Perhaps the trauma of losing his parents was considerably intensified by the previous loss during combat of comrades on whom Al had come to depend. His sense of being extremely vulnerable, dangerously out of control, and in need of a restraining figure in his life appears to be the unconscious meaning of his dream involving the interviewer. This dream also demonstrates the unconscious organizing power of a transference (and, in this case, an idealizing selfobject transference) in the context of a therapeutic interviewing setting.

Al's two dream versions of a major traumatic combat event seem to reflect an important unconscious meaning of his entire tour in Vietnam. In the nightmare version, he exposes himself to certain death at the hands of the enemy as part of an exhibitionist enactment of a grandiose fantasy of dying a hero's death in a blaze of glory. In the other dream version of the incident, in which he "flipped out," Al gallantly leads his men in a victorious assault against the enemy. Both the nightmare and dream version of this combat episode seem reflective of Al's unconscious efforts at defensively and exhibitionistically restoring shattered fantasies of grandiosity.

In summary, Al's case clearly illustrates a number of our central points. It shows that even a youngster with a relatively normal childhood may enter adolescence still under the sway of archaic and therefore untransformed, unintegrated narcissistic fantasies. Thus, if exposed to a traumatic environment such as existed in Vietnam, even the normal adolescent male is extremely vulnerable to the shattering and faulty restoration of central organizing fantasies.

Unlike Chuck, in whom the developmental transformation of fantasies of grandiosity was derailed by an unempathic lack of stimulation, Al's derailment occurred because of unempathic overstimulation. In addition, Al's case also suggests that fantasies of grandiosity may fail to undergo adequate developmental transformation in conjunction with the absence of a sustaining selfobject experience of merger in fantasy with idealized and omnipotent parental imagos. Al's case illustrates therefore how together these two interrelated sets of fantasies may operate as meaning structures defining the personal significance and import of traumatic occurrences.

As in Chuck's case, Al's combat and postcombat histories abounds with clear evidence of both the shattering and the faulty restoration of fantasmagorical meaning structures. Likewise, his case is exemplary in demonstrating that PTSD is a dissociative disorder. However, Al's case illustrates that some persons may create a lifestyle that temporarily restores shattered fantasies. The traumatic shattering of Al's central organizing fantasies produced, however, a searing and disorganizing sense of shame that precluded any permanent self-restitution. States of dissociation connected with rageful reliving experiences may stem from efforts to blunt intensely painful shame. In other words, dissociative reliving experiences may represent the unconscious attempt to magically change shame into grandiosity through narcissistic rage. In this sense, narcissistic rage became an agent for self-restitution, however faulty.

"Junior"

Junior, a single, 38-year-old, Hispanic Army combat veteran of medium height and stocky build, boldly displays "macho" military tattoos on his arms. He has wavy black hair, a thick beard, and sad, dark eyes. Speaking in a deep and husky voice, he laced his speech with distinct obscenities and colorful vulgarities. During the lengthy period of the therapeutic interviews, which were interrupted by a year-long prison sentence, he often became extremely animated and agitated, occasionally bursting into tearful and angry tirades.

Prior to a recent series of hospitalizations at a V.A. hospital, Junior resided for 12 year in the South, living on and off with his girlfriend and working as a long distance moving man. In his initial screening interview, he said that he had come north seeking care for a drinking problem at a V.A. hospital alcohol treatment unit. He stressed that his alcohol problem had recently "gotten totally out of hand" and was seriously interfering with both his personal life and ability to work.

Junior was admitted to a V.A. hospital alcohol treatment unit and, following the diagnosis of PTSD, was transferred to a special posttraumatic stress treatment unit at the same facility. In the course of his treatment on the PTSD unit, Junior was transferred on several occasions to a regular medical unit for alcohol detoxification following unauthorized use of alcohol.

Eventually, Junior was discharged from the PTSD unit for repeated violations of its strict regulation forbidding the use of any unauthorized substances. Following his discharge, he had to be readmitted on two subsequent occasions to the hospital intensive care unit as a result of alcohol and drug overdoses. After recovering from the second overdose, he left the area and returned to the South, where he was arrested for assault and battery. He spent almost a year in a state prison and then returned to the hospital for further care.

During the initial interviews, Junior was tense, suspicious, and reluctant to discuss the details of his combat tour in Vietnam. He emphasized that he had never talked about them with anyone. On several occasions, he alluded to very disturbing incidents in Vietnam but was unable to describe them, insisting that he was too upset to continue. The interviewer assured Junior that he understood how difficult it was for him to talk about these events and that Junior could proceed with the interviews at his own speed.

As the interviews continued, Junior spoke of a growing trust, respect, and admiration for the interviewer. This reassuring emotional ambience facilitated Junior's ability to describe every aspect of his combat tour in remarkable detail and with great feeling. The interviewer told Junior that his recall for the details of all these events attested to the indelible impression made by the war, which continued to rage in all its original fury in his mind.

In discussing his early history, Junior said that he was born and raised in a tough Hispanic inner-city neighborhood. His biological father abandoned his mother when he was an infant, and he saw him again only once, when he was eight years old. His mother remarried, and Junior grew up with her, his stepfather, and a half-sister. His mother worked as the superintendent of their apartment building, and his stepfather as a freight loader.

Junior described a tense, troubled relationship with his mother, who he said was an alcoholic. (He explained that alcoholism ran in his family and that as he grew up his mother, maternal grandfather, and two uncles all died from physical complications of the disease.) With great sorrow and bitterness, he recalled the many times that his mother both at home and in public had gone into alcoholic rages, humiliating and embarrassing him.

Junior had far more pleasant memories of his stepfather, whom he remembered as warm, supportive, and encouraging. Junior reported with obvious pleasure that his stepfather had always "treated me like I was his real son." He joyfully recalled that his stepfather taught him to play baseball and football; they often went together to professional sporting events.

However, Junior's positive relationship with his stepfather did not compensate for his negative relationship with his mother. Junior felt that she dominated the household with her ill humor, drinking, and rages. However, in marked contrast to his unhappy life at home, Junior spoke with great pride and enthusiasm of his involvement as a teenager with a neighborhood street gang. Junior stated that as a gang member he had "found a happy, new home" in which he always felt special and powerful. He noted that one of the leaders of the gang, an older adolescent named Hector, "took me under his wing, so to speak" and "treated me like his kid brother and best friend." Junior described Hector in glowing and worshipful terms, conveying that he viewed Hector as an almost godlike figure.

Junior recalled with great relish and glee the details of all the secret gang rituals and elaborate ceremonies. He said that as a gang member he had savored the fear and awe accorded him by everyone in the neighborhood. Junior bragged about his many street fights and rumbles. "Zip guns," "Saturday night specials," and switchblade knives were all weapons commonly used in these clashes, resulting, according to Junior, in many serious injuries and even fatalities. He noted that his gang relationships and activities totally eclipsed the importance of his family and home life.

The themes of abandonment, death, and violence seemed to structure Junior's account of his childhood and adolescence. For example, his biological father had abandoned him as an infant, and his mother, grandfather, and two uncles all died while he was growing up. In addition to the violent deaths of fellow gang members, Junior also mentioned several other early instances of violence. For example, during junior high school, a classmate was abducted from the schoolyard by a stranger and taken to the rooftop of an abandoned building, where he was brutally raped and murdered. During this same period, a fellow gang member, who was driving a stolen car, was killed in an automobile crash.

In spite of the predominance of the themes of abandonment, violence, and death during his childhood and adolescence, Junior insisted that he was unaware of much pain or a sense of loss. He claimed that his mother's death one year before he was drafted and entered the Army had had little effect on him. However, he spoke in grave terms of Hector's sudden and unexpected death in Vietnam, which was a crushing blow and shattering loss.

Junior and Hector had joined the Army together on the "buddy system." (The buddy system was an arrangement designed by the Army to increase enlistment. It allowed two friends to enlist together, remain together throughout boot camp, and be assigned to the same overseas combat unit.) Junior and Hector were recruited into an airborne rangers unit. However, during basic training, Junior suffered a hernia, which forced him to remain behind as Hector advanced to paratrooper school. Hector graduated from "jump school" and was sent to Vietnam while Junior was still receiving his parachute training.

Junior sobbed as he recalled the day that he learned of Hector's death. Hector had died in a helicopter crash only ten days after arriving in Vietnam. Barely holding back the tears, Junior described attending Hector's funeral back in the States. It was obvious by Junior's reaction during the interviews that Hector's death remained an extremely painful loss from which he had failed to recover.

Junior acknowledged that he became very despondent and disillusioned following Hector's death. Apparently, Junior had tried to defend against his overwhelming fear of dying in combat with a comforting illusion. He imagined that he and Hector would survive the war because of their vastly superior fighting prowess and skills, gained in years of bloody gang warfare.

Junior also acknowledged that he had fortified and protected himself with this illusion. The shattering impact of Hector's death left Junior feeling unprotected and vulnerable. Junior was so disillusioned and fearful that he went AWOL, drank, and smoked marijuana, and even seriously considered desertion.

Eventually, however, Junior pulled himself together. He returned to his unit and successfully graduated from jump school. It appears that he attempted to defend against Hector's loss with a highly inflated and grandiose sense of his own specialness as a member of an elite airborne ranger's unit. Comparing this feeling with those he had had as a member of the street gang, he realized that his ranger training had been designed to instill in him the overriding conviction that he was indeed indestructable and immortal, especially in comparison to the lowly and subhuman enemy. To emphasize the godlike superiority of the American combat soldier, the enemy, and in fact all Asians, were constantly referred to by both drill instructors and recruits in the most racist and derogatory terms such as "gooks," "dinks," and "slopes."

Junior mentioned that on the plane to Vietnam he sat next to a soldier who had been assigned to a morgue as a graves registration clerk. The soldier described his role in the identification and tagging of bodies to be flown back to the States. As they got off the plane at the Saigon airport, the soldier innocently remarked that he hoped to see Junior again. Junior immediately retorted that he certainly hoped not, meaning, he said, that he did not want to end up "as a stiff on a morgue slab."

During the first part of his combat tour, Junior served as a member of an airborne ranger unit that fought in the treacherous and steaming jungle mountain ranges of the infamous Ashau Valley. Junior proudly reported that although only a corporal he was made a squad leader, a position usually reserved for sergeants. He explained that he was elevated to this position because he had distinguished himself as a "crack" jungle fighter, or, as he said, "a grunt who had his shit together" [that is, a superior combat soldier].

During the second part of his tour, he requested and was granted a transfer to a special and elite reconnaissance team, known as the LURPS (slang for long-range reconnaissance patrols). Junior became extremely attached to a young officer, Lieutenant King, whom he followed from the airborne rangers to the LURPS. Junior's glorious description of King made him sound like Hector's reincarnation.

As a member of the airborne ranger unit, which operated from an LZ (landing zone) base camp situated in the jungle of the Ashau Valley, Junior went on many patrols deep into the heart of enemy territory. During a number of these dangerous patrols he developed a close personal relationship with a more experienced soldier, an "old-timer," in his squad. This relationship was comforting and reassuring; apparently, it helped to ground Junior after the loss of Hector. Referring to his comrade as a "fatherly type and teacher," Junior told how his senior partner "showed me the ropes." Having this soldier as his personal mentor and guide bouyed Junior's spirits and enabled him to achieve a reputation as a crack jungle fighter.

Junior sadly recounted the incident in which his buddy was seriously wounded during a patrol. As the two men were returning with their squad from a night patrol, the other man accidentally stepped on a landmine. The force of the explosion ripped off his leg; he was "medivacted" (flown by rescue helicopter) to a field hospital for emergency surgery. He was subsequently flown back to the States for additional surgery and rehabilitation therapy.

Junior said he was devastated by the loss of his buddy and was disconsolate for weeks. He had consoled himself with the belief that his close personal relationship with his more experienced and wiser comrade would protect him from harm, and without this relationship, he once again felt exposed and vulnerable.

Desperate, Junior sought out another senior member of his squad whose companionship and comraderie provided him with a renewed sense of calm and confidence. His new relationship made it easier for him to endure the daily hell of fighting the enemy in the treacherous terrain of the Ashau Valley. Junior recounted numerous firefights during which he and his comrades fought an almost invisible enemy. The thick jungle underbrush provided the enemy with cover for deadly booby traps and ambushes, both of which took the lives of many of Junior's fellow squad members.

During a patrol, Junior's new partner discovered a booby trap, which he attempted to destroy. He tossed down a grenade into a hole that he thought was rigged with only light explosives. Unfortunately, the enemy had planted a much larger and more powerful bomb underneath the visible and less powerful explosives. Consequently, the exploding grenade set off a massive blast, seriously wounding Junior's buddy, who was medivacted to a field hospital in the rear.

Junior was inconsolable at the loss of still another powerful authority figure on whom he depended for his own sense of well-being and security. He felt deserted, abandoned, and without hope of surviving. Lost and hopeless, he resorted to smoking marijuana. High on pot, Junior temporarily regained the illusion of safety and security.

Increasingly dependent on pot and "stoned" throughout the day, Junior began to smuggle it into his base camp for distribution to other soldiers. During one of his smuggling runs, Junior was "busted," detained, and then returned to the rear for a court martial. However, a series of character witnesses persuaded the court martial board to discipline him with only a minor reprimand.

Just before his detention for drug smuggling, Junior's company had been placed under the command of a new officer, Lieutenant King. Shaken by the loss in rapid succession of three close and important figures (Hector and his two other buddies), Junior quickly developed an intense attachment and loyalty to King. According to Junior, King was that rare and exceptional officer who really identified with enlisted men and was able to relate to them in a very close and personal way. Junior pointed out that King was always in the "thick of it" during combat. Moreover, after the fighting, he allowed his men to unwind and relax in their own distinctive ways. Under the influence of what Junior described as an increasingly close and powerful bond with King, he regained his previous composure. He stopped smoking pot and resumed his role within the squad as the crack jungle fighter.

Following a brief "R&R" (rest and relaxation) in Australia, King was reassigned to command the LURP team. He immediately followed King. As King's "right-hand man," Junior prided himself on his supreme competency in handling any combat situation. He proudly announced that he had remained "calm, cool and collected" even under murderous enemy fire. He said that he and King were inseparable; they always accompanied each other on dangerous reconnaissance patrols deep into enemy territory.

Junior confided, however, that as his tour was ending, or, as he said, "getting short," he became increasingly reluctant to go out on these risky missions. Instead, he asked King to allow him to remain behind as a resupply man. Normally, King permitted Junior to stay behind. However, in preparing for a particularly dangerous outing, King pleaded with Junior to accompany him. Junior confessed that he was too scared and refused to go.

Junior provided a vivid and moving description of King and the team as they prepared to leave on their mission. He said that just as King was moving out, he turned around and looked Junior straight in the eyes. He read the expression on King's face as a final plea to accompany him. Junior walked over to King, shook his hand, and embraced him, warning him not to "fuck up."

Remaining at the LZ resupply area, Junior paced back and forth as he anxiously awaited radio reports from the patrol on its latest position and the progress of the mission. Several hours into the mission, word came over the radio that the team had been ambushed—some members had been seriously wounded and others killed. Precise information on the identity of those hit was unavailable. Junior waited for what seemed an eternity for the arrival of the rescue helicopter.

As the helicopter landed, Junior rushed up to see the casualties. The dead were already enclosed in body bags, but Junior recognized King's M-16 automatic rifle by the special tapping on the gun butt. Junior grabbed the rifle only to drop it instantly in horror as King's blood-spattered brains oozed through his fingers.

Shocked, Junior fell into a deeply dissociated state. He only dimly recalls wandering around, dazed and confused, drinking and smoking pot. After several days of nonstop drinking and smoking, Junior regained enough composure to ask one of the survivors of the ambush about the circumstances surrounding King's death.

The survivor told Junior that for some inexplicable reason King had assigned a soldier named Dennis, a member of the LURP team with a reputation for being clumsy and noisy, to "walk point" (that is, to lead the patrol). According to Junior, as might have been expected Dennis led the patrol directly into the middle of an ambush. Dennis was immediately hit several times in the chest. However, instead of staying down, he repeatedly tried to get up, only to be shot several more times.

According to the survivor's account, King went berserk as he watched Dennis struggling. Ripping off his combat helmet, he single-handedly charged the enemy. He was shot through the head and killed instantly.

Junior said he was enraged with King for foolishly assigning Dennis to "walk point" and for recklessly charging the enemy. But, he moaned, his anger at King was dwarfed by his own self-hate and self-loathing. Accusing himself of inexcusable cowardice, he blamed himself for King's death. He has remained convinced throughout the postcombat period that had he accompanied King, he, and not Dennis, would have walked point, thus avoiding the ambush and sparing King's life.

Just before returning to the States, Junior was ordered to the morgue to identity the bodies of Dennis and King. Ironically, he was assisted by the graves registration clerk whom he had vowed never to meet again. With tears rolling down his cheeks, he spoke of staring, horrified, at King's twisted and contorted face, disfigured almost beyond recognition by the force of the bullet exploding in his skull. Junior cried as he divulged that this terrible image has remained with him as if burned indelibly into his mind.

Following the scene at the morgue, Junior flew back to the States. Still dazed and disoriented, he immediately went to stay with his half-sister and her husband. Desperate to forget about King's death as well as his sense of shame and guilt, Junior drank heavily and got high on pot.

Even though drunk and "stoned," Junior still flew into uncontrolled and destructive rages. On several occasions, he violently confronted his half-sister and her husband. In one instance, he broke down their bedroom door and threatened to kill them.

Realizing that both his half-sister and brother-in-law feared for their lives, Junior left their home. He drifted aimlessly toward the South, where he spent the next 12 years. Except for a stormy relationship with his girlfriend, which included several extended periods of separation, he remained a loner.

Junior spent hours in the cab of the moving van, which he drove for a living, ruminating about Vietnam. Obsessing about King's death and consumed by his intense shame, disgrace, and guilt, he repeatedly conjured up his image of the ambush in which King was killed. Junior despaired that the grotesque image of King's twisted and contorted face, rather than fading with time, would always haunt him.

Junior's sleep is often disturbed by terrifying nightmares in which he repeats his secondhand version of the ambush in which King was killed. He also has nightmares of identifying King's body at the morgue and staring at his bullet-shattered head. Junior often has nightmares of the incidents in which his two comrades were seriously wounded. He awakes from these nightmares feeling abandoned, deserted, and despondent.

In relating these recurrent traumatic nightmares, Junior reported a series of nocturnal productions including one nightmare and three dreams, apparently stimulated by his participation in the therapeutic interviews. The nightmare and dreams illuminate transference within the intersubjective field that existed between the interviewer and Junior. (See the case of Al for another example of the intersubjective field created by interviewer and research subject.)

According to Junior, in the nightmare beginning the series:

People are handing me a plate with bloody brains on it. I get blood all over my hands and scream: 'What are you doing, why are you giving me all this stuff, what's wrong with you? Take this shit away! I don't want it!'

Junior awoke from this nightmare in a cold sweat. Declaring "I've got King's blood on my hands!" Junior connected the dream image of King's blood on his hands with his overwhelming shame and guilt.

In the second dream in the series:

> You [the interviewer] and I are both back in 'Nam. You are telling me that the enemy couldn't beat me because my "shit is too strong" [that is, Junior was too good a combat soldier]. I'm asking myself how you could know this since you had never seen me fighting in the field.

At this point, the dream changes:

> I'm with King, who is asking me about the best site for setting up an ambush. I point out a spot alongside the road and King orders the other men to take cover in the area I've suggested.

Junior referred to the obvious connection he had made between the interviewer and King: In the two dream scenes involving first the interviewer and then King, Junior experiences himself as once again praised and admired by a respected authority figure. Junior also recognized that the dream represented the first time since King's death he had appeared alive in a dream.

Junior stressed the importance of this last point by reporting a third dream in the series:

> I see King in the chopper just as it is preparing to take off on the patrol in which he was killed. We are shouting good-bye to each other.

The dream changed into the following scene:

> King and I are sitting together in a jungle clearing and "bullshitting" with each other. We are talking about being back home, work, and women.

Together, Junior and the interviewer raised the possibility that King had come back to life in Junior's dream world through Junior's (transference) relationship with the interviewer.

In the fourth and final dream of the series:

> I'm at the hospital and I'm packing my things to leave. My brother-in-law, Richie, is coming in a moving van to pick me up. I meet Richie in

front of the hospital and discover that I don't have the belongings I just packed. Dismayed, I realize that I only have a "fucked up" monkey wrench. Despite its condition, I offer it to Richie, who accepts it, saying that he will try to use it to fix the van.

Junior reported this dream following one of his many drinking episodes on the hospital PTSD unit. In connection with his violation of the unit's strict regulations forbidding drinking, the interviewer interceded on Junior's behalf; the interviewer succeeded in persuading the treatment team to allow Junior to remain on the unit. Junior linked his brother-in-law, Richie, with the interviewer, whom he affectionately called by his first name, Richard.

Junior connected the dream image of giving Richie a "fucked up" monkey wrench with his belief that he had "fucked up" the interviewer's efforts to help him. In this context, Junior recalled that King had left his new field command over the ranger's unit to testify as a character witness in Junior's behalf at his court martial proceeding. He associated his feeling of letting down a trusted and valued authority figure (the interviewer) with his shame and guilt over having failed to accompany King on the ill-fated reconnaissance patrol.

In addition to suffering from intrusive thoughts and recurrent traumatic nightmares, Junior also reported a history of reliving experiences. He began suffering from these dissociative episodes soon after he returned from Vietnam. For example, several weeks after arriving back in the States, while walking casually down a street, he suddenly heard the sound of gunfire. Looking down the street, he saw a policeman firing at a speeding car. Junior became dissociated and, thinking that he was back in combat, automatically reached for his imaginary M-16 rifle as he dove for cover under a nearby car.

Several years later, as he and a friend strolled down a beachfront boardwalk, a helicopter unexpectedly swooped down from the dark night sky. It hit them with a burst of light from a powerful spotlight. Dissociated and disoriented, Junior frantically sought cover from the "enemy." Dragging his friend with him under the boardwalk, Junior said he remained dissociated for 15 minutes while his friend desperately tried to reorient him.

In connection with his history of reliving experiences, Junior also referred to episodes in which he had sensory "flashbacks" involving visual, auditory, and olfactory reexperiences. For instance, he often thought that he saw woodlines similar to those in the Ashau Valley. He also mentioned instances in which he imagined that he smelled "Gooks."

Junior remained a loner throughout the postcombat period, obsessed with his traumatic combat experiences and consumed with shame and guilt over King's death. He had little interest in making anything of himself. He was alienated and estranged from other people and institutions and never talked with anyone about his combat experiences in Vietnam. As further evidence of this pattern of numbing, during the 12-year period of his relationship with his girlfriend Junior never spoke to her about Vietnam.

Junior often worried that his intrusive thoughts, recurrent traumatic nightmares, and reliving experiences were proof that he had gone mad and had lost control over all his mental faculties. This further intensified the sense of gross incompetence of the once proud crack jungle fighter who had fancied himself King's powerful right-hand man. Junior admitted that he was afraid to speak to anyone about his confused mental state for fear that he would be locked up in a mental institution.

Instead, Junior drank alcohol and smoked marijuana in an attempt to blot out the images of Vietnam. Apparently this fostered the illusion of control and mastery over his haunting memories. But Junior's alcohol and pot binges provided only temporary relief from the pain of Vietnam and triggered violent and explosive rages ending in the destruction of property and physical assault.

Case Summary

Abandoned at an early age by his biological father and emotionally abused by his alcoholic mother, Junior turned to his stepfather in a desperate attempt to compensate for the absence of empathic parental mirroring. He was fortunate that the relationship with his stepfather facilitated the selfobject experience of merger in fantasy with an idealized imago, thus somewhat compensating for the absence of mirroring parental selfobjects.

As a teenager, Junior recreated in his relationship with Hector an adolescent version of his fantasy of idealized merger with an omnipotent paternal selfobject. Junior's fantasized merger with Hector and the street gang enabled him unconsciously to organize himself in accordance with fantasies of his own grandiosity.

Apparently Hector's totally unexpected death in Vietnam traumatically shattered his fantasy of idealized merger with an omnipotent imago. As a result, Junior went into combat already traumatized, disillusioned, and extremely vulnerable. He desperately and repeatedly sought out idealizable figures with whom he could recreate a sustaining selfobject merger unconsciously organized in accordance with fantasized omnipotence.

Unfortunately, however, each time Junior reestablished such a fantasized merger, it was shattered by the loss of a buddy. Junior was repeatedly overwhelmed by the feeling that he had been abandoned and deserted by an all-powerful and protective male authority figure, thus recapitulating the trauma of early childhood. Devastated and disillusioned by these traumatic losses, Junior resorted to a drug induced illusion of safety.

Traumatized and shaken, Junior rediscovered, in the person of Lieutenant King, the lost idealized imago with whom he could merge in fantasy. Viewing Junior within the intersubjective context of this relationship, we see the compensatory although temporary, restoration of archaic narcissistic fantasies. He exhibited outstanding skill and ability as a combat soldier until his fantasized merger with King was traumatically shattered by King's death.

Unable to recreate a relationship facilitating the restoration of such central organizing fantasies in the postcombat period, Junior remained subjectively suspended in time, doomed to repeat his traumatic combat experiences in his mind. His futile attempt at self-medication through the use of alcohol and marijuana, as well as isolating himself, led only to loneliness and despair. Emotionally cut off from all around him, he periodically burst into narcissistic rages directed at both King and himself. Junior's wrath at King reflects his narcissistic rage at King for failing to continue to function as an omnipotent and idealized selfobject. Junior's self-hatred and self-destructiveness stem from narcissistic rage over failing to live up to his own grandiose fantasies.

In the intersubjective field created within the research setting of the therapeutic interviews, Junior psychologically recreated for the first time in the postcombat period a fantasized merger similar to that which he had with King. On the basis of this relationship, Junior once again enjoyed a selfobject experience of merger in fantasy with a soothing and calming omnipotent imago. Unfortunately, the transient quality of this transference relationship proved inadequate in effectively modulating the narcissistic rage that was part of both the shattering and the faulty restoration of Junior's fantasy of idealized merger with a series of omnipotently endowed paternal imagos, the last of whom was King.

As we demonstrate in chapters six and seven, the intersubjective field structuring the therapeutic relationship becomes a clinical setting for: (1) interpreting the unconscious meaning of traumatic occurrences;

and (2) facilitating the transformation of traumatically shattered and faultily restored archaic narcissistic fantasies.

CONCLUSION

We have presented three representative case studies of PTSD in Vietnam combat veterans in support of our self-psychological theory of the narcissistic trauma of combat. The case studies of Chuck, Al, and Junior suggest that military training inflates already highly volatile and unstable adolescent male fantasies. They also demonstrate that the unconscious meaning of traumatic combat occurrences may be analytically interpreted as the shattering and faulty restoration of these adolescent male fantasies.

The psychological aftereffects of combat may be read in the reexperiencing and numbing symptoms of PTSD. The case studies suggest that these symptoms are reflective of states of dissociation and, more specifically, depersonalization, and derealization. In this context, the cases indicate that many survivors of trauma are likely to abuse various substances (psychoactive drugs and alcohol) in a desperate but unsuccessful effort at self-medicating for the sense of fragmentation and disintegration anxiety so characteristic of PTSD.

The cases also demonstrate that narcissistic rage (including violent antisocial behavior) may be viewed both as a disintegration product of the shattering of fantasies and as an agent of integration reflecting the faulty attempt at restoring these fantasies (See the case of ".44 Mike" in chapter one.) The shattering of fantasies of grandiosity left both Chuck and Al narcissistically rageful in response to the absence of expected and desperately needed mirroring. Both Chuck and Al were prone to dissociative reliving experiences involving violent narcissistic rage. Apparently, these reactions were unconsciously intended magically to change shame and guilt into a grand and exhibitionistic triumph. The shame and guilt that consumed Junior triggered dissociative reliving experiences in which narcissistic rage was directed at both himself and others experienced as failing selfobjects.

All three case studies also suggest that the experience of death and dying is critical to understanding the unconscious meaning of traumatic combat occurrences. Although he lived through combat, Chuck experienced himself as having died as a result of the shattering and faulty restoration of fantasies of grandiosity. Ironically, Al saw death by suicide as a mystical rebirth and restoration of a shattered fantasy of exhibitionistic grandiosity. And, for Junior, life became a living torment because of the death of an omnipotent paternal figure whose loss shattered a fantasy of idealized merger.

Finally, two of our case studies (Al and Junior) provide clinical evidence of a selfobject transference within an intersubjective field created in the context of a therapeutic interviewing setting. In these two cases, the selfobject transferences although transient were none-theless important clinical sources for interpreting the unconscious meaning of traumatic combat occurrences.

CHAPTER 6

A Self-Psychological Approach to Analytic Therapy of the Trauma Patient

W e approach the treatment of the trauma patient in the same way that we approach analytic therapy with any other patient. Years of treating survivors of incest, rape, and combat trauma have convinced us that as a group these patients are responsive to self-psychologically oriented analytic therapy. Our treatment approach relies on the selfobject transference as a means of restoring and transforming shattered and faultily restored central organizing fantasies of self in relation to selfobject. The selfobject transference permits the reconstruction and working through of the unconscious meaning of psychic trauma. A careful reading of Kohut's (1971) *The Analysis of the Self* reveals that he originally conceived of selfobject transference as the primary therapeutic medium within which to restore and transform (via transmuting internalization) archaic narcissistic fantasies (pp. 83-4, 107-8).

Consistent with our psychoanalytic research methodology, we employ Kohut's (1971, p. 219) "vicarious introspection" or "empathic-introspective observational stance" (Kohut, 1977, p. 309) as our basic "mode of analytic listening" (Schwaber, 1981). According to Kohut, there is a fundamental difference between the extrospective mode of observation employed in the biological, physical, and medical sciences and the empathic-introspective mode of observation employed in the human sciences, including psychoanalysis. In the former, the human observer is outside the field of study; in the latter, the observer is "inside" (Kohut, 1971, p. 219, n. 8) the field of study (See chapter 1). In other words, both observer and observed constitute the field of inquiry in psychoanalysis. Hence, the analyst must attempt to understand the patient's relationship to him or her from the patient's subjective frame of reference.

It is an inescapable psychological given that the analyst's presence within the field of psychoanalytic inquiry affects both the patient and the treatment. There is therefore no escape for the analyst to a hypothetical but illusory Archimedean vantage point outside the psychological field of study from which to make so-called objective observations about the patient's unconscious mental life. Psychoanalytic interpretation and explanation occur within the intersubjective context created by the respective subjectivities of therapist and patient. They cannot be objectified as if they were independent of that context.

Consistent with our use of vicarious introspection, our approach to treatment relies heavily on the theory of intersubjectivity (Atwood and Stolorow, 1984). Atwood and Stolorow argue that the involvement of two persons in a relationship—whether child and parent, patient and therapist, or two friends—psychologically structures that relationship in accordance with the separate but interrelated subjectivities of the two participants. Subjectivity refers to the unique ways in which each individual organizes experience and imbues it with personal (and unconscious) meaning according to what Atwood and Stolorow call "organizing principles" or "structures of subjectivity." Within our theoretical framework, central organizing fantasies of archaic narcissism (that is, fantasies of self in relation to other as selfobject or fantasies of other as selfobject in relation to self) have the ontological and psychological status accorded by Atwood and Stolorow to structures of subjectivity (see chapter 1).

For example, one participant in a relationship may operate under a central organizing fantasy of exhibitionistic grandiosity. He therefore imbues experience with unconscious meaning in accordance with illusions of self-entitlement, perfection, and omnipotence. The second party in the relationship may operate on the basis of a central organizing fantasy of idealized merger with omnipotent imagos. She therefore imbues experience with unconscious meaning in accordance with illusions of others as perfect, omniscient, and omnipotent selfobject extensions of herself. The different subjectivities of these two persons codetermine their relationship.

Of course, the two participants in any relationship are often psychologically organized at different developmental levels and in accordance with different central organizing fantasies. However, despite these differences, the respective subjectivities of each participant must always be taken into account in understanding the nature and explaining the meaning of psychological phenomena arising within the intersubjective context of that relationship. Kohut's (1977) empathic-introspective observational stance requires that the analyst maintain, simultaneously, empathic attunement with the patient's subjective frame of reference and his or her own personal frame of reference. Atwood and Stolorow (1984, p. 47), borrowing a term from Piaget, refer to this as the analyst's ability to "decenter." In a sense, the theory of intersubjectivity constitutes an important theoretical and clinical refinement and expansion of the concept of the self-selfobject matrix (see chapter 1).

Because our treatment approach relies on vicarious introspection and the theory of intersubjectivity, it clearly is different from much of the other work in the field. The prevailing opinion seems to be that it is neither advisable nor possible to treat the trauma patient using standard analytic therapy techniques, especially transference and transference neurosis analysis. There are those, however, who support our approach. In fact, others have already begun to apply the analytic principles and techniques of self psychology to the treatment of the trauma patient.

In essence, we use the intersubjective field created by the analyst and the trauma patient as a therapeutic context from within which to reconstruct and work through the unconscious meaning of trauma. Reconstruction involves the restoration within the selfobject transference of shattered and faultily restored archaic narcissistic fantasies, whereas working through entails the therapeutic transformation of these central organizing fantasies of self in relation to selfobject. These fantasies are transformed as part of the survivor's structural growth and increasing insight into the unconscious meaning of past traumatic occurrences. This transformation occurs in the course of the analysis of selfobject transference fantasies and resolution of transference neurosis, or the "traumatic transference-neurosis" (Glover, 1955; Forman, 1984). The basic "therapeutic action" (Strachey, 1934; Loewald, 1960; Modell, 1976; Kohut, 1984) of our analytic therapy consists of the transference restoration and transformation of shattered and faultily restored fantasmagorical meaning structures.

In line with the theory of intersubjectivity, we need to point out that a trauma patient's selfobject transference fantasy sometimes elicits from the therapist an unconscious countertransference response, which, if unanalyzed, may interfere with the further unfolding of the transference fantasy. However, the patient's selfobject transference fantasy may also conflict with a selfobject countertransference fantasy of the therapist about the patient. The simultaneous presence

of competing and conflicting selfobject transference and countertransference fantasies creates what Ulman and Stolorow (1985) refer to as
the "transference-countertransference neurosis" (p. 39; see also Ulman, forthcoming).

Ulman and Stolorow (1985) developed this clinical concept as part of
a general theory of intersubjectivity. It is intended to illuminate the
"unfolding of patient's and therapist's developmentally arrested psychological structures, in particular the mirroring and idealizing selfobject functions that the two participants in the therapeutic dialogue
serve for each other" (p. 37). In a refinement of this concept, we
conceive of these "developmentally arrested psychological structures"
as archaic narcissistic fantasies unconsciously organizing subjective
experience for both patient and analyst (see Ulman and Brothers,
1987).

It is assumed that normally the therapist's central organizing fantasies have undergone sufficient transformation to enable him or her
to facilitate rather than impede the necessary unfolding of the patient's
selfobject transference fantasies. However, in the intersubjective context unconsciously organized by the transference–countertransference
neurosis, the therapist experiences the patient as providing selfobject
functions of mirroring, idealization, or twinship (or alter ego). Such
"counterresistance" (Racker, 1968) interferes with the patient's transference fantasy of the therapist as providing missing selfobject functions of mirroring, idealization, and alter ego or twinship. Yet, if
empathically understood, the transference–countertransference neurosis may be invaluable in reconstructing and working through the
unconscious meaning of trauma. In the representative treatment cases
(see chapter 7) to follow, we offer several examples illustrating how
the therapist's use of the transference–countertransference neurosis
sheds light on the unconscious meaning of trauma for the patient (see
Ulman and Brothers, 1987).

Like many other self-disordered patients, the trauma survivor often
dreads further "narcissistic mortification" (Freud, 1939; Eidelberg,
1959; A. Freud, 1936; Sandler with A. Freud, 1985) and therefore
unconsciously resists the establishment of transference fantasies of
self in relation to mirroring, idealizing, and alter ego or twinship
selfobjects. In the initial phase of treatment, which for purely heuristic
purposes we distinguish from the reconstructive and working through
phases, we therefore devote considerable attention to analyzing the
trauma patient's dread and resistance. This facilitates the transference
organization of the therapeutic relationship in accordance with the
unconscious meaning of selfobject transference fantasies. Because we
use these selfobject transference fantasies as the primary source for

reconstructing and working through the unconscious meaning of trauma, resistance analysis is essential to our analytic therapy.

Following Kohut (1970), we distinguish between "nonspecific narcissistic resistance" to the analytic process and "specific narcissistic resistance" to a selfobject transference. According to Kohut, the former

> resistance is a function of the general narcissistic vulnerability to the patient. Analytic treatment as a whole offends the pride of the analysand, contradicts his *fantasy of his independence,* and that is why he now resists treatment—without reference to the specific details of his psychic illness [p. 549, italics added].

Later, in the same essay, Kohut argues that the latter

> resistances in the analyses of narcissistic personality disturbances are motivated by the anxieties of an insecurely established self which fears the rejection of the narcissistic needs that are reactivated in analysis, i.e., the need to be mirrored and to merge with an ideal. In other words, the specific narcissistic resistances are motivated by anxieties—I will (broadly speaking) refer to them as disintegration anxieties—which focus on the self and on an object experienced as [part of] the self [p. 560].

Kohut concludes that

> the analysand suffering from a narcissistic personality disorder consciously tries to express his needs openly, he nevertheless shies away from doing so because of the danger of the self's disintegration to which a possibly impending traumatic rejection of needs exposes him. In other words, he fears the reactivation of the unempathic rejection by his childhood selfobjects, who did not respond to the need of his growing self for supportive and strengthening sustenance through mirroring and merger with the ideal [p. 560].

We empathically understand the trauma patient's resistances as unconsciously motivated by the disintegration anxiety of the "dread to repeat" (A. Ornstein, 1974, p. 232) the shattering of archaic narcissistic fantasies. In this connection, the trauma patient may initially resist any discussion of the still emotionally charged and disturbing details of the traumatic experience. In the initial phase of treatment, we therefore introduce the discussion of PTSD symptoms, which are often easier to talk about than the actual details of traumatic experiences. Discussion of these symptoms avoids distressing the patient further and yet provides a sense of the nature and meaning of traumatic experience. It also allows us to establish the diagnosis of PTSD, which then serves as a clinical guide for further therapeutic work. Because we reconceptualize PTSD as a dissociative rather than an anxiety disorder (see Chapter 1), our analytic therapy focuses on disturbances arising in the context of failures to empathically understand the patient on the basis of transference fantasies of self in relation to selfobject.

Clinical evidence of resistance to selfobject transference fantasies of exhibitionistic grandiosity and idealized merger with an omnipotent imago appears in trauma survivors' allusions to their own perceived inferiority, frailty, vulnerability, or other supposed flaws in character. Resistance may also be inferred from expressions of concern about the therapist's supposed inadequacies, limitations, and weaknesses. Allusions to a sense of oneself as psychologically defective may be expressions of an unconscious resistance to an archaic mirroring selfobject transference fantasy. Those directed toward the therapist as deficient are usually unconscious expressions of a resistance to either an idealized or twinship (alter ego) selfobject transference fantasy.

If the therapist is empathically attuned to these resistances and the unconscious fears that motivate them, they may be slowly and carefully analyzed. This facilitates the emergence of underlying transference fantasies. Clinical evidence of the emergence of a selfobject transference fantasy appears in trauma survivors' allusions to their own perceived greatness, power, or other unique attributes or to expectations and hopes of merging with the therapist's idealized qualities.

As our representative case studies of incest, rape, and combat trauma illustrate (see chapters 3, 4, and 5), we rely heavily on the interpretation of recurrent traumatic nightmares in reconstructing and working through the unconscious meaning of trauma (see also Wilmer, 1982). Our use of recurrent traumatic nightmares is based on Kohut's (1977) notion of the "self-state dream" (pp. 109-10). Represented within these nightmares are graphic and emotionally charged symbolic depictions of both the shattering and faulty restoration of archaic narcissistic fantasies. These nightmares provide the therapist with a symbolic representation of disturbances in the unconscious organization of the trauma survivor's subjective world. The interpretative use of these nightmare images of trauma also provides the therapist with invaluable clues to archaic selfobject functions of emerging transference fantasies.

For example, a nightmare depicting a shattered and faultily restored fantasy of exhibitionistic grandiosity, should alert the therapist to the possible emergence of a mirroring selfobject transference. Or, a nightmare depicting the shattered and faultily restored fantasy of idealized merger might presage the emergence of an idealizing or alter ego (twinship) selfobject transference. In other words, the trauma survivor will unconsciously try to use the therapeutic relationship to revive faultily restored fantasies of self in relation to selfobject. (See, Simmel, 1944, for an earlier discussion of the trauma patient's attempt at self-restitution through use of the therapeutic relationship.)

Interpreting the "transmutation of meaning" (De Monchaux, 1978, p. 445), signified by the transfiguration of recurrent traumatic nightmares, is particularly useful in documenting the restoration of an archaic narcissistic fantasy within the selfobject transference. For instance, a rape trauma survivor has had a recurrent traumatic nightmare of herself as defenseless and helpless before her attacker. She repeats the traumatic experience of being forced for fear of her life to submit to a degrading and shameful sexual assault. In the course of treatment, however, she dreams of herself as fearlessly subduing her attacker. Or, to take another example, a combat veteran has had a recurrent traumatic nightmare of himself in which he is trembling before an enemy soldier who is about to bayonet and shoot him. In the course of treatment, however, he dreams of himself as triumphantly repelling the enemy soldier and emerging victoriously from battle as a hero. We view the transfiguration of these nightmares and the corresponding transmutation of meaning as evidence of the transference restoration of a previously shattered and faultily restored central organizing fantasy. The recent work of Ulman (forthcoming) supports our use of the intersubjective field as a therapeutic medium within which to facilitate and empathically observe the restoration and transformation of such archaic meaning structures as shattered fantasies of self in relation to selfobject.

In keeping with our emphasis on the importance of narcissistic rage as a reaction to the shattering and as part of the faulty restoration of central organizing fantasies (see chapter 5), we pay special attention to it in treatment. Kohut (1977) saw narcissistic rage as a "disintegration product" (pp. 120–121) of the narcissistic injury to a grandiose sense of omnipotent control of the selfobject environment. Narcissistic rage is directed at others and the environment for failing to provide required selfobject functions.

Kohut also saw narcissistic rage occurring as a result of narcissistic damage to a grandiose sense of omnipotent control of basic mental and physical processes. Here, narcissistic rage is directed at the self for failing to perform in accordance with grandiose expectations of perfection and omnipotence. As we see it, narcissistic rage occurs as a result of the shattering and faulty restoration of archaic narcissistic fantasies. It is directed either at failing selfobjects or at an imperfect and impotent self.

Kohut distinguished between narcissistic rage reactions over loss of a grandiose sense of omnipotent control and shame reactions in response to a narcissistic blow to an exhibitionistic display of grandiosity. A person is ashamed because of the failure to exhibit or display in accordance with grandiose notions. In our terms, Kohut is referring to a sense of shame in reaction to the shattering and faulty restoration of a fantasy of exhibitionistic grandiosity.

However, it has been our clinical experience that a patient may direct narcissistic rage at the self for failing to exhibit or display in accordance with grandiose expectations or for failing to elicit the expected mirroring selfobject response from others or the environment. We understand instances of acute narcissistic rage as a sign of failure to be emphatically attuned to an emerging or shifting selfobject transference fantasy. As long as we can prevent narcissistic rage from becoming chronic, it is an invaluable source of clinical information about the therapeutic course of selfobject transference fantasies and hence the unconscious meaning of trauma.

For heuristic purposes we divide our analytic therapy into three separate yet interrelated phases—initial, reconstructive, and working-through. Dividing treatment in this way is not original; we follow a long analytic tradition. The initial phase of treatment focuses on the patient's vacillations between resistance to and establishment of selfobject transference fantasies. It also involves a discussion of PTSD symptoms and their significance for understanding the unconscious meaning of trauma. The reconstructive phase centers on the analysis of resistances to selfobject transference fantasies as well as both traumatic and genetic reconstruction. Finally, the working through phase involves the consolidation and analysis of selfobject transference fantasies. The therapeutic transformation of these fantasies as part of the resolution of a traumatic transference-neurosis leads to further psychic structuralization of the patient's subjective world and to increased introspection or insight into the unconscious meaning of trauma.

During the initial phase many trauma patients, like other analytic patients, unconsciously communicate both the dread and the hope (A. Ornstein, 1974) of establishing selfobject transference fantasies. However, the trauma patient has a particularly intense dread of further shattering fragmentation and disintegration or narcissistic mortification. The therapist must be empathically attuned to these vacillations in order to avoid attempting to force a selfobject transference "fantasy bond" (Firestone, 1985) against stiff and still unanalyzed resistance or rupturing a "spontaneously developing" (Kohut, 1970, p. 554) selfobject transference fantasy. Failure to be empathically attuned to these often subtle yet critical clinical vacillations may derail treatment before it has really begun. Empathic attunement to these vacillations enables the therapist to help the survivor begin forming the transference fantasy necessary for reconstructing and working through the unconscious meaning of trauma.

Introducing the discussion of PTSD symptoms early in treatment gives these psychological remnants of the shattering and faulty restoration of central organizing fantasies a voice in the "psychoanalytic dialogue" (Leavy, 1980). This strategy is consistent with modern refinements in analytic practice emphasizing the use of symptom analysis not as an end in itself but as a part of character analysis. Unlike a number of prominent authorities (see, for example, Horowitz, 1976; Hendin, 1983, Hendin and Haas, 1984), we do not think that the analysis of PTSD symptoms is sufficient for achieving increased structuralization and introspection. On the contrary, we maintain that significant and lasting therapeutic gains are possible only through the analysis of transference and resolution of transference neurosis. We cite a body of analytic literature in support of our contention.

The distinction between traumatic and genetic reconstruction is an important issue in the reconstructive phase. We base this distinction on the work of Anna Ornstein (1983). She observed that the reconstruction of childhood self-states rather than specific events is essential in illuminating the unconscious meaning of psychic trauma. We extend Ornstein's ideas on reconstruction of the unconscious meaning of trauma to include shattered and faultily restored archaic narcissistic fantasies, core expressions of childhood self-states.

We employ traumatic reconstruction to revive in the transference central organizing fantasies of self in relation to selfobject as they bear on the unconscious meaning of past occurrences. Similarly, we use genetic reconstruction to revive in the transference a survivor's central organizing fantasies of self as they unconsciously existed prior to or at the time of trauma. This provides us with a clinical replication of a specific "intersubjective developmental context" (Atwood and Stolorow, 1984) within which to reconstruct and work through the unconscious meaning of trauma.

We use traumatic and genetic reconstruction in different ways depending upon the stage of psychological development at which a specific trauma occurs in contrast to other traumas. On the one hand, trauma such as incest, which usually occurs at a relatively early stage of development, inevitably involves a blurring of distinctions between traumatic experience and genetic context. On the other hand, traumas such as rape and combat, which usually occur later in life, do not necessarily involve the same blurring of distinctions. Reconstruction requires careful attention to establishing distinctions between trauma and genetic context. However, the therapeutic objective of reconstruction is to arrive at valid empathic inferences about the unconscious meaning of trauma.

We use two clinical sources for reconstructing archaic narcissistic fantasies that form the critical genetic context for interpretations about the unconscious meaning of trauma. First, we use the survivor's personal account of formative family history to reconstruct the genetic context of interferences in the developmentally necessary transformation of archaic narcissistic fantasies. Because we accept as a psychological given that these fantasies are a constant feature of unconscious mental life and activity, we think it entirely possible to indirectly "observe" their unconscious organizing action on the basis of a detailed and comprehensive family history.

Second, we use emerging selfobject transference fantasies as another clinical source for reconstructing archaic narcissistic fantasies. For example, the trauma survivor may need to establish a mirroring selfobject transference in order to restore a fantasy of exhibitionistic grandiosity that was shattered by incest, rape, or combat trauma. Or, to take another typical example, the trauma survivor may need to establish an idealizing or alter ego selfobject transference in order to restore a fantasy of merger with an omnipotent imago or identical twin.

Working through constitutes the third, and final, phase of our analytic therapy. It may be divided into three interrelated subphases: consolidating a selfobject transference fantasy as a means of restoring a shattered and faultily restored archaic narcissistic fantasy; increasing introspection or insight into the unconscious meaning of psychic trauma as symbolically encoded in PTSD symptoms; and analyzing the selfobject transference fantasy and thus transforming archaic narcissistic fantasies into developmentally more advanced meaning structures. Transformation of these fantasies into a mature sense of self is the major goal of our analytic therapy.

The consolidation of a selfobject transference fantasy usually leads to a diminution of the dissociative disturbance in the survivor's "sense of subjective self" (Stern, 1985). We base our reconceptualization of PTSD as a dissociative disorder symptomatically expressing the shattering and faulty restoration of fantasmagorical meaning structures on Kohut's (1971) important distinction between "horizontal" and "vertical splits" in the psyche (p. 185). We linked (see chapter 5) Kohut's distinction with Freud's (1927, 1936, 1940) introduction and discussion of the difference between dissociative splits in the ego maintained by depersonalization and derealization and dynamic splits between conscious recall and unconscious memory maintained by repression. We cite the work of Fairbairn (1952) and others in support of our reconceptualization of traumatic neurosis or PTSD as a dissociative disorder.

Let us briefly review our earlier discussion (see chapter 1) of Kohut's distinction between horizontal and vertical splits. According to Kohut (1971), horizontal splits in the psyche involve the unconscious repression of painful memories of parental failures to respond empathically to developmentally appropriate expressions of archaic narcissism (pp. 183-6). Such repressive horizontal splits do not prevent the development of a cohesive nuclear self, however. Vertical splits have just that effect. They involve the unconscious disavowal of the meaning of experience and lead to a "developmental arrest" (Stolorow and Lachmann, 1980) in the transformation and integration of archaic forms of narcissism into a cohesive nuclear self. These untransformed and unintegrated forms of archaic narcissism remain dissociatively split off realms of self (selfobject) experience. We have argued that the shattering and faulty restoration of archaic narcissistic fantasies constitute a vertical split as maintained by dissociation and disavowal.

We read Kohut as suggesting that trauma results in a vertical split maintained by dissociative splitting of archaic narcissistic fantasies as part of the disavowal of meaning. In propounding our theory of the unconscious meaning of trauma as caused by the shattering and faulty restoration of fantasmagorical meaning structures, we have simply refined Kohut's ideas. Kohut's monumental discovery of the selfobject transference enabled him to employ analysis as a method of transforming via transmuting internalization split-off archaic narcissistic fantasies. For instance, Kohut (1971) concluded that "the idealized parent (*the fantasy of the omnipotent father*, for example) becomes repressed and/or split-off. *No modification of the fantasy can take place (nor can it be integrated with the reality ego) without analysis* (p. 184, italics added). We have built upon Kohut's discovery as the basis for our self-psychological approach to analytic therapy with the trauma patient.

Our treatment approach is designed to mend vertical splits. It does so by transforming archaic narcissistic fantasies and "undoing" disavowal as part of reconstructing and working through the unconscious meaning of trauma. Our approach is markedly in contrast to other forms of trauma therapy. They rest on an implicit conception of trauma as resulting in a horizontal split and therefore requiring the uncovering and lifting of unconscious repression. The difference between conceptions of trauma as resulting in horizontal versus vertical splits underlies, we believe, the symptom versus character analysis dispute in the treatment of survivors.

Reducing dissociative disturbances in self-experience decreases the intensity and frequency of PTSD symptoms. In addition, as survivors unconsciously organize themselves in accordance with a needed selfobject transference fantasy, they are increasingly able to explore the disturbing details of traumatic occurrences. These explorations lead to more introspection or insight into the unconscious meaning of these occurrences. In other words, as the transference deepens, the level of free associative introspection increases.

Analysis of selfobject transference fantasies leads to their transformation into developmentally advanced meaning structures and, concomitantly, a more stable, cohesive sense of self. Previous attempts at restoring shattered fantasmagorical meaning structures failed because they were based on unconscious elaboration, not transformation. The successful analysis of selfobject transference fantasies entails the transformation of shattered and faultily restored archaic narcissistic fantasies. The resulting diminution of PTSD symptoms increases the survivor's ability to handle daily problems of living, which further enhances a sense of competence and well-being.

REVIEW OF THE LITERATURE

Several recent works (see, for example, Horowitz, 1976; Hendin and Haas, 1984; Brende and Parson, 1985) provide excellent historical surveys of the general literature on the analytic treatment of trauma. Focusing on a significant yet less well-known body of literature, we examine what Hillel Klein (1968) declared as the central "therapeutic dilemma" (p. 247) in the treatment of trauma. Analysts have long recognized that "massive traumatization" (Krystal and Niederland, 1968), including incest, rape, and combat trauma, results in severe psychological damage to basic character structures. However, many of these same analysts advocate brief and limited forms of trauma therapy designed to provide only symptomatic relief. (We refer to all of these treatment strategies as trauma therapy, which we distinguish from our analytic therapy of trauma.) They argue that the severely damaged trauma patient, like the schizophrenic patient, can neither tolerate nor benefit from standard analytic therapy.

These analysts become caught in the dilemma of recognizing that trauma damages basic character structures yet advocating brief and limited therapy that provides only symptomatic relief. A way out of this predicament is to argue that massive traumatization leads to irreversible psychic damage that destroys basic character structures and permanently alters personality functioning; hence, only limited treatment is a realistic possibility.

Obviously, we do not accept this dim and pessimistic therapeutic outlook. In citing a significant body of analytic literature supporting our approach, we discuss what we believe is behind the central "therapeutic dilemma" in the treatment of trauma, namely, what we call the symptom versus character analysis dispute.

Before proceeding with our literature review, however, let us briefly describe the basic features of our approach. Our approach consists of the transferential illumination and transformation of shattered and faultily restored central organizing fantasies of self in relation to selfobject as part of the reconstruction and working through of the unconscious meaning of trauma. This constitutes the primary "therapeutic action" of our approach.

As part of our approach, we pay close attention to clinical manifestations of narcissistic rage (Kohut, 1972) as well as recurrent traumatic nightmares, seen, however, as a type of "self-state dream" (Kohut, 1977, pp. 109-10). Both narcissistic rage and the dream depiction of the state of the self are important clinical phenomena illuminating the continued unconscious organizing activity of shattered and faultily restored archaic narcissistic fantasies.

Moreover, our reconceptualization of PTSD as a dissociative rather than an anxiety disorder has important treatment implications. Our approach to treating the reexperiencing and numbing symptoms of PTSD, which we view as dissociative forms of depersonalization, derealization, and disembodiment, uses standard analytic therapy techniques. These include the analysis of resistance, transference, transference neurosis (or, in this case, traumatic transference-neurosis), as well as the use of countertransference. (See Frick and Bogart, 1982, on the use of standard analytic techniques in the group therapy of trauma patients.) More specifically, as a basic feature of our approach, we employ the concept of the transference-countertransference neurosis.

Self-Psychological Literature and the Analytic Therapy of Trauma

Although our effort represents the first exclusive and systematic self-psychological approach to the analytic therapy of trauma, a number of other previous studies incorporate and utilize self psychology in understanding and treating trauma. We have cited Anna Ornstein's (1983) work on the analytic reconstruction of childhood self-states as a means of understanding the unconscious meaning of trauma. In addition, there is the work of Fox (1972, 1974), Horowitz (1974, 1976), Cohen (1980, 1981), Blitz and Greenberg (1984), and Brende and Parson (1985).

Before discussing the studies of these various authors, we return to the early work of Simmel (1944) (see chapter 5). In an important sense, Simmel anticipated our self-psychological approach to the analytic therapy of the trauma patient. Simmel was a "medical officer in the German army and for two years was in charge of a military hospital for war neuroses" (p. 228). In carrying out his respective military and medical duties, he reported, he saw "two thousand war neurotics— half of [whom] I treated myself with a combination of psychoanalysis and hypnosis" (p. 228).

Based on his extensive clinical experience, Simmel found in the dreams (recurrent traumatic nightmares) and "epileptiform seizures" (reliving experiences) of war neurotics evidence of what he described as a "self-curing tendency." In other words, Simmel distinguished himself from Freud and subsequent analysts who saw the symptoms of trauma as instances of a neurotic "repetition compulsion." Simmel, in terms similar to our own, viewed these symptoms as manifestations of narcissistic trauma and faulty attempts at self-cure.

Simmel employed his therapeutic relationship with war neurotics to harness their "self-curing tendency." In fact, Simmel anticipated the self-psychological theory of the selfobject functioning of the therapeutic relationship especially with respect to narcissistic rage. He (1944) argued that (narcissistic) rage resulted from "essential woundings to the soldier's narcissism" (p. 244). He encouraged his patients to vent and work out such rage against a "dummy," which Simmel used as what amounted to a selfobject transference substitute.

As previously noted (see chapter 5), Simmel concluded that his method of modified analytic treatment helped the "soldier to liquidate the war psychologically—i.e., to retransform his 'war ego' into a 'peace ego' " (p. 247).

We have already cited Horowitz's work as part of our discussion of the unconscious meaning of combat trauma (see chapter 5). He was neither exclusively nor systematically self-psychological in his approach to understanding and treating trauma. However, he was one of the first to incorporate and apply Kohut's (1971) early work on the narcissistic character disorder as part of his "stress response short-term trauma therapy." Horowitz used Kohut's work as the basis for treating trauma patients with a preexisting and underlying narcissistic character disorder, one of four major neurotic character types, the others being hysterical, obsessional, and phobic. In keeping with his overall treatment approach, Horowitz argued that the therapy of the traumatized "narcissist" must focus on specific characterological information processing styles as they manifest themselves clinically in resistances to cognitive recall and affective reexperiencing of trauma.

Utilizing Kohut's (1971) original description of the narcissistic character, Horowitz argued that such a person is psychologically organized around an extremely fragile and vulnerable "self-concept" grounded in unconscious illusions of grandiosity, omnipotence, idealization, and merger. Experience is imbued with unconscious traumatic meaning by the narcissist to the degree to which it is cognitively and affectively processed as endangering a precarious sense of self. In an attempt to protect and shore up such an endangered sense of self, the narcissist, according to Horowitz, "slides the meaning" of trauma by a process he refers to as "polarization."

Polarization involves the attempt on the part of the narcissist to buttress and maintain unconscious illusions of grandiosity, omnipotence, idealization, and merger by "externalizing" all bad attributes and "internalizing" all good attributes. To quote Horowitz (1976):

> That which is good is labeled as of the self (internalization). Those qualities that are undesirable, are excluded from the self by denial of their existence, disavowal of related attitudes, externalization, and negation of recent self-experience. Persons who function as accessories to the self may also be idealized by exaggeration of their attributes. Those who counter the self are depreciated [p. 174].

The failure of polarization to "slide the meaning" of trauma sufficiently to maintain a desperately needed but threatened sense of self may lead to more extreme measures, such as a shift in "global being." According to Horowitz, this "state includes changes in self-imagery, demeanor and style" (p. 174). All shifts in meaning are unconsciously motivated by a dread of falling into a "state of self-fragmentation."

Again building upon Kohut's (1971) early work, Horowitz suggested that in treating the traumatized narcissist it is necessary to form one of two types of "quasi-relationship": "One form is characterized by personal grandiosity with the expectation of admiration, the other by idealizing the therapist with the expectation of being all right because he is related to by an ideal figure . . ." (p. 182).

Using these mirroring and idealizing selfobject transferences (although he never explicitly referred to them as such), Horowitz argued that it is possible to analyze the narcissist's "sliding of meaning" via polarization as the latter is reflected in resistances (defenses) to remembering and feeling. The therapist interprets the narcissist's denial of impotence, disavowal of imperfection, and loss of control as part of reconstructing and working through the unconscious meaning of trauma.

We have taken Horowitz's limited and circumscribed use of Kohut's early self-psychological work and expanded it to encompass the analytic treatment of all trauma patients. We have found that the narcissistic issues that Horowitz argued are limited solely to the narcissist are actually at the crux of the unconscious meaning of trauma for most survivors regardless of character type. For example, Horowitz's description of a shift in "global being" represents, we believe, an early attempt to account for the shattering and faulty restoration of central organizing fantasies. In addition, we have made far greater use of Kohut's concept of the selfobject transference in our analytic therapy with the trauma patient.

Narcissistic Fantasies as Agents of Therapeutic Action

In chapter 1, we provided a detailed discussion of the psychoanalytic literature on narcissistic fantasy and its central role in the formation and unconscious organizing activity of the self-as-fantasy. We also discussed (see chapter 4) Freud's important description of the ontogenesis of specific unconscious psychosexual fantasies into pathogenic agents in the development of common psychoneurotic disorders. We linked Freud's thoughts on the ontogenesis and pathogenesis of unconscious fantasy with Kohut's theory of the autonomous developmental transformation of archaic into mature forms of narcissism, and, more specifically, narcissistic fantasies of self in relation to selfobject. This linkage served as a basis for our self-psychological theory of trauma.

We cited (see chapter 1) a number of key studies, including the work of Federn (1952), A. Reich (1960), Tartakoff (1966), Pumpian-Mindlin (1969), Bach and Schwartz (1972), Tolpin (1974), Volkan (1973), Modell (1975, 1976), Silverman (1978/9, 1979, Silverman, Lachmann, and Milich, 1982), Bloch (1978), Grunberger (1979), Rothstein (1984a, b), Eigen (1980, 1982), Schwartz-Salant (1982) and Bach (1985), all documenting what we view as the unconscious organizing activity of archaic narcissistic fantasies throughout life. We noted that these same studies highlight the role of these fantasies in narcissistic disorders. Of these studies those of Volkan, Modell, and Silverman are of particular relevance to our self-psychological approach to the analytic therapy of trauma. We also need to discuss briefly the work of Bloch (1978), Eigen (1980, 1982), and Auerhahn and Laub (1984), all of whom support our use of unconscious fantasy as a primary agent in the therapeutic action of analytic therapy.

Both Volkan and Modell approach the role of archaic narcissistic fantasy from an object relations theoretical perspective specifically, from a Winnicottian framework. Volkan views these fantasies as types of "transitional object" on which patients suffering from narcissistic character disorder rely to shore up fragile and vulnerable self-structures and a precarious sense of self. In describing the treatment of a patient, Volkan (1973) observes:

> In his second year his *narcissistic core* became more apparent; he *fantasized* an iron ball in which he lived and from which he reigned. It offered boundaries and an identity against the outside world . . . [pp. 359-60, italics added]. . . . An examination of some of Mr. Brown's *specific* fantasies disclosed different levels of condensation and what I suggest was their underlying function as transitional objects. He seemed to be addicted to some of them, chosen from an endless store of possibilities; these he used over and over whenever he felt the need. There was some change in superficial content but the basic themes remained unaltered [p. 370, italics in original]. . . . They were clearly *narcissistic;* a glorified self-image underlay them all [p. 371, italics added].

According to Volkan, it is necessary to illuminate these fantasies and analyze their unconscious functioning as transitional objects in order to create a genuine transference relationship:

> Control by the use of transitional fantasies of that area in which inner and outer realities are separated but interrelated had to be worked through in analysis in order for my patient to be able to cross over to the progressive side by utilizing his analyst as a transitional object. A less narcissistic object relationship then became possible [p. 370].

Modell (1976) viewes archaic narcissistic fantasy as an essential element in the narcissistically disordered patient's illusion of the analytic setting and analyst as a "holding environment." He writes:

> The *fantastic elements* include the magical wish to be protected from the dangers of the world and the illusion that the person of the analyst in some way stands between these dangers and shields the patient. It is the illusion that the patient is not "really in the world." There is the wish that the analyst can make the world better for the patient, without the patient's being required to do any work—that mere continguity to this powerful analyst will transfer the analyst's magical powers to himself [pp. 292-3, italics added].

Modell sees the holding environment fantasy or "cocoon fantasy" (p. 302) as part of what Kohut (1971) called a "vertical split" (pp. 183-6) in the psyche resulting from severe environmental trauma.

Adopting a position similar to Volkan's, Modell argues that such a holding environment fantasy, although a necessary part of the initial phase of analytic treatment with the narcissistically disordered patient, must be analyzed if a therapeutic alliance that will sustain a genuine transference relationship is to be created. Failure to analyze sufficiently the holding environment or cocoon fantasy may have dire consequences, Modell warns:

> If these fantasies associated with the holding environment are not sufficiently analyzed, there is a danger, in the narcissistic character disorder, that the analytic process itself may become a transitional object and the patient would then be addicted to an interminable analysis [p. 305].

The works of both Volkan and Modell are relevant to our approach because they are unique in recognizing and discussing the clinical manifestation and role of archaic narcissistic fantasies. However, their object relations perspective limits their conception of these fantasies as primary agents in the therapeutic action of analytic therapy. They do not view the analysis and transformation of these fantasies as basic to the therapeutic action of analytic therapy. Rather, they see them as obstacles to be removed as part of establishing and analyzing genuine transference. The absence of a self-psychological theory of the developmental transformation of archaic into mature forms of narcissism, selfobject functioning, and selfobject transference prevents them from taking full advantage of their own important insights into the use of narcissistic fantasies in analytic therapy.

By adopting a theoretical perspective more congenial to self psychology, Silverman advances beyond some of the limitations in the work of Volkan and Modell. Silverman pioneered the use of the "subliminal psychodynamic activation" method as an experimental means of illuminating a species of archaic narcissistic fantasy he (Silverman et al., 1982) referred to as "symbiotic-like oneness fantasies" (p. 6). He (Silverman, 1978/9) described these fantasies as involving "a *partial* merging of self with mother—in more precise terminology, fantasies in which there is a merging of some but not all self-representation with representations of mother" (p. 564).

Silverman has also been a major proponent of the use of these fantasies as primary "therapeutic agents" in analytic therapy with severely disturbed patients. Writing with coauthors Lachmann and

Milich, Silverman (1982) goes so far as to argue that "there are ways of activating these *fantasies* that not only do not impede the psychoanalytic process, but *facilitate it for certain patients who might otherwise be inaccessible to psychoanalytic treatment*" (p. 197, italics added).

Silverman and his colleagues write: "These oneness fantasies, we believe, are particularly implicated in the analytic 'holding environment' and in the *function of the analyst as empathic mirroring selfobject*" (p. 194, italics added). In this critical passage Silverman linked "oneness fantasies" with Modell's "holding environment" or "cocoon fantasy" and Kohut's selfobject transference fantasy. Silverman et al. go on to maintain:

> What we believe is often at the basis of this [developmental] arrest is the absence of sufficient and sufficiently safe symbiotic experiences during these early phases; *and it is this deficiency that we are proposing must be addressed in treatment through the activation of non-threatening oneness fantasies* [p. 202, italics added].

We believe that the "developmental arrest" (Stolorow and Lachmann, 1980) or "deficiency" referred to by Silverman et al. results from trauma, which produces vertical splits in the psyche that can be analyzed only by facilitating the emergence and development of selfobject transference fantasies.

In support of our approach, Silverman et al. (1982) argue that

> the use of oneness fantasies activated by empathic responses does not preclude the analysis of these fantasies. On the contrary, we think it important that at appropriate times in treatment the analyst help the patient understand not only that he or she seeks to feel at one with the analyst, but that the analyst's empathic responsivity has left the patient feeling that his wish has been gratified [p. 204].

Our approach employs a general expansion as well as specific application of Silverman's work. We have broadened Silverman's ideas on unconscious merger fantasies of symbioticlike oneness to include other types of central organizing fantasies of self in relation to selfobject. We have found that the activation of shattered and faultily restored versions of these fantasies in specific selfobject transferences is critical to their transformation as part of working through the unconscious meaning of trauma. Like Silverman, who discovered that the use of merger fantasies of symbioticlike oneness leads to significant therapeutic improvement in the schizophrenic patient, we have found that the transformation of similar fantasies leads to increased psychic structuralization and introspection in the trauma patient.

Bloch's (1978) work supports our theory of the shattering import of traumatic occurrences for unconscious fantasy life. In addition, her work is also relevant to our treatment approach. Bloch advocated a therapy focusing on what she called the patient's "fantasy-identity," an identity formed in the context of early childhood trauma (p. 4).

Although Bloch did not explicitly refer to this fantasy identity in terms of archaic narcissistic fantasy, her description of it points to a very close similarity between the two. In describing fantasy identity, she observed:

> His feelings of *omnipotence* may lead him to expect deeds to materialize effortlessly, or he may inhibit activity in order to avoid exposing his limitations and risking failure. He may also renounce realistic goals for *grandiose schemes that may unconsciously be designed to establish his absolute control* [p. 5, italics added].

Bloch went on:

> In varying degrees, depending on the intensity of the danger the child has experienced, he frequently transforms himself. He creates the illusion that he is *shadowy or invisible,* or he acts out this *fantasy and assumes an identity that endows him with superpowers or a different sex* [p. 22, italics added].

We shall see this type of adaptation to trauma in all three of our representative treatment studies (see chapter 7).

Our contention that such fantasies continue to unconsciously organize experience in adults also finds support in Bloch's writings:

> What may happen to children's fantasies when the child does not receive psychoanalytic help was revealed in my work with adult patients. In those instances where they were able to disinter them, *the early fantasies appeared to simply have gone underground, and as part of their unconscious, they continued to exact a controlling influence on their lives* [p. 93, italics added].

Bloch contended that the transferential activation of a fantasy-identity allows the therapist to enter into the patient's unconscious mental life. Once inside this world, the therapist can use the analysis of the transference to help the patient reorganize identity around less fantasmagorical mental imagery.

The fantasy that led Patty from schizophrenia into the world of reality progressed through three different phases and a coda, *each one representing a step toward health and marked by evolving identities for both of us*. When she initially delineated me as a 'blur,' an 'angel who can turn bad people into good,' she presented her central preoccupation with feelings of worthlessness and the ephemeral hope . . . *that I possessed supernatural powers that could transform her* and so make her eligible for love [p. 104, italics added].

Our analysis of selfobject transference fantasies as a means of transforming shattered and faultily restored central organizing fantasies is based, in part, on Bloch's ideas on the use of transference to alter trauma induced fantasy-identity.

Eigen (1980, 1982), like Silverman and Bloch, stressed the therapeutic value of the transferential activation of what he described as fantasy "ideal images" of self. He points out that these fantasmagorical self-states were primary therapeutic agents in "clinical healing" and in overcoming arrests in "self-formation." Eigen (1982) wrote: "A regression to a sense of self-creation is sometimes needed in order to generate and maintain a fuller sense of self" (p. 322).

Eigen connected his ideas on fantasmagorical ideal images with Kohut's work on narcissistic selfobject transferences (p. 336). Eigen viewed the transferential activation and analysis of unconscious fantasies of ideal self-states, like the selfobject transference, as critical in contributing to the "personality's overall well-being and ability to function" (p. 336). Going beyond the works of Volkan and Modell, Eigen lends further support to our position of viewing the transference activation of unconscious narcissistic fantasies as critical to the therapeutic action of analysis.

Auerhahn and Laub's (1984) view of the relation between trauma and fantasy is similar to our own. They saw the transference activation of traumatically shattered unconscious fantasy of self and other as a basic mode of therapeutic action in the analytic treatment of the trauma survivor. For example, summarizing the analytic treatment of a traumatized Vietnam combat veteran, they described the patient's transference fantasy of the analyst as an omnipotent parental imago as critical to both reconstructing and working through the unconscious meaning of the trauma. In this particular case, the meaning involved the destruction and loss of a previous unconscious fantasy of merger with an idealized omnipotent other.

Auerhahn and Laub's description of this patient's transference fantasy of the analyst as an omnipotent other, or what they call "elusive helper" and "benign other," is similar to Klein's (1968) description of the Holocaust survivor's transference fantasy of the therapist as the magical "guardian angel." According to Auerhahn and Laub, this transference fantasy enabled their patient to neutralize extreme psychic pain as part of the therapeutic process of restoring and transforming his traumatically shattered self-image. In support of our approach, Auerhahn and Laub contend that such transformation is at the heart of working through the unconscious meaning of trauma.

Narcissistic Rage and Recurrent Traumatic Nightmares

We have repeatedly stressed the importance of narcissistic rage in understanding, reconstructing, and working through the unconscious meaning of trauma. Earlier (see chapter 1), we pointed out that narcissistic rage is implicitly included in *DSM* III (1980) as a secondary symptom of PTSD. It is described as unprovoked, explosive, and sometimes destructive outbursts.

The nature and function of aggression in treating survivors of trauma has been discussed by several authors. De Wind (1971), a colleague and collaborator of Krystal's in developing methods of treating Holocaust survivors, indicated that these patients are often extremely well-defended against any expression of aggression. She argued that this inability to express aggression must be understood in the context of the trauma of imprisonment in concentration and death camps. According to De Wind part of the unconscious meaning of this traumatic occurrence centers, paradoxically, on the illusion of possessing a malevolent and lethal form of aggression.

Behind such unconscious illusions is, De Wind concludes, the phenomenon of the omnipotence of thought. In the context of the traumatic experiences in the camps, the survivor imagines that thoughts, and, in this case, the wish to survive, are omnipotent; the wish automatically begets the deed. Wishing to survive is translated into the unconscious belief that survival is always at another's expense.

This belief is further unconsciously elaborated into the idea of having "caused" the other's death as part of the wish to survive. Surviving becomes imbued therefore with the unconscious meaning that one possesses a malevolent and lethal form of aggression. Such violent destructiveness must be unconsciously defended against to avoid causing the death of others who arouse anger.

De Wind also links the omnipotence of thought and its bearing on experiencing aggression as malevolence with unconscious "survivor guilt," a common symptom of trauma typically found among Holocaust survivors and Vietnam combat veterans suffering from PTSD. Unconscious survivor guilt leads, according to De Wind, to the masochistic wish to suffer. Such a wish may seriously jeopardize therapy in the form of a negative therapeutic reaction.

De Wind's discussion of the omnipotence of thought and its role in imbuing the trauma of the Holocaust with a malevolent unconscious meaning (see also H. Klein, 1968) has relevance for our understanding of the role of narcissistic rage in the analytic therapy of incest, rape, and combat trauma survivors. What she describes as malevolent aggression we view as a manifestation of narcissistic rage. In our therapeutic work with trauma patients we have found that narcissistic rage often takes on omnipotent and malevolent unconscious meaning. As we document in several of our treatment cases (see chapter 7), interpreting the omnipotence and malevolence associated with narcissistic rage, both when it is defended against in resistances and when it is expressed in acute outbursts, is crucial to reconstructing and working through the unconscious meaning of trauma.

In addition to De Wind, a number of other authors have commented on the importance of aggression and rage in treating trauma patients, especially Vietnam combat veterans suffering from PTSD (e.g., Fox, 1972, 1974; Haley, 1974, 1978; Frick and Bogart, 1982; Hendin and Haas, 1984). For our purposes, the work of Fox is most relevant. He introduced Kohut's (1972) concept of narcissistic rage as critical to understanding and treating the trauma patient.

According to Fox, an important unconscious meaning of combat trauma for the soldier involves the loss of an admired and idealized buddy or field commander. On the basis of Kohut's (1971) concept of the selfobject, Fox contends that the buddy or officer is often experienced by the soldier as providing desparately needed soothing and calming selfobject functions. The idealized selfobject functioning of such a person, with whom the soldier unconsciously merges in fantasy, helps the soldier to hold himself together despite the enormous strain of battle. The unexpected and often horrifying loss of the person throws the surviving soldier into a frightening and chaotic state of self-fragmentation, accompanied by painful disintegration anxiety. It is as if the soldier had suddenly lost a part of his own body.

The absence of the buddy or field commander entails the loss for the surviving soldier of the ability to sooth and calm himself by unconsciously merging in fantasy with an omnipotent and idealized parental imago. As part of impending self-fragmentation, the loss of the capacity for self-control throws the soldier into a blind and wild fury, that is, a narcissistic rage. In the rage, the soldier indiscriminately strikes out at his immediate surround, feeling that it has deprived him of his ability to sooth and calm himself.

In the representative case studies of Alexander and Junior (see chapter 5), we presented examples of this type of narcissistic rage and interpreted its significance for understanding the unconscious meaning of combat trauma. In both cases, the unconscious meaning of combat trauma revolved around the shattering and faulty restoration of a fantasy of grandiose and omnipotent control of the immediate environment, which was experienced as a selfobject extension of self. The shattering and faulty restoration of this central organizing fantasy was manifested symptomatically in chronic narcissistic rage appearing in periodic violent and destructive outbursts.

Fox (1974) followed Kohut's recommendations for dealing with narcissistic rage. Fox maintained that it is necessary to transform the "underlying narcissistic structures over an extended period of psychoanalytic work with patients who have narcissistic character problems" (p. 810). He based his position on Kohut's contention that narcissistic rage is a symptom, or a "disintegration product," of the breakup of the "nuclear self."

We have extended and refined Kohut's and Fox's thinking on the symptomatic nature of narcissistic rage. We view it as both a disintegration product of the shattering and agent for the (faulty) restoration of central organizing fantasies of self in relation to selfobject. Like Fox, we have found that treating the chronic narcissistic rage connected with PTSD requires an in-depth and long-term analytic therapy capable of transforming "underlying narcissistic structures," that is, archaic narcissistic fantasies. This is one of the main reasons behind our argument that the treatment of the trauma patient requires an analytic therapy going beyond symptomatic relief of PTSD to structural growth.

As a major feature of our approach, we incorporate the self-psychological work of Blitz and Greenberg (1984). In treating Vietnam combat veterans suffering from PTSD, they focused on the use of recurrent traumatic nightmares, viewed as what Kohut (1977, pp. 109-10) called "self-state dreams." Blitz and Greenberg built upon the previous self-psychological work of Fox. Like Fox, they interpreted the unconscious meaning of combat trauma as a narcissistic loss of buddies or field commanders who were experienced by surviving soldiers as providing critical idealizing selfobject functions.

Blitz and Greenberg presented clinical evidence that the self-fragmentation and disintegration anxiety that accompany traumatic loss may be seen in self-states symbolically portrayed in recurrent traumatic nightmares. They offered a self-psychological alternative to the prevailing view that these nightmares were unconscious attempts at belated mastery of trauma by mental repetition of the experience. On the basis of their self-psychological view of these nightmares, they insisted that it was necessary to establish a selfobject transference as a means of helping the trauma patient to reinstate a sense of self-cohesion. A renewed experience of wholeness is often portrayed in the transfiguration of recurrent traumatic nightmares into dream imagery symbolically depicting the trauma patient's revived experience of cohesiveness.

We view recurrent traumatic nightmares as means of gaining empathic access to the trauma survivor's symbolic representation of the shattering and faulty restoration of central organizing fantasies of self in relation to selfobject. We use the selfobject transference to illuminate and transform these fantasies as they are symbolically depicted in recurrent traumatic nightmares (see Ulman and Brothers, 1987). We find clinical evidence of the therapeutic transformation of these fantasies in the transfiguration of these nightmares into dream imagery symbolically depicting self-states of greater cohesion and wholeness. We interpret this dream imagery as the survivor's having successfully worked through the unconscious meaning of trauma. (See De Monchaux, 1978, for a similar analysis of the significance of the transfiguration of dream imagery in posttraumatic nightmares for understanding the "transmutation of meaning.")

"Horizontal" versus "Vertical" Splits

Our reconceptualization of PTSD as a dissociative disorder has important implications not only for understanding the unconscious meaning of trauma but for treating trauma. We find support for our reconceptualization and treatment approach in the self-psychological work of Basch (1981, 1983), Cohen (1980, 1981) and Brende and Parson (1985). Basch developed Kohut's thoughts on disavowal of meaning as the basis for a vertical split in self-experience. Such disavowal entails dissociative splitting of vital realms of self-experience, the reintegration of which is necessary for the transformation of archaic forms of narcissism. Specifically, Basch viewed disavowal as arising in the context of narcissistic trauma, that is, occurrences the unconscious meaning of which represents a threat to the cohesion of self-concept and sense of self.

Basch argued convincingly that disavowal is not, as traditionally described in psychoanalytic theory, equivalent to denial. It does not entail the denial of the perception of a "piece" of external reality. Rather, according to Basch, it involves the failure to imbue the internal percept arising from such perception with personal meaning.

In this connection, Basch criticized A. Freud (1936; see also J. Sandler with A. Freud, 1985) for contributing to the confusion within psychoanalytic theory about disavowal and denial. This confusion resulted, Basch contended, in the failure to analyze adequately disavowal as part of psychoanalytic treatment. In light of Basch's distinction between disavowal and denial, Anna Freud's (1936) important concept of "denial-in-fantasy" must be reassessed. The role of unconscious fantasy in this defensive process does not involve the denial of the perception of external reality. Rather, it serves to disavow and therefore alter the meaning of the internal percept.

In unconsciously organizing experience, fantasy substitutes one meaning for another, usually a meaning that is less threatening to a fragile and vulnerable sense of self. A core sense of self is fragile and vulnerable to the extent that it is unconsciously organized in accordance with archaic narcissistic fantasies. Of course, the disavowal of meaning is never entirely successful, which helps to account for the faulty restoration of these fantasies.

Our reliance on the standard analytic therapy techniques of reconstruction and working through (the unconscious meaning of trauma) is intended to facilitate the reintegration of vertically and dissociatively split-off areas of self-experience. Such reintegration occurs in the course of undoing disavowal and transforming archaic narcissistic fantasies. According to Basch, the undoing of disavowal and transformation of archaic narcissistic structures involves more than the lifting of unconscious repression and recovering meaningful memories lost to conscious recall (Basch, 1981, p. 172; 1983, p. 150). It entails the creation of new meaning, meaning necessary for mending vertical splits and reintegrating dissociatively split off self-experience.

Cohen (1981) and Brende and Parson (1985) rely heavily on self psychology in their respective approaches to the analytic treatment of trauma. These authors support our reconceptualization of trauma as a dissociative disorder, the treatment of which requires mending vertical splits. In this connection, we are all deeply indebted to the pioneering work of Fairbairn (1952), whose elaboration of Freud's ideas on dissociative ego splitting is critical to our understanding and treatment of trauma.

Cohen (1981) expanded his earlier work (1980) on the pathological effect of early childhood trauma on normal memory functioning. The latter, he argued is critical to the development of psychic structures necessary for self-regulation. Cohen (1981) presented the details of the analytic treatment of an incest trauma survivor in support of his theory.

According to Cohen, early and severe trauma leads to a pathological state in which memory and affect are registered on a somatic rather than a mental level of conscious awareness (see, for example, the case of Jean in chapter 3). Such registration seriously interferes with the development of repression as a primary unconscious ego mechanism of defense. We have found that even in young adult trauma survivors, severe trauma interferes with repression as a method of coping with the unconscious meaning of the experience. Instead, these people rely on disavowal of meaning and the dissociative splitting of self-experience.

The translation of traumatic memories and affects originally registered primarily through somatic channels entails, according to Cohen, the use of transference, specifically, selfobject transference. Only within the therapeutic context of the selfobject transference is it possible, Cohen (1981) asserts, to help the survivor relive the traumatic past in an immediate and *meaningful* way. Transferentially including the therapist as part of this reliving aids the trauma survivor in translating somatically registered traumatic memories and affects into mental imagery. Such translation enables the survivor to put into words the meaning of traumatic occurrences as part of participating in the "psychoanalytic dialogue," thus facilitating the development of normal memory functioning.

According to Cohen, the development of the normal functioning of memory is essential to the "growth" of the previously missing psychic structure necessary for mature self-regulation. He links this process with Kohut's concept of transmuting internalization. A close reading of Kohut (1971) reveals that he originally conceptualized transmuting internalization as entailing the unconscious transformation of archaic narcissistic fantasies ("prestructural objects") into healthy and mature psychic structures (pp. 50-5, 106-7, 165-6). Such structures are necessary for a sturdy and stable sense of self and a reliable means of regulating self-esteem.

According to Kohut, trauma interferes with the normal developmental process of transmuting internalization and psychic structure formation (pp. 106, 165). To correct this developmental arrest, it is necessary to revive archaic narcissistic fantasies in the form of selfobject transferences, the slow and gradual analysis of which constitutes transmuting internalization. As Cohen (1981) correctly notes, in introducing the concept of transmuting internalization, Kohut advanced psychoanalysis from a theory and technique of structural change to one of structural growth (p. 95).

Like Cohen, Brende and Parson (1985; Brende, 1981, 1982, 1983; Brende and Benedict, 1980; Brende and McCann, 1984; Parson, 1984) conceptualized trauma as resulting in a vertical split involving a dissociative disturbance in subjectivity. They describe these dissociative disturbances in subjectivity as involving splits in basic identity, or "identity splits." According to Brende and Parson, the treatment of such traumatically induced identity splits requires the use and analysis of selfobject transferences. In the therapeutic context of such a selfobject transference, the trauma survivor undergoes what they refer to as a "reintegrative regression," or "regression in the service of self-cohesion." In our terms, the trauma survivor must revive and reexperience dissociatively split-off areas of self-experience within the transference as part of reconstructing and working through the unconscious meaning of trauma.

The Symptom versus Character Analysis Dispute

We believe that the basic therapeutic dilemma in treating trauma, or the symptom versus character analysis dispute, arises from two fundamentally different conceptions of the very nature of psychic trauma. One group of analysts (e.g., Kardiner, 1941, 1959; Kardiner and Spiegel, 1947; Rado, 1942; Niederland, 1968a,b; Krystal, 1971; Krystal and Niederland, 1968, 1971; Horowitz, 1974, 1976; Hendin and Haas, 1984b; Hendin et al., 1984a) implicitly view trauma as resulting in a horizontal split in the psyche maintained by unconscious repression. For these analysts, especially Horowitz and Hendin and Haas, treatment consists mainly in the analysis of symptomatic forms of resistance and defense (that is, "repetitive-intrusive flooding" and "denial-numbing blocking"). The analysis of the reexperiencing and numbing symptoms of PTSD is, according to these authors, supposed to lead to relatively quick and lasting symptomatic relief.

In addition, these authors claim that such relief is possible without engaging in the analysis of transference and transference neurosis. In fact, a number of them insist that analyzing transference and transference neurosis in severely traumatized patients is counterindicated and, if attempted, is countertherapeutic.

A second group of analysts (for example, Basch, Cohen as well as Brende and Parson) support our conception of trauma as resulting in vertical splits in the psyche. They view such splits as maintained by unconscious dissociation, including forms of depersonalization, derealization and disavowal. In marked contrast to the first group of analysts, this second group recommends treating trauma by standard analytic therapy techniques and, especially, the analysis of transference and transference neurosis. According to these authors, the use of these analytic therapy techniques is necessary to reintegrate basic character structures (in our terms, archaic narcissistic fantasies of self in relation to selfobject) dissociatively split off in the context of the unconscious meaning of trauma.

We do not question the usefulness of symptom analysis. In fact, we

follow Hendin et al. (1981, 1983a,b, 1984a,b) in using the analysis of
PTSD symptoms as a basis for understanding the unconscious meaning
of trauma. Our representative case studies of trauma (see chapters 3,
4, 5) illustrate the utility of this method of symptom analysis.

However, we seriously question the implicit view that trauma results
in horizontal splits maintained by unconscious repression. This view
has lead to a form of treatment that does not use transference and
transference neurosis analysis. We present our three representative
treatment studies (see chapter 7) in support of our central contention
that an analytic therapy utilizing transference analysis and resolution
of transference neurosis is necessary to transform archaic narcissistic
structures that unconsciously organize character.

We find additional support for our approach to treating trauma on
the basis of character rather than symptom analysis in the work of
Kelman (1945, 1946) as well as in the more recent work of Glenn (1984)
and Forman (1984). Originally, Kelman (1945, p. 132) treated World
War II combat veterans using Kardiner's form of trauma therapy,
with its exclusive reliance on symptom analysis. However, Kelman
wrote, he was discouraged by the limited and temporary therapeutic
results (p. 132). In response, he devised a type of character analysis
based on Karen Horney's work. (See chapter 2 for our previous
discussion of the relevance of Kelman to our overall theoretical position.) Kelman reported that the results of his Horneyan character
analysis were superior to those he had previously achieved with Kardiner's form of symptom analysis (p. 132). In fact, Kelman went so far
as to suggest that a number of the cases reported by Kardiner as
being "helpless could have been helped by the technique of character
analysis" (p. 127).

More recently, both Glenn (1984) and Forman (1984) have presented
extensive treatment material demonstrating the efficacy and effective-
ness of standard analytic therapy techniques in treating trauma. In
fact, Forman reintroduced Glover's (1955) classical concept of the
"traumatic transference neurosis." Both Glenn and Forman maintain,
in contrast to Horowitz as well as Hendin and Haas, that rather than
character defining trauma, trauma defines character. A view of trauma
as defining character leads naturally to a therapy using the analysis of
the unconscious meaning of trauma as method of changing character.

Resistance and Countertransference

The role of resistance is central to the dispute between analysts using
symptom analysis in the treatment of trauma and those employing
character analysis. In arguing for symptom analysis, Horowitz (1974,

1976) as well as Hendin and Haas (1984) placed great emphasis on the analysis of resistance as central to their respective trauma therapies. On the basis of the classical psychoanalytic framework, these authors view resistance as a clinical manifestation of unconscious defenses buttressing the repression of traumatic memories and affects. Analysis of resistance (and defense) to remembering and feeling becomes the basic mode of reconstructing and working through the unconscious meaning of trauma, as well as alleviating the symptoms resulting from repression.

In the work of Horowitz and Hendin and Haas, who elaborate Horowitz's view of trauma as a failure in completing cognitive–affective information processing, the primary focus of resistance analysis is on amnestic loss of the conscious recall of the memories associated with trauma and the numbing loss of related feelings. Amnesia and numbing prevent successful cognitive–affective information processing of traumatic occurrences as symptomatically expressed by repetitive-intrusive flooding of painful memories and images as well as denial-numbing blocking of all feeling. In the clinical setting, repetitive-intrusive flooding and denial-numbing blocking manifest themselves as resistances to completing cognitive–affective information processing. They appear either in the form of being overwhelmed by recollection yet emotionally numb or overwhelmed by feeling with no recollection. By analyzing these resistances to remembering and feeling, the therapist helps the trauma patient to: (1) recover repressed memories and affects; (2) gain insight into the unconscious meaning of trauma; and, (3) significantly reduce repetitive-intrusive flooding and denial-numbing blocking as expressed in the reexperiencing and numbing symptoms of PTSD.

We view resistance analysis as critical to facilitating the unfolding of selfobject transference fantasies, the illumination and transformation of which are critical to the reconstruction and working through of the unconscious meaning of trauma. We find support for our approach to resistance analysis with the trauma patient in the work of Klein (1968). Klein found that survivors of the Holocaust often formed primitive transference fantasies in which the therapist was imagined as a "guardian angel" who had magically saved the patient from extermination in the camps.

However, Klein also stressed that for such primitive transference fantasies to emerge it is usually necessary first to analyze intense resistance to the transference. She noted that the survivor may unconsciously resist treatment because it may pose a threat to a cherished illusion of personal grandeur and omnipotent control upon which the survivor has unconsciously organized a fragile and vulnerable posttraumatic sense of self. In other words, Klein was describing a specific form of narcissistic resistance that must be empathically understood as an attempt to maintain the unconscious organization of self-experience. The need for extended periods of slow and gradual analysis of narcissistic resistance is another major reason we advocate and use long-term analytic therapy of the trauma patient rather than short-term trauma therapy.

Countertransference is less an issue for those authors, like Horowitz and Hendin and Haas, who use forms of limited and brief trauma therapy. However, there is a considerable literature warning about particular countertransference problems in the treatment of the trauma patient. For example, in discussing the treatment of the Holocaust survivor, Krystal (1971) wrote about the therapist's unconscious countertransference reaction to the incomprehensible and unbelievable nature of the accounts of the torture and slaughter that were common in the daily routines of the camps. In reaction to this highly charged and upsetting material, the therapist might unwittingly collude with the Holocaust survivor in what Krystal called a "conspiracy of silence" (p. 225). Caught up in such a conspiracy, therapist and patient together either avoid entirely, or fail to discuss in sufficient detail, important material. The countertransference pitfall of a conspiracy of silence is equally dangerous in the treatment of other trauma survivors.

Paradoxically, avoiding the conspiracy of silence may lead to other countertransference problems in analytic therapy with trauma patients. The sexually and aggressively charged nature of the accounts by survivors of the traumatic occurrences of incest, rape, and combat may result in countertransference voyeurism. This type of countertransference reaction may lead to needless and countertherapeutic repetition of the details of traumatic occurrences so that the lurid scenes may be visualized and heard.

Therapists may also become frightened of the trauma patients' possible loss of control of either sexual or aggressive feelings. Such countertransference reactions interfere with the transference reenactment of the sexual and aggressive experiences as part of the therapeutic revival and reliving of trauma. This is particularly true, as Haley (1974, 1978) and Frick and Bogart (1982) point out, in dealing with the violent aggression so prevalent in Vietnam combat veterans suffering from PTSD (see also, Boulanger, 1986).

However, for our purposes, the most significant countertransference issue concerns the therapist's unconscious selfobject fantasies of the patient. Such countertransference selfobject fantasies may, if empathically understood by the therapist, enhance the illumination and transformation of shattered and faultily restored archaic narcissistic fantasies as they organize a reciprocal selfobject transference. Countertransference may therefore be used as part of reconstructing and working through the unconscious meaning of trauma (see Ulman and Brothers, 1987).

In this connection, we cite the work of De Wind (1984). In terms similar to our use of the transference–countertransference neurosis, De Wind recognizes that the intense and emotionally charged "transference/countertransference relations" (p. 298) that inevitably develop between analyst and trauma patient are invaluable in reconstructing and working through the unconscious meaning of trauma.

Klein (1968) discusses countertransference "therapeutic enthusiasm" in working with survivors of trauma, a reference to the therapist's countertransference belief in the unlimited possibilities to help the trauma survivor. This represents a failure to take adequately into account the shattering import of the meaning of the survivor's traumatic experiences. We view such therapeutic overenthusiasm as a form of narcissistic countertransference. The therapist, in responding to the trauma patient's communication of an intense need for help, becomes a captive of his or her own unconscious fantasy of exhibitionistic grandiosity.

In seeking to avoid countertransference therapeutic overenthusiasm, it is important to avoid the equally dangerous countertransference pitfall of "therapeutic pessimism." Such pessimism appears in the writings of number of outstanding authorities on treating trauma. For example, Krystal (1971) maintains that the Holocaust survivors' severely damaged ego and extremely limited capacity for reality testing necessitated a treatment approach of dealing with "psychiatric emergencies" in which the trauma patient may be "restored" to his or her "chronic 'survivor syndrome' state" (p. 224). It is imperative in treating the trauma patient that the therapist avoid the countertransference pitfalls of both therapeutic overenthusiasm and therapeutic pessimism.

CHAPTER 7

Treatment Case Studies of Incest, Rape, and Combat

I n earlier chapters we presented representative case studies of incest, rape, and combat survivors to illustrate our self-psychological theory of trauma. However, the explanatory power of our theory must ultimately be tested by the results of its therapeutic application. To demonstrate the therapeutic value of our treatment approach as outlined in chapter Six, we now offer three representative analytic therapy case studies.

Our therapy patients—Marge, an incest survivor; Thea, a rape survivor; and Nick, a combat survivor—were all seen in analytic therapy for extended periods of time, ranging from three to six years. The results of these ongoing treatment cases provide encouraging support that severe trauma can be successfully treated using self-psychological analytic therapy techniques.

MARGE

Marge, a vivacious 26-year-old, single, white woman, sought treatment specifically to find relief from florid symptoms of PTSD, which, because of their disturbingly dissociative quality, had convinced her that she was "at the edge of a nervous breakdown." Although she had been sexually molested by her brother 11 years earlier, most of her symptoms appeared only after she had viewed a television drama about incest. She has been seen in weekly analytic treatment sessions for two and a half years.

In keeping with our approach to treatment, the presentation of Marge's therapy is divided into three phases—initial, reconstruction, and working through—each corresponding to approximately ten months of treatment.

Initial Phase

Marge called for her first appointment after learning from another incest survivor that the therapist was conducting a research project on incest. Breaking into tears during the early moments of her first session, Marge seemed amazed by her own display of emotion. "I never cry at home," she said, "I'm supposed to be the happy-go-lucky kid." In her loud, animated voice, with its strident "New York accent," she infused even her most poignant descriptions of her distress with humor. Although she dressed in tight jeans and sweaters that showed off her shapely figure, Marge's manner was far from stereotypically feminine. After an initial period in which she presented herself in a distant, rather formal, and self-consciously "ladylike" way, she typically sat with her legs flung carelessly apart, used large, sweeping gestures, and peppered her conversation with mild obscenities.

During the first few sessions, Marge revealed her anxiety about "fitting in" with the therapist's views on incest. She announced her intention to become so well versed in the therapist's theories that she would serve as her "disciple." A graduate student in a mental health field, Marge said she planned to help other victims of sexual abuse.

Marge's air of worshipful devotion to the therapist suggested that, from the very beginning of treatment, she sought a transference relationship in which she might experience herself as merged in fantasy with an idealized imago. Moreover, her avowed determination to serve as the therapist's disciple indicated that an important aspect of this experience was her fantasy of being granted a special position in relation to her therapist. However, a dream she reported in the second week of treatment revealed Marge's association of such a relationship with incest:

My biology notes were stolen from my handbag in a large stadium filled with people.

Marge associated the biology notes with her innermost thoughts and feelings. She noted that she was a very "private person," who seldom shared her feelings in public as other survivors had done at a meeting she had recently attended. Hesitantly, Marge expressed her fear that she might be "robbed" of her privacy if the therapist were indiscreet in using her story for research purposes. She acknowledged that the crowded stadium in her dream might represent her fear of public exposure. Asked what such exposure might be like for her, Marge said she would feel abused, exploited, and furious—"Like I feel about what my brother did," she added.

In subsequent sessions, for which she always appeared exactly on time, Marge responded to the therapist's every question as if to a command for total compliance. She frequently bemoaned the fact that her recall for her early life was scanty. Although the therapist noted Marge's strenuous efforts to behave like a model patient, the meaning of these efforts remained unclear during the initial phase of treatment.

Marge's scrupulously thorough description of her symptoms permitted a firm diagnosis of PTSD. She reported a host of frightening reexperiencing symptoms, including intrusive recollections of her experiences with her brother and reliving experiences that occurred on waking from sleep. She described experiencing an urgent need to wash herself associated with an eerie feeling that she was once again in bed with her brother. Consequently, Marge said, she scrubbed herself over and over as she showered each morning.

Marge also described the following traumatic nightmare, which had recurred repeatedly since her viewing of the television drama on incest:

> You know the morning "cheeses" in the corner of your eye? Well, I grab the cheese between my thumb and pointer and my eyeball unravels.

Associating to this nightmare, Marge said that since watching the television program on incest she had experienced a sense of excruciating vulnerability, "like I have a gaping wound." She revealed her fear that her PTSD symptoms portended her "unravelling" and fragmentation (disintegration anxiety). Marge also observed that since her traumatic incestuous experiences with her brother "my vision of reality has blurred" (derealization). She voiced her suspicion that she had been terrified of seeing her situation clearly.

Numbing symptoms, some of which dated back to her incest, were also prominent in Marge's PTSD. She described highly dissociated states in which she felt "detached from my feelings" and "numb." Even during frequent rage reactions ("anger is the only feeling I really know"), Marge noted that she often felt as if she were observing herself "from a great height" (depersonalization). Since watching the television program on incest, Marge confessed, her rage had been focused almost exclusively on her brother. "I just can't pretend we're the 'Brady Bunch' anymore," Marge commented, "I want to kill Victor."

Among her other PTSD symptoms was a severe sleep disorder. According to Marge, she had not slept through the night since she was molested by her brother. She noted that she often worried that her room would be broken into while she slept. She also described intense startle reactions whenever a family member entered her room without knocking.

The initial phase of treatment was devoted to reconstructing the unconscious meaning of Marge's traumatic incestuous experiences. Marge reported experiencing some relief from her PTSD symptoms in the course of this therapeutic process. She provided the following account of the traumatic episodes.

She recalled several occasions, beginning somewhere between Marge's 12th and 13th birthdays, on which she had awakened during the night to find her 16-year-old brother, Victor, lying beside her in bed, talking to himself. One night, shortly after she had turned 13, she awoke to find her hand on her naked brother's penis. Marge described screaming and "becoming hysterical." Despite the intensity of her reaction, she remembered feeling completely ignored by her parents. "They acted as though nothing had happened to me," Marge said. "Victor became the center of attention—as usual."

According to Marge, Victor frequently occupied center stage in the family because of his penchant for "getting into trouble." As she described a number of his exploits at school and in the neighborhood that had aroused her parents' concern and anger, a note of pride crept into Marge's voice. As the therapeutic work continued and Marge recaptured more and more of the childhood memories for which she had at first been amnestic, it became evident that Marge had once looked up to her older brother with awe and reverence.

Because Marge experienced a great deal of pain in remembering details of her early life, particularly insofar as these involved recollections of being neglected and ignored by her parents, the following account of Marge's childhood was pieced together only after slow and careful therapeutic work. The third of four children in a middle-class Italian-American family, Marge initially described herself as a "model child in your average American family." After a number of transference interpretations regarding her expectation that the therapist, like her parents, required her to maintain a happy, untroubled demeanor and emphasize only the positive aspects of her life, Marge realized that she had grown up with the feeling that her emotional needs were burdensome to her parents. "By the time my mother had me," she said ruefully, "the novelty must have worn off." "Besides," she added, "my mother was always more involved with my father than with us kids."

In one tearful session, Marge reported that the only photograph in the family album showing her as a baby included all the other family members. Yet, the album was filled with individual pictures of the other children. "I was 'the wash-and-wear kid'," Marge observed, "I was supposed to do well without causing any trouble."

On the other hand, Victor, as the oldest male child, received the lion's share of the attention. "Victor was always treated as the special child," Marge said, "and I always thought he was special." She explained that all her father's hopes and dreams had been pinned on Victor's success in life. Marge remembered, until Victor dashed these hopes with his rebellious behavior, that her father—whom she had regarded as a somewhat remote yet loving and protective figure—had often related to her in a playfully affectionate way. Utterly disillusioned by Victor's adolescent escapades, he sullenly withdrew from the family and abruptly called a halt to the lighthearted, teasing interactions Marge had treasured. She recalled that despite her pleas, he ended their Sunday outings to the hardware store he owned and operated. Reminiscing about these "magical Sundays," Marge recalled how delighted she had been to be chosen as his "assistant." Looking back, she speculated that her mother had probably insisted that he take Marge "out of my mother's hair." She also recalled daydreams in which she imagined herself grown up, standing beside him behind the store counter, while he told customers that Marge was indispensible to him.

Marge recalled her painful sense of disillusionment in her father for failing to comfort and console her in the days that followed the molestation. "How could he let this happen to me?" she had asked herself repeatedly. After her incestuous sexual experience with Victor, no outsider could have detected changes within the family, except possibly that Marge seemed even more admiring of her brother.

Hopeless about regaining her place in her father's affections, Marge suddenly found herself behaving "like my brother's groupie." She described following Victor everywhere, watching him play sports and rooting for him when he got into fights. However, Victor, she sadly recalled, regarded her as a nuisance and often disparaged and criticized her. Nevertheless, Marge remembered feeling proud just to be "Victor's little sister." Letters she wrote to Victor in the Navy several years later were full of assurances of her love, support, admiration, and devotion.

Until Victor came home on leave shortly before the television drama on incest, Marge said she never thought about the molestation. However, when she found him "looking at me like I was a girl, not a sister" and when he commented on the appearance of her breasts in a sweater, her memories returned. Even then, Marge noted, she tried to convince herself that she was "flattered" that Victor appreciated her development as a young woman.

After several months of treatment, Marge reported the following dream:

I rub my arm and realize that bumps under my skin are worms.

Associating to this dream, Marge confided that the therapist was "getting under my skin" and that increasingly, her waking thoughts and feelings centered around therapy. Marge assumed that her preoccupation with therapy had been engineered by the therapist, just as she imagined that the therapist had magically caused the recovery of her memories. Although Marge expressed a sense of awe at the therapeutic process, she admitted feeling that perhaps the therapist was becoming too important to her.

Once again, Marge confessed to some apprehension that the therapist might expose her secrets to public scrutiny without adequately protecting her identity. She worried that by becoming "enthralled" with therapy she put herself in danger of being "robbed" of her privacy. Marge did not connect the phallic image of worms under her skin with her sexual molestation. Nevertheless, the therapist wondered if the dream also expressed Marge's unconscious association of the therapist's clinical intrusiveness with Victor's sexual intrusiveness.

Still associating to the dream, Marge wondered if the therapist spent much time thinking about her, if, in other words, she was getting under the therapist's skin. Marge worried that the therapist would find such a situation repugnant. The therapist understood this aspect of the dream as relating specifically to her countertransference. Although she had welcomed Marge's idealization with a sense of pride in her ability to facilitate the therapeutic revival of Marge's fantasy of idealized merger, the therapist had felt offended by Marge's shift from respectful and distant admiration to an attitude of greater ease and familiarity. She had experienced a sense of being intruded upon, for example, when Marge put her feet on an office chair and reached for the therapist's appointment book when a change in appointment time was discussed.

The therapist realized that much as she had welcomed Marge's idealization of her, she had resisted her efforts at merger. She became aware of a fantasy of herself as a lofty and infallible healer with exclusive possession of a cure for incest survivors. Such a fantasy did not permit the sharing of her gradiose omniscience with a patient. Caught up in this selfobject countertransference fantasy, the therapist had resisted Marge's unconscious efforts to merge as part of a selfobject transference fantasy, thereby creating a transference–countertransference neurosis (Ulman and Stolorow, 1985).

The therapist's difficulty in becoming aware of her countertransference fantasy prevented her from noticing indications that Marge had unconsciously perceived her withdrawal. Looking back, however, it is evident that such indications abounded. Around the time of the "worms" dream, Marge had complained of feeling depressed and listless. She had expressed a sense of hopelessness about herself as a fledgling therapist. "I'll never learn to work the way you do," she had moaned.

In a session following a cancellation because of the therapist's illness, Marge jokingly suggested that she had worn the therapist down. Further exploration revealed Marge's distressing conviction that the therapist, like her father and brother, was unable to tolerate her need for a selfobject experience of herself as merged in fantasy with an idealized imago. The therapist presumed that just as Marge was narcissistically enraged with Victor and her father for interfering with her fantasies of idealized merger, she must also feel enraged with the therapist.

A great deal of the working through of this aspect of the transference–countertransference neurosis involved the therapist's attention to Marge's disavowal of any angry feelings. When, for example, Marge seemed to accept the therapist's absence with an exaggerated show of cheerful good humor, the therapist expressed her understanding of Marge's dread of jeopardizing the therapeutic relationship by expressing any displeasure with the therapist.

After a number of similar interventions addressing Marge's fears about expressing her narcissistic rage in the treatment situation, Marge reported a series of dreams that further elucidated the unconscious traumatic meaning of her incestuous experiences. The manifest content of all these dreams involved the discovery of precious jewelry that has been lost or buried, as in the following example:

> You [the therapist] find a tiny ring buried in some soil that my father bought before I was born

Associating to this dream, Marge said that through therapy, she had recaptured a sense of herself as deserving the expensive presents her father continued to buy for her. In the past, Marge said, these presents had only made her more painfully aware of the emotional void between the two of them, a void she attributed to her own deficiencies. Proud of her commitment to therapy and her decision to learn the "magical" techniques the therapist employed to help her feel so much better about herself, Marge said her life now had purpose and direction. She noted feeling "like a treasured heirloom." It seems likely that Marge's fantasy of merger with the therapist's idealized attributes enabled her to restore a sense of herself as a precious gem.

The dreams also heralded the emergence in the transference of fantasies of mirrored grandiosity. Concurrent with the "jewelry" dreams, Marge came to sessions dressed in skirts, silk blouses and dresses instead of her usual jeans. She bleached her hair a soft blond shade and wore it in a more becoming style. She beamed and expressed delight when the therapist commented on this change. "I used to feel that Victor thought I was pretty, even if it would break his teeth to admit it," Marge mused. She described her desperate attempts, when she was 13, to understand why Victor had incestuously molested her. "I told myself that I was so sexy and pretty, he couldn't resist me," she said.

The reconstructive therapeutic process at this point in treatment can be summarized as follows: Because of failures in maternal mirroring, Marge's subjective world had been organized primarily in accordance with the unconscious meaning of narcissistic fantasies of merger with an idealized paternal imago. When her father's abrupt withdrawal seriously disrupted these fantasies and interfered with their developmental transformation, Marge unconsciously attempted to shore up these threatened fantasies by substituting her brother as the idealized paternal imago.

However, Victor's contemptuous treatment of Marge prevented her from experiencing herself as securely merged in fantasy with his idealized qualities. Victor's abusive sexual contact with her shattered her fantasies of him as an idealizable paternal imago. In addition, her father's failure to prevent the abuse and provide her with protective solace dashed her hopes of recapturing a desperately needed experience of idealized merger with him.

The faultiness of Marge's compensatory restoration of her fantasy of idealized merger with either her brother or father led to unconscious efforts at defensive restoration via fantasies of grandiose-exhibitionism. By imagining that she was so "pretty and sexy" that her brother could not resist her, Marge not only attempted the compensatory restoration of her fantasy of idealized merger with her brother, she also sought unconsciously to defensively restore her shattered fantasy by imagining that she was irresistible.

Treatment revived Marge's unconscious wish to restore a fantasy of idealized merger that had been shattered and faultily restored in the course of her development. Her initial resistance to forming such a selfobject transference fantasy stemmed mainly from her dread of becoming vulnerable to abuse and exploitation, just as she had been sexually abused and exploited by her brother. The therapist's counter-transference resistance to merger as part of an idealizing selfobject transference fantasy repeated Marge's childhood experience of rejection by her father and brother. With the eventual establishment of a merger transference fantasy, Marge experienced considerable relief from the dissociative (depersonalization and derealization) manifestation of PTSD and gained a sense of personal worth and well-being.

The emergence of a selfobject transference fantasy of mirrored grandiosity toward the end of the initial phase shed more light on Marge's faulty restorative efforts following her traumatic incestuous experiences. As our study of incest survivors indicates (see chapter 3), Marge's fantasy of herself as an irresistible seductress did not precede the sexual abuse. Rather, her fantasy of provoking the incestuous molestation was a reflection of an unconscious effort at defensive restoration.

Reconstructive Phase

Clinical attention during this treatment phase was focused on the analysis of disturbances in Marge's selfobject transference fantasy of idealized merger. The work of reconstruction begun in the initial phase was carried further, providing a richer genetic context for understanding the unconscious meaning of Marge's trauma.

Having experienced a significant degree of symptomatic relief during the first ten months of treatment, Marge felt more competent in her graduate studies and more confident in dating men. In the context of a selfobject transference fantasy of idealized merger, these positive changes in her life appeared to convince Marge that the therapist possessed uncanny healing powers. She confided her belief that she had found the therapist in accordance with a divine plan. Because of the intensity of Marge's fantasy, any occurrence that undermined the idealizability of the therapist had enormous impact on the treatment.

The first major disruption occurred when the therapist used a friend's apartment for several sessions during the renovation of her office. Although Marge's only complaint was that she disliked changes in a familiar routine, a temporary resurgence of her PTSD symptoms indicated that, on an unconscious level, Marge found the move very distressing. The following recurrent traumatic nightmare, which Marge reported during this period, revealed the unconscious meaning of this disruption and led to a deeper reconstruction of Marge's traumatic experiences:

> I am in my bathroom, naked except for a towel wrapped around my body. My brother is banging on the door. I am terrified that he will force it open.

Only after sessions were resumed in the therapist's office did the connection between the nightmare and the disruption in the analytic setting gradually become apparent. Marge explained that she had hated having sessions in a stranger's apartment because she had learned more about the therapist than she wanted to know. Further inquiry revealed that Marge had not wanted to find out that the therapist, being "merely human," required friends and office space— "like everyone else." Such knowledge detracted from Marge's experience of the therapist as possessing uncanny healing powers.

In the course of exploring the meaning of her nightmare, Marge remembered that on one occasion, after finding her brother in bed with her, she had awakened to find blood on the sheet. She recalled that her mother had taken her to a gynocologist but had never discussed his findings. Marge tearfully recovered a hazy memory of her brother touching her genitals and inserting his fingers into her vagina. She associated the nightmare image of her brother attempting to force his way into the bathroom with his forcing his fingers into her vagina. Marge suggested that, at the time, she had "not wanted to wake up and find out what was happening." She apparently experienced the episode in a highly dissociated state.

Marge confirmed the therapist's interpretation that in her sessions in the strange apartment she had experienced much that was similar to her traumatic contacts with her brother. In both instances Marge felt that intimacy had been forced upon her. She had experienced the therapist as unempathically thrusting the fact of her "mere humanness" into her awareness, much as she had experienced her brother as imposing sexual intimacy upon her.

As the image of the stolen biology notes in her earlier dream suggests, she felt robbed by both her brother and the therapist of essential psychological material, that is, her central organizing fantasy of idealized merger. Both times, Marge was disillusioned by an idealized imago. However, following the reconstruction of the meaning of this disturbance in the transference, Marge's selfobject transference fantasy of idealized merger with the therapist was restored.

The therapist's initial selfobject countertransference response to the disruption in Marge's fantasy of idealized merger was an impulse to withdraw as a means of defending against a narcissistic injury. The therapist's fantasy of herself as omniscient was once again threatened by Marge's disillusionment. However, she soon understood her reaction as another manifestation of the transference–countertransference neurosis and regained her empathic stance, thus facilitating the reconstruction of this important aspect of Marge's traumatic experience.

The therapist's incorrect completion of one of Marge's insurance forms created the second major disturbance in the transference. The content of several subsequent sessions revolved around Marge's rage at Victor for robbing her of closeness with her father. She retold the stories of Victor's delinquent escapades, this time suggesting that, motivated by jealousy, he had deliberately caused her father's withdrawal. Marge connected the fact that she would literally have to pay for the therapist's "mistake" on the insurance form with the feeling that she had to "pay" for her brother's mistakes with the loss of her father's affection. She also expressed disappointment in the therapist for falling short of her fantasy of her as perfect and infallible.

Shortly thereafter, Marge reported "exploding" in rage at Victor for burning a hole in the upholstery of her car, which he had borrowed on a recent visit home. She connected a feeling of being "damaged goods," because of Victor's molestation, with the damage to her car. She said she couldn't bear the thought that Victor had gotten off "scott free" after the molestation while she continued to pay the emotional toll. She confided that she had been fairly promiscuous in early adolescence because she felt that she was no longer "a true virgin."

Suddenly tearful and trembling, Marge recalled an incident that had occurred when she was about 14. She had fallen down the cellar steps and twisted her ankle. Only Victor was strong enough to carry her up the steps. When he stood over her reaching down to pick her up, Marge remembered screaming "don't touch me." "I must have been scared of him, even though I tried not to show it," she said quietly. "He must have tried to have intercourse. Why else would I be so frightened?"

Several dreams Marge reported over the next few sessions, as well as a host of fresh memories, confirmed that Victor had attempted intercourse, but Marge, still in a groggy, dissociated state, had nevertheless fought him off. The therapist noted that while Marge expressed rage at Victor as she recaptured these painful memories, she spared the therapist from all expressions of anger, apparently still fearful that her rage would destroy the needed transference bond.

Working-Through Phase

Treatment proceeded in accordance with two main themes during the most recent phase of treatment—the consolidation of Marge's selfobject transference fantasy of mirrored grandiosity and the continued working through of barriers to the expression of her narcissistic rage.

At the age of 25, Marge still lived at home with her parents and younger brother. Earlier in treatment she had mentioned feeling "uncomfortable" about living with her family because most of her friends lived alone and were self-supporting. However, Marge rationalized her living situation on the grounds that she could not afford her own apartment. Her only source of income was a graduate school teaching assistantship. As graduation approached, Marge reported feeling "torn" about moving out.

In sessions exploring her ambivalence, Marge tentatively revealed her fear that her family could not get along without her. After the therapist responded empathically to Marge's grandiose claim, she increasingly revealed a secret fantasy of herself as essential to the family's survival. She feared that without her competence, good humor, and mental stability, her parents would be forced to confront their intolerable failures. All their children except Marge had failed to live up to their expectations. Nothing Victor did could compensate for their earlier disappointments in him. Her sister had been divorced, and her younger brother had recently completed a substance abuse program. "I'm the only one left to keep up the family reputation," she said. "If I leave home, it's goodbye 'Brady Bunch'. It became apparent that in addition to a grandiose-exhibitionistic fantasy of being irresistibly sexy and alluring, Marge's unconscious efforts at defensive restoration following her shattering trauma centered on another grandiose-exhibitionistic fantasy, that of herself as a model child on whom the family's survivial depended.

During this period Marge complained of pervasive anxiety and difficulty falling asleep. She disclosed her fear that the therapist was disappointed because she had not moved out of her parents home. Further exploration revealed Marge's concern that, like her parents, the therapist required Marge to behave like a model patient in order to sustain the therapist's sense of competence.

The therapist interpreted Marge's experience of being caught in an unresolvable dilemma. On one hand, her unconscious efforts at defensive restoration depended on her staying home in order to sustain a fantasy of herself as the indispensable model child. On the other hand, she imagined that only by moving out could she live up to the therapist's expectations of a model patient. Her fantasy of becoming the therapist's disciple apparently depended on her serving the therapist's selfobject needs as she served the selfobject needs of her parents.

With the exploration of this transference configuration, Marge gained further insight into the "blurring of her vision" with respect to her brother's incestuous abuse. "How could I spoil my parents' image of being 'The Brady Bunch' by talking about the incest?" she asked, "I was the only one who could keep that myth alive." Experiencing herself as mirrored within the transference, Marge, by the end of the reconstructive phase, no longer depended on a fantasy of herself as responsible for maintaining her parents' (and the therapist's) self-esteem. She expressed a sense of satisfaction and pride after finding a low-rental apartment as well as a good job in her field within weeks of obtaining her Master's degree.

Marge announced her engagement to an old boyfriend with obvious pride in her ability to take such a major step. She claimed that she owed this accomplishment to the "miracles" worked by therapy. Marge described Joe, her fiance, in glowing terms, noting that her unresolved problems had been the primary cause of their past difficulties. She spoke of experiencing herself as beautiful and desirable whenever she was in his company.

Despite her protestations of "complete happiness," however, Marge increasingly seemed strained and depressed. She attributed her negative feelings to the "distance" she was experiencing in her relationship with her closest friend, Sue, since her engagement. Over the course of the next several sessions, Marge realized that her relationship with Sue had actually ended months earlier but that she had denied the reality of the breakup.

During this period, Marge complained of feeling exhausted and mentioned having to "drag" herself to analytic sessions. Finally, choking with emotion, Marge revealed that she had asked Joe to move out of her apartment because of his extremely exploitative and abusive behavior. He had persuaded her to lend him money and had bought himself expensive appliances they could not afford. More devastating for Marge, however, was the continual barrage of criticism to which he subjected her and his habit of addressing her in a coarse, demeaning way. The "last straw" for Marge had been her realization that Joe never shared in her joy over her successes. Instead he seemed to experience her accomplishments as threats to his masculinity.

Marge acknowledged experiencing Joe's critical, hostile, and exploitative behavior much as she had her brother's. "My vision must have gotten a little blurred again," Marge remarked, apparently recognizing that just as she had once disavowed the reality of her brother's abusiveness in order to maintain a fantasy of idealized merger, she had disavowed the reality of Joe's abusiveness. Still, Marge was reluctant to end her engagement and clung to the hope that by talking to Joe she could "make him see the light."

Responding to the therapist's inquiry about why she had waited so long before revealing her distress, Marge said, "I guess it was so wonderful to make you feel proud of me, I was afraid to spoil it." Once again Marge had expected that she could sustain transference fantasies of idealized merger and mirrored grandiosity only by fulfilling the therapist's selfobject needs. She feared that such fantasies would be jeopardized if she failed to make the therapist "look good" because of her progress.

Following interpretations that connected her behavior in the transference with past actions vis-à-vis parental selfobjects, Marge, for the first time, expressed anger at the therapist. "How could you let this happen to me?" she demanded. She angrily voiced her disillusionment with the therapist for failing to prevent the painful breakup of her engagement. In her transference interpretation, the therapist linked Marge's anger at her for failing to live up to her idealized image with her rage at Victor and her father for shattering her illusions about them. The therapist commented that when Marge had felt let down by her father at the time of the molestation she had been unable to let him know. "I guess I know you won't desert me," Marge said. She added that she could see that the therapist was not perfect, but that "somehow it doesn't matter."

Marge acknowledged that such an admission would have been impossible earlier in treatment. The therapist understood this change in terms of two therapeutic processes. First, the continued transformation of her selfobject transference fantasies of idealized merger had lessened her requirement for the absolute perfection of the therapist as an idealized imago. And second, with the transformation of her grandiose-exhibitionistic fantasies, Marge no longer feared that the expression of her rage would deprive her of desperately needed selfobject functions provided within the transference.

In the following session, Marge announced that she had broken her engagement. She also reported the following dream fragment:

I am my present age but Victor looks much younger than I. I am scowling at him.

Associating to the dream, Marge commented, "I feel so much older and wiser than Victor." Evidently her newly found confidence in herself no longer depended on her connection to an idealized male. She explained that scowling at Victor in the dream signified that she no longer needed to blur her vision of reality. "I am scowling because I see clearly that what he did to me was wrong. I guess I'm not afraid of being angry now. I know I won't kill anyone."

As the working-through phase of treatment progresses, Marge's insight into the traumatic unconscious meaning of her incestuous experiences continues to grow deeper, as does her pride in her strengthened capabilities. No longer involved in a desperate struggle to restore archaic narcissistic fantasies traumatically shattered by incest and faultily restored, Marge looks forward to a richly fulfilled future, which now includes pursuing a doctorate in psychology.

THEA

Thea, a slim, athletic-looking, single, white woman of 20, was referred by her brother for treatment several months after a brutal rape. At the end of a year of weekly sessions, she decided to discontinue therapy. Relieved of many florid symptoms of her PTSD, Thea announced that she would "see how I get along without therapy." Three years later, Thea contacted the therapist. Explaining that the murder of her best friend had triggered a resurgence of PTSD symptoms, she expressed her desire to resume therapy. Thea was seen in weekly analytic sessions for three more years. The initial phase of Thea's treatment consists of her first year of sessions; the reconstructive and working-through phases each lasted approximately 18 months.

Initial Phase

Thea appeared composed and cheerful in her first meetings with the therapist. Wearing faded overalls with a worn shirt (her "uniform") and a hairstyle that all but covered her face, she seemed dressed to hide rather than enhance her appearance. Her choice of clothing appeared to reflect a pervasive attitude of self-concealment. "I don't usually like to talk about myself," she said, "It makes me nervous when people pay too much attention to me." The therapist perceived Thea as a "diamond in the rough," someone who would shine in a therapeutic milieu of empathic mirroring. This "Pygmalion" fantasy, an important dimension of the therapist's countertransference, played a major role in the treatment; it will be amplified later in the discussion.

Thea did not present the rape as her main reason for seeking therapy. She seemed reluctant to describe the details of her trauma. Instead she spoke of a desire to clear up some "confusions" about her family and a wish to overcome "my fears and my discomforts." Nevertheless, it is evident from reviewing her complaints that she suffered from severe PTSD, with a full range of reexperiencing and numbing symptoms. For example, Thea revealed that as she struggled to "forget what happened," she was plagued by intrusive recollections of the attack and obsessed with murderous thoughts about the rapist. Although at first she claimed not to remember her dreams, Thea later reported recurrent nightmares that woke her from sleep. Describing these nightmares, Thea said:

> I see him [the rapist] coming at me—sometimes with a raised fist, sometimes with a knife in his hand. He looks really angry at me. He is coming to get me.

Thea's apparent composure following the rape can be understood, in part, as a symptom of numbing characterized by emotional constriction. Another of her numbing symptoms was a sense of alienation and estrangement, which led her to avoid old friends and shun social gatherings. After several weeks in treatment, Thea also admitted that she had experienced uncontrollable outbursts of rage. During one of these outbursts, she seriously injured her hand by smashing it against a wall. She also confided that for weeks after the rape "suicide seemed attractive" but noted that since beginning therapy, she no longer entertained thoughts of killing herself.

It soon became apparent that Thea's tranquil pose covered an excruciating sense of humiliation, which became particularly unbearable whenever she attempted to recount the details of her rape. "I hate myself for being raped," she said, "It could have been avoided." The therapist found that Thea's anguish subsided whenever she was permitted to regulate the timing and duration of her disclosures. Thea chose to relate small portions of her traumatic experience over the course of several sessions.

Even during these brief "installments," Thea spoke in a cool, detached way, as if describing another person's experience (depersonalization). She explained that the rape had occurred on the West Coast where six months earlier she had relocated in the hope of finding a technical job in film production. Unable to obtain such a position, she had taken a clerical job in a large insurance company.

In the company parking lot one evening as she was leaving work, Thea spotted a tall, good-looking, young white man signalling that he wanted to "hitch" a ride. Mistaking him for a co-worker, Thea stopped her car. Although she quickly realized that she did not know him, she agreed to give him a ride. After several minutes, the man ordered Thea to drive up and down certain streets to look for "a guy who owes me money." Thea refused, stopped the car, and asked him to get out. She was stunned when he raised his fist and said, "do what I say or I'll punch your face."

After riding around for several minutes, the man told Thea that he would not hurt her so long as she obeyed him. He told her confusing stories of having been paid to kill the man he was purportedly looking for. Terrified, Thea tried to get out of the car. The man stopped her, saying, "Now I'm going to have to hurt you." After hitting her several times, he pushed her into the back seat of the car and took the wheel. He then ordered Thea to remove her clothes, ostensibly to prevent her from hurling herself out of the moving car.

Arriving at a deserted wooded area, the man stopped the car and climbed into the back seat. "I thought he was going to kill me," Thea said. Suddenly realizing that he intended to rape her, she begged him to take her to her apartment on the pretext that they would be more comfortable there. When her frantic efforts to "talk him out of it" proved unsuccessful, Thea screamed and struggled. Although she described resisting him with all her strength, she was totally overpowered. After raping and sodomizing her for over an hour, the man told her to lie face down on the floor of the car while he drove away. Finally stopping the car in an area of the city unfamiliar to Thea, he allowed her to dress and get out of the car.

Threatening to hunt her down and kill her if she reported him, the rapist drove off, leaving Thea in a state of terror, pain, and shock. Thea recalled staggering for many blocks before locating a telephone and calling the police. She described being treated gently and tactfully by police detectives, who disclosed that a number of similar rapes had recently been reported in the area.

Aided by a sketch made from her description, the police apprehended the rapist within days of the rape. Thea said she was furious to learn that because he pleaded guilty to a number of rapes the charges of kidnapping and assault were dropped. Although the man was sentenced to prison, Thea said she "lives in fear" that he will attack other women when he is released.

Thea recalled that the thought of returning to work and facing the scene of her kidnapping was so upsetting, she immediately made plans to return to the East Coast. She lost her composure as she described her efforts to gain support from her family and friends on her arrival. "My mother and my sister just brushed it off," she sobbed, "like it was no big deal." She explained that her friends seemed to misunderstand her reluctance to describe what had happened as a sign that she needed no support or comfort from them. Only Paul, her brother, realizing that despite her seeming composure she had suffered a severe trauma, recommended that she get professional help.

Thea remarked that because she felt so angry with herself for "being stupid enough to pick up a hitchhiker" she could not bear talking about the rape. Yet, she noted, she felt relieved after telling the therapist the whole story. "You seem to understand what it was like", she said, adding, "No one ever paid that much attention to me before."

However, Thea did not always experience the therapist's attentiveness as desirable. Often, following a session in which she expressed similar sentiments, Thea would not show up for the next session. In response to these missed sessions, the therapist was taken aback, believing that she had been particularly "in tune" with the patient. Although the therapist was unable to appreciate its significance at the time, in retrospect this emerging transference–countertransference neurosis proved crucial in understanding the unconscious meaning of Thea's rape trauma.

After completing her account of the rape, Thea refused to discuss it further. Instead she focused on her "questions" about her parents' relationship with her and with each other, providing the following picture of her family background. Thea is the youngest of three children. Her father, an actor of some reknown, died of cancer when Thea was nine years old. Because her parents separated when she was four years old, Thea treasured her memories of infrequent meetings with her father. She described him as a gentle, caring man, who was beloved by all who knew him, including his many famous show business friends.

Initially, Thea explained her parents' separation as motivated by her father's wish to spare his family the emotional pain of watching him deteriorate from the ravages of cancer. She insisted that her parents loved each other deeply. However, recent conversations with a family friend had suggested that her parents lived apart because of continual friction in their marriage. Thea admitted that she was preoccupied with finding out the "truth" about her parents' relationship.

Thea observed that her father's death ushered in a bleak period in her life. Her mother, who had been somewhat dependent on alcohol for many years, drank more heavily and chose Thea as the main target of occasional drunken rages. Prior to her father's death, Thea explained, she had felt "overlooked" by her mother, who seemed more interested in Liz, the oldest and clearly her favorite, and Paul, the studious, well-behaved middle child. Thea recalled her unsuccessful attempts as a young child to attract her mother's attention by pretending to be a "little actress." She sadly remarked, "I just can't figure out how I became the one she had it in for when she drank."

Thea recalled her desperate efforts to hide during her mother's drinking binges. "I tried to be as inconspicuous as possible," she said. Thea suddenly remembered her enchantment with a magic show she was taken to see as a child. "I played 'magician' all the time," she said, "pretending I could do an amazing disappearing act." She observed that only by "disappearing" could she adequately protect herself against her mother's angry storms. She described sneaking out of the apartment vanishing into the streets at night as an example of her "disappearing act." "You could say I became a 'street kid'," she added, "because I felt safer on the streets than home with my mother."

During this period of treatment, Thea lived in the home of one of her father's closest show business friends, Jim. In exchange for free room and board while she completed a degree at a junior college, Thea babysat for the man's three-year-old son and helped his wife with the housework. Within months of beginning therapy, she learned that Jim was dying of cancer. Thea's reaction to Jim's death shed a great deal of light on her reaction to the loss of her father.

In therapy on the day Jim died, Thea said nothing about him until three quarters of the session had elapsed. "I can't stand feeling that there was nothing I could so to keep him alive," she blurted out after a long silence. Reconstructive work over the next several sessions revealed that Thea had reacted in a similar way following her father's death. She recalled that on the day her father died, he had visited the family at a seaside resort where they were spending the summer. Thea said that she had spent only a few minutes sitting on his knee, chatting with him before running off to play with friends. That evening, when she was told that he had died, Thea was inconsolable. She was convinced that if only she had stayed near him he would not have died. It seems likely that her illusion was expressive of a childhood fantasy of herself as omnipotently in control of the life and death of others.

Thea's grandiose fantasy of omnipotent control over others also manifested itself in the transference. While the therapist was away on a vacation, Thea arrived at her accustomed hour; following the therapist's return, she failed to keep several scheduled appointments. Only after persistent questioning by the therapist did Thea reveal what had happened. Extremely embarrassed, she said, "I guess I expected you to be there because I hadn't decided it was all right for you to go on vacation." She admitted staying away from sessions to avoid having to confront her impotence at failing to keep the therapist in her office.

The content of the sessions that followed revolved around Thea's memories of always having occupied a background role in the family. She described playing the part of "Cinderella" and living in the shadows while her sister, singled out by her mother as "the beauty," was groomed to become the "belle of the ball." Thea revealed that, as a child, she had nursed fantasies of herself as a performer but on reaching adolescence had decided to become skilled in working behind the scenes in film production. Once again, the therapist imagined that with her help, Thea would emerge from the shadows and shine in her own right.

The therapist was very surprised by Thea's announcement that she was dropping out of treatment at this point. Looking back, however, Thea's decision can be understood to be a consequence of the therapist's failure to understand the transference–countertransference neurosis and to appreciate its significance with respect to the traumatic meaning of Thea's rape. Only after Thea resumed treatment did the following picture of Thea's initial phase of treatment become apparent.

Judging from Thea's account of her early childhood, her mother's failure to provide sufficiently responsive mirroring, as well as her father's absence, interfered with the developmental transformation of her archaic narcissistic fantasies. Instead, her subjective world appears to have been organized by grandiose fantasies of omnipotent control over herself and others. It seems likely that her father's death and her mother's abusiveness threatened Thea's fantasies.

Furthermore, it is possible to infer that the unconscious embellishment of her fantasies included the illusion of performing magical "disappearing acts" as a means of protecting herself from her mother's abusive attacks. Her attempt to control the extent to which she showed herself to others appears to have influenced her choice of body-camouflaging clothing and her characteristic attitude of self-concealment. Her fantasy of omnipotent control over the appearances and disappearances (e.g. the death) of others also appears to have been unconsciously embellished.

During Thea's first year in treatment, the therapist did not fully appreciate the extent to which PTSD symptoms represent the shattering and faulty restoration of archaic narcissistic fantasies. However, in retrospect, it is possible to infer that the rape shattered Thea's fantasies and gave rise to the dissociative symptoms of PTSD. After she was kidnapped, beaten, and raped, Thea's illusion of possessing magical powers to "disappear" at will was dashed. Her impotence in controlling the rapist's behavior proved equally shattering.

Because the therapist failed to comprehend the unconscious fantasmagorical meaning of Thea's rape, she was unaware of the ways in
which Thea attempted to defensively restore her shattered fantasies
in the transference. Thea's urgent need to control her self-revelations,
as reflected, for example, in her choosing to provide "installments" of
the account of the rape over several sessions, was a manifestation of
her wish to enact a fantasy of omnipotent control over herself. Appearing for a session during the therapist's vacation as a means of disavowing the therapist's freedom to leave at will was a reflection of her
fantasy of omnipotent control over others.

It seems likely that Thea unconsciously perceived the therapist's
countertransference "Pygmalion" fantasy as a serious threat to her
grandiosity. The therapist's intent to move her from the shadows into
the spotlight against her own inclinations and without regard for her
own timetable forced Thea to confront her own impotence. It can be
inferred that Thea chose to drop out of treatment because of her
unconscious rage at these threats to her narcissistic fantasies. By
leaving therapy, she appears to have unconsciously enacted her "disappearing act," which may be understood both as means of protecting
the therapist from her rage and as an effort to restore her fantasies.
The therapist's failure to understand this aspect of the transference–
countertransference neurosis interfered with Thea's need to restore a
selfobject transference fantasy of mirrored grandiosity. Her unconscious efforts at self-restitution thwarted, Thea had little reason to
remain in treatment.

Reconstructive Phase

When Thea returned to therapy following the murder of her best
friend, she made no effort to conceal her distress. Tearful and clearly
shaken, she described her reaction to the tragedy. Once again, in
response to the death of a significant person in her life, Thea was
enraged with herself for failing to prevent the loss. She berated herself
for not revealing all the details of her rape to her friend. "Maybe Katie
would have been more careful if she knew everything that happened to
me," she sobbed.

Among her numerous PTSD symptoms was the following recurrent
nightmare:

I am driving on a highway. My car stops dead. Suddenly I am all alone
running along the side of the road. Somehow I know that the rapist is
trying to catch me. I try to keep hidden but the lights of passing cars
keep shining on me. I can't escape.

Thea's first associations to the nightmare revealed the extent to which Katie's death had revived memories of her own trauma. She shuddered as she described how the nightmare image of driving on the highway revived her memory of being driven to a deserted area where she had been raped. Although the details of Katie's abduction and murder bore only slight resemblances to her ordeal, Thea said she often imagined that Katie had lived through the events of her own rape. "In my mind, I even confuse my rapist with Katie's murderer," she added. She wept as she described newspaper accounts of Katie's unsuccessful efforts to escape from her murderer.

Still associating to the nightmare, Thea described an incident that had recently occurred in her mother's home, where she was living temporarily. After returning late from a party, Thea had failed to wake up at her accustomed hour. When her mother noisily entered her room to wake her, Thea had raised her arms as if to shield her face and head and screamed, "Don't hit me."

In her groggy state, Thea recalled, she apparently relived an episode from her childhood in which her mother had barged into her room, screamed at her for some minor offense, and hit her before she had fully awakened. Thea associated the terror in her nightmare at not being able to hide from the headlights of passing cars to her feeling, as her mother approached, that she could not "disappear" to avoid her mother's rage. She also connected this experience with her rape, recalling her mounting desperation as the rapist foiled all of her frantic efforts to avoid being beaten and raped.

The therapist's understanding of the nightmare as a symbolic representation of the shattering and faulty restoration of central organizing fantasies enabled her to offer preliminary interpretations of the meaning of the rape trauma to Thea. She commented on Thea's obvious pride in her ability to perform "disappearing acts" to avoid danger, such as vanishing into the streets to escape her mother's abusive attacks. She also communicated her understanding of Thea's shattering disappointment in herself when she failed to disappear magically at the time of the rape as she had previously failed to vanish before her mother could hit her.

As a result of these interpretations, Thea's selfobject transference fantasy of mirrored grandiosity tentatively emerged in the treatment. She seemed eager to report on a number of positive changes in her life. For example, she had found the courage to contact show business friends of her father's for help in securing a job in film production. Her new wardrobe of flattering clothing also revealed her greater willingness to exhibit herself.

However, the following dream Thea presented during this period illustrated her resistance to consolidating her selfobject transference fantasy:

> I am standing on a subway platform. A woman hands me a baby which I try to take through the turnstile. Suddenly, the woman pushes the turnstile, and I am whirled around and around. I realize that the baby is slipping out of my hands, and I scream with fear. I see the baby in a recess below the platform, but I can't rescue it because the turnstile is revolving too quickly.

Thea described the woman in the dream as resembling the therapist and associated the underground subway with the "uncovering" work of therapy. She connected whirling around in the turnstile to a familiar and distressing feeling of being out of control. Asked to describe the baby, Thea said, "It was a very cute, alert-looking baby that captivates grownups." She added that it was dressed in an outfit she had worn as a child.

Responding to the therapist's suggestion that perhaps the dream expressed some feeling she experienced with the therapist, Thea said, "Maybe I feel that you are a little pushy sometimes." Asked to elaborate, Thea revealed her worry that the therapist wanted her to take more risks in calling attention to herself than she felt was wise. She mentioned that the therapist's insistent inquiry about her job hunting had made her feel pressured to be more aggressive than she would normally have been.

The therapist understood the dream image of the captivating baby, which reappeared in a number of Thea's subsequent dreams, as a symbolic representation of Thea's selfobject transference fantasy of mirrored grandiosity. Thea seemed to fear that the maintenance of this fantasy depended on her surrendering control over her visibility to the therapist. Thea responded to transference interpretations on this theme by announcing, "There's something I never told you about the rape." She explained that from the time of her arrival on the West Coast until the rape, she had not dated men. She described her extreme reluctance to accompany her female friends to "singles bars." "I hated the thought of being ogled like so much flesh," she said.

Ashamed, Thea described her sense of excitement at "picking up" the rapist. "I hate to admit it," she said, "but he was so handsome and had such a nice smile, I really flirted with him in the parking lot." Thea acknowledged that the rape had confirmed her worst fears about what she was "letting myself in for" by attracting a man's interest. For Thea, being raped after calling attention to herself replicated earlier experiences of being beaten by her mother. These terrifying feelings associated with her impotent loss of control were also evoked in therapy when she experienced the therapist as "pushing" her to exhibit herself.

Following reconstructive work along this theme, Thea's selfobject transference fantasy of mirrored grandiosity, which now contained elements of exhibitionism, continued to unfold. She proudly reported on her bold efforts to find jobs in her field. She also pointed to significant changes in a number of her relationships. No longer needing to "blend into the wallpaper," Thea had become increasingly assertive in calling attention to her needs and feelings and to exhibiting her strengths.

The therapist's next vacation disrupted Thea's selfobject transference fantasy. Again, she failed to show up for several scheduled sessions following the therapist's return. When she did appear, Thea reported feeling extremely depressed and rageful. Exploration of the meaning of Thea's absences revealed that as a result of her impotent rage at the therapist's apparent flaunting of omnipotent control, she retaliated by doing her "disappearing act."

Thea reported that in addition to feeling mad at the therapist for leaving, she also felt enraged with Katie for dying. "I know she didn't want to die," Thea said, "but I can't help feeling furious with her for leaving me." The therapist's interpretations about Thea's rage as arising from what she experienced as a threat to her fantasy of omnipotent control over others did nothing to relieve her depression; rather, it seemed to be worsening.

Finally, Thea tearfully spoke of becoming so enraged with herself for failing to prevent the therapist's "disappearance" that she had gone on a prolonged drinking binge. For Thea, drinking was associated with extreme self-destructiveness because she dreaded becoming an alcoholic like her mother. Therapeutic work over the next few sessions uncovered the connection between Thea's reaction of narcissitic rage at herself for failing to prevent the deaths of her father, Jim, and Katie and her rage at not being able to exert absolute control over the therapist's comings and goings.

Thea's self-directed rage following the rape was also explored. She remembered that as a youngster, she had been extremely proud of her "street smarts." Because of her skill in negotiating with neighborhood toughs, she had felt safe staying out late at night. Thea recounted an episode in which she had not only talked the leader of a neighborhood gang out of starting a fight with her and her friends but had convinced him to protect her when she was threatened by a school bully. Thea's inability to talk the rapist out of raping her had profoundly shaken her, she said, noting that it was her rage at herself for failing in this attempt that had caused her to smash her hand against a wall. Thus, Thea's narcissistic rage, directed both at herself and at others experienced as failing selfobjects, may be understood as a consequence of her shattered fantasy of omnipotent control.

Thea's disappearing acts and her resistance to consolidating a selfobject transference fantasy of mirrored grandiosity triggered an intense narcissistic countertransference reaction in the therapist. The more Thea threatened to "blend into the wallpaper" or disappear, that is, skip sessions, the more the therapist felt inclined to demonstrate her omnipotent mirroring capacity by keeping Thea in the spotlight. In other words, the transference–countertransference neurosis involved a struggle between patient and therapist over who would maintain omnipotent control over the other. As the therapist became increasingly aware of the manifestations of this struggle, she was able to empathize more fully with Thea's therapeutic requirements. Understanding the unconscious dynamics of the transference–countertransference neurosis facilitated the consolidation of Thea's transference fantasy.

Working-Through Phase

The consolidation of Thea's selfobject transference fantasy of mirrored grandiosity was marked by a number of dreams about highly intelligent and appealing babies. Unlike her earlier "baby" dream, in which Thea's fears over loss of omnipotent control predominated, in these dreams, Thea triumphantly rescued the baby from a variety of dangerous situations. In one dream, for example, Thea hid the baby behind a post to avoid being noticed by a mugger. Her disappearing act was successful.

During this period, an old friend of Thea's father arranged an interview for her at a leading film production company. In spite of considerable anxiety about having to "sell" herself, Thea landed the entry level job she had thought impossible to obtain. However, because of problems in the industry, she was told that she could count on only three months employment.

At the end of the three-month period Thea was laid off. Although she was complimented on having been an excellent trainee and told that she might be called back for per diem work, Thea experienced the layoff as a narcissistic blow. When, after some time, she was called back on a temporary basis, Thea told the therapist she would not show up for work. Following interpretations about her need to disappear as an expression of her rage at what she considered an insult to her grandiose fantasies, Thea accepted the work. Evidently the working-through process had facilitated the transformation of her grandiose fantasies to some degree and thereby diminished her narcissistic vulnerability and rage.

In order to support herself between film jobs, Thea worked part time at a small advertising agency. She confided that she was highly attracted to Ted, the director of the agency, and often daydreamed about dating him even though his girlfriend, Sarah, worked with him. Since Thea worked evenings, she often found herself alone with Ted. Eventually, they developed a clandestine sexual relationship, Thea's first sexual contact since her rape.

At first Thea seemed pleased with her role as "behind-the-scenes girlfriend." She was content to allow Sarah to be the "leading lady." Exploration of this triangle revealed that Thea felt "safely in control of the relationship" from her accustomed place in the shadows. After a while, however, Thea reported feeling enraged with Ted. She claimed that he saw her only when it was convenient for him and that he "rubbed his relationship with Sarah in my face." Thea said she could hardly bear her painful sense of humiliation when Ted embraced Sarah in her presence. Ted had begun flaunting his relationship with Sarah, and Thea experienced an enraging loss of control. "Nothing I do makes the slightest bit of difference," Thea said, noting that she had tried dressing in "sexy" clothes and wearing makeup in order to appear more attractive.

In spite of her distress, Thea allowed the relationship to continue. She admitted feeling that to break it off would mean "admitting defeat." She announced her intention to "win Ted away from Sarah" and thus retaliate for her humiliating loss of control.

During this period, Thea called to cancel several sessions and changed appointments repeatedly. She seemed unusually irritable and preoccupied during sessions. Surmising that Thea's uncharacteristic attitude was related to her difficulties with Ted, the therapist made an interpretation about a possible connection. Initially, Thea strongly denied any change in her feelings about therapy and attempted to rationalize her erratic behavior. She angrily accused the therapist of "putting me on the spot." After the therapist empathized with Thea's feeling of being "pushed" to reveal herself, Thea acknowledged needing to feel more in control of herself and the therapist after her humiliating experiences with Ted.

Thea also spoke of her bitter disappointment in herself for failing to win Ted's love. "I should have known I'd be done in for trying to attract a man's attention," Thea said. With little assistance from the therapist, she linked her despair at losing control over her relationship with Ted and her traumatic rape. Both times she had "stepped out of the shadows" and displayed her interest in a man, and both times her fantasies of omnipotent control had been compromised. She noted that being ignored by Ted when Sarah was present was particularly painful. At these times Ted was unaffected by her disappearing acts. Noting that this situation, unlike the rape, allowed her the freedom to leave the "scene of this crime," Thea broke off her relationship with Ted and quit her job at the agency.

Depressed over not having a man in her life, Thea recalled having similar feelings around the time of her rape. "It's times like this that I miss my father," she said. She described an "out-of-body experience" (disembodiment) occurring during the rape when she thought she might be killed. She clearly visualized her father extending a hand toward her while, at the same time, she observed herself struggling with the rapist.

Further exploration revealed that since the rape Thea had experienced a number of these disembodiment fantasies with dead loved ones. She explained that these experiences were associated with a sense of enormous well-being insofar as they confirmed her possession of supernatural, magical powers. These experiences can be understood as both a reflection of her deeply dissociated traumatic state and another of her desperate efforts at self-restitution.

Having gained more insight into the unconscious motivation behind her efforts to restore her shattered fantasies, Thea expressed her understanding of the "myth" she had created about her parents' separation. She observed that it was easier to accept her father's absence by imagining that he had acted to shield her from his death from cancer than to feel that she had so little power over him that he simply disappeared at will. Her disembodiment fantasies of reunion with her father restored her sense of omnipotent control.

Thea's involvement in a serious car accident provided the context for further working through of the traumatic meaning of her rape. On a highway in a snowstorm one evening, Thea's car skidded out of control and crashed into the center divider. Thea was thrown against the windshield. She seriously cut her head and briefly lost consciousness.

Regaining consciousness, Thea was terrified to see a man approaching her wrecked car. Thea's immediate thought was that she would be raped or killed. Only her shakiness following what turned out to be a concussion prevented her from running away. To her distress, she realized that the man had been drinking. Apparently hoping to steal anything of value, he gruffly ordered Thea to open the trunk of her car. Just then, another car pulled up. The man ran off as a middle-aged couple got out of their car. Thea gratefully allowed them to drive her to a nearby hospital for treatment.

After commenting on the eerie similarity between her car accident and the image in her recurrent traumatic nightmare of being alone and exposed on a highway, terrified of being caught by the rapist, Thea crashed her fists against the arm of her chair. "I can't live this way," she cried. She described feeling "disgusted" with herself for failing to control her car and placing herself in such a dangerous situation. "I would have killed myself if I got raped again," she said.

After the therapist expressed empathic understanding of her self-directed rage for falling short of her grandiose fantasies of omnipotent control, Thea stopped berating herself. "I just can't let myself be human," Thea said. She acknowledged that even the best driver might have lost control under the snowy conditions. "I guess I had good reason to be scared." Thea compared her reaction to the car accident with many of her frightening experiences as a "street kid," when she had mingled with gangs, drug addicts, and drunks. "I guess I had to believe that no one or nothing could frighten me," she said.

Thea's ability to accept her fear and her vulnerability in response to her terrifying accident indicated considerable progress in treatment and the significant transformation of her archaic narcissistic fantasies. The almost complete cessation of her PTSD symptoms was another sign of marked therapeutic improvement. Because her self-experience is less organized in accordance with the unconscious meaning of fantasies of omnipotent control, her need to remain in the shadows has diminished. As a result, Thea has sought and obtained work that calls attention to her skills and talents. In addition, she has established a number of satisfying personal relationships in which she has demonstrated her ability to exhibit her emotional availability.

NICK

Nick, a handsome, well-built, and articulate 38-year-old Vietnam combat veteran and former Air Force sergeant, began treatment in the summer of 1981 and, with the exception of a six-month period in 1982, has remained in treatment continuously until the present. During this six-year period, Nick attended regular weekly analytic therapy sessions. The number of sessions per week varied depending upon Nick's overall emotional state and the phase of treatment. The initial phase of treatment covered the first year of therapy; the reconstructive and working through phases both consisted of approximately 30-month periods.

Initial Phase

In his first session, Nick spoke of being subject to extremely disorganizing panic attacks in which "I feel like I'm coming apart at the seams." He said that he increasingly found himself overwhelmed by memories of traumatic combat experiences in Vietnam. He mentioned that he had been using both cocaine and marijuana on a heavy and regular basis in an unsuccessful attempt to self-medicate for what sounded like dissociative PTSD symptoms. He conceded that recently neither cocaine nor marijuana were providing relief from these symptoms.

Nick had been referred to the therapist by a friend and fellow Vietnam combat veteran, who had been in treatment with the therapist for PTSD. Nick related that his friend had spoken very highly of the therapist, presenting him to Nick in glowing terms. Throughout the initial phase of treatment, Nick always referred to the therapist with the same awe and admiration. He wanted the therapist to know that he was aware of his reputation as an expert in treating Vietnam combat veterans suffering from PTSD. Nick emphasized that he shared his friend's great respect for the therapist and was extremely grateful to the therapist for agreeing to treat him. He was absolutely certain, he exclaimed, that the therapist would "save my life."

Nick's spontaneous (Kohut, 1970) transference idealization of the therapist was empathically understood as arising in the context of his experience of self-fragmentation and accompanying disintegration anxiety. Therefore, no effort was made at this time to analyze the emerging transference idealization fantasy. However, as becomes evident, this selfobject transference fantasy plays an important role in understanding the unconscious meaning of Nick's traumatic combat experiences as it emerged in the intersubjective context of the therapeutic relationship.

In the initial phase, the following picture gradually emerged of Nick's life both before and after Vietnam. Nick grew up in a lower middle-class Italian-American family in the suburbs of a large northeastern city. Prior to the birth of his younger brother, Nick was an only child for the first ten years of his life. During these early childhood years, his father, a long-distance trucker, was on the road for weeks at a time, leaving Nick alone with his mother, a housewife.

Nick recalled that he missed spending time with his father but felt somewhat compensated for the loss by all the attention he received from his mother. Nick has vivid memories of his mother doting on him. He said that she made him feel like a "little king." As a child he had entertained a superman fantasy in which he imagined himself performing miraculous, superhuman feats just like his cartoon hero.

As we shall see, Nick's superman fantasy, a typical and early conscious manifestation of an unconscious fantasy of grandiosity with both exhibitionistic and omnipotent features, was critical in understanding the personal meaning of his traumatic combat experiences in Vietnam.

As a result of spending so little time with his father during childhood, Nick concocted an embellished fantasy version of him. His fantasies were fueled by a highly romantic vision of his father's job as a long-distance truck driver. Nick spoke of feeling awed by the sight of his father's imposing diesel cab and rig, which was parked in the family driveway. Nick fondly recalled spending hours alone inside the cab, playing with the steering wheel, gear shift, and pedals. He would pretend in his daydreams that he was a "rough-and-ready cowboy of the freeways" who had one exciting and hair-raising adventure after another.

Nick's romantic fantasies of his father were further magnified by his father's position as a captain in the local volunteer fire department. He imagined his father as a brave and heroic fireman, who rescued people from burning buildings and gave them mouth-to-mouth resuscitation. Nick said that all of his neighborhood friends were envious of him because of his father's role as a fire captain. Nick recalled that one of his favorite games was acting out fantasy scenarios of fire scenes in which he and his friends pretended to be firemen. The entire community had great respect and admiration for his father, Nick proudly announced.

During adolescence, Nick was active in several high school varsity sports including football and baseball. Nick said he was particularly gifted as a baseball pitcher. He remembered imagining himself, throughout high school, as the star pitcher for a major league baseball team. He got great satisfaction from pitching as his father watched and rooted for him in the stands. Unfortunately, Nick lamented, his mediocre grades prevented him from getting any significant athletic scholarship offers from colleges. After graduating from high school, Nick became very concerned about being drafted. Rather than risk being drafted into the Army, he joined the Air Force in the hope of avoiding the war in Vietnam.

Nick's unconscious fantasy life as a child and an adolescent appears to have been organized in accordance with typical boyhood magical illusions. In early childhood he fantasized himself as superman and later in childhood fashioned his fantasy life according to his romantic notions of his father as an adventurous truckdriver and heroic fireman. In adolescence, he fantasized becoming a major league baseball star.

However, even Nick's normal childhood and adolescent fantasies proved to be vulnerable to extreme trauma. Moreover, once shattered, these same fantasies were defensively and compensatorily elaborated as part of an unconscious and faulty effort at their restoration.

After serving in Vietnam, Nick returned to the States, where he completed the remainder of his military tour of duty. On being discharged from the Air Force, Nick resettled in his old neighborhood and, following in his father's footsteps, went to work as a long-distance truck driver and joined the same volunteer fire department. In the postcombat period, he was married and divorced three times, having two children with his first wife. (During the six-month break from treatment Nick, married and separated from his third wife.) Nick also started but quickly dropped out of college.

Throughout the postcombat period, Nick had extreme difficulty in relating to others. He was easily angered and prone to violent outbursts in all his marriages. He described himself as a loner who had little patience for others. He noted that his job as a long-distance truck driver was particularly well suited for isolation and solitude.

Because of Nick's long and extensive history of reexperiencing and numbing symptoms, it was possible even in the initial sessions to make a definitive diagnosis of PTSD. Nick reported a postcombat pattern of abusing a variety of drugs including LSD, quaaludes, and amphetamines. He had no history, however, of alcohol abuse or heroin use, two forms of substance abuse commonly found among Vietnam combat veterans suffering from PTSD (see, for example, Roth, 1986).

In discussing his current substance abuse problems, Nick described the past effects of cocaine and marijuana, neither of which was now having its desired result. Nick reported that while high on cocaine he often imagined himself back in combat as a fighter pilot bombing Hanoi. Apparently, cocaine heightened Nick's sense of potency. It thus helped to defend against what he described as an at times disillusioning and enraging sense of ineffectiveness and impotence.

Nick smoked marijuana both during the day and at night in an effort to "blot out" intrusive waking thoughts of combat and recurrent traumatic nightmares. He explained that marijuana functioned as a tranquilizer during the day and a sedative-hypnotic at night. He had started smoking marijuana heavily and regularly while in Vietnam to escape from the terrifying reality of daily combat. It was evident that both cocaine and marijuana provided temporary relief from the distressing symptoms of PTSD by buttressing faultily restored fantasmagorical meaning structures.

At the beginning of treatment, Nick was working as a laboratory technician for a manufacturer of sophisticated industrial electronic equipment. Nick said that he was frustrated at work because he did not receive the promotions and raises he felt he deserved. Although he maintained strict secrecy about his past as a Vietnam combat veteran, Nick was still worried that somehow his past interfered with his progress. At this early point in treatment, Nick was dating a woman, a fellow cocaine abuser, whom he later married and divorced during his break from therapy.

During the early sessions, Nick presented the following account of his year-long combat tour of duty in Vietnam. After completing basic and advanced technical training, Nick spent a year as a cockpit technician at an Air Force base in the South. In the fall of 1967, he received his overseas orders to report to Tan Son Nhut Air Force Base, just north of Saigon.

Nick was shocked and distressed at the prospect of serving in Vietnam. He had joined the Air Force for the explicit purpose of avoiding the war; now he was being catapulted into the middle of the fighting. His only solace was that at the time, Tan Son Nhut, which was the largest American Air Force base in Vietnam, was relatively safe. However, halfway through his tour, all of this would change dramatically with the TET enemy counteroffensive.

Prior to TET, Nick had managed to avoid most of the fighting. He was responsible for maintaining the explosive charges used in emergencies to eject pilots from the cockpit of their planes. Nick described himself as an indispensable member of the ground crew, part of an invincible team. His sense of himself as merged with such a powerful entity was reassuring and comforting to Nick. Yet he complained that the combat pilots did not fully appreciate the importance of his job to their safety and hence to the success of their missions. He resented being ignored and was bitter that his special talents and skills went unacknowledged.

Nick said he still had vivid memories of standing awestruck on the airfield, watching the giant B-52 bombers and sleek F-4 Phantom jet fighters fly off on their combat missions. He spent hours daydreaming about himself as a combat pilot, striking against the enemy from the safety of the clouds. He noted that he got a vicarious thrill from his daydreams. Sometimes, Nick recalled, he got so caught up in his reverie that he became disoriented and confused about "what was real and what was fantasy."

Nick remembered that prior to TET and the enemy counteroffensive, he had come to view himself in relation to the pilots, planes, and airfield of Tan Son Nhut as virtually invulnerable and invincible. He had been promoted to the rank of sergeant, which, he acknowledged, further exaggerated his already intense sense of personal grandeur. Nick reminisced about strutting around the airfield, wearing dark aviator sunglasses, attired in full combat fatigues, and feeling "I was a godlike warrior." Nick consciously thought of himself as part of a mighty and unstoppable military juggernaut. In this context, he imagined that he could not be hurt or injured. He was, in his own words, "immortal."

Nick's experience of himself in relation to his immediate surround changed dramatically with the onset of TET. With TET, Tan Son Nhut suddenly changed from what he had previously experienced as a completely impregnable fortress into a bloody battlefield. The first night of TET, Tan Son Nhut was completely overrun by enemy ground forces.

Nick described the terror and bedlam that swept over the base like a giant tidal wave. Totally unprepared and unarmed, Nick and many of the other men were forced to seek cover in their barracks. Without weapons, they lay defenseless underneath their cots as the battle raged outside. Nick remembers his fear that at any moment enemy soldiers would burst into the barracks and kill everyone. He also was afraid of being blown to bits by incoming enemy mortar and rocket fire.

With the outbreak of TET, Nick underwent a dramatic change in his day-to-day activities and duties, which also affected his sense of himself. Despite having had no previous advanced infantry training or combat experience, Nick was assigned to nightly guard duty on the perimeter of the airfield. He was involved in a number of terrifying and bloody firefights with the enemy forces, most of whom he could not see in the darkness of the night. The early events of TET seem to have begun to shatter his fantasy of idealized merger with Tan Son Nhut, and he no longer experienced himself as united with an unassailable bastion (that is, an omnipotent selfobject).

After TET, Ton Son Nhut was subjected to daily rocket and mortar attacks. Nick reported that enemy mortar and rocket attacks occurred with such regularity that the American airmen referred to them as "Twelve O'clock Charlie." Usually, Nick said, the warning sirens sounded only seconds before the rockets and mortars landed and exploded. Those airmen, like Nick, working in exposed areas had to duck for cover wherever possible. Often this meant jumping into a crater bombed out from previous attacks.

Many American soldiers were seriously wounded or killed during these enemy attacks. Nick remembered one particularly gruesome incident in which a fuel truck was set afire by an enemy rocket. Nick watched in horror as the truck driver burned to death before his eyes. He said that he has never been able to get the image of the man being incinerated out of his mind.

As the enemy air and ground attacks continued around the clock,

Nick underwent a psychological metamorphosis. He no longer experienced himself as a godlike warrior, delivering deadly blows against the enemy from the safety of the clouds or from behind the impenetrable walls of Tan Son Nhut. Now he was "scared shitless" and lived in constant fear that any second and without warning he would be blown to bits.

Nick and the therapist touched on the underlying meaning of this personal metamorphosis. They linked his original sense of being securely merged in fantasy with the pilots, planes, and airfield of Tan Son Nhut with his early childhood fantasies of himself as a rugged truck driver behind the wheel of a mighty diesel rig or as a heroic fireman rescuing people from burning buildings. They spoke about his fantasy vision of himself as a godlike warrior and key member of an invincible team as related to earlier fantasies of himself as superman and a major league baseball star. They commented upon the fact that Nick's fantasy inspired vision of himself in relation to his immediate surround had been shattered by the events of TET.

At this point in treatment, the therapist did not offer interpretations about a possibly deeper, unconscious meaning of this shattering occurrence. However, he formulated several potential explanations. He inferred that Nick's pre-TET experiences in Vietnam had added fuel to his preexisting unconscious childhood and adolescent fantasies. His experience of himself and Tan Son Nhut seemed to reflect a central organizing fantasy of idealized merger with an omnipotent selfobject. This narcissistic fantasy, in turn, facilitated the exhibitionistic display of his own grandiosity. His post-TET experience of himself and Tan Son Nhut seemed to be unconsciously organized in accordance with the personal meaning of the shattering of these fantasies.

As the initial phase of treatment proceeded, Nick's condition improved. He reported feeling less agitated and disorganized. He was effusive in expressing his appreciation and gratitude to the therapist. Nick described his rapid and dramatic improvement as a miracle confirming his original feeling that the therapist would "save my life!"

Naturally, the therapist was encouraged by Nick's improvement. He assumed it was directly attributable to Nick's detailed and emotional account of traumatic combat occurrences within the intersubjective context of an emerging idealizing transference fantasy. The therapist sensed that Nick was enjoying a soothing and calming selfobject experience of himself as merged in fantasy with an omnipotent imago. As part of this selfobject transference experience, Nick felt less fragmented and vulnerable to the disintegration anxiety of his panic attacks. Nick's ability to recall traumatic combat occurrences in detail seemed to confirm the therapist's reading of the transference.

Nick was unconsciously trying within the intersubjective context of the therapeutic relationship to transferentially restore a fantasy of idealized merger that had been shattered by combat. This was part of the unconscious meaning of his traumatic combat experiences. At this juncture in treatment, the therapist did not attempt to connect Nick's effort to restore within the transference a traumatically shattered idealized merger fantasy to its possible genetic roots in his childhood relationship with his father. However, this selfobject transference fantasy played an important role in understanding the unconscious meaning of Nick's traumatic combat experiences as it emerged in the intersubjective context of the therapeutic relationship.

Nick now reported an incident in which he had personally struck back at the enemy. During a daylight enemy ground assault, Nick, lying in a foxhole on the airfield perimeter, had shot and killed three enemy soldiers as they tried to dart for cover. In describing this incident, Nick recalled the fantastic feeling of exhilaration and power that he experienced. He said he felt as if his M-16 automatic rifle had magically become an awesome part of his own body. Having this deadly force in his control empowered Nick with a sense that he was the master of the fate of others. It seemed that killing the enemy soldiers and personally striking back at the enemy enabled Nick to recapture, if only fleetingly, a sense of omnipotent grandeur.

For reasons that the therapist did not fully understand at the time, Nick began to resist any further discussion of combat and expressed a corresponding desire to drop out of treatment. The therapist was uncertain about how to proceed. He encouraged Nick to explore his concerns. In this context, Nick reported a recurrent traumatic nightmare that had recently increased in frequency:

> I step inside a Quonset hut and see a soldier, dressed in full combat fatigues, standing in the middle of the hut. He is smiling sadistically at me. I realize that I am back in Vietnam and that the soldier's sadistic smile means that I've got to go back into battle. I start to scream "I don't want to be here, I don't want to be here!"

Nick associated the nightmare to his current feelings about the therapist and the course of treatment. He was upset that the detailed discussion of traumatic combat occurrences felt overwhelming to him. The therapist commented: "It is as if you are screaming at me that you do not want to be taken back any further into the disturbing memories and painful feelings of your Vietnam combat experiences." Using the nightmare as an intersubjective point of reference, the therapist tried to help Nick better understand his dread of further therapeutic exploration of combat.

However, the analysis of dreads motivating Nick's resistance proved to be insufficient. He continued to voice strong reservations about remaining in treatment. He also referred to a dream that, in hindsight, illuminated the intersubjective context of an emerging transference–countertransference neurosis that was fueling his resistance:

> I'm back at Tan Son Nhut and walking on the airfield toward several combat pilots. As I walk by them they seem to ignore me. I'm enraged but continue walking without saying a word.

Nick's only associations were to the feeling, which he had previously mentioned, that the pilots at Tan Son Nhut never acknowledged the significance of his job to their safety and the success of their missions. A selfobject countertransference fantasy of mirrored grandiosity prevented the therapist from making the critical connection between these feelings and the intersubjective configuration that was structuring the therapeutic relationship. The therapist did not recognize, therefore, that Nick felt that he was once again being taken for granted and ignored by an idealized figure.

As a result, Nick's need for a selfobject experience of himself within the transference as having his own grandiosity mirrored was going unrecognized and unaddressed. In the intersubjective context of this transference–countertransference neurosis, Nick did not feel empathically understood, and, in a narcissistic rage, he abruptly dropped out of treatment. As Nick and the therapist later realized, his sudden disappearance had significance for reconstructing the unconscious meaning of his traumatic combat experiences.

Reconstructive Phase

Nick returned to treatment approximately six months after leaving. He was having serious personal problems and difficulties at work. He also described what sounded like an intensification of the dissociative symptoms of PTSD.

Nick explained that he and his new bride (Nick's third wife and the woman whom he had been dating while still in treatment) had recently separated because of constant fighting. (Nick was divorced for the third time shortly after resuming therapy.) Nick described falling into dissociated states of depersonalization and derealization in which he experienced himself as back in combat. Nick confided that as part of these reliving experiences, he went into wild rages, destroying furniture and other household objects. On several occasions, he threw his wife against the wall, mistaking her for an enemy soldier.

On the job, Nick became so anxious that he was unable to concentrate on his work assignments. He was so "stressed out," that he was barely able to get through a day of work. Nick admitted that in this state of mind he had resorted to using even more cocaine and marijuana, without, however, much sustained symptomatic relief.

Despite his return to treatment, Nick complained of the increasing intensity and severity of his dissociative PTSD symptoms. At Nick's request, the therapist wrote a report enabling him to receive a two-week medical leave of absence. On leave, Nick began to recuperate.

As Nick improved, he repeatedly stated that he owed his recovery and well-being to the therapist. He was sure, he emphasized, that without the therapist's quick and decisive intervention, he was headed for a "nervous breakdown." Once again he spoke of being in awe of the therapist's expertise and competence. He referred to the therapist as "my guardian angel," a phrase used by concentration camp survivors to describe their therapists (Klein, 1968). It appeared that Nick was unconsciously reorganizing himself in accordance with the meaning of a selfobject transference fantasy of idealized merger with an omnipotent imago.

As Nick felt more at ease, he resumed talking about combat. The therapist faciliated this discussion by using Nick's PTSD symptoms and, especially, reexperiencing symptoms, as clinical points of reference. For example, Nick brought up a particularly terrifying occurrence. He had been dropped by plane during the night in the middle of enemy territory to disarm the explosive device of the cockpit ejection system of a downed jet fighter.

Nick immediately discovered that he was trapped in "no man's land" between enemy and American lines. He was afraid that he would be shot and killed if either side spotted him. He feared that the Americans would mistake him for an enemy soldier.

Nick recalled imagining, in what sounded like a trauma induced dissociated state, that he had literally "melted into the ground and become invisible" (depersonalization and disembodiment). He reported that he spent the entire night lying flat and perfectly still on the ground, convinced that he had actually become invisible. Thereafter, he remained convinced of his fantastic ability to become invisible whenever threatened by overwhelming danger.

What Nick referred to as the "Invisible Man phenomenon" continued into the postcombat period. In discussing his fantastic powers of invisibility, he mentioned a recurrent traumatic nightmare that had become especially persistent just before he left treatment:

I'm back in combat in Vietnam. A group of soldiers is marching together
in a closed formation in an exposed area. I'm not part of the formation;
instead, I'm off to the side, watching them as if I were invisible. All of a
sudden enemy snipers ambush the group, killing everyone but me.

In associating to the nightmare, Nick noted that he had learned in
Vietnam that if he kept to himself and remained very quiet, "I was
invisible and safe from danger."

Discussing the nightmare's resurgence just prior to leaving treatment, Nick and the therapist better understood why he had discontinued therapy. They realized that the therapist had failed to acknowledge Nick's courage and bravery for returning emotionally to the hell
of combat. Apparently, under the influence of a then prevailing selfobject countertransference fantasy of mirrored grandiosity, the therapist
had mistakenly thought that Nick was content with an experience of
himself organized in accordance with the meaning of a transference
fantasy of idealized merger.

Within the intersubjective context of this transference–countertransference neurosis, Nick felt himself once again in danger of being
overwhelmed by malevolent forces, in this case the traumatic memories and feelings associated with combat. He also felt ignored and
slighted. In an attempt to save himself psychologically, and in a
narcissistic rage, he once again became invisible by dropping out of
treatment. Nick had, in other words, unconsciously enacted his grandiose fantasy by becoming invisible.

Understanding the unconscious dynamics of the transference–countertransference neurosis proved, therefore, to be critical in reconstructing an important dimension of the fantasmagorical meaning of
Nick's traumatic combat experiences. Throughout the remainder of
his treatment, Nick and the therapist repeatedly returned to these
same dynamics as they reconstructed and worked through the unconscious meaning of trauma.

At this juncture in the treatment, Nick reported another traumatic
combat occurrence. During a surprise enemy mortar and rocket attack
on Tan Son Nhut, Nick was caught in an open and unprotected area.
As he dove to the ground for cover, a mortar round landed with a thud
directly in front of him. Amazingly, it did not explode, thus miraculously sparing his life. Nick explained that as he heard the whistle of
the incoming mortar round hurtling toward him, he immediately
concentrated all of his powers of thought on the idea of preventing it
from exploding.

Nick was quite emphatic that the mortar round had not exploded
because of the concentration of his powers of thought. He acknowl-

edged that this experience had added to his already strong belief in his supernatural psychic powers and the paranormal. He equated this episode in its personal significance with the import of the incident in which he had first come to believe in the Invisible Man phenomenon. In addition to being able to make himself invisible in situations of danger, Nick also believed that through the powers of his own thoughts he could directly affect physical objects and change the outcome of events.

The therapist did not express skepticism about Nick's belief in his uncanny psychic powers. Instead, the therapist maintained his empathic listening stance. He understood that in describing his superhuman powers and experiences with the paranormal, Nick was unconsciously attempting to revive in the selfobject transference a previously shattered grandiose fantasy of omnipotent control.

Facilitating the unfolding of these selfobject transference fantasies was critical to further reconstruction of the unconscious meaning of Nick's traumatic combat experiences. In this empathic therapeutic milieu, Nick revealed that he had killed four soldiers of the Army of the Republic of Viet Nam, or ARVN. Nick described a firefight at the perimeter of Tan Son Nhut in which he found himself pinned down by intense enemy automatic rifle fire. As he looked around for assistance, he noticed out of the corner of his eye that four ARVN troops, located in a foxhole about 100 yards in front of his own, were pointing out his position to the enemy. He waited several minutes until there was a lull in the fighting, and then opened fire on the ARVN, killing all four.

Nick expressed no remorse or regret about killing the ARVN. He remained convinced that he had acted purely in self-defense; moreover, he insisted that the ARVN had gotten only what they deserved. In addition, he cited this incident as further evidence of his magical psychic powers. He was unswerving in his belief that catching the ARVN in the corner of his eye was due to uncanny, prescient powers. Their deaths, he asserted, were testament to the omnious nature of his retaliatory powers.

In pursuing this theme, Nick described a number of instances in the postcombat period, in which he suspected others of attempting to sabotage and harm him. In each case, Nick conjured up evil and diabolical forms of revenge, or what he referred to as "jinxes and hexes." According to Nick, all of his jinxes and hexes befell each of the intended victims.

In addition to believing in magical powers of self-transformation (that is, the power to become invisible), psychokinesis, and prescience, Nick also claimed to possess clairvoyant powers. As an example, he cited eerie premonitions of the death of a specific person, who, only days later, suddenly and unexpectedly died. Or, as another example, he spoke of strange episodes of déjà vu, in which he believed he changed the course of an event on the basis of prior knowledge of its outcome.

The predominance of the omnipotence of thought in Nick's unconscious fantasy life and his belief in paranormal phenomena are consistent with findings (see, for example, Klein, 1968; De Wind, 1971, Terr, 1984, 1985) on the prevalence of this same unconscious thought process among survivors of other forms of trauma. It seems that the unconscious process of the omnipotence of thought is central to the original formation of archaic narcissistic fantasies as well as their attempted but faulty restoration following traumatic shattering. The omnipotence of thought phenomenon should not be equated or confused with psychotic or schizophrenic thought processes. The latter consist of a formal thought disorder including loosening of associations, flight of ideas, and tangentiality. They also manifest themselves in hallucinations and delusions. Finally, there also appears to be a close connection between shattering traumatic occurrence and belief in the uncanny, supernatural, and paranormal.

The therapist's empathic stance toward Nick's ever increasing array of supernatural psychic powers and paranormal experiences facilitated the exhibitionistic display of omnipotence as part of his selfobject transference fantasy of mirrored grandiosity. This considerably enhanced the reconstruction of the unconscious meaning of traumatic combat experiences. In line with our self-psychological theory of treatment, the emergence of a selfobject transference fantasy in the context of an account of traumatic occurrences seemed especially pertinent to understanding the unconscious meaning of trauma.

In Nick's case, a selfobject transference fantasy of idealized merger conveyed meaning about Nick's expereinces at Tan Son Nhut prior to and during TET. In other words, Nick's need to experience himself within the transference in accordance with the unconscious meaning of an idealized merger fantasy paralleled and, therefore, shed light on the unconscious meaning of traumatic combat occurrences. Nick had gone from an experience of himself as unconsciously organized in accordance with fantasies of his own invincibility, invulnerability, and immortality to an experience of himself as a helpless, defenseless, and passive victim of overpoweringly malevolent forces seemingly bent on his personal destruction.

As a result of the shattering of his fantasy of idealized merger with Tan Son Nhut, Nick had apparently attempted to defend against the loss with a grandiose fantasy of omnipotent control. This latter fantasy underwent further unconscious elaboration during combat and in the postcombat period. Its inherent fragility left Nick extremely vulnerable to the dissociative symptoms of PTSD. In shifting from an idealized merger to a selfobject transference fantasy of mirrored grandiosity within the intersubjective context of his therapeutic relationship, Nick had recreated the unconscious meaning of his traumatic combat experiences.

The second half of the reconstructive phase of Nick's treatment (covering approximately one and a half years of therapy) produced a clearer picture of the genetic context of the unconscious meaning of the traumatic shattering and faulty restoration of central organizing fantasies. As Nick felt more comfortable in exhibiting his own grandiosity, he started to speak of missing his father. Nick's father had died several years after he returned from Vietnam. Nick commented that he had joined his father's volunteer fire department to win his respect and admiration. Unfortunately, Nick sighed, his father had already been dead for several years when he was promoted to the rank of fire department lieutenant. Nick expressed great regret at not being able to share his achievement with his father.

In further discussion of the feelings surrounding his father's absence, Nick and the therapist were able to understand better some of the genetic roots of the Invisible Man phenomenon. They linked the death of Nick's father to his earlier disappearances during Nick's childhood. Although unconsciously connected, there was a major difference in these forms of disappearance. Nick remembered feeling upset by his father's long absences on the road when he was a child. Nick said it was as if his father had suddenly disappeared only to reappear magically several days or weeks later. Perhaps, Nick suggested, this partially accounted for his belief in his own power to become invisible. In the postcombat period, apparently Nick was still patiently waiting for his father to reappear magically.

In reminiscing about his father, Nick also provided a genetic context for understanding his idealized merger fantasy with Tan Son Nhut as well as its replication in the transference. Nick connected early childhood fantasies of merger with his idealized father and his huge diesel truck rig with similar fantasies of idealized merger with Tan Son Nhut. He recognized that as these fantasies were shattered by the events of TET, he evoked superman fantasies modeled on similar and earlier childhood versions.

In talking about his father and how much he longed for his praise and admiration, Nick confided that he was beginning to have similar feelings in his relationship with the therapist. In fact, he said, for the first time since his father's death, he had a sense of having achieved such an experience with the therapist. As if to confirm this sense, Nick reported the following dream:

I'm walking with an older man along a street or path. We're walking at a brisk pace. I sense that we're not walking from something, like we're scared, but toward something. I'm wondering who the man is; I think that he must be Frank.

In associating to the dream, Nick indicated that Frank, an official of his hometown and an old friend of the family, had been his father's best buddy. After his father died, Nick often thought of Frank as a fantasy substitute for his father.

In further associations, Nick remembered that in the dream he was struck by one feature of Frank's appearance that did not conform to his real looks. Unlike the real Frank, the dream version had very thin hair. In response to a query from the therapist about this physical discrepancy, Nick connected Frank to the therapist, whose hair was in fact thinning. Nick then linked the dream image of walking with Frank (toward, not away from, something) with his sense that the therapist was leading him from his psychological entrapment in the traumatic past of combat in Vietnan to a new life rooted in the present and future.

Working-Through Phase

The working-through phase of Nick's still ongoing therapy covered the last two and a half years of the treatment. At the beginning of this phase, Nick reported further dramatic improvements in his life. He had recently moved in with a mature and responsible career woman whom he had been dating. Rather than joining him in a deeper and more self-destructive involvement with drugs, as had his third wife, his new girlfriend encouraged him to return to school on a part-time basis to get his college degree in computer science.

In turning to the therapist for guidance in this matter, Nick was especially pleased by what he felt was the therapist's approval and support of such a course of self-improvement. Nick's sessions became filled with glowing reports of his academic and personal achievements as well as success at work. For the first time since returning from Vietnam, Nick spoke of feeling "full of myself" on the basis of a new type of achievement. In the past, he observed, he had gained a sense of accomplishment by exercising his superhuman psychic powers. However, their illusory nature left him unsatisfied and still in need of further confirmatory experiences. He had sought such experiences in drugs. Now, for the first time, he was able to gain a sense of self-confirmation by exercising his intellectual powers and technical competence.

We cannot describe the details of the course of treatment of Nick's dual substance abuse. Suffice it to say that as treatment proceeded, Nick progressively experienced himself as organized within the transference in accordance with the unconscious meaning of restored fantasies. Nick's substance abuse subsided in the intersubjective context of a series of selfobject transference fantasies. And, in the course of analyzing these selfobject transference fantasies, as part of working through the unconscious meaning of traumatic combat occurrences, Nick's abuse of both cocaine and marijuana abated. The "intersubjective absorption" of the selfobject functioning of cocaine and marijuana in the transference fantasies enabled Nick to give up dependence on these drugs. (For an explanation of this self-psychological understanding and approach to the treatment of substance abuse, see Ulman and Paul, 1986, 1987a, b.)

Nick reported a brief but significant dream. It symbolically represented the working through of the unconscious meaning of trauma in the context of the therapeutic transformation of his selfobject transference fantasies into developmentally advanced meaning structures. In the dream:

I'm standing confidently and triumphantly on top of a very tall building.

Nick first associated the dream imagery to traumatic combat occurrences taking place at Tan Son Nhut during the early days and nights of TET. Nick recalled that at that time the enemy ground forces regularly broke through the airfield perimeter and occupied sniper positions atop the roofs of hangers and silos from which they then pinned down American troops. Nick still has terrifying memories of being pinned down by these snipers as they fired on him from their protected perches on the roofs. He remembers wishing that he could fly like superman to a position above the enemy snipers, thus magically reversing positions and gaining the upper hand.

According to Nick, his dream pictorially communicated his sense that he had "finally gotten on top of and gained the upper hand with Vietnam and my life!" Nick related this feeling to his growing confidence and pride in his ability to succeed in life without having to resort to his superhuman psychic powers. For example, when a college instructor gave Nick a lower grade than he thought he deserved, he went to his faculty advisor to register an official complaint. Nick commented on the marked contrast between this action and his previous pattern of relying on guns, jinxes, and hexes to retaliate against those who he felt had attacked or wronged him.

In discussing his new found method of success, Nick spoke of his growing fascination with computers. He described spending hours mesmerized, almost in a self-hypnotic trance, at his computer terminal as if he were merged in fantasy with the seemingly omnipotent computer. Whereas in the past he had felt empowered only by drugs or fantastic powers, now he referred to feeling empowered by the computer. He laughed as he told the therapist about his favorite computer game, which simulated the bombing of Hanoi and other targets in North Vietnam. He jokingly called this his "Rambo in the Sky" fantasy, an allusion to the popular movie hero and the famous Beatle song lyric, "Lucy in the sky with diamonds."

As Nick exhibited a healthier (that is, tempered and moderate) sense of his own grandiosity as part of his idealized merger fantasy with the computer as omnipotent selfobject, his need for the simultaneous stimulation of cocaine and sedation of marijuana diminished. He no longer depended on these drugs to activate and artifically intensify archaic narcissistic fantasies; instead, he increasingly relied on his computer skills to sustain a healthy sense of his own competence and prowess. Nick's sense of self became unconsciously organized more on the basis of demonstrated intellectual ability and computer skill than on illusory and fantastic powers. As a result, he experienced ever greater freedom and relief from the dissociative and disorganizing effects of PTSD symptoms.

Nick noted that instead of feeling as if he were suffocating from the stranglehold of the symptoms of PTSD, he finally felt able to breath freely. This comment reminded him of a recent dream:

> I'm lying on the ground and I've stopped breathing. A man, whose face I can barely make out as I'm losing consciousness, kneels over, and gives me mouth-to-mouth resuscitation. He restores my breathing and brings me back to life.

In associating to the dream, Nick remembered that throughout his combat tour he had been haunted by what seemed like an irrational and inexplicable fear of suffocating to death. He continued to be bothered by this dread in the postcombat period, which probably contributed to his chronic insomnia. (In other words, he unconsciously dreaded sleep because of a fear that if he lost consciousness he would stop breathing and suffocate to death.) Nick connected the therapist with the man in his dream. He then made the link between the therapist and his father, whom he associated with mouth-to-mouth resuscitation and breathing life back into victims of fire who were suffocating from smoke inhalation.

Now, Nick said, he understood for the first time his fear of dying from suffocation. The loss in Vietnam of fantasy substitutes for his father had been expressed in a dread of being without oxygen. He felt that the therapist had figuratively breathed new life into him, thus restoring him and giving "me a second chance to live again."

CONCLUSION

We have presented the clinical details of three representative analytic therapy cases of incest, rape, and combat trauma illustrating our approach to the treatment of PTSD (see also Ulman and Brothers, 1987). The three cases illustrated the reconstruction and working through of the unconscious meaning of: (1) incest trauma caused by the shattering of an idealized merger fantasy and its faulty compensatory and defensive restoration (Marge); (2) rape trauma caused by the shattering of a grandiose-exhibitionistic fantasy and its faulty defensive restoration (Thea); and (3) combat trauma as caused by the shattering of an idealized merger fantasy and its faulty compensatory and defensive restoration (Nick).

The cases of Marge, Thea, and Nick exemplified key aspects of our central thesis regarding treatment. First, they demonstrated that the intersubjective context created by inevitable and therefore unavoidable transference–countertransference neuroses is an ideal therapeutic medium for reconstructing and working through the unconscious meaning of trauma.

Second, these cases demonstrated that the clinical process of reconstruction and working through facilitates the therapeutic transformation of faultily restored (defensive or compensatory) fantasmagorical meaning structures. Such transformation entails lasting structural change (in contrast to temporary symptomatic relief) in the unconscious organization of self-experience. Evidence for such increased psychic structuralization is found in the dimunition of PTSD symptoms as the pathological expression of the dissociative disturbance in the unconscious organization of self-experience. It is also found in increased introspection or insight into the unconscious meaning of trauma.

Third, these cases illustrated the presence of a critical clinical process structuring each of the three therapeutic relationships. In each of the cases, a selfobject countertransference fantasy led to various degrees of counterresistance (Racker, 1968), which, in turn, led to different levels of "misunderstanding" (Ulman and Stolorow, 1985, p. 39) and resulting empathic failures. These misunderstandings and empathic failures created a specific transference–countertransference neurosis, which, in two of the three cases, generated such acute narcissistic rage that the patient temporarily dropped out of treatment. Yet it was precisely these transference–countertransference neuroses that provided the intersubjective context within which to reconstruct and work through the unconscious meaning of traumatic occurrences through the transformation of shattered and faultily restored central organizing fantasies.

Finally, the three cases demonstrated that even normal childhood and adolescent narcissistic fantasies typically fail to undergo sufficient developmental transformation, thus leaving most persons vulnerable to their traumatic shattering and faulty restoration. Faulty restoration of these fantasies, whether defensive or compensatory, often appears in the form of a belief in the possession of uncanny, supernatural, and magical psychic powers. These powers may be experienced as emanating from either the self or the other (animate and inanimate) as selfobject. The traumatically induced belief in the paranormal should not, however, be confused with schizophrenic thought processes or psychotic disorders. Rather, it is an expression of the unconscious organization of self-experience in accordance with the meaning of archaic narcissistic fantasies.

CHAPTER 8

Final Considerations

THEORETICAL ISSUES

We argue (see chapter 2) that Freud more or less abandoned the seduction theory of trauma in favor of the oedipal theory of pathogenesis. We contend that in this dramatic shift he altered the focus of psychoanalysis from the former to the latter. It is difficult to determine if this momentous shift was motivated by personal reasons related to Freud's so-called suppression of the truth (Masson, 1984) about seduction, that is, the prevalence of actual sexual molestation and abuse in childhood.

It is clear, however, that in making this shift, Freud obscured the importance of trauma and failed to appreciate crucial aspects of the relationship between trauma and fantasy. He presented fantasy as merely a product of infantile wish and childhood imagination. Yet, he also argued that psychic reality should take precedence over material or factual reality. In other words, according to Freud, psychoanalysis ought to concern itself with what is imagined or fantasized to have happened rather than with what did occur.

Notwithstanding Freud's position, psychoanalysis has become mired in confusion (see chapter 2) in its attempt to solve a critical theoretical puzzle: Do actual occurrences or fantasies cause trauma? In offering our solution to this psychoanalytic conundrum, we argue that neither reality nor fantasy causes trauma; rather, the unconscious meaning of events shatters central organizing fantasies of self in relation to selfobject. The shattering and faulty restoration of archaic narcissistic fantasies result in PTSD, the present-day version of traumatic neurosis.

Our theory of trauma as the pathological alteration of self experiences caused by unconscious meaning is based on our conception of psychoanalysis as a hermeneutic science of mental action and meaning (see chapter 1 and Ulman and Zimmerman, 1985, 1987). To Rothstein's (1986) typology of psychoanalytic definitions of trauma as hermeneutic, developmental, and adaptational, we add our self-psychological theory of trauma to the "hermeneutic perspective" (p. 225).

Moreover, our solution to the psychoanalytic conundrum represents a self-psychological addition to what Cohen (1980, 1981) refers to as the emergence of a "trauma paradigm" in psychoanalysis. In Kuhnian terms, the "transition" from the prevailing conflict paradigm to a trauma paradigm would constitute a "fundamental paradigm shift" (Kuhn, 1970, p. 89) and hence a "scientific revolution" within psychoanalysis.

We see our work as furthering this transition to a trauma paradigm. We also intend it as a self-psychological contribution to the psychoanalytic literature on fantasy (see, for example, Kohut, 1966, 1968, 1971; Tolpin, 1974; A. Ornstein, 1983; Strozier, 1983). According to the classical psychoanalytic view, unconscious fantasy is solely a product of instinctual desire and grossly distorts the objectively true meaning of events taking place in the external world. In marked contrast, we conceive of archaic narcissistic fantasy as the central meaning structures unconsciously organizing the sense of self in relation to selfobject and hence defining the personal significance of events occurring in the social world of shared experience.

Applying our self-psychological conception of fantasy to the study of trauma led us to rethink Freud's formulations on the self-preservative instinct and the repetition compulsion. We view these concepts as Freud's effort to account for the imperative psychological need to organize, maintain, and restore self- (including selfobject) experience and its unconscious meaning (see Atwood and Stolorow, 1984, p. 35 on the "supraordinate motivational principle"). Our theory of trauma as the shattering and faulty restoration of central organizing fantasies of self in relation to selfobject is based on the unconscious operation of such an imperative psychological need. We employ Kohut's (1966, p. 433, n. 6) ideas on defensive and compensatory reinforcement of archaic narcissistic structures as the foundation of our formulation of either defensive or compensatory restoration of shattered fantasies (see chapter 1).

From the perspective of our theory, the compulsive repetition of the traumatic is not a manifestation of the death instinct, as Freud (1920) speculated, but a reflection of the need for self-restitution. Trauma is dissociatively relived in a faulty attempt to defensively and/or compensatorily restore shattered fantasies of self in relation to selfobject. During development, fantasies of self are unconsciously formed in the intersubjective context of those fantasized as selfobjects. Following trauma, therefore, efforts to restore and transform shattered fantasies of self are often best undertaken in the intersubjective context created by selfobject transference and countertransference fantasies.

Freud's concepts of the self-preservative instinct and the repetition compulsion provide an important link between classical psychoanalysis and self psychology. Connections exist among Freud's classical concepts, Kohut's "principle of the primacy of the preservation of the self" (Tolpin, 1985, p. 87) as reflected in the restoration of the self (Kohut, 1977), and Atwood and Stolorow's (1984) "supraordinate motivational principle" (1984, p. 35). Freud, Kohut, and Atwood and Stolorow all presume the unconscious operation of an imperative psychological need to organize, maintain, and restore self-experience. This presumption also underlies our theory of trauma.

Stolorow (1984) has argued persuasively against viewing the self as personal agent and in favor of a conception of the "self-as-structure." Stolorow's concept of the self-as-structure goes far in solving self psychology's problem of personification. However, it does not go far enough in overcoming the difficulty of reification and experience-distant theorizing.

We believe that our view of archaic narcissistic fantasy as unconscious organizing activity giving structure and meaning to subjective experience helps to correct the error of personifying and reifying self and selfobject. The conception of the self-as-fantasy underlies our experience-near theory of trauma.

In addition, our theory builds on Kohut's (1971) important distinction between horizontal and vertical splits. Kohut's view of the latter is the basis for our self-psychological reconceptualization and diagnostic reclassification of PTSD as a dissociative disorder. We believe that our research findings justify diagnostically reclassifying PTSD as a dissociative disorder. Such a reclassification enables us to understand (and treat) the anxiety so characteristic of PTSD as a disintegration product of the fragmentation of the self rather than as a symptom of unconscious conflict between psychic agencies (that is, the id, ego, and superego).

Moreover, the reclassification of PTSD goes well beyond technical diagnostic issues. It has important implications for the treatment of trauma. Classifying PTSD as an anxiety disorder leads to short-term and brief treatment of symptoms. Reclassifying PTSD as a dissociative disorder necessitates the long-term analytic treatment of traumatic disorders in self-experience.

METHODOLOGICAL ISSUES

Freud's shift from the seduction theory to the theory of the Oedipus complex created not only serious conceptual problems for psychoanalysis but methodological ones as well. With few early exceptions, psychoanalysts joined Freud in totally discounting the material or factual reality of sexual trauma. This unfortunately led them to view sexual trauma only as a psychic (not material or factual) reality reflecting the fantasies of hysterical females and other neurotics (see chapter 2). This mistaken view resulted in the limiting of psychoanalytic research on trauma to combat, the Holocaust, or loss of a loved one. Consequently, the actual occurrence (material or factual reality) of sexual trauma and its unconscious meaning for women was largely ignored by most psychoanalytic researchers.

Instead, many psychoanalytic researchers limited their investigations to the traumatic experiences of young men serving in the military and fighting in war. This emphasis on combat trauma in men and disregard for sexual trauma in women created a false dichotomy between traumatic and anxiety neurosis. Male survivors of combat, as well as survivors of the Holocaust, suffered from traumatic neurosis, the survivor syndrome, or PTSD. Female hysterics and other similarly disturbed people were thought to be suffering from anxiety neurosis.

Utilizing a research design that combined samples derived from male and female survivors of combat, incest, and rape enabled us to arrive at findings on trauma relevant to the lives of both men and women. We were able, therefore, to correct a serious methodological flaw in the sampling techniques of previous psychoanalytic researchers on trauma. We provided ample evidence that the prototypical traumas experienced by men and women result not in two different forms of neurosis but in the same form of neurosis—PTSD. Our findings argue against a theory of pathogenesis based on the dichotomy between traumatic and anxiety neurosis and in favor of a comprehensive and unified theory of traumatogenesis.

We bring to the traditional case study method the applied psychoanalytic research technique of empathic or vicarious introspection as a self-psychological mode of data gathering and analysis. Utilizing Kohut's empathic-introspective observational stance within the therapeutic research setting enabled us to explore the unconscious fantasy lives of our survivors. Our psychoanalytic explorations confirmed the value of the research technique of empathic introspection as a reliable means of arriving at valid inferences about the unconscious meaning of traumatic experience.

Utilizing vicarious introspection as a mode of psychoanalytic inquiry broadens the scope of the standard case study method. Traditionally, this method has relied heavily on structured research interviewing techniques as a means of gathering life history and psychiatric data. In contrast, we used unstructured interviewing techniques based on the sustained empathic immersion in our research subjects' unconscious fantasy lives. This enabled us to gather and analyze introspective data such as dreams and nightmares, related associative material, and self-reports on dissociative states of reexperiencing and numbing. We believe that the research results of our therapeutic interviews substantiates our claim that empathic introspection is a scientific mode of observation that may be reliably applied to fields of study outside the confines of the traditional psychoanalytic treatment setting.

In several of our clinical case studies, for instance, Jean, Al, and Junior, our sustained empathic immersion manifested itself in vague yet recognizable selfobject transferences. Analytically reading these transferences was particularly helpful in interpreting the unconscious meaning of trauma in these three cases. However, we were aware of more subtle and less visible transferences on the part of all our clinical research subjects. (See Hendin, Gaylin, and Carr, 1965, pp. 6, 44, on the use of transference with volunteer subjects in clinical research.)

CLINICAL ISSUES

Our clinical findings support our main thesis that PTSD is a dissociative disorder resulting from the shattering and faulty restoration of central organizing fantasies of self in relation to selfobject. The shattering and faulty (defensive and/or compensatory) restoration of these archaic narcissistic fantasies determines the unconscious meaning of actual occurrences.

We also conclude from our study that these fantasies, although imbuing occurrences with unconscious meaning unique to the individual, are themselves universal. Because the complete transformation of archaic narcissistic fantasies is a developmental ideal rarely attained, virtually everyone is vulnerable to the psychological catastrophe of psychic trauma. Our clinical case studies of Nettie, .44 Mike, Violet, Maggie, Alexander, Thea, and Nick, all of whom had relatively normal developmental histories, illustrate the ubiquitous threat posed by trauma.

We presented clinical evidence of the defensive and/or compensatory restoration of shattered fantasies both in our representative cases and in our treatment studies. The breakdown of the 15 cases is as follows: four (.44 Mike, Nettie, Maggie, and Chuck, are examples of faulty defensive restoration; three (Jean, Tina, and Junior) are instances of faulty compensatory restoration; and eight (Fran, Sybil, Rosa, Violet, Al, Marge, Thea, and Nick) are illustrations of faulty defensive and compensatory restoration.

In contrast, our clinical case studies of Sybil, Jean, and Chuck illustrate the effects of trauma on the lives of persons whose archaic narcissistic fantasies have, as a result of developmental arrests, undergone relatively little transformation. In these cases, the symptoms of PTSD assumed psychotic proportions.

The trauma survivors in a number of our clinical case studies, for example, Jean, Maggie, Thea, and Nick, reported paranormal experiences. We maintain that these experiences do not in themselves indicate the presence of psychosis. Rather, our findings suggest that for some trauma survivors belief that they possess uncanny psychic powers plays a vital role in efforts at self-restitution.

This conclusion is consistent with the findings of Klein (1968), DeWind (1971), and Terr (1984, 1985) that some survivors report significantly increased episodes of paranormal experience following trauma. Perhaps, for some trauma survivors, the paranormal experience of clairvoyance, telepathy, psychokinesis, prescience, or premonition gives expression to unusually archaic forms of narcissism involving a sense of possessing supernatural powers.

Our clinical findings also support previous research on the prevalence of substance abuse among survivors of trauma (see, for example, Krystal and Raskin, 1970; Hendin and Haas, 1984). For some extended period following trauma, 8 of our 15 cases, or 53%, (Sybil, Jean, Rosa, Maggie, Chuck, Alexander, Junior, and Nick) suffered from serious substance-abuse problems with a wide variety of drugs including heroin, cocaine, amphetamines, LSD, marijuana, and alcohol. We view substance abuse in the trauma survivor as uncontrolled self-medication for the dissociative symptoms (reexperiencing and numbing) of PTSD. Survivors are at high risk to develop substance-abuse disorders because they turn to highly addictive drugs, the psychoactive effects of which enhance the unconscious organizing activity of faultily restored fantasmagorical meaning structures. Substance abuse is therefore another example of failed self-restitution following trauma.

A careful review of our clinical findings suggests a revision in the current self-psychological view of narcissistic rage. We understand narcissistic rage both as a disintegration product of the fragmentation of self (that is, traumatic shattering of archaic narcissistic fantasies) and as an agent of self-restitution. In a number of our cases (Maggie, Violet, Chuck, Alexander, Junior, and Nick) we found that survivors of trauma unconsciously attempted to restore shattered fantasies by grand exhibitions of narcissistic rage. That such conspicuous displays of rage usually occurred as part of dissociated reliving experiences attests to the extent to which narcissistic rage was part of failed efforts at self-restitution.

Finally, our clinical results lend support to previous findings on the relation of trauma and fantasy to gender-identity disturbances (see, for example, Stoller, 1975, 1979). Such disturbances consist of a developmental failure to integrate culturally defined feminine and masculine traits into a mature and healthy sense of self. For example, in many of our cases the shattering and faulty restoration of archaic narcissistic fantasies led to gender identity disturbances in the form of highly exaggerated and stereotypic expressions of femininity and masculinity.

In attempting to restore central fantasy images of themselves, a number of our incest and rape trauma survivors, for instance, Jean, Rosa, Maggie, and Marge, displayed exaggerated and caricatured sexual behavior, which left some of them vulnerable to exploitation in prostitution and pornography. For these young women, the highly sexualized nature of the attempted restoration of fantasies of self was a manifestation of a gender-identity disturbance.

All our combat trauma cases (.44 Mike, Chuck, Alexander, Junior and Nick) utilized violently aggressive behavior in attempting to restore central fantasy images of themselves. For these young men, the violently aggressive nature of the attempted restoration of fantasies of self was a manifestation of a gender-identity disturbance.

Our findings suggest that the failure of archaic narcissistic fantasies to undergo healthy developmental transformation accounts, in part, for gender-identity disturbances manifested in stereotypic and caricatured expressions of femininity and masculinity.

The prevalence of paranormal experiences, substance abuse, chronic narcissistic rage, and gender identity disturbances in so many of our cases attests to the failure of efforts at self-restitution following trauma. Yet these failed efforts also attest to the operation of the imperative psychological need to maintain and restore the unconscious organization of experience.

TREATMENT ISSUES

Our self-psychological approach to the treatment of PTSD was an integral part of our research design. Using the representative case study method, we based our selection of individual therapy cases on the degree to which a specific survivor graphically illustrated key features of other survivors of incest, rape, and combat. We also carefully assessed the likelihood of their benefiting from analytic therapy. We believe that our methodological control of the therapy sample warrants the inclusion of the results of our treatment study in the increasing body of scientific (in contrast to purely anecdotal) information on the outcome of forms of analytic therapy (see, for example, Dewald, 1972; Wallerstein, 1986; Horowitz, 1987).

Although we are greatly indebted to Kohut as well as Stolorow and coworkers for our approach to treatment, we have arrived at our own understanding of "how analysis cures" (see Kohut, 1984). We believe that analysis "cures" or is mutative in the transformation of archaic narcissistic fantasies that have become (vertically) split off from the personality. We have argued that such therapeutic transformation occurs primarily in the intersubjective context of the transference-countertransference neurosis (Ulman and Stolorow, 1985). We broadened the original definition of this concept to include the respective archaic narcissistic fantasies of patient as well as therapist (see Ulman and Brothers, 1987).

RESEARCH APPLICATIONS

In concluding our remarks, we briefly allude to applications of our theory to other areas of research interest. First, we have applied specific theoretical and clinical principles derived from our work to understanding and treating substance abuse disorders (see the case of Nick, chapter 7). A report on this research is in preparation (see Ulman and Paul, 1986, 1987a,b). This report indicates that certain self-disordered patients experience substances such as psychoactive drugs and alcohol, as well as food, as inanimate selfobjects. For these patients, the substance-as-selfobject provides desperately needed states of elation and euphoria, or soothing and calming, to temporarily offset the empty depression of unmirrored grandiosity or the fragmented mania of failed merger with the idealized and omnipotent. The report also documents the successful treatment of substance abuse through the "intersubjective absorption" of the selfobject functions of abused substances in the context of the analysis of a selfobject transference fantasy.

Second, we conducted a pilot research project extending our work to the study of accident trauma. For example, one case involved a 60-year-old man who had survived a hit-and-run car accident. Another case was that of a 40-year-old woman who had been near death but survived a small plane crash. In both cases, the unconscious meaning of trauma was determined by the shattering and faulty restoration of a central organizing fantasy of grandiosity. We successfully treated both of these trauma survivors by utilizing the form of analytic therapy developed in this study.

Third, we are planning a research project studying the shattering and faulty restoration of archaic narcissistic fantasies of prostitutes suffering from PSTD, caused by the unconscious meaning of sexual trauma in childhood and adolescence. And, finally, the relationship between trauma and trust disturbance is also under investigation (Brothers, in progress).

We have noted only a few areas of applied psychoanalytic research to which we believe our theory might have relevance. The research already undertaken suggests that a wide range of self-disorders might better be explained by taking into account disturbances in the functioning of central organizing fantasies of self in relation to selfobject. We hope that our study will stimulate other researchers to test our theory of trauma in areas of their special expertise.

References

Abraham, K. (1907a), The experiencing of sexual traumas as a form of sexual activity. In: The *Selected Papers of Karl Abraham*. London: Hogarth Press, 1948, pp. 47–63.
—— (1907b), On the significance of sexual traumas in childhood for the symptomatology of dementia praecox. In: *Clinical Papers and Essays on Psycho-Analysis*. New York: Basic Books, 1955, pp. 13–20.
—— (1921), Comments from symposium on the war neuroses. In: *Psycho-Analysis of the War Neuroses*, ed. S. Ferenczi, K. Abraham, E. Simmel, & E. Jones. London: International Psycho-Analytical Press, pp. 22–29.
Adler, A. (1927), *Understanding Human Nature*. New York: Permabooks.
Alacorn, A. D. Dickinson, W. A., & Dohn, H. H. (1982), Flashback phenomena: Clinical and diagnostic dilemmas. *Journal of Nervous and Mental Disorders*, 170:217–223.
American Psychiatric Association (1980), *Diagnostic and Statistical Manual of Mental Disorders*, 3rd ed. Washington, D.C.: American Psychiatric Association.
—— (1987), *Diagnostic and Statistical Manual of Mental Disorders*, 3rd ed.-rev. Washington, DC: American Psychiatric Association.
Arlow, J. A. (1966), Depersonalization and derealization. In: *Psychoanalysis—A General Psychology*, ed. R. M. Lowenstein, L. M. Newman, M. Schur, & A. J. Solnit. New York: International Universities Press, pp. 456–478.
—— (1969a), Unconscious fantasy and disturbances of conscious experience. *Psychoanalytic Quarterly*, 38:1–27.
—— (1969b), Fantasy, memory, and reality testing. *Psychoanalytic Quarterly*, 38:28–51.
Atwood, G. E., & Stolorow, R. D. (1984), *Structures of Subjectivity*. Hillsdale, NJ: The Analytic Press.
Auerhahn, N. C., & Laub, D. (1984), Annihilation and restoration: Post-

traumatic memory as pathway and obstacle to recovery. *International Review of Psycho-Analysis*, 11:327–344.

Bach, S., & Schwartz, L. (1972), A dream of the Marquis de Sade: Psychoanalytic reflections on narcissistic trauma, decompensation, and the reconstruction of a delusional self. *Journal of the American Psychoanalytic Association*, 20:451–475.

——— (1985), *Narcissistic States and the Therapeutic Process.* New York: Aronson.

Balson, P. M., & Dempster, C. R. (1980), Treatment of war neuroses from Vietnam. *Comprehensive Psychiatry*, 21: 167–175.

Bard, M., & Ellison, D. (1974), Crisis intervention and investigation of forcible rape. *Police Chief*, 5:68–74.

Basch, M. F. (1981), Psychoanalytic interpretation and cognitive transformation. *International Journal of Psycho-Analysis*, 62:151–175.

——— (1983), The perception of reality and the disavowal of meaning. *The Annual Psychoanalysis*, 11:125–153.

——— (1985), Interpretation: Toward a developmental model. In: *Progress in Self Psychology, Vol. 1*, ed. A. Goldberg. New York: Guilford Press, pp. 33–42.

Becker, J., Skinner, L., Abel, G., & Treacy, E. (1982), Incidence and types of sexual dysfunctions in rape and incest victims. *Journal of Sex and Marital Therapy*, 8:65–74.

Beres, D., & Arlow, J. A. (1974), Fantasy and identification in empathy. *Psychoanalytic Quarterly*, 43:26–50.

Berg, C. (1947), *Deep Analysis: The Clinical Study of an Individual Case.* New York: Norton.

Blank, A. S., Jr. (1985), The unconscious flashback to the war in Viet Nam veterans: Clinical mystery, legal defense, and community problem. In: *The Trauma*, ed. S. M. Sonnenberg, A. S. Blank, Jr., & J. Talbott. Washington, DC: American Psychiatric Press, pp. 295–308.

Blos, P. (1962), *On Adolescence.* New York: Free Press of Glencoe.

——— (1963), The concept of acting out in relation to the adolescent process. *Journal of the American Academy of Child Psychiatry.* 2:118–143.

——— (1967), The second individuation process of adolescence. *The Psychoanalytic Study of the Child*, 22:162–186. New York: International Universities Press.

Blitz, R., & Greenberg, R. (1984), Nightmares of the traumatic neuroses: Implications for theory and treatment. In: *Psychotherapy of the Combat Veteran*, ed. H. J. Schwartz. New York: Spectrum, pp. 103–123.

Bloch, D. (1978), *So the Witch Wont Eat Me.* Boston: Houghton Mifflin.

Blum, H. P. (1986), The concept of the reconstruction of trauma. In: *The Reconstruction of Trauma*, ed. A. Rothstein. New York: International Universities Press, pp. 7–27.

Blumenthal, R. (1981), Did Freud's isolation, peer rejection prompt key theory reversal? Science Times, *The New York Times*, August 25.

——— (1984), Freud: Secret documents reveal years of strife. (Evidence points to anguish over seduction theory). *The New York Times*, Science Times, January 24.

Bonaparte, M. (1953), *Female Sexuality*, New York: International Universities Press.

Boulanger, G. (1986), Violence and Vietnam veterans. In: *The Vietnam Veteran Redefined*, ed. G. Boulanger & C. Kadushin. Hillsdale, NJ: Lawrence Erlbaum Associates, pp. 70–90.

Brende, J. O. (1981), Combined individual and group therapy for Vietnam veterans. *International Journal of Group Psychotherapy*, 31:367–378.

——— (1982), Electrodermal responses in post-traumatic syndromes: A pilot study of cerebral hemisphere functioning in Vietnam veterans. *Journal of Nervous and Mental Disorders*, 170:352–361.

——— (1983), A psychodynamic view of character pathology in Vietnam combat veterans. *Bulletin of the Menninger Clinic*, 47:193–216.

——— Benedict, B. D. (1980), The Vietnam combat delayed stress response syndrome: Hypnotherapy of "dissociative symptoms." *American Journal of Clinical Hypnosis*, 23:34–40.

——— McCann, I. L. (1984), Regressive experiences in Vietnam veterans: Their relationship to war, post-traumatic symptoms and recovery. *Journal of Contemporary Psychotherapy*, 14:57–75.

——— Parson, E. R. (1985), *Vietnam Veterans: The Road to Recovery*. New York: Plenum Press.

Brandchaft, B., & Stolorow, R. D. (1984), The borderline concept: Pathological character or iatrogenic myth? In: *Empathy*, Vol. 2, ed. J. Lichtenberg, M. Bornstein, & D. Silver. Hillsdale, NJ: The Analytic Press, pp. 333–357.

Breuer, J., & Freud, S. (1893–95), Studies on hysteria. *Standard Edition*, 2, London: Hogarth Press, 1955.

Bromley, D. B. (1977), *Personality Description in Ordinary Language*. New York: Wiley.

Brothers, D. (1982), *Trust Disturbances Among Rape and Incest Victims*. Unpublished doctoral dissertation. Yeshiva University. *Dissertation Abstracts International*, 1247, Vol. 43 (4-B).

Brown, S. (1980), *Political Subjectivity: Applications of Q-Methodology in Political Science*. New Haven, T: Yale University Press.

Brownmiller, S. (1975), *Against Our Will*. New York: Simon & Schuster.

Burgess, A. W. (1980), Rape typology and the coping behavior of rape victims. In: *The Rape Crisis Intervention Handbook*. ed. S. McCombie. New York: Plenum Press, pp. 27–40.

——— Holmstrom, L. L. (1973), The rape victim in the emergency ward. *American Journal of Nursing*, 73:1740–1745.

——— ——— (1974), Rape trauma syndrome. *American Journal of Psychiatry*, 131:981–986.

Burstein, A. (1985), Post-traumatic flashback, dream disturbances, and mental imagery. *Journal of Clinical Psychiatry*, 46: 374–378.

———— ———— (1974), Rape trauma syndromw. *American Journal of Psychiatry*, 131:981–986.

Butler, S. (1978), *Conspiracy of Silence: The Trauma of Incest*. San Francisco: New Glide.

Chassan, J. B. (1961), Stochastic models of the single case as the basis of clinical research design. *Behavioral Science*, 6:42–50.

———— (1970), On psychodynamics and clinical research and methodology. *Psychiatry*, 33:94–101.

———— (1979), *Research Design in Clinical Psychology and Psychiatry*, 2nd ed. New York: Wiley.

Cohen, J. (1980), Structural consequences of psychic trauma: A new look at "Beyond the Pleasure Principle." *International Journal of Psycho-Analysis*, 61:421–432.

———— (1981), Theories of narcissism and trauma. *American Journal of Psychotherapy*, 35:93–100.

Cooper, A. M. (1986), Toward a limited drfinition of psychic trauma. In: *The Reconstruction of Trauma: Its Significance in Clinical Work*, ed. A. Rothstein. New York: International Universities Press, pp. 41–56.

De Fazio, V. J. (1978). Dynamic perspectives on the nature 8and effects of combat stress. In: *Stress Disorders Among Vietnam Veterans*, ed. C. R. Figley. New York: Brunner/Mazel, pp. 23–42.

De Francis V. (1969), *Protecting the Child Victim of Sex Crimes Committed by Adults*. Denver, CO: American Humane Association, Children's Division.

De Monchaux, C. (1978), Dreaming and the organizing function of the ego. *International Journal of Psycho-Analysis*, 59: 443–453.

Demott, B. (1980), The pro-incest lobby. *Psychology Today*, 3:11–16.

Deutsch, H. (1944), *The Psychology of Women*. Vol. 1 & 2. New York: Grune and Stratton.

Dewald, P. A. (1972), *The Psychoanalytic Process*. New York: Basic Books.

De Wind, E. (1971), Psychotherapy after traumatization caused by persecution. In: *Psychic Traumatization*, ed. H. Krystal & W. Niederland. Boston: Little, Brown, pp. 93–114.

———— (1984), Some implications of former massive traumatization upon the actual analytic process. *International Journal of Psycho-Analysis*, 65:273–281.

De Young, M. (1982), *The Sexual Victimization of Children*. Jefferson, NC: McFarland.

Donaldson, M. A., & Gardner, R., (1985), Diagnosis and treatment of traumatic stress among women after childhood incest. In: *Trauma and Its Wake*, ed. C. R. Figley. New York: Brunner/Mazel, pp. 356–377.

Edelson, M. (1984), *Hypnosis and Evidence in Psychoanalysis*. Chicago: University of Chicago Press.

Egendorf, A. (1982), The postwar healing of Vietnam veterans: Recent research. *Hospital and Community Psychiatry*. 33:901–908.

———— Kadushin, C., Laufer, R., Rothbart, G., & Sloan, L. (1981), *Legacies of Vietnam*. Washington, DC: United States Govt. Printing Off.

Eigen, M. (1980), Instinctual fantasy and ideal images. *Contemporary Psychoanalysis*, 16:119–137.

—— (1982), Creativity, instinctual fantasy and ideal images. *Psychoanalytic Review*, 69:317–339.

—— (1986), *The Psychotic Core*. Northvale, NJ: Aronson.

Eidelberg, L. (1959), The concept of narcissistic mortification. *International Journal of Psycho-Analysis*, 40:163–169.

Eisnitz, A. J. (1985), Father-daughter incest. *International Journal of Psychoanalytic Psychotherapy*, 10:495–503.

Eissler, K. R. (1986), *Freud as an Expert Witness*. New York: International Universities Press.

Erikson, E. H. (1968), *Identity: Youth and Crisis*. New York: Norton.

Fairbairn, W. R. D. (1952), *Psychoanalytic Studies of the Personality*. London: Routledge & Kegan Paul.

Federn, P. (1952), On the distinction between healthy and pathological narcissism. In: *Ego: Psychology and the Psychoses*. New York: Basic Books, pp. 323–364.

Ferenczi, S. (1913), Stages in the development of the sense of reality, In: *Sex in Psychoanalysis*. New York: Brunner, 1950, pp. 213–239.

—— (1916–17), Two types of war neuroses. In: *Further Contributions to the Theory and Technique of Psycho-Analysis*. London: Hogarth Press, 1950, pp. 124–141.

—— (1921), Comments from the symposium on the war neuroses. In: *Psycho-Analysis and the War Neuroses*, ed. S. Ferenczi, K. Abraham, E. Simmel, & E. Jones. London: International Psycho-Analytical Press, pp. 5–21.

—— (1930), Trauma and striving for health. In: *Final Contributions to the Problems and Methods of Psycho-Analysis*. New York: Basic Books, 1955, pp. 230–231.

—— (1949), Confusion of tongues between the adult and child. *International Journal of Psycho-Analysis*, 30: 225–230.

Firestone, R. W. (1985), *The Fantasy Bond*. New York: Human Sciences Press.

Fisher, C. (1945), Amnesic states in war neuroses: The psychodyamics of fugues. *Psychoanalytic Quarterly*, 14:437–469.

—— (1947), The psychogenesis of fugue states. *American Journal of Psychotherapy*, 1:211–220.

Forman, M. (1984), A trauma theory of character neuroses and traumatic transferences, In: *Psychoanalysis, Vol. 2*, ed. G. H. Pollack & J. E. Gedo. New York: International Universities Press, pp. 321–345.

Forward, S., & Buck, C. (1978), *Betrayal of Innocence: Incest and Its Devastation*. Los Angeles, CA: Tarcher.

Fox, R. P. (1972), Post-combat adaptational problems. *Comprehensive Psychiatry*, 13:435–443.

—— (1974), Narcissistic rage and the problem of combat aggression. *Archives of General Psychiatry*, 31:802–811.

Frances, A., Sacks, M., & Aronoff, M. S. (1977), Depersonalization: A self-relations perspective. *International Journal of Psycho-Analysis*, 58:325–331.

Frankel, V. (1963), *Man's Search for Meaning*. New York: Washington Square Press.

Freud, A. (1936), *The Ego and the Mechanisms of Defense*, New York: International Universities Press, 1966.

——— (1958), Adolescence. *The Psychoanalytic Study of the Child*, 13:255–278. New York: International Universities Press.

——— (1967), Comments on trauma. In: *Psychic Trauma*, ed. S. S. Furst. New York: International Universities Press, pp. 235–245.

Freud, S. (1900–01), The interpretation of dreams. *Standard Edition*, 4 & 5. London: Hogarth Press, 1953.

——— (1905), Fragment of an analysis of a case of hysteria. *Standard Edition*, 7. London: Hogarth Press, 1953.

——— (1905), Three essays on the theory of sexuality. *Standard Edition*, 7. London: Hogarth Press, 1953.

——— (1906), My views on the part played by sexuality in the aetiology of the neuroses. *Standard Edition*, London: Hogarth Press, 1953.

——— (1908), Hysterical phantasies and their relation to bisexuality. *Standard Edition*, 9. London: Hogarth Press, 1959.

——— (1909a), Analysis of a phobia in a five-year-old boy. *Standard Edition*, 10. London: Hogarth Press, 1955.

——— (1909b), Notes upon a case of obsessional neuroses. *Standard Edition*, 10. London: Hogarth Press, 1955.

——— (1913), Totem and taboo. *Standard Edition*, 13. London: Hogarth Press, 1953.

——— (1916–17), Introductory lectures on psycho-analysis. *Standard Edition*, 15 & 16. London: Hogarth Press, 1963.

——— (1918), From the history of an infantile neuroses. *Standard Edition*, 17. London: Hogarth Press, 1955.

——— (1919a), "A child is being beaten." *Standard Edition*, 17. London: Hogarth Press, 1955.

——— (1919b), Introduction to psycho-analysis and the war neuroses. *Standard Edition*, 17. London: Hogarth Press, 1955.

——— (1920), Beyond the pleasure principle. *Standard Edition*, 18. London: Hogarth Press, 1955.

——— (1924), The economic problem of masochism. *Standard Edition*, 19. London: Hogarth Press, 1961.

——— (1927), Fetishism. *Standard Edition*, 21. London: Hogarth Press, 1961.

——— (1936), A disturbance of memory on the acropolis. *Standard Edition*, 22. London: Hogarth Press, 1964.

——— (1939), Moses and monotheism. *Standard Edition*, 23. London: Hogarth Press, 1964.

——— (1940), Splitting of the ego in the process of defense. *Standard Edition*, 23. London: Hogarth Press, 1964.

Frick, R., & Bogart, L. (1982), Transference and countertransference—group therapy with Vietnam veterans. *Bulletin of the Menninger Clinic*, 46:429–444.

Futterman, S., & Pumpian-Mindlin, E. (1951), Traumatic war neuroses five years later. *American Journal of Psychiatry*, 108:401–408.

Gaylin, W. (1974), *Partial Justice*. New York: Random House.

Gedo, M. (1984), Looking at art from the empathic viewpoint. In: *Empathy*, Vol. 1, ed. J. Lichtenberg, M. Bornstein, D. Silver. Hillsdale, NJ: The Analytic Press, pp. 267–300.

Geleerd, E. R., Hacker, F. J., & Rapaport, D. (1945), Contribution to the study of amnesia and allied conditions. *Psychoanalytic Quarterly*, 14:199–220.

Glenn, J. (1984), Psychic trauma and masochism. *Journal of the American Psychoanalytic Association*, 32:357–386.

Glover, E. (1955), *The Technique of Psycho-Analysis*, New York: International Universities Press.

Goleman, D. (1984), Freud: Secret documents reveal years of strife. (Psychoanalysis appears stung but little harmed.) *The New York Times*, Science Times, January 24.

Goodwin, J. (1985), Post-traumatic symptoms in incest victims. In: *Post-traumatic Stress Disorder in Children*, ed. S. Eth & R. S. Pynoos. Washington, DC: American Psychiatric Press, pp. 155–168.

——— McCarty, T., & DiVasto, P. (1981), Prior incest in abusive mothers. *Child Abuse and Neglect*, 5:1–9.

Greenacre, P. (1949), A contribution to the study of screen memories. In: *Trauma, Growth and Personality*. New York: International Universities Press, pp. 188–203.

——— (1950), The prepuberty trauma in girls. In: *Trauma, Growth and Personality*. New York: International Universities Press, pp. 204–223.

——— (1967), The influence of infantile trauma on genetic patterns. In: *Psychic Trauma*, ed. S. S. Furst. New York: International Universities Press, pp. 108–153.

——— (1980), A historical sketch of the use and disuse of reconstruction. *The Psychoanalytic Study of the Child*, 35:35–40. New Haven: Yale University Press.

——— (1981), Reconstruction: Its nature and therapeutic value. *Journal of the American Psychoanalytic Association*, 29:27–46.

Greenwald, A. G. (1980), The totalitarian ego: Fabrication and revision of personal history. *American Psychologist*, 35:603–618.

——— Pratakanis, A. R. (1984), The self. In: *Handbook for Social Cognition*, ed. R. S. Wyer, & T. K. Scrull. Hillsdale, NJ: Lawrence Erlbaum Associates, pp. 129–176.

Grossman, W. I. (1982), The self as fantasy: Fantasy as theory. *Journal of the American Psychoanalytic Association*, 30:919–937.

——— (1984), The self as fantasy: Fantasy as theory, In: *Psychoanalysis*, Vol. 1, ed. J. E. Gedo & G. H. Pollack. New York: International Universities Press, pp. 395–412.

Grunberger, B. (1979), *Narcissism: Psychoanalytic Essays*. New York: International Universities Press.

Haas, A. P., Hendin, H., & Singer, P. (1987), Psychodynamic and structured interviewing: Issues of validity. *Comprehensive Psychiatry*, 28:40–53.

Haley, S. A. (1974), When the patient reports atrocities. *Archives of General Psychiatry*, 30:191–196.

——— (1978), Treatment implications of post-combat stress response syndromes for mental health professionals. In: *Stress Disorders Among Vietnam Veterans*, ed. C. R. Figley. New York: Brunner/Mazel, pp. 254–267.

Hendin, H. (1964), *Suicide and Scandinavia*. New York: Grune Stratton.

——— (1969), *Black Suicide*. New York: Basic Books.

——— (1975), *The Age of Sensation*. New York: Basic Books.

——— (1982), *Suicide in America*. New York: Norton.

——— (1983), Psychotherapy with Vietnam veterans with posttraumatic stress disorders. *American Journal of Psychotherapy*, 37:86–99.

——— Gaylin, W., & Carr, A. C. (1965), *Psychoanalysis and Social Research*. New York: Doubleday.

——— Haas, A. P. (1984), *The Wounds of War*. New York: Basic Books.

——— ——— Singer, P., Ellner, M., & Ulman, R. (1987), *Living High*. New York: Human Sciences Press.

——— ——— ——— Gold, F., Trigos, G.-G., & Ulman, R. B. (1983), Evaluation of posttraumatic stress in Vietnam veterans. *Journal of Psychiatric Treatment and Evaluation*, 5:303–307.

——— ——— ——— Houghton, W., Schwartz, M., & Wallen, V. (1984), The reliving experience in Vietnam veterans with posttraumatic stress disorder, *Comprehensive Psychiatry*, 25:165–173.

——— Pollinger, A., Singer, P., & Ulman, R. B. (1981), Meanings of combat and the development of posttraumatic stress disorder. *American Journal of Psychiatry*. 138:1490-1493.

——— Ulman, R., & Carr, A. C. (1981), *Adolescent Marijuana Abusers and Their Families*. National Institute on Drug Abuse Monogr. 40, Washington, DC: United States Gov Printing Off.

——— Siegel, K. (1981), Psychodynamic and structured interviewing: A synthesis I. Rationale. *Comprehensive Psychiatry*, 22:153-161.

Herman, J., & Hirshman, L. (1977), Father-daughter incest, *Signs: Journal of Women and Culture*, pp. 735–746.

——— ——— (1981), *Father-Daughter Incest*. Cambridge, MA: Harvard University Press.

Hilberman, E. (1976), *The Rape Victim*. New York: Basic Books.

Horney, K. (1924), On the genesis of the castration complex in women. In: *Feminine Psychology*, ed. H. Kelman. New York: Norton, pp. 37–53.

——— (1926), The flight from womanhood: The masculinity-complex in women as viewed by men and women. In: *Feminine Psychology*, ed. H. Kelman. New York: Norton, pp. 54–70.

——— (1933), The problem of feminine masochism. In: *Feminine Psychology*, ed. H. Kelman, New York: Norton, pp. 214–233.

Horowitz, M. J. (1969), Psychic trauma: return of images after a stress film. *Archives of General Psychiatry*, 20:552–559.

—— (1973), Phase oriented treatment of stress response syndromes. *American Journal of Psychotherapy*, 27:506–515.

—— (1974), Stress response syndromes: Character style and dynamic psychotherapy. *Archives of General Psychiatry*, 31:768–781.

—— (1975), Sliding meanings. A defense against threat in narcissistic personalities. *International Journal of Psychoanalytic Psychotherapy*, 4:167–180.

—— (1975), A prediction of delayed stress response syndromes in Vietnam veterans. *Journal of Social Issues*, 31:67–80.

—— (1976), *Stress Response Syndromes*. New York: Aronson.

—— (1987), *States of Mind*, 2nd ed. New York: Plenum Medical Books.

—— Becker, S. S. (1971), The compulsion to repeat trauma. *Journal of Nervous and Mental Disorders*, 153:32–40.

—— Wilner, N., Kaltreider, N., & Alvarez, W. (1980), Signs and symptoms of posttraumatic stress disorder. *Archives of General Psychiatry*, 37:85–92.

Jacobson, E. (1949), Observations on the psychological effect of imprisonment on female political prisoners. In: *Searchlights on Delinquency*, ed. K. R. Eissler. New York: International Universities Press, pp. 341–368.

—— (1959), Depersonalization. *Journal of the American Psychoanalytic Association*, 7:581–610.

—— (1961), Adolescent moods and the remodeling of psychic structures in adolescence. *The Psychoanalytic Study of the Child*, 16:164–183. New York; International Universities Press.

Jaffe, R. (1968), Dissociative phenomena in former concentration camp inmates. *International Journal of Psycho-Analysis*, 49:310–312.

Janoff-Bulman, R. (1985), The aftermath of victimization: Rebuilding shattered assumptions. In: *Trauma and Its Wake*, ed. C. R. Figley, New York: Brunner/Mazel, pp. 15–35.

Joseph, E. D. (1959), An unusual fantasy in a twin with an inquiry into the nature of fantasy. *Psychoanalytic Quarterly*, 28:189–206.

Josephs, L., & Josephs, L. (1986), Pursuing the kernel of truth in the psychotherapy of schizophrenia. *Psychoanalytic Psychotherapy*, 3:105–119.

Justice, B., & Justice, R. (1979), *The Broken Taboo*. New York: Human Sciences Press.

Kadushin, C., & Boulanger, G. (1986), Introduction. In: *The Vietnam Veteran Redefined*, ed. G. Boulanger & C. Kadushin. Hillsdale, NJ: Lawrence Erlbaum Associates, pp. 1–12.

Kardiner, A. (1941), *The Traumatic Neuroses of War*. New York: Paul Hoeber.

—— (1959), Traumatic war neuroses of war. In: *American Handbook of Psychiatry*, ed. S. Arieti. New York: Basic Books, pp. 245–257.

—— Oversey, L. (1951), *The Mask of Oppression*. New York: World.

—— Spiegel, H. (1947), *War Stress and Neurotic Illness*. New York: Hoeber.

Katz, S., & Mazur, M. (1979), *Understanding the Rape Victim*. New York: Wiley.

Kaufman, I., Peck, A. L., & Tagiuri, C. K. (1954), The family constellation and overt incestuous relations between father and daughter. *American Journal of Orthopsychiatry.* 24:266–277.

Kelman, H. (1945), Character and the traumatic syndrome. *Journal of Nervous and Mental Disease,* 102:121–153.

———— (1946), The traumatic syndrome. *American Journal of Psychoanalysis,* 6:12–19.

Klein, G. (1976), *Psychoanalytic Theory.* New York: International Universities Press.

Klein, H. (1968), Problems in the psychotherapeutic treatment of Israeli survivors of the Holocaust, In: *Massive Psychic Trauma,* ed. H. Krystal. New York: International Universities Press, pp. 233–276.

Kligerman, C. (1984), The empathic approach to biography. In: *Empathy, Vol. 1,* ed. J. Lichtenberg, M. Bornstein, & D. Silver. Hillsdale, NJ: The Analytic Press, pp. 317–330.

Kline, N. A., & Rausch, J. L. (1985), Olfactory precipitants of flashbacks in posttraumatic stress disorder: Case reports. *Journal of Clinical Psychiatry,* 46:383–384.

Kohut, H. (1959), Introspection, empathy, and psychoanalysis: An examination of the relationship between mode of observation and theory. In: *The Search for the Self,* Vol. 1, ed. P.H. Ornstein, New York: International Universities Press, 1978, pp. 205–232.

———— (1961), Discussion of "The Unconscious Fantasy" by David Beres. In: *The Search for the Self,* Vol. 1, ed. P. H. Ornstein. New York: International Universities Press, 1978, pp. 309–318.

———— (1966), Forms and transformations of narcissism. In: *The Search for the Self,* Vol. 2, ed. P. H. Ornstein. New York: International Universities Press, pp. 427–460.

———— (1968), The psychoanalytic treatment of narcissistic personality disorders. In: *The Search for the Self,* Vol. 1, ed. P. H. Ornstein. New York: International Universities Press, pp. 477–509.

———— (1970), Narcissism as a resistance and as a driving force in psychoanalysis. In: *The Search for the Self,* Vol. 2, ed. P. H. Ornstein. New York: International Universities Press, 1978, pp. 547–561.

———— (1971), *The Analysis of the Self.* New York: International Universities Press.

———— (1972), Thoughts on narcissism and narcissistic rage. In: *The Search for the Self,* Vol. 2, ed. P. H. Ornstein. New York: International Universities Press, 1978, pp. 615–658.

———— (1974), Remarks about the formation of the self: Letter to a student regarding some principles of psychoanalytic research. In: *The Search for the Self,* Vol. 2, ed. P. H. Ornstein. New York: International Universities Press, pp. 737–770.

———— (1976), Creativeness, charisma, group psychology: Reflections on the self-analysis of Freud. In: *The Search for the Self,* Vol. 2, ed. P. H. Ornstein. New York: International Universities Press, pp. 793–843.

——— (1977), *The Restoration of the Self*. New York: International Universities Press.

——— (1984), *How Does Analysis Cure?* Chicago: University of Chicago Press.

——— (1985), *Self Psychology and the Humanities*, ed. C. B. Strozier. New York: Norton.

——— Wolf, E. (1978), The disorders of the self and their treatment: An Outline. *International Journal of Psycho-Analysis*, 59:413–425.

Kris, E. (1956), The personal myth. *Journal of the American Psychoanalytic Association*, 4:653–681.

Krystal, H. (1971), Psychotherapy after massive traumatization. In: *Psychic Traumatization*, ed. H. Krystal & W. G. Niederland. Boston: Little, Brown, pp. 223–229.

——— (1975), Affect tolerance. *The Annual of Psychoanalysis*, 3:179–219. New York; International Universities Press.

——— (1978), Trauma and affects. *The Psychoanalytic Study of the Child*, 33:81–116. New Haven; Yale University Press.

——— (1988), *Integration and Self Healing*. Hillsdale, NJ: The Analytic Press.

——— Niederland, W. G. (1968), Clinical observations of the survivor syndrome. In: *Massive Psychic Trauma*, ed. H. Krystal. New York: International Universities Press, pp. 327–348.

——— Raskin, H. (1970), *Drug Dependence*. Detroit: Wayne State University Press.

Kuhn, T. S. (1970), *The Structure of Scientific Revolutions*. 2nd ed. Chicago: University of Chicago Press.

Lagache, D. (1964), Fantasy, reality, and truth. *International Journal of Psycho-Analysis*, 45:180–189.

Laufer, M. (1976), The central masturbation fantasy, the final sexual organization, and adolescence. *The Psychoanalytic Study of the Child*, 31:297–316. New Haven: Yale University Press.

Laufer, R. S., Brett, E., & Gallops, M. S. (1985), Dimensions of posttraumatic stress disorder among Vietnam veterans. *Journal of Nervous and Mental Disorders*, 173:538–545.

——— (1985), War trauma and human development: The Viet Nam experience. In: *The Trauma of War*, ed. S. M. Sonnenberg, A. S. Blank, Jr., & J. Talbott. Washington, DC: American Psychiatric Press, pp. 33–57.

Leavy, S. (1980), *The Psychoanalytic Dialogue*. New Haven, CT: Yale University Press.

Lerner, M. J. (1970), The desire for justice and reactions to victims. In: *Altruism and Helping Behavior*, ed. J. R. Macauley & L. Berkowitz. New York: Academic Press, pp. 205–229.

——— (1980), *The Belief in a Just World*. New York: Plenum Press.

Lifton, R. J. (1967), *Death in Life*. New York: Random House.

——— (1972a), Experiments in advocacy research. In: *Science and Psychoanalysis*, ed. J. E. Masserman. New York: Grune & Stratton, pp. 259–271.

—— (1972b), The "Gook syndrome" and "numbed warfare." *Saturday Review*, December.

—— (1973), *Home from the War, Vietnam Veterans*. New York: Simon & Schuster.

—— (1975), The postwar war. *Journal of Social Issues*, 31:181–195.

—— (1976), *The Life of the Self*. New York: Simon & Schuster.

—— (1982), Psychology of the survivor and the death imprint. *Psychiatric Annals*, 12:1011–1020.

—— Olson, E. (1976), The human meaning of total disaster. *Psychiatry*, 39:1–18.

Loewald, H. W. (1960), On the therapeutic action of psychoanalysis. *International Journal of Psycho-Analysis*, 41:16–33.

Maisch, H. (1972), *Incest*, trans. C. Bearne. New York: Stein & Day.

Malcolm, J. (1983a), Annals of scholarship (psychoanalysis—part I), *The New Yorker*, December 5.

—— (1983b), Annals of scholarship (psychoanalysis—part II), *The New Yorker*, December 12.

—— (1984), *In the Freud Archives*. New York: Knopf.

Masson, J. M. (1984), *The Assault on Truth*. New York: Farrar, Strauss & Giroux.

Meiselman, K. (1978), *Incest*. San Francisco: Jossey-Bass.

Mellman, T. A., & Davis, G. C. (1985), Combat-related flashbacks in posttraumatic stress disorder: Phenomenology and similarity to panic attacks. *Journal of Clinical Psychiatry*, 46:379–382.

Modell, A. H. (1975), A narcissitic defense against affects and the illusion of self-sufficiency. *International Journal of Psycho-Analysis*, 56:275–282.

—— (1976), "The holding environment" and the therapeutic action of psychoanalysis. *Journal of the American Psychoanalytic Association*, 24:285–307.

Morrison, C. H. (1980), A cultural perspective on rape. In: *The Rape Crisis Intervention Handbook*, ed. S. McCombie. New York: Plenum Press, pp. 3–16.

Moskos, C. C., Jr. (1975), The American combat soldier in Vietnam. *Journal of Social Issues*, 31:25–37.

Murphy, W. F. (1959), Ego integration, trauma, and insight. *Psychoanalytic Quarterly*, 28:514–532.

Muslin, H. L. (1984), On empathic reading. In: *Empathy, Vol. 1*, ed. J. Lichtenberg, M. Bornstein, & D. Silver, Hillsdale, NJ: The Analytic Press, pp. 301–316.

MacKinnon, R. A., & Michels, R. (1971), *The Psychiatric Interview in Clinical Practice*. Philadelphia: Saunders.

Nadelson, C. C., & Notman, M. T. (1979), Psychoanalytic considerations of the response to rape. *International Review of Psycho-Analysis*, 6:97–102.

—— —— (1982), A follow-up study of rape victims. *American Journal of Psychiatry*, 139:1266–1270.

Neu, J. (1973), Fantasy and memory: The aetiological role of thoughts according to Freud. *International Journal of Psycho-Analysis*, 54:383–398.

Niederland, W. G. (1968a), The psychiatric evaluation of emotional disorders
in survivors of Nazi persecution. In: *Massive Psychic Trauma*, ed. H.
Krystal. New York: International Universities Press, pp. 8–22.

———— (1968b), Clinical observations on the 'survivor syndrome'. *International Journal of Psycho-Analysis*, 49:313–315.

Notman, M. T., & Nadelson, C. C. (1976), The rape victim: Psychodynamic
considerations. *American Journal of Psychiatry*, 133:1408–1413.

Noy, P. (1969), A revision of the psychoanalytic theory of the primary process.
International Journal of Psycho-Analysis, 50:155–178.

———— (1980), The psychoanalytic theory of cognitive development. *The Psychoanalytic Study of the Child*, 35:169–216. New Haven; Yale University
Press.

Nurnberg, G. H., & Shapiro, L. M. (1983), The central organizing fantasy.
Psychoanalytic Review, 70:493–503.

Nydes, J. (1950), The magical experience of the masturbation fantasy, *American Journal of Psychotherapy*, 4, 303–310.

Oremland, J. O. (1984), Empathy and its relation to the appreciation of art.
In: *Empathy, Vol. 1*, ed. J. Lichtenberg, M. Bornstein, & D. Silver.
Hillsdale, NJ: The Analytic Press, pp. 239–265.

Ornstein, A. (1974), The dread to repeat and the new beginning: A contribution to the psychoanalysis of the narcissistic personality, *The Annual of
Psychoanalysis*, 2:231–248. New York: International Universities Press.

———— (1983), Fantasy or reality? The unsettled question in pathogenesis and
reconstruction in psychoanalysis, In: *The Future of Psychoanalysis*, ed. A.
Goldberg. New York: International Universities Press, pp. 381–396.

———— (1985), Survival and recovery. *Psychoanalytic Inquiry*, 5:99–130.

Ornstein, P. H. (1978), Introduction: The evolution of Heinz Kohut's psychoanalytic psychology of the self. In: *The Search for the Self*, Vol. 1, ed. P. H.
Ornstein. New York: International Universities Press, pp. 1–106.

———— (1980), Self psychology and the concept of health. In: *Advances in Self
Psychology*, ed. A. Goldberg. New York: International Universities Press,
pp. 137–159.

Ostow, M. (1974), The role of early experiences. In: *Sexual Deviation*, ed. M.
Ostow, New York: Quandrangle, pp. 7–21.

Parson, E. R. (1981), The reparation of the self: Clinical and theoretical
dimensions in the treatment of Viet Nam combat veterans. Read at grand
rounds, Queens Hospital Center, Jamaica, NY.

———— (1984), The role of psychodynamic group therapy in the treatment of
the combat veteran. In: *Psychotherapy of the Combat Veteran*, ed. H. J.
Schwartz. New York: Spectrum Medical & Scientific Books, pp. 153–220.

———— (1984), The reparation of the self: Clinical and theoretical dimensions
in the treatment of Vietnam combat veterans. *Journal of Contemporary
Psychotherapy*, 14:4–56.

Piaget, J. (1959), *The Language and Thought of the Child*. London: Routledge & Kegan Paul.

—— (1962), *Play, Dreams and Imagination in Childhood*. New York: Norton.

—— (1970), *Structuralism*. New York: Basic Books.

Peters, J. J. (1976), Children who are victims of sexual assault and the psychology of the offenders. *American Journal of Psychotherapy*, 30:398–421.

Poland, W. S. (1984), On empathy in and beyond analysis. In: *Empathy, Vol. 1*, ed. J. Lichtenberg, M. Bornstein, & D. Silver. Hillsdale, NJ: The Analytic Press, pp. 331–349.

Pumpian-Mindlin, E. (1969), Vicissitudes of infantile omnipotence. *The Psychoanalytic Study of the Child*, 24:213–226. New Haven: Yale University Press.

Pynoos, R. S., & Eth, S. (1984), Developmental perspective on psychic trauma in childhood. In: *Trauma and Its Wake*, ed. C. R. Figley. New York: Brunner/Mazel, pp. 36–52.

Racker, H. (1968), *Transference and Counter-transference*. New York: International Universities Press.

Rado, S. (1942), Pathodynamics and treatment of traumatic war neurosis (traumatophobia). *Psychosomatic Medicine*, 4:362–368.

Reich, A. (1932), Analysis of a case of brother-sister incest. In: *Annie Reich*. New York: International Universities Press, 1973, pp. 288–311.

—— (1960), Pathological forms of self-esteem regulation. In: *Annie Reich*. New York: International Universities Press, 1973, pp. 288–311.

Rosen, V. H. (1955), The reconstruction of a traumatic childhood event in a case of derealization. *Journal of the American Psychoanalytic Association*, 3:211–231.

Roth, L. M. (1986), Substance use and mental health among Vietnam veterans. In: *The Vietnam Veteran Redefined*, ed. G. Boulanger & C. Kadushin. Hillsdale: NJ: Lawrence Erlbaum Associates, Publishers, pp. 61–77.

Rothstein, A. (1984a), Fear of humiliation. *Journal of the American Psychoanalytic Association*, 32:99–116.

—— (1984b), *The Narcissistic Pursuit of Perfection*. New York: International Universities Press.

—— (1986), Conclusion. In: *The Reconstruction of Trauma*, ed. A. Rothstein. New York: International Universities Press, pp. 219–230.

Rowland, J. (1985), *The Ultimate Violation*. Garden City: NY: Doubleday.

Runyan, W. Mc. (1980), Alternative accounts of lives: An argument for epistemological relativism. *Biography*, 3:209–224.

Runyan, W. Mc. (1982), In defense of the case study method. *American Journal of Orthopsychiatry*, 52:440–446.

—— (1984), *Life Histories and Psychobiographies*. New York: Oxford University Press.

Rush, F. (1980), *The Best Kept Secret*. New York: McGraw-Hill.

Russell, D. E. H. (1986), *The Secret Trauma*. New York: Basic Books.

Ryan, W. (1971), *Blaming the Victim*. New York: Random House.

Rycroft, C. (1984), Review of *The Assault on Truth: Freud's Suppression of the Seduction Theory* by Jeffrey M. Masson. *New York Review of Books*, 31(6).

Schad-Somers, S. P. (1982), *Sadomasochism: Etiology and Treatment*. New York: Human Sciences Press.

Sandler, J., & Nagera, H. (1963), Aspects of the metapsychology of fantasy. *The Psychoanalytic Study of the Child*, 18:159–194. New York: International Universities Press.

—— with A. Freud (1985), *The Analysis of Defense*. New York: International Universities Press.

Sarlin, C. N. (1962), Depersonalization and derealization. *Journal of the American Psychoanalytic Association*, 10:784–804.

Schafer, R. (1976), *A New Language for Psychoanalysis*. New Haven, CT: Yale University Press.

—— (1978), *Language and Insight*. New Haven, CT: Yale University Press.

Schimek, J. G. (1975), The interpretation of the past: Childhood trauma, psychical reality, and historical truth. *Journal of the American Psychoanalytic Association*, 23:845–865.

Schwaber, E. (1981), Empathy: A mode of analytic listening. *Psychoanalytic Inquiry*, 1:357–392.

Schwartz-Salant, N. (1982), *Narcissism and Character Transformation: The Psychology of Narcissistic Character Disorders*. Toronto, Canada: Inner City Books.

Sebastiano, S. (1977), Action, fantasy and language: Developmental levels of ego organization in communicating drives and affects. In: *Communicative Structures and Psychic Structures*, ed. N. Freedman & S. Grand. New York: Plenum Press, pp. 331–354.

Shainess, N. (1984), *Sweet Suffering*. Indianapolis, IN: Bobbs-Merrill.

Shatan, C. F. (1972), Post-Vietnam syndrome. *The New York Times*, May 6.

—— (1973), The grief of soldiers: Vietnam combat veterans self-help movement. *American Journal of Orthopsychiatry*, 43:649–653.

—— (1974), Through the membrane of reality: Impacted grief and perceptual dissonance in Vietnam combat veterans. *Psychiatric Opinion*, 2:6–15.

—— (1977), Bogus manhood, bogus honor: Surrender and transfiguration in the United States Marine Corps. *Psychoanalytic Review*, 64:585–610.

—— (1978), Stress disorders among Vietnam veterans: The emotional content of combat continues. In: *Stress Disorders Among Vietnam Veterans*, ed. C. R. Figley. New York: Brunner/Mazel, pp. 43–52.

—— (1985), Have you hugged a Vietnam veteran today? The basic wound of catastrophic stress. In: *Post-traumatic Stress Disorder and the War Veteran Patient*, ed. W. E. Kelly. New York: Brunner/Mazel, pp. 12–28.

Shengold, L. (1980), Some reflections on a case of mother/adolescent son incest. *International Journal of Psycho-Analysis*, 61:461–476.

Silver, R. L., Boon, C., & Stones, M. H. (1983), Searching for meaning in misfortune: Making sense of incest. *Journal of Social Issues*, 39:81–102.

Silverman, L. H. (1977), Experimental data on the effects of unconscious fantasy on communicative behavior. In *Communicative Structures and Psychic Structures*, ed. N. Freedman & S. Grand. New York: Plenum Press, pp. 237–254.

—— (1978/9), Unconscious symbiotic fantasy: A ubiquitous therapeutic agent. *International Journal of Psychoanalytic Psychotherapy*, 7:562–585.

—— (1979), The unconscious fantasy as therapeutic agent in psychoanalytic treatment. *Journal of the American Academy of Psychoanalysis*, 7:189–218.

—— Lachmann, L. M., & Milich, R. H. (1982), *The Search for Oneness*, New York: International Universities Press.

Simmel, E. (1921), Comments from the symposium on war neuroses, Fifth International Psycho-Analytical Congress, Budapest, 1918. In: *Psycho-Analysis and the War Neuroses*, ed. S. Ferenenzi, K. Abraham, E. Simmel, & E. Jones. London: International Psycho-Analytical Press, pp. 30–43.

—— (1944), War neuroses. In: *Psychoanalysis Today*, ed. S. Lorand. New York: International Universities Press, pp. 227–248.

Sloane, P., & Karpinski, E., (1942), Effects of incest on the participants. *American Journal of Orthopsychiatry*, 12:666–667.

Solloway, F. J. (1983), *Freud, Biologist of the Mind*. New York: Basic Books.

Spitz, R. A. (1965), *The First Year of Life*. New York: International Universities Press.

Spotts, J. V., & Shontz, F. C. (1976), *The Life Styles of Nine American Cocaine Users*. Research Issues No. 16, National Institute on Drug Abuse. Washington, DC: United States Govt. Printing Office.

—— (1980), *Cocaine Users*. New York: Free Press.

Stephenson, W. (1954), *Psychoanalysis and Q-Method: A Scientific Model for Psychoanalytic Doctrine*. Unpublished manuscript, rev. 1979.

Stern, D. (1985), *The Interpersonal World of the Infant*. New York: Basic Books.

Stoller, R. J. (1975), Perversion. New York: Pantheon.

—— (1979), *Sexual Excitement*. New York: Pantheon.

Stolorow, R. D. (1984), Self psychology is not soul psychology: Notes on the self-as-structure vs. the person-as-agent. Society for the Advancement of Self Psychology *Newsletter*, 2 (1).

—— Atwood, G. E. (1982), Psychoanalytic phenomenology of the dream. *The Annual of Psychoanalysis*, 10:205–220. New York: International Universities Press.

—— Brandchaft, B., & Atwood, G. E. (1983), Intersubjectivity in psychoanalytic treatment: With special reference to archaic states. *Bulletin of the Menninger Clinic*, 47:117–128.

—— Lachmann, F. M. (1980), *The Psychoanalysis of Development Arrest*. New York: International Universities Press.

—— —— (1985), Transference: The future of an illusion. *The Annual of Psychoanalysis*, 12/13:19–37. New York: International Universities Press.

Storr, A. (1984), Review of *The Assault on Truth: Freud's Suppression of the*

Seduction Theory by Jeffrey M. Masson, *New York Times Book Review*, February 12.

Strachey, J. (1934), The nature of the therapeutic action of psycho-analysis. *International Journal of Psycho-Analysis*, 15:127–159.

Strozier, C. B. (1982), *Lincoln's Quest for Union.* New York: Basic Books.

——— (1983), Fantasy, self psychology and the inner logic of cults. In: *The Future of Psychoanalysis*, ed. A. Goldberg. New York: International Universities Press, pp. 477–493.

Symonds, P. M. (1949), *Adolescent Fantasy.* New York: Columbia University Press.

Tartakoff, H. H. (1966), The normal personality in our culture and the nobel prize complex. In: *Psychoanalysis—A General Psychology.* New York: International Universities Press, pp. 222–252.

Terr, L. (1979), Children of Chowchilla: Study of psychic trauma. *The Psychoanalytic Study of the Child*, 34: 547–623. New Haven: Yale University Press.

——— (1984), Time and trauma. *The Psychoanalytic Study of the Child*, 39:633–665. New Haven: Yale University Press.

——— (1985), Remembered images and trauma. *The Psychoanalytic Study of the Child*, 40:493–533. New Haven: Yale University

Tolpin, M. (1974), The Daedalus experience: A developmental vicissitude of the grandiose fantasy. *The Annual of Psychoanalysis*, 2:213–228. New York: International Universities Press.

Tolpin, P. H. (1985), The primary of preservation of self. In: *Progress in Self Psychology, Vol. 1*, ed. A. Goldberg. New York: Guilford Press, pp. 83–87.

Tsai, M., & Wagner, N. N. (1978), Therapy groups for women sexually molested as children. *Archives of Sexual Behavior*, 7:417–427.

Ulman, R. B. (1987), Horneyan and Kohutian theories of psychic trauma: A self-psychological reexamination of the work of Harold Kelman. *American Journal of Psychoanalysis*, 47:154–160.

——— (forthcoming), The "transference-countertransference neurosis" in psychoanalysis: The intersubjective context of dream formation. In: *The Borderline and Narcissistic Patient in Therapy*, ed. N. Slavinska-Holy. New York: International Universities Press.

——— Brothers, D. (1987), a self-psychological reevaluation of posttraumatic stress disorder (PTSD) and its treatment: Shattered fantasies. *Journal of the American Academy of Psychoanalysis*, 15:175–203.

——— Paul, H. (1986), A self-psychological understanding and approach to the treatment of substance abuse disorders: The "intersubjective absorption" hypothesis. Presented at the Society for the Advancement of Self Psychology 1985–6 Lecture and Seminar Series, New York.

——— ——— (1987a), A self-psychological understanding and approach to the treatment of substance abuse disorders: The "intersubjective absorption" hypothesis. Presented at the Society for the Advancement of Self Psychology 1986–7 Lecture and Seminar Series, New York.

——— ——— (1987b), A self-psychological understanding and approach to the treatment of substance abuse disorders: The "intersubjective absorption" hypothesis. Presented at the 10th Annual Conference on the Psychology of the Self, October 23–25, 1987, Chicago.

——— Stolorow, R. D. (1985), The "transference-countertransference neurosis" in psychoanalysis: An intersubjective viewpoint. *Bulletin of the Menninger Clinic*, 49:37–51.

———, & Zimmerman, P. B. (1985), Psychoanalysis as a hermeneutic science and the new paradigm of subjectivity: A prolegomenon. Presented at the Eighth Annual Scientific Meeting of the International Society of Political Psychology, June 18–21, George Washington University, Washington, DC.

——— Zimmerman, P. B. (1987), Psychoanalysis as a hermeneutic science and the new paradigm of subjectivity: Evolution of a research tradition. Presented at the Tenth Annual Scientific Meeting of the International Society of Political Psychology, July 4–7, Cathedral Hill Hotel, San Francisco.

Volkan, V. (1973), Transitional fantasies in the analysis of a narcissistic personality. *Journal of the American Psychoanalytic Association*, 21:351–376.

Wallerstein, R. S. (1986), *Forty-Two Lives in Treatment*. New York: Guilford Press.

Weber, E. (1979), Sexual abuse begins at home. *Ms. Magazine* April, pp. 64–67.

Weinberg, S. K. (1955), *Incest Behavior*. Secaucus, NJ: Citadel Press.

Weiner, I. B. (1962), Father-daughter incest: A Clinical Report. *Psychiatric Quarterly*, 36:607–632.

Williams, M. (1987), Reconstruction of an early seduction and its aftereffects. *Journal of the American Psychoanalytic Association*, 35:145–163.

Wilmer, H. A. (1982), Vietnam and madness: Dreams of schizophrenic veterans. *Journal of the American Academy of Psychoanalysis*, 10:47–65.

Wilson, J. P. (1977), Identity, Ideology and Crisis: The Vietnam Veteran in Transition, Part I. Paper presented to the Disabled American Veteran Association, Forgotten Warriors Project, Cleveland State University, Cleveland, OH.

——— (1978), Identity, Ideology and Crisis: The Vietnam Veteran in Transition, Part II, Psychosocial Attributes of the Veteran Beyond Identity. Patterns of Adjustment and Future Implications. Paper presented to the Disabled Veterans Association, Forgotten Warriors Project, Cleveland State University, Cleveland. OH.

——— (1980), Conflict, stress, and growth: The effects of war on psychosocial development among Vietnam veterans. In: *Strangers at Home*, ed. C. R. Figley & S. Leventman. New York: Praeger, pp. 123–165.

Wolf, E. S., Gedo, J. E., & Terman, D. M. (1972), On the adolescent process as a transformation of the self. *Journal of Youth and Adolescence*, 1:257–272.

Wolff, R. P. (1963), *Kant's Theory of Mental Activity*. Cambridge, MA: Harvard University Press.

Woodbury, J., & Schwartz, E. (1977), *The Silent Sin*. New York: Signet Books.

Zetzel, E. R. (1965), Depression and the Incapacity to bear it. In: *Drives, Affects, Behavior*, Vol. 2, ed. M. Schur. New York, International Universities Press, pp. 243–274.

——— Meissner, W. W. (1973), *Basic Concepts of Psychoanalytic Psychiatry*. New York: Basic Books.

Index